# Discourse and Diversionary Justice

Michele Zappavigna • JR Martin

# Discourse and Diversionary Justice

## An Analysis of Youth Justice Conferencing

Michele Zappavigna
School of the Arts & Media
UNSW Australia
Sydney, NSW, Australia

JR Martin
Department of Linguistics
University of Sydney
Sydney, NSW, Australia

ISBN 978-3-319-63762-4    ISBN 978-3-319-63763-1  (eBook)
DOI 10.1007/978-3-319-63763-1

Library of Congress Control Number: 2017954308

© The Editor(s) (if applicable) and The Author(s) 2018
This work is subject to copyright. All rights are solely and exclusively licensed by the Publisher, whether the whole or part of the material is concerned, specifically the rights of translation, reprinting, reuse of illustrations, recitation, broadcasting, reproduction on microfilms or in any other physical way, and transmission or information storage and retrieval, electronic adaptation, computer software, or by similar or dissimilar methodology now known or hereafter developed.
The use of general descriptive names, registered names, trademarks, service marks, etc. in this publication does not imply, even in the absence of a specific statement, that such names are exempt from the relevant protective laws and regulations and therefore free for general use.
The publisher, the authors and the editors are safe to assume that the advice and information in this book are believed to be true and accurate at the date of publication. Neither the publisher nor the authors or the editors give a warranty, express or implied, with respect to the material contained herein or for any errors or omissions that may have been made. The publisher remains neutral with regard to jurisdictional claims in published maps and institutional affiliations.

Cover credit: Image Source Plus / Alamy Stock Photo

Printed on acid-free paper

This Palgrave Macmillan imprint is published by Springer Nature
The registered company is Springer International Publishing AG
The registered company address is: Gewerbestrasse 11, 6330 Cham, Switzerland

*For Diana Eades, with great respect*

# Preface

The research we are documenting here grew out of a research seminar organized by Ghassan Hage at the University of Sydney in 2003, a seminar focusing on social hope as an analytical category and object of research (see Hage 2006 for his conception of social hope). Paul Dwyer was attracted to this seminar in relation to his work on ritual reconciliation ceremonies in Bougainville; and Jim Martin was attracted in relation to his interest in what he calls 'positive discourse analysis', where this is understood as involving a focus on what is going right in the world (that we can learn from and perhaps participate in; Martin 2004) rather than what is going wrong (the usual focus of critical discourse analysis, aka CDA, research).

At the time, Paul had his eye on the possibility of exploring a form of restorative justice which had recently been introduced in New South Wales (hereafter NSW), Australia—the diversionary justice programme known as Youth Justice Conferencing. Youth Justice Conferences dealt with adolescent offenders who would meet with their victim and other relevant members of the community to discuss relatively minor offences and work out some form of community service by way of reparation (instead of going to court, getting a criminal record and possibly serving time in juvenile detention). Paul invited Jim to join him in this research, and thanks to some seed funding from the University of Sydney in 2007 they were able to secure an Australian Research Council Discovery Grant

(DP0881513) for the period 2008–2011. The funding enabled Michele Zappavigna to join the project, initially as a research associate and then as a postdoctoral fellow, and with audiovisual recording support from staff in the Department of Performance Studies at the University of Sydney we got under way.

In general terms, the project involved a combination of ethnographic and functional linguistic research. On the ethnography side, Paul sat in on the training offered for convenors of Youth Justice Conferences, observed many conferences, interviewed practitioners and, along with Michele, undertook the audiovisual recording of the eight conferences we focused on in detail in our study. Jim drew on his background in discourse analysis (Martin 1992; Martin and Rose 2003/2007, 2008) and its applications in educational linguistics (Rose and Martin 2012) to explore with Michele the language and paralanguage of these conferences. The team met regularly over four years to contextualize the detailed linguistic analysis in relation to understandings arising from our ethnographic research.

We append a list of publications arising from this research at the end of this Preface (many were republished in Martin 2012 and are cross-referenced to that volume). Our understanding of conferencing naturally evolved during the research. Martin and Zappavigna (2016) provide a partial overview of its trajectory. The present volume consolidates our current understandings.

The authors are deeply indebted to Paul Dwyer for his critical role in this research, for his contribution to Chap. 1 of this volume and for suggestions elsewhere. We would also like to thank Yaegan Doran for his painstaking editing of this monograph and his critical feedback on each chapter (and Sue Hood for her help with proofing). Finally, we would like to thank the conference participants who agreed to participate in this research. Their goodwill resonates strongly with the restorative justice mission of the designers and proponents of Youth Justice Conferencing, an inspirational mission we are proud to endorse.

We respectfully dedicate this book to Diana Eades, one of Australia's forensic linguistics pioneers, in recognition of her tireless work on behalf of Indigenous Australians, who all too often find themselves struggling for survival in retributive justice proceedings.

School of the Arts and Media  Michele Zappavigna
UNSW Australia
Sydney, NSW, Australia

Department of Linguistics  JR Martin
University of Sydney
Sydney, NSW, Australia

# List of Related Publications by the Authors

Martin, J. R. (2009). Realisation, instantiation and individuation: Some thoughts on identity in youth justice conferencing. *DELTA – Documentação de Estudos em Linguistica Teorica e Aplicada, 25*, 549–583. [Reprinted in *Forensic Linguistics* 2012. 75–101].

Martin, J. R. (2012). In W. Zhenhua (Ed.), *Forensic linguistics, Vol. 8: Collected works of J R Martin*. Shanghai: Shanghai Jiao Tong University Press.

Martin, J. R., & Zappavigna, M. (2013). Youth justice conferencing: Ceremonial redress. *International Journal of Law, Language and Discourse, 3*, 103–142.

Martin, J. R., & Zappavigna, M. (2014). Beyond redemption: Choice and consequence in youth justice conferencing. In F. Yan & J. J. Webster (Eds.), *Developing systemic functional linguistics: Theory and application* (pp. 18–47). London: Equinox. [Reprinted in *Forensic Linguistics* 2012, 227–257].

Martin, J. R., & Zappavigna, M. (2016). Exploring restorative justice: Dialectics of theory and practice. *International Journal of Speech, Language and the Law, 23*(2), 217–244.

Martin, J. R., & Zappavigna, M. (in press). Rites of passion: Remorse, apology and forgiveness in youth justice conferencing. *Linguistics and the Human Sciences*. (Special Issue on Legal Discourse edited by Wang Zhen Hua).

Martin, J. R., Zappavigna, M., & Dwyer, P. (2007a). Negotiating narrative: Story structure and identity in youth justice conferencing. *Linguistics and the Human Sciences*, *3*(2), 221–253. [Reprinted in *Forensic Linguistics* 2012. 129–159].

Martin, J. R., Zappavigna, M., & Dwyer, P. (2007b). *"Just like sort of guilty kind of": The rhetoric of tempered admission in youth justice conferencing*. Proceedings of the 2007 Australian Systemic Functional Linguistics Congress, Wollongong. http://www.asfla.org.au/category/asfla2007/. [Reprinted in *Forensic Linguistics* 2012. 39–57].

Martin, J. R., Zappavigna, M., & Dwyer, P. (2009). Negotiating shame: Exchange and genre structure in youth justice conferencing. In A. Mahboob & C. Lipovsky (Eds.), *Studies in applied linguistics and language learning* (pp. 41–73). Newcastle upon Tyne: Cambridge Scholars Press. [Reprinted in *Forensic Linguistics* 2012. 102–128].

Martin, J. R., Zappavigna, M., Dwyer, P., & Cléirigh, C. (2013). Users in uses of language: Embodied identity in youth justice conferencing. *Text & Talk*, *33*(4/5), 467–496. [Reprinted in Forensic Linguistics 2012. 258–288].

Zappavigna, M., & Martin, J. R. (2014). Mater Dolorosa: Negotiating support in NSW youth justice conferencing. *International Journal for the Semiotics of Law*, *27*(2), 263–275. (Special Issue 'Fresh Waters from an Old Spring: The semiotics of restorative justice, recognizing harm and healing communities anew with old ways' edited by J. B. Hamlin).

Zappavigna, M., Martin, J. R., & Dwyer, P. (2008). Syndromes of meaning: Exploring patterned coupling in a NSW youth justice conference. In A. Mahboob & N. Knight (Eds.), *Questioning linguistics* (pp. 164–185). Newcastle upon Tyne: Cambridge Scholars Publishing. [Reprinted in Forensic Linguistics 2012. 58–74].

Zappavigna, M., Cléirigh, C., Dwyer, P., & Martin, J. R. (2010a). The coupling of gesture and phonology. In M. Bednarek & J. Martin (Eds.), *New discourse on language: Functional perspectives on multimodality, identity and affiliation* (pp. 219–236). London: Continuum. [Reprinted in *Forensic Linguistics*. 192–209].

Zappavigna, M., Martin, J. R., & Dwyer, P. (2010b). Negotiating evaluation: Story structure and appraisal in youth justice conferencing. In A. Mahboob & N. Knight (Eds.), *Applicable linguistics* (pp. 44–75). London: Continuum. [Reprinted in Forensic Linguistics 2012. 160–191].

Zappavigna, M., Martin, J. R., & Dwyer, P. (2010c). Visualising appraisal prosody. In A. Mahboob & N. Knight (Eds.), *Applicable linguistics* (pp. 150–167). London: Continuum. [Reprinted in Forensic Linguistics 2012. 210–226].

Zappavigna, M., Dwyer, P., & Martin, J. R. (2016). Consent and compliance in youth justice conferences. In D. Eades, S. Erhlich, & J. Ainsworth (Eds.), *Coercion and consent in the legal system: Discursive and linguistic perspectives* (pp. 186–212). Oxford: Oxford University Press.

# Contents

**1 Approaching Restorative Justice** — 1
  1 Youth Justice Conferencing and the Purpose of This Study — 1
  2 The Contested Field of Restorative Justice — 5
  3 Researching a New Paradigm — 11
  4 Fieldwork and Ethnographic Methodology — 19
  5 'Context and Text': A Brief Introduction to Systemic Functional Linguistics (SFL) — 25
  6 Multimodal Discourse and Performance — 33
  7 A Road Map for Readers — 37
  References — 41

**2 Conference Design: Genre and Macro-Genre** — 49
  1 Youth Justice Conferences: Talk and Interaction — 49
  2 Pathways to a Conference — 51
  3 Conference Openings: From Script to Genre — 56
  4 The Socio-legal Framing Genre in the YJC Macro-Genre — 62
  5 From Genre to Macro-Genre: The Whole Conferencing Sequence — 71
  6 The Commissioned Recount — 73

| | 7 | The Reflective Recount | 84 |
|---|---|---|---|
| | 8 | The Rejoinder Macro-Genre | 91 |
| | 9 | The Impact Genre | 92 |
| | 10 | The Avouchment Genre | 95 |
| | 11 | The Apology | 100 |
| | 12 | The Admonition Genre | 104 |
| | 13 | The Reintegration Macro-Genre | 117 |
| | 14 | Genre and Macro-Genre | 124 |
| | References | | 125 |
| **3** | **Conference Interaction: Exchange Structure** | | **129** |
| | 1 | Regulative and Integrative Discourse | 129 |
| | 2 | Analysing Exchange Structures | 131 |
| | 3 | Conferencing as a Pedagogical Practice | 138 |
| | 4 | Guided Storytelling in the Commissioned Recount | 145 |
| | 5 | Conferencing as Pedagogic Discourse | 154 |
| | References | | 155 |
| **4** | **Expressing Feeling: Appraisal Systems** | | **157** |
| | 1 | Introduction | 157 |
| | 2 | Introducing Appraisal | 158 |
| | 3 | Adding Evaluative Language to the Commissioned Recount | 162 |
| | 4 | The Commissioned Recount as a Storytelling Genre | 176 |
| | 5 | The Rejoinder: 'Outsourcing' Evaluation to Support Persons and Carers | 187 |
| | 6 | Scaffolding Evaluation | 190 |
| | References | | 195 |
| **5** | **Negotiating Feeling: The Role of Body Language** | | **199** |
| | 1 | Introduction | 199 |
| | 2 | From Feeling to Belonging: The Role of 'Coupling' in Affiliation | 200 |
| | 3 | A Metafunctionally Organized Model of Body Language | 202 |

|   |   |   |
|---|---|---|
| 4 | Linguistic Body Language | 205 |
| 5 | Epilinguistic Body Language | 208 |
| 6 | Protolinguistic Body Language | 211 |
| 7 | Body Language and the Small Target Young Person Identity | 212 |
| 8 | The Role of Body Language in Negotiating Coupling: A 'Bond by Bond' Analysis | 215 |
| 9 | Belonging and Community | 227 |
| 10 | Conclusion | 240 |
|   | References | 241 |

**6  Performing Identity: A Topological Perspective** — 245
   1  Introduction: Users in Uses of Language — 245
   2  How Can Young Persons Enact a 'Sincere' Persona in YJCs? — 247
   3  Modelling Identity: A Topological Perspective — 251
   4  YP Identities in the Commissioned Recount — 254
   5  YP Identities and the Admonition — 257
   6  Support Person Identities — 263
   7  Conclusion — 265
      References — 266

**7  Ceremonial Redress: How Conferencing in Fact Achieves Its Goals** — 269
   1  Introduction — 269
   2  Discourse Iconography — 270
   3  Iconization — 272
   4  Conferencing as Ritual: The Power of Ceremonial Redress — 287
   5  Ceremonial Redress — 292
   6  Envoi — 296
      References — 299

**Appendix A: Anonymized Cast of Characters and Youth Justice Conference Locations** — 303

Appendix B: Conventions Used in This Book          307

References          317

Index          333

# List of Figures

| | | |
|---|---|---|
| Fig. 1.1 | Examples of a youth justice conference (This image has been stylized to aid in preserving anonymity) | 21 |
| Fig. 1.2 | Basic English MOOD systems | 29 |
| Fig. 1.3 | English MOOD and MODALIZATION | 29 |
| Fig. 1.4 | A stratified model of language | 31 |
| Fig. 1.5 | Types of meaning (metafunction) and levels of abstraction (strata) | 32 |
| Fig. 2.1 | Diagrammatic convention for macro-genres, genres and stages used throughout this chapter | 62 |
| Fig. 2.2 | The socio-legal framing genre | 63 |
| Fig. 2.3 | Canonical structure of the youth justice conferencing macro-genre | 72 |
| Fig. 2.4 | The commissioned recount genre (a step within the testimony macro-genre, itself a step in the YJC macro-genre) | 74 |
| Fig. 2.5 | The reflective recount genre | 84 |
| Fig. 2.6 | The rejoinder macro-genre | 91 |
| Fig. 2.7 | The impact genre in the rejoinder macro-genre | 93 |
| Fig. 2.8 | The avouchment in the rejoinder macro-genre | 95 |
| Fig. 2.9 | The admonition genre | 105 |
| Fig. 2.10 | Future irrealis YP, positively judged | 113 |
| Fig. 2.11 | Future irrealis YP, negatively judged | 114 |
| Fig. 2.12 | Domains of potentially negative outcomes | 115 |
| Fig. 2.13 | Domains of potentially positive outcomes | 116 |

| | | |
|---|---|---|
| Fig. 2.14 | The reintegration macro-genre | 118 |
| Fig. 3.1 | System network for knowledge and action exchanges (Martin 1992) | 136 |
| Fig. 3.2 | Regulative discourse projecting integrative discourse in youth justice conferencing | 142 |
| Fig. 4.1 | Dimensions of evaluation (Adapted from Martin and White (2005: 45)) | 158 |
| Fig. 4.2 | APPRAISAL systems (After Martin and White (2005)) | 159 |
| Fig. 4.3 | Some story genres (After Martin and Rose (2008)) | 184 |
| Fig. 4.4 | Commissioned recount as a story genre (After Martin and Rose (2008)) | 185 |
| Fig. 4.5 | Some story genres—a topological perspective | 186 |
| Fig. 5.1 | An example of tone group analysis performed using ELAN | 204 |
| Fig. 5.2 | YP body language during the commissioned recount, Mobile Phone YJC | 213 |
| Fig. 5.3 | YP body language during the commissioned recount, Guide Dog YJC | 214 |
| Fig. 5.4 | YP body language during the commissioned recount, School Library YJC | 214 |
| Fig. 5.5 | Three kinds of Gemeinschaft (Adapted from Tann 2010b: 96) | 228 |
| Fig. 6.1 | The Specialization plane (Maton 2007: 97) | 252 |
| Fig. 6.2 | Enacting Maton's 'specialization plane' to analyse identities in YJC | 254 |
| Fig. 6.3 | YP personae topology for commissioned recount and rejoinder steps in the YJC macro-genre (retrospective) | 255 |
| Fig. 6.4 | YP personae topology for admonition step in the YJC macro-genre (prospective) | 261 |
| Fig. 6.5 | Retrospective and prospective identity profiles for the commissioned recount and admonition genres | 262 |
| Fig. 6.6 | Support person personae topology for the avouchment step in the YJC macro-genre (retrospective) | 264 |
| Fig. 7.1 | Tann's topological perspective on discourse iconography (Adapted from Tann 2010b) | 271 |
| Fig. 7.2 | Obama iconography (Based on Tann 2010b) | 272 |
| Fig. 7.3 | Extended Oracle dimension of discourse iconography resources in discourse | 272 |
| Fig. 7.4 | Well-known bondicons for peace | 275 |

| | | |
|---|---|---|
| Fig. 7.5 | The parent–child dyad as Communitas | 279 |
| Fig. 7.6 | Reintegration iconography (family, self-respect and pride, 'line in the sand' parable) | 281 |
| Fig. 7.7 | Reintegration iconography (Muslim community, respect for mother, hijab bondicon) | 282 |
| Fig. 7.8 | Reintegration iconography (ethical citizen, empathy and obeying the law, 'Victim') | 284 |
| Fig. 7.9 | Youth justice conferencing and court as a level of liminality | 292 |
| Fig. 7.10 | Youth justice conferencing as a form of ritual redress | 293 |

# List of Tables

| | | |
|---|---|---|
| Table 1.1 | The sample of video-recorded NSW youth justice conferences used in this study | 23 |
| Table 3.1 | Adapted from transcript of Mobile Phone YJC—Version 1 | 143 |
| Table 3.2 | Adapted from transcript of Mobile Phone YJC—Version 2 | 143 |
| Table 3.3 | Simultaneity of regulatory and integrative moves | 144 |
| Table 3.4 | Exchange structure of the commissioned recount genre in Mobile Phone YJC, extract 3.1 | 145 |
| Table 3.5 | Exchange structure of the commissioned recount genre in Mobile Phone YJC, extract 3.2 | 146 |
| Table 3.6 | Exchange structure of the commissioned recount genre in Mobile Phone YJC, extract 3.3 | 147 |
| Table 3.7 | Exchange structure of the commissioned recount genre in Mobile Phone YJC, extract 3.1 | 148 |
| Table 3.8 | Extension in the commissioned recount genre, Mobile Phone YJC | 149 |
| Table 3.9 | Interpretation in the commissioned recount genre, Mobile Phone YJC | 150 |
| Table 3.10 | Discussion of moral responsibility in the commissioned recount genre, Mobile Phone YJC | 150 |
| Table 3.11 | 'What's your mum wearing on her head?', Affray YJC | 151 |
| Table 3.12 | 'Who's sitting here right now?', Affray YJC | 152 |

| | | |
|---|---|---|
| Table 3.13 | 'What the perception going to be?', Affray YJC | 152 |
| Table 3.14 | Distancing the YP from his mates, Affray YJC | 153 |
| Table 3.15 | Ethnic Community Liaison Officer's disgust, Affray YJC | 153 |
| Table 4.1 | Inscriptions of affect in the Interpretation stage of the Mobile Phone commissioned recount | 167 |
| Table 4.2 | Inscriptions of judgement in the Interpretation stage of the Mobile Phone commissioned recount | 168 |
| Table 4.3 | Inscriptions of honesty in the ECLO's Interpretation stage of the affray commissioned recount | 170 |
| Table 4.4 | Inscriptions of capacity in the ECLO's Interpretation stage of the affray recount | 171 |
| Table 4.5 | Inscriptions of propriety in the ECLO's Interpretation stage of the affray commissioned recount | 171 |
| Table 4.6 | Inscriptions of impropriety by the YP in relation to his mother | 173 |
| Table 4.7 | Inscriptions of impropriety by the YP in relation to the Muslim community | 173 |
| Table 5.1 | Linguistic body language (Cléirigh 2011) | 205 |
| Table 5.2 | Increased salience realized as increased frequency of gestural beats | 207 |
| Table 5.3 | Increased salience scaling up evaluation | 207 |
| Table 5.4 | Epilinguistic body language (Cléirigh 2011) | 208 |
| Table 5.5 | Gesture representing a process | 209 |
| Table 5.6 | Gesture realizing deixis | 210 |
| Table 5.7 | Protolinguistic body language (Cléirigh 2011) | 212 |
| Table 5.8 | YP's body language during the commissioned recount, Mobile Phone YJC—'Do you think your father was disappointed in you?' | 215 |
| Table 5.9 | YP1's body language—'I'm not a rat from Bridgeton' | 217 |
| Table 5.10 | YP1's body language—'I'm not one of those friggin' retarded people' | 218 |
| Table 5.11 | YP1's body language—'I'll do everything that I can to…' | 218 |
| Table 5.12 | YP1's body language—'Walk the streets, mate' | 220 |
| Table 5.13 | YLO's body language—'See you two guys are a bit like the old farmyard rooster' | 221 |
| Table 5.14 | YP2's body language—rejecting YLO's bond | 222 |

| | | |
|---|---|---|
| Table 5.15 | YP1's body language—imitating YLO's 'fluffed-up rooster' gesture | 222 |
| Table 5.16 | YP1's body language in response to YLO | 223 |
| Table 5.17 | YP1's body language—'Happy now?' | 224 |
| Table 5.18 | YP1's & YP2's body language—rejecting YLO's bond | 224 |
| Table 5.19 | YP1's body language—accusing YLO | 225 |
| Table 5.20 | YLO's & YP1's body language—'Well, we're not here to sling comments at you' | 226 |
| Table 5.21 | Examples of 'mate' in initial position with Tone 3 | 235 |
| Table 5.22 | Instances of the use of 'man' by ECLO | 236 |
| Table 5.23 | Examples of the use of 'brother' by the ECLO | 236 |
| Table 7.1 | Criteria for distinguishing types of events on a continuum of ritual, ritual-like, not ritual-like (Adapted from Lewis 2013) | 289 |

# 1

# Approaching Restorative Justice

## 1    Youth Justice Conferencing and the Purpose of This Study

Imagine a late Friday night in a fairly large regional city. People are pouring out of the pubs and clubs, looking for a way to get home. A fight breaks out between two young women, one of whom is soon on the ground trying to shield herself from frequent kicks to the belly. Her assailant (who doesn't know the other girl is pregnant) is later charged with assault and resisting arrest. Imagine two groups of boys meeting near a suburban train station 'to sort things out'. One boy chases another down the street, and then realizes his adversary has pulled out a knife. The pursuer, now pursued, grabs some rubble from a derelict building and soon a volley of bricks and obscenities are flying across the street, over the tops of cars, alarming drivers and onlookers alike. Both boys will be charged with causing an affray. Imagine other scenes of young people, fuelled with too much booze and bravado, getting themselves arrested for

---

An early draft of this chapter was revised by Paul Dwyer, and subsequently reworked for inclusion in this monograph.

© The Author(s) 2018
M. Zappavigna, JR. Martin, *Discourse and Diversionary Justice*,
DOI 10.1007/978-3-319-63763-1_1

swearing, spitting and lashing out at police or else being caught in acts of shoplifting, trespass and vandalism. Wherever you live, it's probably not too hard to imagine similar, or indeed worse, scenarios. Harder, of course, is to imagine ways of addressing the consequences of such crimes.

In the state of New South Wales (NSW), Australia, where these incidents occurred and where the research for this book was undertaken, the response to juvenile crime seems typical of the way Western liberal democracies are responding to crime in general. It is a response in which, as Bourdieu (1998: 2) once put it, 'the right hand [of the state] no longer knows, or, worse, no longer really wants to know, what the left hand does'. As our major political parties have sought to outdo each other in trumpeting their tough law and order credentials (policies of 'zero tolerance', restricted access to bail, mandatory sentencing and the like), the number of young people incarcerated in juvenile detention centres in NSW has been climbing.[1] At the same time, among many legal reform advocates, policy advisers, welfare agencies, police and some politicians, it is also understood that a custodial sentence for a juvenile offender mostly represents systemic failure—failure to support a family and kids in crisis through early intervention, failure in parenting, failure in schools, failure to learn from previous, lesser offences and failure when it comes to imagining alternative pathways to rehabilitation.[2] Gradually, the push for new ways of doing justice has gained momentum. Governments in many jurisdictions worldwide have begun to experiment with a range of alternative legal processes and diversionary sentencing programmes as a way to address systemic failures.

Throughout this book, we offer detailed descriptions and analyses of one such process, known as 'youth justice conferencing', which was established as a key part of the NSW juvenile justice system through passage of the 1997 Young Offenders Act. A typical youth justice conference brings the Young Person (YP) face to face with the Victim of his or her crime (or someone chosen to represent the victim's perspective), in the presence of each party's family members, friends, a Police Youth Liaison Officer (YLO) or Ethnic Community Liaison Officer (ECLO)[3] and perhaps one or two workers from local community organizations (schools, sporting clubs, youth centres and so on). The conference is convened by a private citizen who, while trained and accredited by the

## 1 Youth Justice Conferencing and the Purpose of This Study

state to do this work, is not acting in a direct judicial or law enforcement capacity. Rather, the Convenor's role is to facilitate a 'structured conversation' (Moore and McDonald 2000: 14) in which participants are encouraged to discuss not only how the crime occurred but also how they have been personally affected by any material damages, emotional/psychological distress or harm to relationships. Expressions of remorse and forgiveness may be exchanged and, together, participants negotiate the design of an 'outcome plan' in which the YP commits to carrying out certain tasks (for instance, some unpaid community work for a welfare organization) as a way of making amends for their offending behaviour.

Given the pervasive 'get tough on crime' rhetoric of so many politicians, the introduction of youth justice conferencing represents a remarkable investment of hope in what we might almost think of as a talking cure for the consequences of crime. Certainly, there is an understanding here that speech (and not only speech) is performative—a way of getting things done. The difficult negotiations of a conference unfold through the interplay of words, facial expression, gesture, movement, dress and seating arrangements. Through these multiple modes of communication, a YP is called upon to demonstrate acceptance of his or her responsibility for a crime while a victim, it is hoped, experiences relief from fear and anxiety. The expectation of legal reform advocates seems to be that a better quality of justice is possible in a setting that is less alienating or intimidating than a courtroom and without the mediating influence of litigating lawyers.[4] To have participants sit together in a circle, looking one another in the eye (or perhaps momentarily shunning eye contact out of a certain sense of shame) and to have them talk about their feelings is taken to be a major step towards shifting attitudes and future behaviour.

Such assumptions warrant further investigation. Despite the relative informality, there is no guarantee that conference participants are meeting on a 'level playing field' in terms of access to meaning-making resources. Indeed, the interactions in a conference are likely to be every bit as complex as some of the elements of courtroom discourse (the cross-examination tactics of lawyers; judges' instructions to juries and so on) that have been so usefully analysed in the field of forensic linguistics (see Gibbons 2003 for excellent overviews of this research; see also Conley and O'Barr 2005; Eades 2008, 2010). To date, however, diversionary forms of justice such as conferencing have received almost no attention from forensic linguists; nor has there been much in the way of discourse analysis in the large body of criminological research into these forms.

The purpose of this book is to offer a fully grounded, empirical account of how the participants in a youth justice conference use the resources available to them—literally, the way they make meanings and interact with one another through spoken discourse and other embodied modes of communication—in the process of negotiating new 'identity scripts' and promoting reintegration of the offender into family and community networks. In pursuing this agenda, we aim at the following:

- To raise consciousness of the language structures and embodied modes of communication that practitioners of restorative justice processes such as YJCs are responsible for managing
- To show how close-up discourse analysis illuminates, but also calls into question, some key notions in current restorative justice theory and research
- To encourage a wider focus of research within the field of forensic linguistics, including greater attention to diversionary processes such as conferencing
- To expand the range of tools available to linguists engaged in similar sorts of 'multimodal' discourse analysis, particularly in relation to projects concerned with how identities are jointly constructed and performed within the constraints and possibilities afforded by different genres

As noted in the Preface to this book, we come to this project as outsiders to the disciplines of criminology, transitional justice and social psychology within which the bulk of research on restorative justice has been carried out. There are bridges to be built between this body of research and the discipline of linguistics. In addition, there are pathways that we will need to signpost for linguists with complementary theoretical orientations who we hope will follow us in this interdisciplinary endeavour. To begin, we will contextualize the practice of conferencing with respect to key ideas, processes and research traditions within the broader restorative justice movement of which YJCs are a part. We will then outline the key theoretical and methodological perspectives that have informed our particular approach to discourse analysis.

## 2  The Contested Field of Restorative Justice

The range of practices to which the label 'restorative justice' has been attached in recent decades has become so eye-blurringly wide that no single definition or simple genealogy can adequately account for all usages. It is a contested term but it is nevertheless useful as a 'sensitizing theory' (Zehr 1990: 227)—a clustering of concepts that, at the very least, encourage persistently useful questions about what we might want a justice system to deliver for victims, offenders and other parties.

In practice, most attempts to define restorative justice involve a 'process conception' or a 'values conception' or a combination of both (Braithwaite and Strang 2001: 11–12). For example, the initial description of youth justice conferencing we offered earlier has process features that would be immediately recognizable to restorative justice practitioners working in many different jurisdictions worldwide. Precursors to conferencing can be readily found in the programmes of Victim–Offender Mediation (VOM) or Victim–Offender Reconciliation Programmes (VORPs) that started in North America and Europe during the 1970s and 1980s (see Maxwell and Morris 2001; Aertsen and Willemsens 2001). Parallel developments include the growing use of Circle Sentencing among indigenous communities of Canada and Australia (see Dickson-Gilmore and La Prairie 2005). A key process issue around which these programmes differ has to do with defining interests: who needs to be brought into the circle of stakeholders? On this scale, we might see conferencing as more expansive than VOMs but often less inclusive of wider community participation than Circle Sentencing. Nevertheless, the family resemblances between mediation, conferencing and circles are clear enough.

The conduct of YJCs in NSW closely resembles that of other conferencing programmes across Australia, as well as in the UK, the USA, Canada, South Africa and elsewhere. Particularly significant for the development of YJCs was a precedent set in New Zealand whereby a model of 'Family Group Conferencing' was established under the Children, Young Persons and their Families Act of 1989.[5] There are, of course, differences in the way conferencing programmes operate in these jurisdictions. They may vary in terms of the range of offences that are referred to a conference: for instance, some programmes exclude sexual assault or drug-related crime. They may also vary in the role that police play: for example, in the Australian Capital Territory and Thames Valley, UK, conferences are convened by police officers; in most other jurisdictions, as in NSW, conferences are facilitated by citizen Convenors (see Daly 2001) for commentary on the significance of these and other jurisdictional variations.[6] Again, however, the similarities between programmes are quite clear. None of them emerged in a vacuum. Without going so far as to say that YJCs are the paradigmatic example of a restorative justice process, we can at least note that juvenile conferencing in NSW is one of the largest statutory restorative justice programmes in the world today, with over 2000 referrals per year. Conferencing in NSW has also been typical insofar as its deployment in the juvenile justice sector has been the prelude to the development of conferencing schemes in the adult criminal justice system—either as a diversionary sentencing option or, in the case of crimes that lead to a custodial sentence, as a post-sentencing option that some offenders and victims seek out for purposes of rehabilitation and reconciliation.

All of the programmes mentioned here fit comfortably within Marshall's influential minimal definition of restorative justice as 'a process whereby all the parties with a stake in a particular offence come together to resolve collectively how to deal with the aftermath of the offence and its implications for the future' (in Van Ness et al. 2001: 5). This is obviously a very inclusive rubric. Not surprisingly, many practitioners and theorists in the field of restorative justice have begun connecting canonical processes like VOMs, conferencing and circles with a much wider range of practices, from initiatives such as anti-bullying schemes in primary and secondary schools to workplace-based community conferences, all the way up to larger processes of transitional justice like the South African Truth and Reconciliation Commission. This expansion of restorative justice upwards and downwards has placed some pressure on the way in which its core values and principles have been theorized (Lambert et al. 2011: 142–159). We turn to some of these key ideas now and briefly canvass the critiques that have been most relevant in the course of our research.

Following McLaughlin (2003), we can say that, broadly speaking, the value systems of restorative justice represent a convergence of four influences. First, there has been a persistent effort to trace historical connections between restorative justice and forms of dispute resolution that are believed to have existed in some pre-modern European contexts or still occur among Melanesian societies, New Zealand Maori, Australian Aboriginal and Torres Strait Islander peoples, and other 'traditional' cultures (see, for example, Weitekamp 1999; Consedine 1999). Braithwaite (2003: 58) writes of the universality of 'deep-seated restorative traditions' across human cultures, arguing that 'in the world of the twenty-first century […these] restorative traditions [are] a more valuable resource than [the equally prevalent] retributive traditions'. Second, there is the influence of faith-based traditions. Many practitioner-scholars have sought to draw parallels between restorative justice and the values of repentance and forgiveness as expressed in Old and New Testament writings, or in the foundational texts of Buddhism, Islam and other religions (see Hadley 2001). Third, there is the influence of what has been called the 'new communitarianism' (Etzioni 1998). Here, the emphasis is on rebuilding 'community associations and attachments to bolster a highly localized democratic culture' (McLaughlin 2003: 3). This is seen as a corrective to the excessive emphasis on individual rights and entitlements that has developed under a culture of laissez-faire liberalism, particularly in the USA. The aim is to strengthen civil society by balancing individual rights with greater respect for social responsibilities. Fourth, there have been borrowings from critical criminology and abolitionism. A seminal article by Christie, 'Conflicts as Property' (1977), captures the tenor of this line of thinking. His key argument—that conflict presents an opportunity for repairing and strengthening social bonds but that modern legal systems have effectively robbed victims, offenders and grassroots communities of their rightful place in managing conflict—is still widely cited in the restorative justice literature. Christie's argument rings true particularly insofar as the experience of victims is concerned, absent as they often are from court proceedings, and many restorative justice initiatives have also developed in close interaction with victim support movements (Strang and Braithwaite 2001).

Undoubtedly, it is expecting too much for any neat synthesis to have formed out of the convergence of these influences on restorative justice. Braithwaite perhaps comes closest to enunciating a core value that all practitioners would acknowledge: 'Restorative justice is about the notion that because crime (or any other kind of injustice) hurts, justice should heal' (in Ahmed et al. 2001: 4). In line with the assumption that conventional court proceedings typically fail to achieve this, Howard Zehr offers another popular shorthand definition when, like Braithwaite, he sets restorative justice against dominant forms of retributive justice:

> Retributive Justice [sees crime as] a violation of the state, defined by lawbreaking and guilt. Justice determines blame and administers pain in a contest between the offender and the state directed by systematic rules.
> Restorative Justice [sees crime as] a violation of people and relationships. It creates obligations to make things right. Justice involves the victim, the offender, and the community in a search for solutions which promote repair, reconciliation, and reassurance. (Zehr 1990: 181)

As noted at the start of this section, such working definitions of restorative justice are always going to raise as many questions as they answer. One line of critique is to question whether Zehr's binary opposition between retributive and restorative justice is as clear-cut as he implies. To make an obvious point, the largest and best-known restorative programmes are nearly always operating under statutory regulations that place them within, rather than outside, the criminal justice system. Youth justice conferencing in NSW is again quite typical in this regard. Referral to a YJC comes via the police before a matter goes to court, or via a court if a children's magistrate thinks that a YJC will be of more rehabilitative benefit to the YP. Whatever the referral route, the outcome plan from a YJC must be submitted to the children's magistrate's court for approval. The NSW Young Offenders Act explicitly states that sanctions imposed on a YP as part of an outcome plan should have regard to the severity of sanctions 'that might have been imposed in court proceedings for the offence concerned' (Section 52 (6)). They are not to be more severe, and will often be accompanied by forms of symbolic reparation such as an apology; nevertheless, outcome plans—and, indeed, the experience of the conference itself—do constitute a form of punishment, no matter how gently administered. Should a YP fail to complete their YJC outcome plan, the matter comes back before the magistrate's court, reinforcing the point that this is where the ultimate sanction lies. Of course, it is also possible to view in a positive light the way restorative justice is embedded within conventional criminal justice systems. The courts can provide a necessary check and balance against any community conferencing practices that might otherwise veer towards vigilantism. Alternatively, magistrates, through their engagement with community-based practices, might become more attuned to the restorative values that allow offenders, victims and communities to reconcile. This, in turn, might garner more support from legal agents for restorative justice as a social movement aiming to move beyond the 'get tough on crime' politics that fuels a culture of retribution.

Another difficulty with the attempts of Zehr, Braithwaite and others to define restorative justice concerns the problematic status of 'community' as a concept, let alone as a lived reality. Who represents 'the' community and on what basis? In what sense can restorative justice help heal communities? If, as many criminologists would argue, the high levels of social dysfunction in certain communities are one of the causes of crime, how much hope can we have of finding respected individuals with the necessary resources to make conferencing and other restorative programmes the kind of democratic grassroots decision-making forum envisaged by communitarian theory? As poststructuralist critiques (for example, Pavlich 2005) and feminist analyses (Daly and Stubbs 2007; Hudson et al. 1996) of restorative justice have emphasized, the experience of community is as much about exclusion as inclusion. Special interests based on race, gender, class or other forms of social stratification cannot be so easily dissolved as the homogenizing discourse of community in the rhetoric of restorative justice sometimes seems to imagine. From our point of view as discourse analysts, this issue is particularly pertinent. In the analysis of actual discourse samples, we see conference participants negotiating forms of solidarity that are not simply 'there', as fixed values to be plugged into a conference, but that are always 'at risk' and needing to be made anew.

On the issue of how restorative justice relates to dispute resolution processes across a range of indigenous cultures, critics have been particularly vocal. For Daly (2001), these origin stories are mostly mythical and misguided. For a start, they trivialize important differences between cultures, as well as the impact of colonialism on the social structures that sustain traditional practices:

> To say that conferences are 'like' indigenous justice practices is to re-engage a white-centred view of the world. It erases the many histories of indigenous justice practices, some of which would not be comprehensible or acceptable in the modern world. And, as Blagg (1997) suggests, it may lead to a 'double failure' for indigenous groups: not only will they have failed to act in a law-abiding fashion [...] they will appear to have 'failed' to act appropriately as indigenous people according to a white-centred justice script. (Daly 2001: 66; see also Dickson-Gilmore and La Prairie 2005)

Blagg (1997, 2008) further argues that proselytizers of conferencing often give inadequate attention to the specific, local characteristics of political campaigns by indigenous activists who have forced the issue of legal reform, including the development of restorative justice programmes, on sometimes reluctant state institutions. Australian practitioners, he suggests, have drawn superficially on the New Zealand Maori experience when promoting conferencing as a means to help divert Indigenous Australian youth from deeper entanglement with the criminal justice system.[7] Not only have they ignored the range of other policy initiatives that accompanied and bolstered the original implementation of conferencing in New Zealand; they have also downplayed the risk that conferencing programmes could result in 'net-widening' (minor matters that police may have previously ignored or dealt with via an on-the-spot warning could be scaled up to a matter for conferencing just because this option exists) and thereby lead to greater police control over the lives of young people. As Cuneen and White (2007: 344) explain, diversionary justice generally involves 'diversion *to* other parts of the criminal justice system, rather than diversion *from* the system itself' and the informality of some processes, if abused by police, could mean a YP misses out on protections offered by the courts and professional legal assistance.[8]

Foreshadowing an argument to which we will return several times in this book, we suggest that critics are right to question whether conferencing is always such a close cultural fit for disenfranchised indigenous youth or, indeed, for any YP without the appropriate cultural capital (including the necessary linguistic resources) to engage in it. As Daly puts it, conferencing can be practised in ways that are

> *flexible and accommodating* toward cultural differences [but it is] better understood as a fragmented justice form: it splices white, bureaucratic forms of justice with elements of informal justice that may include non-white (or non-Western) values or methods of judgment. (Daly 2001: 65)

Having noted some of the complexities in the values associated with restorative justice, we should also point out that critics like Daly, Cuneen and other criminologists cited earlier are, nevertheless, sympathetic—as are we—to much of what advocates of restorative justice have sought to achieve. Indeed, as a social movement, it has cut through with policy makers to an impressive degree. To understand this, we turn now to the promise through which restorative justice has been promoted, the evidence adduced to support claims and the theoretical frameworks offered to explain results.

## 3    Researching a New Paradigm

For many proponents of restorative justice, the processes and values described in the preceding section are part and parcel of an ambitious reform agenda, constituting a 'radical alternative to our current way of viewing and responding to crime' (Johnstone 2011: 6). On the other hand, for some critics, as Johnstone notes, restorative justice 'still takes for granted most of the language, assumptions and structures of criminal justice' and seems to underestimate the structural violence that sustains unequal social relations (2011: 7). As Braithwaite himself acknowledges, restorative justice cannot resolve the deep structural injustices that cause problems like hunger [though] we should hope from restorative justice for micro-measures that ameliorate macro-injustice [... at the very least, it] should restore harmony with a remedy grounded in dialogue which takes account of underlying injustices. (Braithwaite 2003: 57)

In any case, the fact that gaps are sometimes apparent between the rhetoric and the realities of particular restorative justice initiatives does not, in and of itself, invalidate these initiatives. It is not unreasonable for proponents of restorative justice to rally around a possibly utopian social vision while, at the same time, resigning themselves to the hard slog of having to engage with existing bureaucracies in order to secure small, incremental changes.

In practice, the 'promotion' of restorative justice has involved the promise of improvements that are easily enough reconciled with the pragmatic concerns of bureaucrats and policy makers. Four specific claims have been repeatedly advanced: (i) that restorative justice processes should prove more satisfying to both victims and offenders than court-based remedies; (ii) that there should be strong, positive perceptions of procedural fairness in relation to restorative justice and that this, in turn, should fuel greater respect for the justice system; (iii) that restorative justice programmes are likely to be less expensive to run than court-based programmes; and (iv) that offenders who go through a restorative justice process should be less likely to reoffend than those who go through a conventional court hearing. Criminologists have focused a great deal of their attention on testing these claims and the research literature on restorative justice now includes numerous evaluations of conferencing schemes in Australia, New Zealand, North America and Europe (see, for example, Campbell et al. 2005; Maruna et al. 2007; Maxwell and Morris 2001; McCold and Wachtel 1998; Palk et al. 1998; Sherman et al. 2000; Trimboli and New South Wales 2000).

Not surprisingly, a lot of the political debate around restorative justice has centred on the claim that conferencing can help lower recidivism rates. A number of early studies did offer encouragement for this view. Braithwaite (2002) reviews the findings on recidivism of over 20 evaluations of restorative programmes. He notes the methodological problems with some studies and a good deal of variation in results but concludes that, even at the lower end of the scale, it would be reasonable to predict 'modest benefits in the order of 10 to 20 percent lower levels of reoffending' when matters are dealt with through a restorative process rather than through the courts (Braithwaite 2002: 61). The most promising results he cites are from randomized controlled studies in Indianapolis (McGarrell 2000) and in Canberra (the landmark 'Re-Integrative Shaming Experiments' or RISE project: see Sherman et al. 2000; Ahmed et al. 2001). Results from the former showed a rate of re-arrest that was 40 per cent lower (after 6 months) or 25 per cent lower (after 12 months) when first-time juvenile offenders went through a conferencing process rather than a court process. The RISE results suggested that violent offenders who went through a conference were 38 per cent less likely to re-offend than those who went to court. As Braithwaite (2002: 69) argued in his 2002 review, such studies appeared to have validated the 'the great promise [of restorative justice] as a strategy of crime reduction'.

However, the picture emerging from more recent research is less clear. Smith and Weatherburn (2012) stress, even more than Braithwaite, the methodological difficulties involved in comparing the rates of recidivism by offenders who go through a conference to those of offenders who are dealt with in the courts. They argue that, even in randomized controlled trials such as the RISE study, researchers have often failed to take account of differences between the treatment and control groups (ignoring, for example, a range of variables that are associated with a propensity to re-offend) and have potentially skewed results through inappropriate statistical methods, through a lack of clarity about whether the treatment group includes all offenders assigned to a conference or only those who completed a conference, or else through an overly restrictive definition of re-offending Smith and Weatherburn (2012: 6). Their own analysis of re-offending outcomes across a large sample of juvenile offenders in NSW carefully adjusts for such factors and concludes that youth justice conferences are, in fact, no more effective (nor any less effective) than proceedings in the NSW Children's Court when it comes to reducing the risk of recidivism (2012: 17).[9]

Such findings will no doubt disappoint some proponents of restorative justice but it is also possible to see them as justification for a salutary refocusing of the debate on restorative justice options. Simply put, if the only arguments that ever carry weight are those that deal with 'hard' issues like recidivism rates, then we are quite likely missing whatever is new about the 'new paradigm' of restorative justice. As Smith and Weatherburn (2012) themselves argue, whatever the impact on re-offending, conferencing still merits support if it delivers justice to both offenders and victims:

> If conferencing gives victims of crime some measure of closure and relief while at the same time restraining the public appetite for expensive but ineffective punishments, then it serves a valuable purpose. The challenge for policy makers is to devise a legal and administrative framework that allows police and/or courts to refer juvenile offenders to conferencing – while at the same time ensuring that those who need effective intervention and support to reduce the risk of further offending receive it. (Smith and Weatherburn 2012: 17)

In this regard, the more encouraging and more robust findings from the plethora of evaluations of conferencing concern the high levels of satisfaction that participants report in relation to conference outcomes and their positive perceptions of conferencing as procedurally fair. An evaluation by Trimboli (2000) of the NSW youth conferencing programme, for instance, reported that 79 per cent of victims, 90 per cent of offenders and 95 per cent of offenders' Support Persons agreed or strongly agreed with a statement about being satisfied overall with the way the case was handled. While other researchers have found a little more variation between the responses of offenders and those of victims, even the least optimistic studies report results that are in line with Trimboli's findings (see, for example, Wagland et al. 2013).

Criminologists and social psychologists have offered various theoretical perspectives on the social interaction that they believe is contributing to these largely positive evaluations of conferencing. The theory of 'reintegrative shaming', first articulated in Braithwaite's landmark publication *Crime, Shame and Reintegration* (1989a), has been particularly influential. In brief, Braithwaite argues that societies with low rates of crime (such as Japan) mobilize the power of shame as a form of social sanction in different and more effective ways than societies with high crime rates (such as in the USA). However, as he readily acknowledges, shaming is a dangerous game. It is clearly counterproductive when it results in stigmatizing labels being applied to offenders, thereby confirming their deviance as a kind of master identity trait and 'push[ing them] into the clutches of criminal subcultures' (1989a, b: 4). According to Braithwaite, it is essential to distinguish between shaming that produces stigmatization of this kind and shaming that has a useful reintegrative effect. Reintegrative shaming is

> shaming which is followed by efforts to reintegrate the offender into the community of law-abiding or respectable citizens through words or gestures of forgiveness or ceremonies to decertify the offender as deviant. [...] It is shaming which labels the act as evil while striving to preserve the identity of the offender as essentially good. (Braithwaite 1989: 100–101)

Shortly after publishing *Crime, Shame and Reintegration*, Braithwaite was able to observe family group conferences in New Zealand and the early trials of youth conferencing in Wagga Wagga (NSW), with these having since been interpreted as exemplary practices of reintegrative shaming.

However, the notion of reintegrative shaming has not been uncontested in the restorative justice literature. Critics have questioned whether shame is really as central to the efficacy of conferencing as Braithwaite suggests. Tangney (1991), for instance, has argued that shame induction can be destructive of self-esteem (which is already low in many young offenders) and actually contributes to criminal pathologies. In her account, guilt is the more 'moral emotion' stemming from a sense of responsibility for one's actions. Maxwell and Morris (2002) take a similar position when they argue that the key to reintegration of an offender is remorse, not shame. The trigger for remorse, they suggest, is an experience of empathy with the victim that comes as the offender starts to understand the consequences of their actions. Scheff and Retzinger (1991), in their critique, stress the role of pride as a counterpoint to shame: the former suggests enjoyment of social bonds that are intact, while the latter arises from bonds that are threatened or broken. In their view, conferences are successful not because of shaming that is instigated by others but because the offender has a chance to discharge their own internal feelings of shame through a 'core sequence' of remorse and forgiveness (Retzinger and Scheff 1996).

In response to such criticisms, Braithwaite and his associates have readily acknowledged the need for 'repair work' to the theory of reintegrative shaming (Ahmed et al. 2001: 41). However, the statistical analyses conducted by Harris and Burton (1997) as part of the RISE study of conferencing in Canberra suggest that what Tangney is calling guilt and what Maxwell and Morris understand by remorse will co-occur with an offender's experience of shame (Harris in Ahmed et al. 2001: 106–130). As a consequence, one adjustment to the theory has been to make more careful distinctions between shaming as *a practice* (that can be either stigmatizing or reintegrative), shame as *an emotional response* to a particular set of circumstances and shame-proneness as *a personality trait*. Braithwaite clearly accepts the need to avoid stigmatizing an offender who is already prone to a generalized sense of shame and low self-esteem. He also acknowledges that no matter how much conscious effort is applied towards criticizing the deed not the doer, it is hard to disentangle completely other people's assessment of your actions from your own self-assessment in relation to identity; what we do usually does say something about who we are. Picking up on the arguments of his critics, Braithwaite now stresses the importance of finding ways within a conference to resolve the shame a young offender may be feeling in relation to self. In addition, he highlights the fluidity of identity that is involved in this process. Restorative justice is seen, in part, as 'restorative storytelling', helping an offender to break with a 'criminal self-story' and fostering, instead, 'an ethical conception of the self' (Ahmed et al. 2001: 10). The interaction between offenders and victims is clearly important here insofar as it encourages an offender's sense of empathy and remorse. However, the offender's Support Persons—if these are people whom the offender respects—have an equally crucial role to play in making sure that the complex experience of remorse, shame and guilt has a positive side to it. The young offender must be encouraged to see that their actions are out of character with the person who they and their supporters want them to be.

Looking further, Moore and McDonald offer not so much a critique as an extension to the idea of reintegrative shaming by drawing on the affect theory of Tomkins (Tomkins 2009). Shame, in Tomkins' work, is about 'inferiority' and is regarded as an auxiliary to other affects, amplifying or reducing their strength; it is experienced as an interruption to the impulses that would otherwise allow us to express interest and enjoyment in the company of another person. Hence, as Braithwaite would agree, McDonald and Moore (2001: 138) see shame as not all negative: at the very least, it serves as a 'visceral reminder' that what we most desire is to engage positively with other people. For McDonald and Moore, Tomkins's theory helps to explain how other emotions beyond shame are at work in conferencing, as well as the collective and embodied nature of our emotional experiences. They suggest that successful conferences will move through the following stages of emotionality:

- A stage marked by contempt, anger and fear, directed at individuals, as a result of their actions in the past
- A stage marked by disgust, distress and surprise, evoked by present revelations about those actions, and associated thoughts and emotions
- A transitional stage of shame, experienced individually as deflation and collectively as vulnerability, once the group has a fuller picture of how they have all been affected
- A stage marked by interest and then by relief, as plans for the future are developed (Moore and McDonald 2001: 138 emphasis in original)

This account is broadly in line with what Harris et al. (2004: 199) have offered as an 'ideal-typical theoretical construction' of the emotional dynamics of conferencing. Harris et al. acknowledge, however, that the order in which emotions occur in actual conferences is likely to fluctuate more than such models suggest. The intention behind their modelling of ideal–typical practice is to 'orient theoretical thinking on what really happens in a conference' as well as to encourage 'research to complement the quantitative evaluations through in-depth qualitative observations and descriptions of conferencing' (Harris et al. 2004: 199).

As a response to such an invitation (and as a point of departure for our own research) one point to make is how linguistic and paralinguistic behaviour regularly 'falls below the radar' in the empirical studies used to examine the efficacy of conferencing. If the emotional dynamics of conferencing are as crucial as the authors cited here suggest, surely we should expect to see at least some of this complex emotional work being realized through language? To their credit, researchers on the RISE project did include several language-related items on a 'Global Ratings Questionnaire' as one means of structuring their observations of a large sample of conferences. However, given the sheer volume of cases these researchers were dealing with, most of these questions were very broad in focus, significantly limiting their usefulness (for example, 'How much respect for the offender was expressed?' 'How emotionally powerful was the account given of consequences of the offender's act?' 'How much was the offender's speech affected by irregularities, pauses or incoherence? (Harris and Burton 1997: 14–31)). Such items either scored low in terms of inter-rater reliability or else scored high only because observers reported few if any instances of the phenomena in question.

Qualitative studies of conferencing practice allow more scope for analysing communication strategies but here, too, research has been patchy. Retzinger and Scheff (1996), for instance, usefully draw attention to the subtlety with which fleeting gestures of remorse and forgiveness might support symbolic reparation in a conference. However, in making this argument, they also make an unnecessarily crude distinction between the 'mostly verbal' process of negotiating an outcome plan and the 'crucial non-verbal elements, the exchange of emotions and changes in the relationships between participants' that they see as constituting the bulk of the conference—as if participants could be doing all this interpersonal work in complete silence. Further, qualitative studies that have attempted some discourse analysis, using actual transcripts and tag-and-retrieve style coding, have been limited to fairly general commentary on items of thematic interest. The most engaging work so far has been bolstered by Foucault's social theory and has attended to discourses, in the broadest sense of the term, as forms of power and control that are open to abuse (see, for instance, Young 2001; Hoyle et al. 2002).

The lack of close-up attention to discourse in restorative justice research contrasts starkly with the interest in language we have observed in our interactions with conference Convenors, as well as the trainers of Convenors. Convenors do want to understand the variety of ways in which participants use language and other communicative modes to 'tell their side of the story' or to 'show their feelings'. The *Conference Convenor Training Package*, developed by the NSW Youth Justice Conferencing Directorate, for instance, recognizes that the ordering and precise wording of questions asked by a Convenor are powerful resources for encouraging respondents to thematize certain issues. Training consultants suggest that a 'deliberately mannered use of voice, face and body' may be necessary if a Convenor is to be 'perceived as both authoritative and neutral by all participants' (Moore et al. 2000: 71; Moore and McDonald 2000). They also recommend a number of specific techniques, such as 'try not to raise the pitch of your voice; do not add "yes", "I see", "hmmm", "sure" while people are speaking' and so on, which highlight just how far the conversation in a conference can differ from the conventions of casual conversation, workplace conversations or, indeed, courtroom discourse with which the participants may be more familiar. This close attendance to language that Convenors and trainers espouse warrants closer investigation.

## 4 Fieldwork and Ethnographic Methodology

Our particular approach to qualitative research combines ethnography with methods of discourse analysis that derive from a linguistic tradition known as systemic functional linguistics (SFL). SFL is a wide-ranging theory that offers a number of tools for understanding the meaning-making practices that occur in both language and embodied communication. Before outlining some of the key concepts of SFL, however, it is important we first describe the nature and scope of our fieldwork, and highlight the methodological issues that have informed the way we see the ethnographic work linking up with the discourse analysis.

Following consultation with the NSW Youth Justice Conferencing Directorate in late 2005, this project began with one member of our team (Dwyer) attending (as a participant-observer) the workshops through which new Convenors are trained. Through discussion and detailed simulations, these workshops provided valuable insights into how Convenors are encouraged to think about their role within a conference. In addition, these four days of workshops provided a substantial introduction to the legislative and regulatory frameworks within which conferences operate. The NSW Young Offenders Act contains strict provisions to ensure the confidential nature of conference proceedings. Accordingly, access to outside observers for training or research purposes is carefully controlled. A research protocol was developed in consultation with the NSW Attorney General's Department allowing us to observe conferences but also, in some cases, to document proceedings on video. In line with this protocol, names of participants, localities and other identifying features have been altered or deleted in transcripts; video frame-grabs have also been digitally altered to mask faces.

With our ethics protocol approved, Dwyer and our project's post-doctoral fellow, Zappavigna, attended several professional development days at which the project was introduced to the administrators who manage conferencing in different metropolitan and regional areas (most of them were former Convenors themselves). Introductions to Convenors who were willing to have their conferences observed were made through these managers. The Convenors were given information statements and consent forms which they, in turn, supplied to participants during their normal pre-conference briefing sessions. While recognizing that it would have been valuable for us to observe the ways in which Convenors help to frame participants' expectations prior to a conference, we chose not to attend these briefings. We did not want the fundamental process whereby Convenors negotiate agreement to attend a conference among participants to be clouded by the further issue of negotiating consent for us, as researchers, to attend and document proceedings. Convenors would simply mention our interest in attending; consent for our presence as observers and documenters was negotiated in a separate meeting just prior to the conference and was based on an explicit agreement that we would leave the conference and switch off recording equipment at any point should any participant so desire (no such request was ever made).

As well as striving to avoid any form of coercion in recruiting participants for the research, video-recording equipment was set up in a way that was unobtrusive but nevertheless clearly visible; we wanted to avoid turning the conference into a TV studio but also avoid any impression that we were doing covert surveillance.[10] Two cameras were mounted on specially adapted microphone stands that have a smaller base than standard camera tripods and could thus be set well back into opposite corners of the room. The cameras were left to run unattended, on a fixed, wide-focus setting. At the suggestion of Convenors, the researchers in attendance (never more than two people) sat within the circle of other conference participants, usually opposite the Convenor in a place where 'third-party' participants such as teachers or social workers tend to sit. Apart from introducing ourselves to the other participants at the start of the conference, we did not participate verbally. Field notes were written directly after, but not during, each conference. Figure 1.1 shows the typical conditions in which observation and documentation occurred. The camera recording the conference is visible in the corner of the room in the centre of the left-hand image.

One issue that is sometimes raised in regard to video documentation of such sensitive processes is whether or not the presence of recording equipment induces people to alter their behaviour. While this possibility certainly deserves consideration it is worth recalling that audio and

**Fig. 1.1** Examples of a youth justice conference (This image has been stylized to aid in preserving anonymity)

video-recording equipment has been used for decades by conversation analysts and sociolinguists, and more recently by researchers conducting ethnographic studies of intimate theatre rehearsal processes (McAuley 2008), without any apparent disruption to normal behavioural patterns. Simply put, participants in a youth justice conference have a more than full-time job on their hands just dealing with the immediate communicative demands of keeping the conference going. Apart from an occasional remark or glance at the cameras in the first minute or two of a conference, participants seemed fully absorbed in the matter at hand. The following comment, made by the Mother of a YP after a conference had just ended and cameras were about to be switched off, is typical in this regard (transcription conventions are explained in Appendix B).

### Extract 1.1, Shopping Trolley YJC

**Mother:** I forgot they were even there, (...) you like don't even think, just like say what you have to say and that's it.
**Convenor:** And that's excellent, that's exactly what these guys want to hear.
**Mother:** (That's it). You forget that the camera's sitting there on.

Between 2007 and 2010, we worked with four different Convenors: a retired school principal, a former police officer, a currently serving police officer who convenes conferences as a private citizen on her days off and a community worker with a background in conflict resolution and human rights advocacy. A total of 14 conferences were observed, of which 8 were documented on video. Table 1.1 gives a brief summary of these video-recorded conferences. Each conference has been given a shorthand title that we will use throughout the book when labelling transcript excerpts.

This is, of course, a very small number of conferences compared to the thousands of cases that occurred during the period of our fieldwork; notably, it is not a statistically representative sample.[11] Due to the sensitive nature of the context in which our research was embedded we were not able to create a sample of recorded conferences that is representative

Table 1.1 The sample of video-recorded NSW youth justice conferences used in this study

| YJC | Offence |
| --- | --- |
| Affray | The Young Person (YP) committed an affray offence |
| Batteries | The YP stole a packet of batteries from a supermarket |
| Guidedog | The YP stole the wallet of a blind woman |
| Mobile phone | The YP swapped his mobile phone for a stolen mobile phone |
| Running shoes | The YP stole some running shoes from a shopping centre |
| School library | Two YPs entered a school library and 'roughed up' a student |
| Shopping trolley | The YP threw a shopping trolley near railway tracks |
| Train tracks | The YP stole a packet of chips from her local service station and ran away onto train tracks when pursued by police |

of all demographic dimensions. However, for the analysis we are presenting, this sample was sufficient. The cases we observed were extremely rich in a variety of phenomena that conferencing, as a social practice, obviously provides for, and the range of data allowed for models to be tested and modified as needed. And the sample does cover a range of YPs reflective of broader demographic patterns. In terms of gender, from 13 cases, 2 YPs are women and 11 are men; and in terms of ethnicity, the backgrounds of the YPs span Aboriginal and Torres Strait Islander (3), Pacific Islander (1), Asian (2), Lebanese (1) and Anglo-Celtic (6).

Using a small dataset such as ours allows for a comprehensive treatment: there is scope to test ideas against all the data, not simply those instances for which statistically significant correlations can be calculated (Silverman 2006: 298–299). There is also more ability to explore in detail the most relevant of the many thousands of meanings that are being made in the discourse of each conference across multiple modes of communication.

The research discussed in this book is informed in part by an ethnographic approach. Ethnographic research, as a form of qualitative inquiry, is by its very nature open-ended and exploratory. The researcher often spends a considerable amount of time as a 'participant observer', usually in a single small-scale setting, essentially trying to answer two questions: What do I see (and hear, smell, taste, touch) is going on here? How do these activities make sense for those involved in them? Inherently, the approach is more about generating, rather than testing, hypotheses.

Through close-up, in-depth study of a small number of cases, the researcher tries to explain, for instance, whatever is particular to the way certain cultural activities are carried out in a given setting or to account for the ways in which practices may have evolved over time. Such explanations are necessarily provisional. Implicitly or explicitly, any ethnographic study is part of a larger comparative project which might be summed up as the long-term effort to understand the many different ways of 'being in the world' which humans have devised in response to a range of common challenges.

In ethnographic research, when we talk to people about the practices they are engaged in, what they reveal are not universal truths but situated responses to the researcher's questions. From the many hours of informal conversation with Convenors, as well as the formal interviews conducted during our research, we certainly gained insights into the perceptual frameworks and exemplary conference experiences that help Convenors orient themselves to the role they must play. However, the views expressed in interviews are, of course, representations of experience; they do not offer direct, unmediated access to the heart of what may be occurring in practice (Silverman 2006: 118). As the anthropologist Jackson so aptly remarks, 'the knowledge whereby one lives is not necessarily identical with the knowledge whereby one explains life' (Jackson 1996: 2). It follows that to make sense of how the people engaged in a practice are, themselves, making sense of their activities requires more than simply echoing their common-sense explanations.

Geertz addresses this methodological challenge in his famous definition of ethnography as 'thick description', an elaboration of the multiple 'structures of signification' or 'frames of interpretation' which combine to shape a person's (not always conscious) understanding of what particular actions might mean (Geertz 1973: 6–9). This kind of analysis requires, in Geertz's view, the use of both 'experience-near' and 'experience-distant' concepts. Concepts that are experience-near are those that an insider might 'naturally and effortlessly' apply to a situation, whereas experience-distant concepts are those that 'specialists of one sort or another […] employ to forward their scientific, philosophic or practical aims' (Geertz 1983: 57). For instance, a YP might gloss their experience of a conference as 'a bit of a lecture but fair enough'; the specialist observer might describe it as 'a reintegrative shaming ceremony'. Clearly, there is some overlap but also some semantic slippage here. Any suggestion that some young people experience reintegrative shaming as lecturing would, of course, be revealing and ethnographic analysis would want to keep both descriptions in play for this very reason. As Geertz (1983: 57) puts it, '[c]onfinement to experience-near concepts leaves an ethnographer awash in immediacies, as well as entangled in vernacular. Confinement to experience-distant ones leaves him [sic] stranded in abstractions and smothered in jargon'. In the same essay, Geertz goes on to describe the 'characteristic intellectual movement' of ethnographic analysis as follows:

> [A] continuous dialectical tacking between the most local of local detail and the most global of global structure in such a way as to bring them into simultaneous view. [...] Hopping back and forth between the whole conceived through the parts that actualize it and the parts conceived through the whole that motivates them, we seek to turn them, by a sort of intellectual perpetual motion, into explications of one another. (Geertz 1983: 69)

For us, this description could well be extended to cover the dialogical practice of research meetings in which the ethnographic fieldworker (Dwyer) and the specialist linguists (Zappavigna and Martin, the other chief investigator on the project) would tack back and forth between fine-grained analyses of small portions of transcript and, for instance, sweeping discussions about the place of ritual in a secular society. Furthermore, a similar kind of dialectical movement is very much built into the model of language, SFL, that guided the discourse analysis work, and to which we now turn.

## 5 'Context and Text': A Brief Introduction to Systemic Functional Linguistics (SFL)

Ethnographic research, as we suggested earlier, is propelled by the question 'What exactly is going on here?'. Whatever else is happening, a youth justice conference involves talk—a lot of it. Our approach to discourse analysis has been informed by SFL, which is a comprehensive theory of language.[12] Here we introduce some of the key principles. The more specific tools used to analyse YJCs will be introduced as they become relevant.

To begin, SFL is considered to be a functional theory of language. For linguists who are trained in this tradition, this means that two of the most important questions to ask about language are

(i) How do people actually use language across a whole range of situations from the everyday to the 'extra-daily'?
(ii) How is language itself structured to make such a diversity of uses possible?

According to Halliday, the foundational figure for SFL theory, these issues are always closely linked: 'The nature of language is closely related to the demands we make on it, the functions it has to serve' (Halliday 1970: 140). To model this, Halliday argues that we can identify three main strands of meaning—or metafunctions—that shape language use (Halliday and Matthiessen 1999, 2004). First, we use language to construe our experience of the world around us. In SFL, this is called the ideational metafunction of language. This strand of meaning is about 'what's going on, including who's doing what to whom, where, when, why and how and the logical relation of one going-on to another' (Martin and Rose 2008: 24). Second, we use language to interact with other language users. This is the interpersonal metafunction, involving the use of resources to negotiate social relations, to share feelings and so on. Third, there are the resources that we use to make a text 'hang together', to control the flow of information. This is the textual metafunction of language. Critically, SFL theory posits that when we use language we are making these three complementary kinds of meaning all at the same time: ideational, interpersonal and textual meanings are 'fused together in linguistic units' (Eggins 1994: 3). The tools for language description developed within SFL help us to analyse these strands of meaning separately as well as cumulatively.

To make this a little more concrete, consider the following brief snippet of talk from a youth justice conference involving two boys who had

## 5 'Context and Text': A Brief Introduction to Systemic Functional... 27

admitted trespassing on, and vandalizing, an unoccupied house. Here is how one of the boys described what occurred:

> We just started running around the place, punching and kicking holes in the walls. ... There's one wall that just kept getting damaged. (Conference transcript from Australian Broadcasting Commission program 'Radio Eye', Davis (2002))

What can we say about the meanings being made by this YP? In terms of ideation, he moves from an initial concern with his own agency (the verbs '*running*', '*punching*' and '*kicking*' are material processes carried out by him and his mate, collaboratively) to a focus on 'one wall' that 'kept getting damaged' by means and by agents that are now no longer named. Interpersonally, the repetition of '*just*', in the phrases '*just running around*' and '*just kept getting damaged*', helps further soften the focus on the boys' actions. The listener is invited to judge them a little less harshly, as if this is simply an example of what boys sometimes do, or of what sometimes happens to walls. Textually, the ideas in this excerpt are organized by taking the YPs as point of departure (*we*) and the damage to the walls as news (*started running around the place, punching and kicking holes in the walls; one wall that just kept getting damaged*).

As experienced language users, a moment's reflection tells us that the speaker could have made other choices. He could have said, for instance: 'I felt this amazing surge of adrenalin as I started smashing the wall – it was a real buzz.' This would make for a very different constellation of ideational, interpersonal and textual meanings. In this version, the speaker would not only be declaring his agency in the act of vandalism; he would also be inviting his listeners to empathize with the strong affectual response that accompanied this action and he would be packaging this information in such a way as to ultimately make the 'buzz' seem more newsworthy than the damage to the wall. Of course, as soon as we take into account the context of a youth justice conference, we are also able to understand how the YP would want to avoid inviting conference participants to share meanings of this kind.

One of the key concerns of SFL is to make language choices explicit. SFL maps the choices language users can make through diagrams known as system networks. The different choices shown in a system network offer options for meaning in a text. In this way, system networks display language as a meaning potential—a set of options that can be taken up for different purposes. This is a perspective that considers language paradigmatically in terms of 'what could go instead of what' (Halliday and Matthiessen 2004: 22), rather than modelling language as a catalogue of structures. As an example, Fig. 1.3 shows a simplified version of the system network used for analysing MOOD in English. This network is based on the analyses of English grammar presented by Halliday and Matthiessen (2013). It distinguishes declarative (information giving), interrogative (information seeking) and imperative (directing) clauses:

[declarative]
We started running round the place.

[interrogative]
Did we start running round the place?

[imperative]
Start running round the place.

Within system network symbolism, a square bracket represents a choice between two options (an 'or' relation). The network in Fig. 1.2 can thus be read procedurally from left to right as 'choose between indicate or imperative, and if indicative, choose between declarative and interrogative'. The network in Fig. 1.2 also includes realization statements (in boxes following a slated arrow) specifying the structural consequences of a particular choice. For example, in Halliday's grammar of English, all indicative clauses (information-negotiating declarative and interrogative ones) have a Subject and a Finite function, while in unmarked imperative clauses (request-negotiating ones) these functions are absent. Further, in declaratives the Subject comes before the Finite, while in interrogatives the Subject follows the Finite.

A brace (curly bracket) in system networks represents simultaneous choices (an 'and' relation). For example, Fig. 1.3 shows that English

## 5 'Context and Text': A Brief Introduction to Systemic Functional...

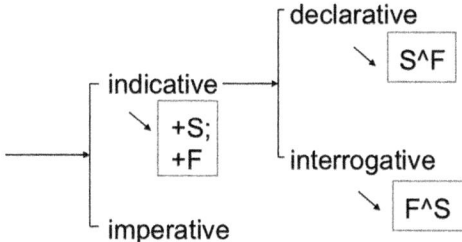

**Fig. 1.2** Basic English MOOD systems

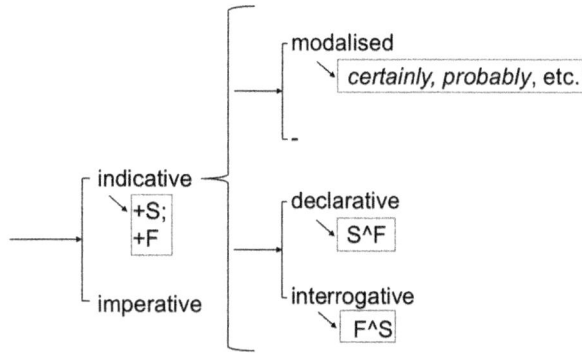

**Fig. 1.3** English MOOD and MODALIZATION

indicative clauses can be modalized, while imperative clauses cannot. This means that indicative clauses choose between declarative and interrogative options at the same time as they allow for the possibility of MODALIZATION (e.g. shown by *certainly* in *We certainly started running round the place*).

As indicated in the preceding paragraphs, by convention the names of systems in SFL are written in small caps (e.g. MOOD, MODALIZATION), while the choices within systems are written in lower case.

The task of mapping system networks and their interrelations is an ongoing challenge for SFL theory, rendered especially complex by the fact that systems are operating at different levels—or 'strata'—of language. At the level of phonology (for speech) or graphology (for written texts), we have systems for producing meaningful sounds or combinations of letters and punctuation marks. Above this, there is the level of lexicogrammar that describes the wordings of clauses, groups and phrases. Further above, there is the level of discourse semantics that maps the meanings made in larger stretches of discourse. And finally, SFL puts forward a model of context, the most abstract levels of meaning in this model. From the perspective of metafunctions, we can think of context in terms of variations in register. In the version of SFL theory we use here, these register variables are field (the setting and social activity in which language is being used; for instance, 'a court case', implicating ideational meaning), tenor (the social relations between interlocutors, variable in terms of status and solidarity; for instance, the 'accused', the 'judge' and the lawyers—or 'learnèd friends', implicating interpersonal meaning) and mode (the role that language plays in the activity, a scale moving from monologue to dialogue and from a constitutive role, as when a witness utters their testimony live in court, to more of an accompanying role, as when police make context-dependent comments while searching a premise, implicating textual meaning). Finally, SFL theory suggests that the broader cultural context in which people are interacting is construed, linguistically (and inter-modally), by systems of genre (the different types of text we produce to achieve different social purposes). Figure 1.4 shows these different language strata as a series of co-tangential circles designed to represent how each different stratum of language is related to the others in terms of degrees of abstraction. What we find at the level of discourse-semantics, for instance, is a patterning of lexicogrammatical resources that are, in turn, a patterning of phonological and graphological resources.

For most of these levels, we need to remember that distinctive contributions are being made by each of the three metafunctions of language described earlier—that is, ideational, interpersonal and textual meanings. Different system networks at different levels are being drawn upon simultaneously, as suggested in Fig. 1.5.

We will be moving around this model of language in terms of the focus of analysis at any given point in the book. The main dimension that allows us to shed light on restorative theory and practice is the interpersonal metafunction, from phonology all the way up to genre.

The final point to emphasize here is that for SFL theorists it makes no sense to think of 'text' apart from 'context'. Context is not a container

# 5 'Context and Text': A Brief Introduction to Systemic Functional...

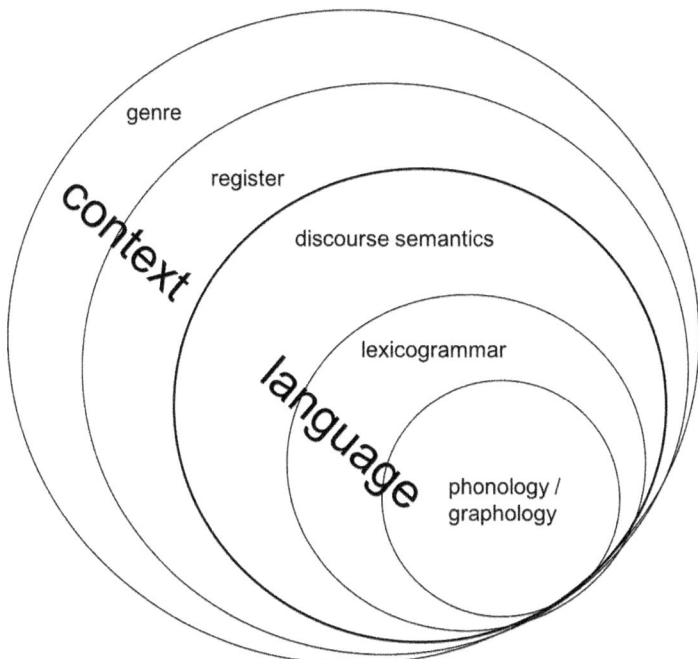

**Fig. 1.4** A stratified model of language

within which text sits. Context itself is a patterning of meanings that affect, and are affected by, the patterns of meanings we find in texts. This dynamic intertwining of text and context explains why, for instance, we may know very little, or nothing at all, about the provenance of a piece of transcribed talk, yet we are able to deduce certain features of its context from what is said (Eggins 1994). 'Man, you just fucking demolished that wall – that's sick!' is clearly more likely to be a comment shared between intimate, youthful mates quite close in time to the act of vandalism being described, rather than a piece of testimony delivered in a children's magistrate's court several months after the event. Alternatively, when we do know a given context well, we can often predict the sort of talk that is likely to occur. When the boss calls you in for an annual performance appraisal, you know that it pays to produce well-coordinated sentences that foreground a causal relation between your activities and the achievement of outcomes aligned with the organization's 'key performance

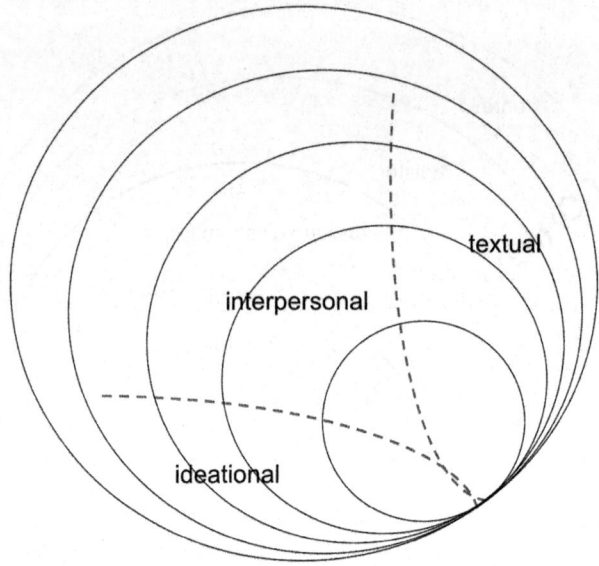

**Fig. 1.5** Types of meaning (metafunction) and levels of abstraction (strata)

indicators' (KPIs); this is probably not the right situation for sharing a risqué joke or chatting about a recent boozy weekend.

SFL provides some very sophisticated tools to describe and analyse text in context, since accounting for the relationships between text and context is so integral to accounting for the social meanings that are made by language users. This position regarding the important relationship between language and context is derived originally from the work of the anthropologist Malinowski and brought into linguistics by Halliday's teacher, Firth:

> [S]ystemicists, like Firthians before them … have always argued … that you cannot understand the meaning of what someone says or writes unless you know something about the context in which it is embedded. Or, looking at this the other way round, if you understand what someone says or writes (a text in technical terms), you can also figure out a great deal about the context in which that text occurred. (Martin 1984: 14)

Of course, not all features of context are encoded in language. For instance, the time of day and the weather at the moment this paragraph was first written are unlikely to be discernible by you, the reader (but if our mode of interaction shifts—if we are friends and start discussing the ideas of this paragraph, for instance, as part of an online Skype chat and if we are on opposite sides of the globe—then these features of context could certainly, at some point, become relevant and leave their imprint in language). So, while allowing for a rich, context-sensitive examination of language, an SFL approach to discourse analysis cannot simply unpack the meaning of social interactions from a close reading of transcripts alone. The method of ethnographic participant-observation described earlier complements the SFL-based discourse analysis by helping us to keep track of the patterns of meaning that are most significant to practitioners of restorative justice and by highlighting the less obvious features of context that might place at risk the values and frameworks within which conference participants are expected to make sense of their encounter.

## 6 Multimodal Discourse and Performance

I think it's genuine … up to a certain point.

This was a comment made by a young man towards the end of one of the first youth justice conferences we observed. The young man had just received an apology from the youth who had bashed him outside a pub one night, an assault that put him in hospital for several days. The Convenor wanted to know how the victim felt about this apology. No discourse analysis can claim to know 'the whole truth' of whatever this victim's thoughts and feelings were at this poignant moment. However, analysis does not have to have the pretensions of psychoanalysis to be of interpretive value.

The conference in question was not a conference where the 'core sequence' of remorse and forgiveness, as Retzinger and Scheff (1996) put it, swept everyone up in a surge of collective empathy. It was a conference of awkwardness, hedging and, above all, mismatched expectations. Some of this was apparent in the spoken discourse but a great deal was palpably evident in the ways that space, dress and gesture were used.

The venue for this conference was a sparse room upstairs and at the back of a Police Citizens Youth Club. To access the room, one had to walk across or around an indoor basketball court where a dozen or so young people, some of them solo, some in small groups, were practising their shooting skills in an ad hoc way. The victim arrived earlier than most and enthusiastically shook the hands of others who were there. He was dressed neatly in trousers, a shirt that had been ironed and a tie. At the appointed time, the Convenor went downstairs to check that the offender had arrived. They came into the room together a few minutes later, the offender all sweaty, in shorts and a singlet—he'd been there all along, among the group of basketballers. At the start of the conference, when we were asked to introduce ourselves, the victim made a short speech in which he explained his motivation for attending was largely to do with the fact that he had previously participated in a conference for an offence he himself had committed:

> I actually got a lot out of it. It helped me turn things around. I think it's a great process.

The speech was addressed directly to the offender who looked down and away. Then the offender gave a recount of the offence, in which a number of other young men were involved, that was short on many crucial details. Unusually, the detective who had investigated the offence was present at this conference. It was through him that we heard of evidence, including CCTV footage, that showed the offender was heavily involved, not simply a half-hearted participant as he had intimated, and that the assault was planned, not spontaneous. Fifteen minutes into the conference, it was pretty clear that wholesale integration or reconciliation was probably aiming too high. Half an hour later, an apology quietly uttered by the offender, with some eye contact now established, and accepted 'up to a certain point' by the victim, seemed quite a bit better than nothing. The retelling of this conference indicates that it is only through an understanding of both the verbal and the non-verbal meanings made by the young people that we can comprehend the victim's hesitation at fully endorsing the genuineness of the apology.

Drawing attention to some of what was happening in this conference, not only verbally but also in terms of space, gaze, gesture and dress, brings us back to one of the larger ambitions of this book, namely to help advance the state of what many linguists now refer to as multimodal discourse analysis. The tools that would enable us to track how participants in an activity like conferencing are making meanings across different modes of communication are emerging but the grammars for some modes are far better developed than for others. Valuable work, adapting SFL for the analysis of non-verbal modalities of communication, has been done in the area of visual images (Kress and Van Leeuwen 2006): advertising, film and websites (Baldry and Thibault 2006; O'Halloran 2004), art, museum displays and architecture (O'Toole 2011). While spoken discourse remains the mode that receives most of our attention in the early part of this book, ethnographic observations concerning other modes are offered throughout. More systematically, in Chap. 5, we propose a theoretical model that refines and extends the grammars that have so far been proposed for description and analysis of gesture (cf. Martinec 2000, 2001); for a complementary activity theory–based perspective on multimodal discourse analysis, see Norris (2012)).

Challenges of this kind of theoretical work in linguistics and semiotics are considerable but, to borrow an analogy from the culinary field, we might also say that a 'slow-food' approach to developing multimodal grammars has its attractions. In the discipline of performance studies, for instance, within which Dwyer normally writes, scholars are still wary of the brisk manner in which textbooks on the semiotics of theatre were regularly pumped out between the 1950s and 1980s. Many of these erroneously assumed that language was a kind of master code for all modes of cultural expression and that the way to 'read' theatre was to break it down into language-like units of structure. Similar grievances exist in many other humanities disciplines (see Bateman and Schmidt (2013) for a critique of how the semiotics of film used to be theorized). As functional linguists working in what we might think of as a 'second wave' of approaches to multimodality, we suggest that it is not the building blocks of language, such as phonemes and morphemes, that we need to bring to other disciplines as possible keys to an analysis of visual, spatial, gestural and other modes of communication. Rather, it is the kind of conceptual framework offered by SFL's focus on the metafunctions of language that can most assist. Ideational, textual and interpersonal meanings can certainly be made through modes such as spatial organization, gesture and facial expression, though the structures that realize the meanings being made may be different to those used by language.

Beyond the challenge of developing grammars for multiple modes of communication, there lies, of course, the even greater challenge of thinking about 'intermodality'; this involves looking at how meanings are co-articulated and coordinated across modes, not simply analysing them as more or less discrete layers of meaning. To date, work on intermodality has focused mainly on text and image relations in print, film and electronic texts (see, for instance, Bateman 2008; Bateman and Schmidt 2013; Painter et al. 2013). In this book, we address intermodality in dialogic face-to-face social interaction, looking at how verbal resources act in tandem with paralinguistic modes, particularly gesture, to construe meanings that align conference participants interpersonally, and keep the activity going.

A final comment about a difficult word, clearly relevant to multimodality, namely 'performance'. Scholars in the interdisciplinary area of performance studies—the meeting point of theatre and anthropology according to some (Schechner 2004)—are notoriously loathe to offer a tight definition of 'performance' and, thus, to demarcate their object of study. Even the phrase 'object of study' implies a considerable level of abstraction from what one is trying to appreciate. We have to consider the rules, but also the special freedoms; we have to consider the organization, but also the typically messy, in-between status of events in which culture is sung, danced or in other ways embodied. We call on performance theory most directly in Chap. 7 where we argue for the notion that conferencing has some characteristics in common with ritual performances. Critical to this understanding is the work of the anthropologist, Turner,; but some of our earlier references to performance bear the trace of other thinkers who are likely to be more familiar to readers coming from linguistics and the social sciences. From Austin we borrow the idea of speech itself being performative, a 'saying' that is also a 'doing' (Austin 1962). As Judith Butler's reworking of this notion emphasizes, in the context of her arguments about gender identity, we construct a sense of self through a 'stylized repetition' of bodily acts, performed under the pressure of prevailing social norms (Butler 1988). In this early work, at least, Butler is close to the usage Goffman makes of the 'drama analogy' in his micro-sociological analyses of how people present themselves in daily life in different institutional contexts (see also Randall Collins, for an elaboration of Goffman's ideas (Collins 2014), and Meredith Rossner, who pursues this line of thinking in her recent analysis of restorative justice practices (Rossner 2011)). More recently, Hinckfuss (2012) has applied Butler's account of identity as a performative accomplishment in an analysis of how students must enact the preferred 'genre identities' of different disciplines in order to succeed in academic writing. As Hinckfuss suggests, Butler's early work on performativity also resonates with what has been the most practical definition of performance for our purposes, namely the position taken by the folklorist and anthropologist, Bauman:

> [P]erformance […] consists in the assumption of responsibility to an audience for a display of communicative competence. This competence rests on the knowledge and ability to speak in socially appropriate ways. […] Performance thus calls forth special attention to and heightened awareness of the act of expression and gives license to the audience to regard the act of expression and the performer with special intensity. (Bauman 1977: 11)

Granting the caveat that in youth justice conferencing the participants are all in a sense actors and audience for each other, the 'special intensity' and reflexivity implied in Bauman's definition of performance aptly capture the way participants must marshal their personal resources (linguistically and otherwise) to enact social roles (as family, police, friends or others) that are geared to specific purposes (integration and reconciliation perhaps, or simply the fixing of an outcome plan).[13]

# 7    A Road Map for Readers

The interpretations of YJCs we engage with in the rest of this book unfold in the following way. Chapter 2 considers youth justice conferencing as a 'macro-genre' (i.e. a genre comprising other elemental genres). We survey what this structure looks like in practice, noting some fluidity in the roles available to participants and taking note of genre elements that appear to have evolved subsequent to the original design of the conferencing model. Chapter 3 zeros in on the 'story' of the offending behaviour, recounted by the YP at the start of a conference; here we focus on how much work is done by the Convenor and other professional participants (such as Police Community Liaison Officers) to draw out this story through interaction with the YP. Chapter 4 continues by considering how the Convenor and other participants fold certain kinds of evaluative language into the story and, in a sense, help construct an identity for the YP as a suitable candidate for reintegration. Chapter 5 introduces the model of gesture analysis mentioned earlier, and uses this to explore how YPs and their Support Persons take up, but also sometimes resist, the preferred roles that the conferencing genre offers—roles explored in more detail in Chap. 6. Chapter 7 returns to our earlier discussion about conferencing as a reintegration ceremony involving highly charged emotional dynamics, and recasts this in the light of what the analyses in Chaps. 2, 3, 4, 5 and 6 are suggesting. We argue that 'passion play' scenarios of remorse, shame, apology and forgiveness are not as obviously present as other theorists have suggested. However, a quieter kind of efficacy that conference participants obviously find satisfying is still possible through the shared labour of ritualizing an informal legal process that, superficially at least, lacks iconic markers of its ritual-like status.

## Notes

1. Across Australia, the rate at which young people (aged 10–17 years) were being held in detention had been consistently falling during the 1980s and 1990s, from a rate of 65 young people per 100,000 in 1981 to a rate of just 28 per 100,000 in 2001. By 2008, the detention rate had climbed back up to 37 young people per 100,000 (Richards 2011). In NSW alone, the number of juveniles in detention rose by 52 per cent between 2005 and 2010 (see McGrath A. and Weatherburn D. (2012) The effect of custodial penalties on juvenile reoffending. *Australian & New Zealand Journal of Criminology* 45: 26–44).

2. In NSW, over two-thirds of young people who receive a custodial sentence are convicted of a further offence within two years (see Weatherburn D., Vignaendra S. and McGrath A. (2009) *The specific deterrent effect of custodial penalties on juvenile re-offending. Report to the Criminology Research Council*).
3. There are a range of Ethnic Community Liaison Officers (ECLOs) associated with the police who are involved with conferences. Throughout the book we will primarily see an example of an ECLO who works with the Islamic community of one YP, but there are others, such as Aboriginal Liaison Officers who are specially devoted to various communities.
4. The Young Persons Act does make provision for a YP attending a conference to be accompanied by a lawyer; however, the lawyer can only advise the YP, not speak for them. In the conferences observed as part of our research, no lawyers were ever present.
5. For an overview of New Zealand Family Group Conferencing, see Hudson J., Morris A., Maxwell G.M., et al. (1996) *Family Group Conferences: perspectives on policy & practice*, Annandale: Federation Press.
6. Note that the category of 'citizen Convenor' can include a police officer who convenes conferences outside the hours of their police work, in a private capacity. This was the case of one of the Convenors whose conferences we observed. She described the appeal of conferencing, compared to her police work, in terms of the opportunity 'to have a different, more hopeful kind of conversation' with a YP, one in which 'you feel like you're making more of a difference to their lives'.
7. A note on our spelling of the word 'indigenous' in this section: when written with a lower-case 'i', it refers to indigenous cultures around the world; when written with an upper-case 'I', following current usage in our own part of the world, it refers specifically to Aboriginal and Torres Strait Islander peoples of Australia.
8. It should perhaps be noted that Blagg is here basing his observations on conferencing in Western Australia where relations between the police and Nyoongar youth are often highly adversarial. Cuneen and White (2007) are most concerned by the police-run conferencing programmes, as well as the role police might play in formal cautions—one step down from a conferencing process—where the YP attends the police station. As Cuneen and White mention, much depends on the way in which diversionary programmes are implemented and regulated (see Cuneen C

and White R. (2007) *Juvenile Justice: Youth and Crime in Australia*, Oxford: Oxford University Press).

9. A recent study of the cost-effectiveness of YJCs has suggested that it is about 18 per cent less than if the YP had been dealt with via the Children's Court (see Webber A. (2012) Youth Justice Conferences versus Children's Court: A comparison of cost-effectiveness *Crime and justice bulletin* 164).

10. There is a fine balance that needs to be achieved between being minimally invasive in terms of the use of equipment without reducing the quality of the recordings that can be produced. For instance, the type of recording used in this project, where participants were not wearing lapel microphones, might be compared with the widely circulated documentary 'Facing the demons' in which a hugely invasive camera set-up was used, involving a full camera crew. While this configuration captures fantastic audio and video recording, the impact on participants may be significant (see Ziegler A. (1999) Facing the demons).

11. For a discussion of issues of validity in relation to criminal justice research, see Chan J. (2013) Ethnography as practice: Is validity an issue? *Current Issues in Criminal Justice* 25: 503–516.

12. Eggins (1994) offers an accessible introduction to SFL and our brief exposition here is indebted to her account. For a short history of the theory, citing key references, see Martin J.R. (2016) Meaning matters: a short history of systemic functional linguistics. *Word* 61: 1–23; foundational papers are collected in Martin J.R. and Doran Y.J. (2015d) Grammatics. *Critical Concepts in Linguistics: Systemic Functional Linguistics, Vol. 1*. London: Routledge; Martin J.R. and Doran Y.J. (2015c) Grammatical descriptions. *Critical Concepts in Linguistics: Systemic Functional Linguistics, Vol. 2*. London: Routledge; Martin J.R. and Doran Y.J. (2015a) Around Grammar: phonology, discourse semantics and multimodality. *Critical Concepts in Linguistics: Systemic Functional Linguistics, Vol. 3*. London: Routledge; Martin J.R. and Doran Y.J. (2015b) Context: register and genre *Critical Concepts in Linguistics: Systemic Functional Linguistics, Vol. 4*. London: Routledge; Martin J.R. and Doran Y.J. (2015e) Language in Education *Critical Concepts in Linguistics: Systemic Functional Linguistics, Vol. 5*. London: Routledge.

13. Bauman's definition of performance connects strongly to the way Dell Hymes used the term in his linguistic anthropology and his 'ethnography

of speaking' framework that has been taken up in applied linguistics and was an early influence on SFL (see Hymes D. (1962) The ethnography of speaking. *Anthropology and human behavior* 13: 11–74). The brief elaboration we offer of Bauman's definition in this paragraph—where performance is seen as whatever behaviour emerges from the dynamic interplay of three variables, namely *roles, resources* and *goals*—is borrowed from Tim Fitzpatrick (see Fitzpatrick T. (1995) *The Relationship of Oral and Literate Performance Processes in the Commedia Dell'arte: Beyond the Improvisation-Memorisation Divide*: Edwin Mellen Press).

# References

Aertsen, I., & Willemsens, J. (2001). The European forum for victim–offender mediation and restorative justice. *European Journal on Criminal Policy and Research, 9*, 291–300.

Ahmed, E., Harris, N., Braithwaite, J., et al. (2001). *Shame management through reintegration*. Cambridge/Oakleigh: Cambridge University Press.

Austin, J. L. (1962). In J. O. Urmson (Ed.), *How to do things with words. The William James lectures delivered at Harvard University in 1955*. Oxford: Clarendon Press.

Baldry, A., & Thibault, P. J. (2006). *Multimodal transcription and text analysis: A multimedia toolkit and coursebook*. Oakville: Equinox.

Bateman, J. (2008). *Multimodality and genre: A foundation for the systematic analysis of multimodal documents*. Basingstoke/New York: Palgrave Macmillan.

Bateman, J., & Schmidt, K.-H. (2013). *Multimodal film analysis: How films mean*. London: Routledge.

Bauman, R. (1977). Verbal art as performance. *American Anthropologist, 77*, 290–311.

Blagg, H. (1997). A just measure of shame? Aboriginal youth and conferencing in Australia. *British Journal of Criminology, 37*, 481–501.

Blagg, H. (2008). *Crime, aboriginality and the decolonisation of justice*. Sydney: Hawkins Press.

Bourdieu, P. (1998). *Acts of resistance: Against the tyranny of the market*. New York: New Press.

Braithwaite, J. (1989). *Crime, shame and reintegration*. Cambridge/Sydney: Cambridge University Press.

Braithwaite, J. (2002). *Restorative justice & responsive regulation.* Oxford/New York: Oxford University Press.
Braithwaite, J. (2003). The fundamentals of restorative justice. In S. Dinnen, A. Jowitt, & T. N. Cain (Eds.), *A kind of mending: Restorative justice in the Pacific Islands* (p. xi, 308 p). Canberra: Pandanus Books.
Braithwaite, J., & Strang, H. (2001). *Restorative justice and civil society.* Cambridge/Melbourne: Cambridge University Press.
Butler, J. (1988). Performative acts and gender constitution: An essay in phenomenology and feminist theory. *Theatre Journal, 40,* 519–531.
Campbell, C., Devlin, R., & O'Mahony, D., et al. (2005). *Evaluation of the Northern Ireland youth conference service.* NIO research and statistical series: Report 12. Belfast: NIO.
Chan, J. (2013). Ethnography as practice: Is validity an issue? *Current Issues in Criminal Justice, 25,* 503–516.
Christie, N. (1977). Conflicts as property. *British Journal of Criminology, 17,* 1–15.
Collins, R. (2014). *Interaction ritual chains.* Princeton: Princeton University Press.
Conley, J. M., & O'Barr, W. M. (2005). *Just words: Law, language, and power.* Chicago: University of Chicago Press.
Consedine, J. (1999). Restorative justice: Could Ireland lead the way? *Studies: An Irish Quarterly Review, 88,* 132–137.
Cuneen, C., & White, R. (2007). *Juvenile justice: Youth and crime in Australia.* Oxford: Oxford University Press.
Daly, K. (2001). Conferencing in Australia and New Zealand: Variations, research findings, and prospects. In A. Morris & G. Maxwell (Eds.), *Restorative justice for juveniles: Conferencing, mediation and circles* (pp. 59–83). Oxford/Portland: Hart Publishing.
Daly, K., & Stubbs, J. (2007). Feminist theory, feminist and anti-racist politics, and restorative justice. *Handbook of Restorative Justice,* 149–170.
Davis, S. (2002). *"Offending behaviour": Episode four of "crime and punishment".* Documentary broadcast on the program Radio Eye, Australian Broadcasting Commission.
Dickson-Gilmore, E. J., & La Prairie, C. (2005). *Will the circle be unbroken?: Aboriginal communities, restorative justice, and the challenges of conflict and change.* Toronto: University of Toronto Press.
Eades, D. (2008). *Courtroom talk and neocolonial control.* Berlin: Mouton de Gruyter.
Eades, D. (2010). *Sociolinguistics and the legal process.* Bristol: Multilingual Matters.

Eggins, S. (1994). *An introduction to systemic functional grammar*. London: Pinter.
Etzioni, A. (1998). *The essential communitarian reader*. Lanham: Rowman & Littlefield.
Fitzpatrick, T. (1995). *The relationship of oral and literate performance processes in the Commedia Dell'arte: Beyond the improvisation-memorisation divide*. Lewiston/Lampeter: Edwin Mellen Press.
Geertz, C. (1973). Thick description. In C. Geertz (Ed.), *The interpretation of cultures: Selected essays*. New York: Basic Books. <<need pages>>.
Geertz, C. (1983). *Local knowledge: Further essays in interpretive anthropology*. New York: Basic books.
Gibbons, J. (2003). *Forensic linguistics: An introduction to language in the justice system*. Oxford/Malden: Blackwell Publishing.
Hadley, M. L. (2001). *The spiritual roots of restorative justice*. New York: State University of New York Press.
Halliday, M. A. K. (1970). Language structure and language function. In J. Lyons (Ed.), *New horizons in linguistics* (pp. 140–165). Harmondsworth: Penguin.
Halliday, M. A. K., & Matthiessen, C. M. I. M. (1999). *Construing experience through meaning: A language-based approach to cognition*. London: Cassell.
Halliday, M. A. K., & Matthiessen, C. M. I. M. (2004). *An introduction to functional grammar*. London: Arnold.
Halliday, M. A. K., & Matthiessen, C. M. (2013). *Halliday's introduction to functional grammar*. London: Routledge.
Harris, N., & Burton, J. (1997). The reliability of observed reintegrative shaming, shame, defiance and other key concepts in diversionary conferences. *RISE Working Papers, Research School of Social Sciences, ANU, 5*, 1–50.
Harris, N., Walgrave, L., & Braithwaite, J. (2004). Emotional dynamics in restorative conferences. *Theoretical Criminology an International Journal, 8*, 191–210.
Hinckfuss, J. (2012). *Rethinking English for academic purposes: Towards a performance-centred pedagogy*. Thesis, Department of Performance Studies, University of Sydney.
Hoyle, C., Young, R., & Hill, R. (2002). *Proceed with caution: An evaluation of the Thames Valley police initiative in restorative cautioning*. York: York Publishing Services.
Hudson, J., Morris, A., Maxwell, G. M., et al. (1996). *Family group conferences: Perspectives on policy & practice*. Annandale: Federation Press.
Hymes, D. (1962). The ethnography of speaking. *Anthropology and Human Behavior, 13*, 11–74.

Jackson, M. (1996). *Things as they are: New directions in phenomenological anthropology*. Bloomington: Indiana University Press.

Johnstone, G. (2011). *Restorative justice: Ideas, values and debates*. London and New York: Routledge.

Kress, G., & Van Leeuwen, T. (2006). *Reading images: The grammar of visual images*. Oxon: Routledge.

Lambert, C., Johnstone, G., Green, S., et al. (2011). *Building restorative relationships for the workplace: Goodwin Development Trust's journey with restorative approaches*. London: Goodwin Development Trust and University of Hull.

Martin, J. R. (1984). Language, register and genre. In: F. Christie (Ed.), *Children writing: Reader* (pp. 21–30). Geelong: Deakin University Press. (ECT Language Studies: children writing), [revised for Burns, A., & Coffin, C. (Eds.). (2001). *Analysing English in a global context: A reader* (pp. 2149–2166). Clevedon: Routledge (Teaching English Language Worldwide)] [Japanese translation by Hiro Tsukada published in Shidonii Gakuha no SFL: Haridei Gengo Riron no Tenkai. Tokyo: Liber Press. 2005.] [further revised for Coffin, C., Lillis, T., & O'Halloran, K. (Eds.). (2010). *Applied linguistics methods: A reader* (pp. 2012–2032). London: Routledge.] [reprinted in J R Martin 2012 Register Studies [Volume 2004 in the Collected Works of J R Martin edited by Wang Zhenhua. Shanghai: Shanghai Jiao Tong University Press. 2047–2068].

Martin, J. R. (2016). Meaning matters: A short history of systemic functional linguistics. *Word, 61*, 1–23.

Martin, J. R., & Doran, Y. J. (2015a). Around grammar: Phonology, discourse semantics and multimodality. In *Critical concepts in linguistics: Systemic functional linguistics* (Vol. 3). London: Routledge.

Martin, J. R., & Doran, Y. J. (2015b). Context: Register and genre. In *Critical concepts in linguistics: Systemic functional linguistics* (Vol. 4). London: Routledge.

Martin, J. R., & Doran, Y. J. (2015c). Grammatical descriptions. In *Critical concepts in linguistics: Systemic functional linguistics* (Vol. 2). London: Routledge.

Martin, J. R., & Doran, Y. J. (2015d). Grammatics. In *Critical concepts in linguistics: Systemic functional linguistics* (Vol. 1). London: Routledge.

Martin, J. R., & Doran, Y. J. (2015e). Language in education. In *Critical concepts in linguistics: Systemic functional linguistics* (Vol. 5). London: Routledge.

Martin, J. R., & Rose, D. (2008). *Genre relations: Mapping culture*. London: Equinox.

## References

Martinec, R. (2000). Types of process in action. *Semiotica, 130,* 243–268.
Martinec, R. (2001). Interpersonal resources in action. *Semiotica, 135,* 117–145.
Maruna, S., Wright, S., Brown, J., et al. (2007). *Youth conferencing as shame management: Results of a long-term follow-up study.* Cambridge: ARCS.
Maxwell, G., & Morris, A. (2001). Family group conferences and reoffending. In A. Morris & G. Maxwell (Eds.), *Restorative justice for juveniles: Conferencing, mediation and circles* (pp. 243–266). Oxford: Hart.
Maxwell, G., & Morris, A. (2002). The role of shame, guilt, and remorse in restorative justice processes for young people. In E. Weitekamp & H. J. Kerner (Eds.), *Restorative justice: Theoretical foundations* (pp. 267–284). Cullompton: Willan Publishing.
McAuley, G. (2008). Not magic but work: Rehearsal and the production of meaning. *Theatre Research International, 33,* 276–288.
McCold, P., & Wachtel, B. (1998). *Restorative policing experiment.* Pipersville: Community Service Foundation.
McDonald, J., & Moore, D. (2001). Community conferencing as a special case of conflict transformation. In H. Strang & J. Braithwaite (Eds.), *Restorative justice and civil society* (pp. 130–148). Cambridge: Cambridge University Press.
McGarrell, E. F. (2000). *Returning justice to the community: The Indianapolis juvenile restorative justice experiment.* Indianapolis: Hudson Institute.
McLaughlin, E. (2003). Introduction: Justice in the round: contextualising restorative justice. In E. McLaughlin, R. Fergusson, G. Hughes, et al. (Eds.), *Restorative justice: Critical issues* (pp. 1–19). London: SAGE.
Moore, D. B., & McDonald, J. M. (2000). *Transforming conflict in workplaces and other communities.* Bondi: Transformative Justice Australia.
Moore, D., & McDonald, J. (2001). Community conferencing as a special case of conflict transformation. In J. Braithwaite & H. Strang (Eds.), *Restorative justice and civil society* (pp. 130–148). Cambridge/Melbourne: Cambridge University Press.
Norris, S. (2012). *Multimodality in practice: Investigating theory-in-practice-through-methodology.* London: Routledge.
O'Halloran, K. L. (2004). *Multimodal discourse analysis: Systemic-functional perspectives.* London: Continuum.
O'Toole, M. (2011). *The language of displayed art.* London: Routledge.
Painter, C., Martin, J. R., & Unsworth, L. (2013). *Reading visual narratives: Image analysis of children's picture books.* London: Equinox Publishing.

Palk, G., Hayes, H., & Prenzler, T. (1998). Restorative justice and community conferencing: Summary of findings from a pilot study. *Current Issues in Criminal Justice, 10*, 138.

Pavlich, G. C. (2005). *Governing paradoxes of restorative justice*. London: Psychology Press.

Retzinger, S., & Scheff, T. (1996). Strategy for community conferences: Emotions and social bonds. In B. Galaway & J. Hudson (Eds.), *Restorative justice: International perspectives* (pp. 315–336). Monsey: Criminal Justice Press.

Rossner, M. (2011). Emotions and interaction ritual: A micro analysis of restorative justice. *British Journal of Criminology, 51*, 95–119.

Schechner, R. (2004). *Performance theory*. London: Routledge.

Scheff, T., & Retzinger, S. (1991). *Violence and emotions*. Lexington: Lexington Books.

Sherman, L. W., Strang, H., & Woods, D. J. (2000). *Recidivism patterns in the Canberra reintegrative shaming experiments (RISE)*. Centre for Restorative Justice, Research School of Social Sciences, Australian National University, Canberra.

Silverman, D. (2006). *Interpreting qualitative data: Methods for analyzing talk, text and interaction*. London: Sage.

Smith, N., & Weatherburn, D. (2012). Youth justice conferences versus children's court: A comparison of re-offending. *Crime and Justice Bulletin. Contemporary issues in crime and justice, 160*, 1030–1046.

Strang, H., & Braithwaite, J. (2001). *Restorative justice and civil society*. Cambridge: Cambridge University Press.

Tangney, J. P. (1991). Moral affect: The good, the bad, and the ugly. *Journal of Personality and Social Psychology, 61*, 598.

Tomkins, S. S. (2009). Affect theory. In K. R. Scherer & P. Ekman (Eds.), *Approaches to emotion* (pp. 163–195). New York/London: Psychology Press.

Trimboli, L. (2000). *An evaluation of the NSW youth justice conferencing scheme*. Sydney: NSW Bureau of Crime Statistics and Research.

Trimboli, L., & New South Wales. (2000). An evaluation of the NSW youth justice conferencing scheme. Sydney: NSW Bureau of Crime Statistics and Research'.

Van Ness, D., Morris, A., & Maxwell, G. (2001). Introducing restorative justice. In A. Morris & G. Maxwell (Eds.), *Restorative justice for juveniles: Conferencing, mediation and circles* (pp. 3–16). Oxford: Hart.

Wagland, P., Blanch, B., & Moore, E. (2013). Participant satisfaction with youth justice conferencing. In *Crime and justice bulletin: Contemporary issues in crime and justice*. Sydney: NSW Bureau of Crime Statistics and Research.

Weatherburn, D., Vignaendra, S., & McGrath, A. (2009). *The specific deterrent effect of custodial penalties on juvenile re-offending*. Report to the Criminology Research Council.

Webber, A. (2012). Youth justice conferences versus children's court: A comparison of cost-effectiveness. *Crime and Justice Bulletin, 164*, 1030–1046.

Weitekamp, E. (1999). The history of restorative justice. In G. Bazemore & L. Walgrave (Eds.), *Restorative juvenile justice: Repairing the harm of youth crime*. Monsey: Criminal Justice Press.

Young, R. (2001). Just cops doing "shameful" business? In A. Morris & G. Maxwell (Eds.), *Restorative justice for juveniles: Conferencing, mediation and circles* (pp. 195–226). Oxford: Hart.

Zehr, H. (1990). *Changing lenses: A new focus for crime and justice*. Scottdale: Herald Press.

Ziegler, A. (1999). Facing the demons.

# 2

# Conference Design: Genre and Macro-Genre

## 1   Youth Justice Conferences: Talk and Interaction

A youth justice conference, as we emphasized in the previous chapter, involves a lot of talk. It also involves, as we will explore in this chapter, different kinds of talk. Convenors are well aware of this, of course, and it was a frequent topic of conversation during the training workshops we attended. Allusions were made to situations that might be comparable to conferencing and thus could help the trainee Convenors understand their role: '[T]here'll be an expectation that it's going to be like court [and] you need to steer [participants] away from this'; 'I imagine it's a bit like counselling [but] you're not social workers, you're not welfare workers.'

What these comments highlight is the fact that conferences are an unusual, potentially unsettling amalgam of different types of social interaction. As Van Stokkom (2002) argues:

> [R]estorative conferences are the scene of an emotional collision that is highly unfamiliar to people nowadays. […] According to Weijers (2001) the combination of a victim–offender confrontation and a family consultation

places a heavy emotional and moral burden on the shoulders of participants. For the offender, the weight of the confrontation is doubled, while the victim is drawn into family discussions and a family history (thus increasing the pressure on him or her to show solidarity and move towards reconciliation). In a liberal culture, people are seldom or never addressed on their acts or their negligence in such a 'confusing' setting.

In a similar manner to the critiques of early reintegrative shaming theory we surveyed in Chap. 1, Van Stokkom (2002) is concerned that young offenders are likely to experience low self-esteem before a conference. If conferences are as confronting and potentially confusing as he fears, then building a deliberate focus on shame induction into the conferencing process strikes Van Stokkom as a highly fraught strategy for reintegration.

Several points need to be made here. First, the amendments to reintegrative shaming theory we mentioned in the last chapter make clear that Braithwaite and his colleagues are not calling for Convenors or other participants to make special, intensive efforts to induce extra feelings of shame in the young offender. Rather, their point is that the conference needs to provide ways of resolving shame and that disapproval of the offender's actions—by persons whom the offender respects—is part of this. Second, part of the impetus behind the development of conferencing has been the recognition that conventional court-based processes are themselves confronting and confusing settings for many young people. Third, a key concern throughout the training of Convenors we observed, including training in how to conduct the pre-conference briefings of other participants, was to help reduce any confusion participants might be experiencing. Finally, Convenors of youth justice conferences are working with a notional 'script' (provided by the Department of Juvenile Justice) that suggests specific prompt questions and a basic outline for the conference to follow. In their opening remarks, Convenors will usually give other conference participants some sense of this outline.

The use of scripts has been somewhat controversial in the restorative justice field, with some critics seeing them as too restrictive. In spite of this, the clear implication in the Convenor-training workshops we observed was that individual Convenors were to use the script flexibly: 'You're working within a structure but we do encourage you to develop your own style.' Nonetheless, even in conferencing programmes that do not provide Convenors with a formally scripted template, there will be structural features that all conferences have in common. The purpose of this chapter is to examine the typical generic structure of conferences and to highlight where different kinds of talk tend to occur within them. We will see that there is some flexibility in the roles that conference participants are able to take up within this broad structure. We will also consider how conferencing practice appears to have evolved somewhat since the introduction of the 1997 New South Wales (NSW) Young Offenders Act—with forms of participation by police, in particular, that do not receive much attention in the legislation. First, however, we look at some of the parameters of conferencing that are defined in the legal framework.

## 2 Pathways to a Conference

The NSW Young Offenders Act applies to summary offences (matters that would otherwise be tried by a magistrate) as well as indictable offences that can be dealt with summarily (matters that could go before a jury but are usually tried by a magistrate, both to expedite the process and because the offence is of a less serious nature than matters that go to the District or Supreme Courts). This means the Young Offenders Act covers matters such as offensive behaviour, dangerous behaviour, resisting police, carrying a knife (without a work-related justification), trespass, breaking and entering, stealing or receiving stolen goods, taking and conveying a vehicle ('joy riding'), assault and disturbances of public order such as rioting or affray.[1] It excludes matters such as assault intentionally designed to cause a Victim very serious injury, manslaughter or murder, sexual offences and crimes related to drug trafficking. The maximum punishment that a magistrate might impose when sentencing someone for a summary offence or an indictable offence dealt with summarily is two years' imprisonment; this gives us some idea of the seriousness of offences that are eligible for conferencing.

The Young Offenders Act sets out a range of options by which police may respond to offending behaviour. The simplest form of intervention, for minor summary offences where no violence is involved, is a Warning that a police officer can give to a Young Person (YP) on the spot. The YP does not need to have admitted the offence, the officer simply records the fact that a Warning has been given and why. The next level of intervention, for offences that are deemed to warrant more than a Warning, is a formal Caution. This requires the YP to have admitted the offence and to have given their informed consent for the matter to be dealt with by this means (the Act stipulates that police must advise the YP of their right to legal advice before making any admissions or giving consent). The YP attends a police station, accompanied by a parent, caregiver or some other Support Person they have chosen, where a specially trained police Youth Liaison Officer (YLO) gives the Caution. No Victims or other parties attend. The general procedures for a Caution include a discussion to clarify the nature of the offence and its impact and another with the YP and his Support Person(s) about future plans and strategies to avoid reoffending (Clancey et al. 2005). As we will see later in this chapter, this kind of talk has also filtered into the practice of conferencing. Apart from requiring a YP to provide a written apology to any Victim(s), no sanctions can be imposed as a result of a Caution. In addition, as is the case for Warnings, no conviction is recorded against the YP although the police keep a record of the fact that a Caution was given and why.

A Youth Justice Conference is the third and most intensive option for intervention in the hierarchy of responses established by the Young Offenders Act. As with a Caution, the YP must admit to the offence and consent to having the matter dealt with via a conference. As we noted in Chap. 1, in many cases a conference referral is made directly by a YLO. In other cases, where police have initially charged the YP and referred the matter to court, it may be the children's magistrate who decides to refer the matter for conferencing instead of to a court. A team of local conference administrators working across different metropolitan and rural regions of NSW is responsible for managing all referrals from police and the courts. The work of administrators includes recruiting, training and supervising Convenors; appointing Convenors to run particular conferences according to their availability and suitability; taking conference outcome plans to the children's magistrate for approval before implementation; keeping records on the YP's progress towards completion of the outcome plan, including obtaining approval from the court for any extensions or variations to the plan; and advising police and the court when the outcome plan has been successfully completed (the Act specifies a six-month time limit for this to occur). If the plan is not completed, as mentioned in Chap. 1, the matter goes back to the children's magistrate to be heard in court. If the plan is completed, police and administrators retain a record of the conference but the offence does not have to be declared in situations where a criminal record check is required.[2]

The Act stipulates that a conference should take place within 28 days of the referral being received by the local conference administrator, which leaves Convenors with a considerable amount of preparation to do in a short space of time. Convenors and Convenor-trainers stress that these preparations do shape participants' expectations considerably. One trainer remarked: 'If you [the Convenor] have prepared people properly, the conference will be fine; it may not fix everything but it certainly won't make anything worse.' Another commented: 'Your work [as a Convenor] is in the preparation. In the conference, you sit back; you're the only one who can be neutral.'

Our interviews and experience of Convenor-training workshops suggest that four factors in the preparation for a conference are particularly challenging. First, it is clear that for a conference to be successful administrators and Convenors need to build good working relationships with police and magistrates in their local area. Among some police and legal agents, there is still scepticism about conferencing, which can result in lower rates of conference referral in some areas of NSW compared to others. Convenors sometimes find themselves having to proselytize and promote the importance of conferencing to show police that conferencing is not just a 'soft option' for young offenders. This means that the first phone call a Convenor will often make after receiving a referral is to the police in order to lock in a time that will enable YLOs and (where relevant) Aboriginal or Ethnic Community Liaison Officers to attend.

The second factor that must be considered by conference Convenors is the role Victims will play in the process. In Convenor-training workshops, it is stated that 'conferences are much more effective when a victim attends' and that Convenors should 'work really hard' to achieve this. The workshops suggest that the presence of a Victim 'puts a face to crime' and 'allows the conference to become emotional if necessary'. Convenors are encouraged to promote the benefits of conferencing to Victims in a number of ways: firstly through the opportunity for acknowledgement (the Victim can 'let the offender know what it feels like to have something done to you'); secondly through the chance to experience relief from anxiety (Victims might be relieved to learn, for instance, that the offending behaviour was opportunistic, not specifically targeted at them: 'sometimes it helps to demystify the offender'); thirdly through the possibility of helping change the YP's outlook (the Victim's presence 'ties the law into the community' and raises awareness of 'community expectations'); and finally through the chance not only to contribute ideas to the outcome plan ('to have a say and be heard') but also to veto any outcome plan that they find unacceptable (this right is only extended to a Victim actually attending a conference). This last point raises the concern that the Victim may become vindictive. To manage this, the practical advice shared in training was to let an angry Victim express their emotions: 'Sometimes they start by feeling very vindictive and, at the end, all they want is an apology.' On the other end of the spectrum, there are some offences that could be considered 'victimless crimes' (such as trespass upon the grounds of a school), and others where the Victim is a large business or organization (like the corporate owners of a chain of grocery stores from which a YP has been caught shoplifting goods), significantly lowering the chance of an emotional response.

In all cases, Convenors are expected to make special efforts to include in the conference someone (or some documentation) who can represent a Victim's perspective. For a 'victimless crime', this might be a respected community leader who can help the YP understand the potential harm to self and others from the offending behaviour. For 'corporate victims', this might be a staff member experienced in community relations who can contextualize the individual offence by explaining how such crimes impact on the community generally. In cases where a directly affected Victim declines to attend, the Victim may suggest someone to attend in their place and/or provide some kind of document that explains the consequences they have suffered as a result of the offence. For instance, in one case where peoples' homes had been damaged by arsonists, the Convenor made sure to include in the conference a slide show illustrating some of the destruction. A recent review of participant profiles in NSW youth justice conferences found that direct Victims were present in 42 per cent of cases and a Victim's Representative attended in 16 per cent of cases (Taussig 2012).

A third key factor is the number and mix of other participants. While it is possible to run a conference with only the YP and the Convenor in attendance, this is a very rare occurrence and the full list of eligible participants identified in the Young Offenders Act (including lawyers, interpreters and researchers) is long. In Convenor-training workshops, it was suggested that 'in general, the more the better'. For example, the Victim(s) and the YP(s) involved in a conference may feel apprehensive and so are encouraged to have Support Persons attend with them. Much of the Convenor's preparation consists of eliciting and following up on suggestions for such Support Persons, including parents, siblings, friends, older relatives or other people who are involved in the life of a YP or Victim in the context of health, education, welfare services and the like. A Convenor will not necessarily meet face-to-face with all Support Persons before a conference but will endeavour to at least have a phone conversation. In particular, a Convenor will want to identify someone who can take on the role of Monitor for the outcome plan that is agreed to at the conference and, possibly, persons who work for community organizations where the YP might be able to do some unpaid work as part of the outcome plan.

A final issue, acknowledged by Convenors and Convenor trainers alike, is the task of briefing the young offender. There is recognition that many offenders will often have low levels of literacy and may not be confident or even capable of speaking at any great length in a conference.[3] To remedy this, it is suggested in the training workshops that part of a Convenor's work in the lead-up to a conference may be to 'help a young offender acquire the language they'll need to express remorse'. As we will see, this is sometimes more easily said than done, but it does bring us back to the issue of conference structure and how participants are able to engage with this process.

## 3 Conference Openings: From Script to Genre

Whatever preparation participants have had beforehand, the first few minutes of a conference are important in terms of shaping expectations. As noted earlier, Convenors are able to adapt the scripted prompts provided by the Department of Juvenile Justice; however, for the purposes of illustration, let us look at an example where the Convenor starts by quoting the script almost verbatim. This is the opening of the 'Guide Dog' conference, dealing with the case of a 15-year-old boy who stole the purse of a woman with severely impaired vision (apart from the observing researcher, all participants have been given pseudonyms; as noted in Chap. 1, transcription conventions are explained in Appendix B).

**Extract 2.1, Guide Dog YJC**

| | |
|---|---|
| **Convenor:** | Welcome everyone. As you know my name's Louise Horton and I'll be convening this youth justice conference in accordance with the provisions of the Young Offenders Act 1997. Before we begin I'd just like everyone to introduce themselves and to indicate their reason for being here. Melanie, could you just start it please? |
| **YLO:** | Yep. I'm Melanie. I'm the Youth Liaison Officer for Davidton so I deal with the young offenders and often come to these things. |
| **Convenor:** | [Points to vacant chair next to YLO] Now Greg's missing at the moment. He said he was coming along. He actually is the president of the Guide Dog Association for [Location B] and he's coming along as a Support Person for Donna and he's also going to ah maybe help Nathan link in with some – something for his outcome plan.[4] |
| **Victim:** | So I'm next == right? |
| **Convenor:** | == Donna. |
| **Victim:** | Donna O'Neill. I live here in [Location C]. |

## 3 Conference Openings: From Script to Genre 57

| | |
|---|---|
| **Convenor:** | And you're the victim in this matter? You had your purse stolen? |
| **Victim:** | Yes. |
| **Convenor:** | Thanks, Donna. |
| **Researcher:** | Paul Dwyer from Sydney Uni. Just observing and I don't say anything after this point. [He makes a 'zipping your lips shut' gesture; smiles from other participants] |
| **Mother of YP's girlfriend:** | Julie, I'm here for him, [laughs], Nathan. |
| **Convenor:** | Could you just tell us how you (how you two == are connected)? |
| **Mother of YP's girlfriend:** | == He's– what? |
| **Convenor:** | He's your daughter's == boyfriend? |
| **Mother of YP's girlfriend:** | == daughter's boyfriend. |
| **Convenor:** | OK, thanks Julie. |
| **YP:** | My name's Nathan and I stole the wallet. |
| **Convenor:** | Thanks Nathan. |
| **Mother of YP:** | I'm Sharon and I'm Nathan's mum. I'm just here to support Nathan and see what it – comes about. |
| **Convenor:** | Thank you. |
| **Girlfriend of YP:** | I'm Chelsea and I'm Nathan's girlfriend. |
| **Convenor:** | Thanks. |
| **Step-Grandfather of YP:** | And I'm Don. I'm Nathan's pop. Nathan's been living with us for the last couple of years so I am here to make sure everything works out for him. |
| **Convenor:** | Terrific thanks. |
| **Arresting Officer:** | I'm Jim and I'm the one that arrested him and his worst nightmare. [Other participants laugh. Jim smiles and looks across to YP] Correct, Nathan? |
| **YP:** | [smiles and nods] |
| **Convenor:** | Thanks Jim. OK well thanks all for making the effort to attend. It's a difficult matter. Your presence here will help us deal with it successfully. The conference will focus on an incident that happened at [Location C] on |

|  |  |
|---|---|
| | [Day of Month] last year about 10 o'clock in the morning. It involved Nathan and Donna. The Young Offenders Act 1997 requires that the Young Person has admitted the offence and agreed to the conference. Nathan, do you confirm your admission to the offence of stealing? |
| **YP:** | Yes. |
| **Convenor:** | And do you give your consent for this conference to proceed? |
| **YP:** | Yes. |
| **Convenor:** | Do you understand that at any time you can elect ah for this matter to be dealt with by the court? |
| **YP:** | Yes. |
| **Convenor:** | Thanks. OK let's proceed. So today we want to explore how people have been affected to see whether we can begin to umm repair the harm that's been done. And I need to remind you of the importance of confidentiality. Everything said at this conference should not be repeated outside this circle and by no means should anyone's name be mentioned when discussing this conference or the outcome. Any previous criminal activity that Nathan may have been involved in is also confidential in these proceedings. I am not suggesting that he has any criminal history but I am obliged to mention this in all conferences before we begin. You may see me referring to this sheet. It's just to ensure that everything is covered during the process and I may ah also take notes which will help me prepare a document for the police or court. Just like to go through a few issues. Obviously the umm the nearest emergency exit is just here, outside here, and the toilets are just located around down the corridor to the right. And we'll have a short adjournment later. If you can just turn your phones off that'd be great. It's a bit of a disruption when they ring and people talk on them and stuff. So it is acknowledged that you may be feeling very emotional at this time. However, I would ah ask that during this conference that you treat everyone with respect. |

In order to demonstrate respect, I ask that only one person speak at a time. During the first stages of the conference you wait to be invited to speak. That you do not use threats or any oth – inappropriate language and that you remain in the seat that you have been allocated. So as I said ah we will determine some positive actions for Nathan which will make up the outcome plan. It's not a punishment but an offer to repair some of the harm caused. There are certain restrictions on outcome plans. They must be reasonable, must not be more than what a court would impose. After the conference you will have the opportunity to complete a comments form of what you thought about the conference and your comments will be valuable and help us improve our service and conferencing program. Ah while we're completing important paperwork after the conference, please stay and join in some refreshments. OK, Nathan, we'll get you to start by telling us exactly what happened on the day.

This extract is very neatly bookended by the Convenor's opening moves at the top of the extract (*'Welcome everyone [...] Before we begin'*) and the final clause (*'OK, Nathan, we'll get you to start…'*) that indicates the conference is moving into a new section. As a starting point for our analysis, this bookending suggests that we can think of the whole extract as constituting a relatively discrete, coherent 'chunk' of the conference. In addition, within the extract there are several points of transition where the Convenor takes care to mark some changes to the direction of the conference (*'OK, well thanks all for making the effort to attend'*, *'OK let's proceed,'* etc.). Once we have noted this, what are we to make of these preliminaries? We could begin by considering a description from an educational brochure produced for the general public by the Juvenile Justice Department. In this brochure, the opening section of a conference is described as follows: 'Step 1. The Convenor asks those present to introduce themselves and explain their relationship to the offence' (NSW Department of Juvenile Justice 1999: 1). From the extract above, it is clear that this is part of what is happening but there is clearly more to it than this. Looking deeper, the *Policy and Procedures Manual* for conference administrators and Convenors uses the same form of words as the educational brochure, but adds usefully:

> The Convenor introduces him/herself and gives a brief overview of the purpose and process for the conference, and the requirements of confidentiality. (NSW Department of Juvenile Justice 2000: 2–27)

While this description brings us closer to what is happening in the opening of the Guide Dog YJC, it still does not tell us much about how these different tasks are woven together as parts of a coherent whole. In order to capture the overall function of the Guide Dog extract, we need a tool for showing how it consists of patterns we can generalize across conferences, while allowing for conference specific variation. In Systemic Functional Linguistics (SFL), this tool is referred to as genre.

In this case of the Guide Dog extract, we have an example of a genre that conference designers have invented in lieu of the formal introduction that would open proceedings in a magistrate's court. In SFL, a genre is characterized as

> a staged, goal-oriented social process. Social because we participate in genres with other people; goal-oriented because we use genres to get things done; staged because it usually takes us a few steps to reach our goals. (Martin and Rose 2008: 5)

A genre, then, is a relatively stable, predictable, recurrent pattern of meaning through which members of a given culture interact with one another in particular situational contexts (an alternative term that some linguists and educators use for genre is 'text type'). Recalling the way SFL models the relations between text and context, we can say the genre configures the language patterns used by the participants enacting the genre.

Martin and Rose (2008: 7) suggest that genre is a tool for mapping the different types of language used in a culture. As they argue, '[t]he number of recognizably distinct genres in any given culture may be quite large,' but they are not unmanageably so. From early childhood through years of schooling and in our adult lives, we are incorporated into the genres we need to achieve certain ends. For instance, we learn how to participate in a *sales transaction*. We learn the genre of *appointment making* and how this differs from a *job interview*. We learn how to behave in a *consultation* with a family doctor and so on. Of course, not everyone will acquire control of all of the genres available in a particular culture, either because there are genres we find we do not need (not everyone wants to be followed on Twitter) or, more insidiously, because educational failure and other forms of social disadvantage can leave people locked out of genres that the more economically and politically powerful members of society deploy to their advantage.

None of this is set in stone. Politicians, activists, educators and parents can, and sometimes do, intervene to redress linguistic and other forms of social disadvantage. Indeed, much of the early work on genre in the SFL tradition was developed within the context of aiding students from disadvantaged backgrounds to achieve educational success.[5] Furthermore, genres change and new/hybrid genres emerge (Miller and Bayley 2016) as a culture changes (witness the sometimes clumsy attempts of politicians to engage with the new genres of social media practice that they must use to interact with younger voters).

Before proceeding with our analysis of YJCs, we need to explain the way we will model the genres involved. Since genres are staged, goal-oriented social processes, each genre has a distinctive structure. We refer to each element of this structure as a stage, and format the stage name with an initial upper case letter (following the SFL convention for function labels). Names of genres on the other hand are written in lower case (following the SFL convention for class labels). So, for example, for a narrative of personal experience (with reference to Labov and Waletzky's (1967) well-known work on story genres), we would say that it has as its canonical stages an Abstract, Orientation, Complication, Evaluation, Resolution and Coda (Labov and Waletzky 1967).

Clearly, the extract we have seen above is part of a longer conference that is made up of a range of genres in succession. We will refer to these longer genre complexes as macro-genres (Martin and Rose 2008) and will describe each genre in such a sequence as a step in the macro-genre.

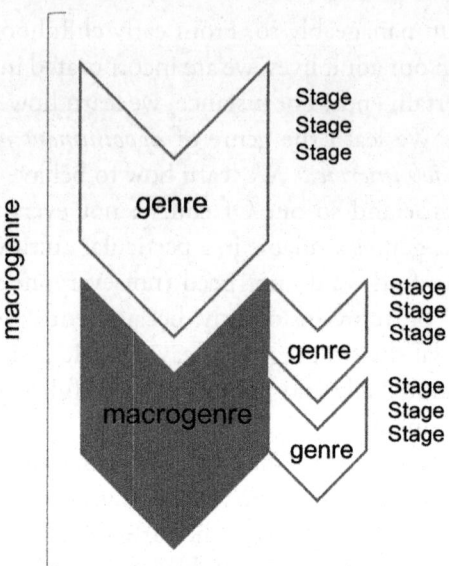

**Fig. 2.1** Diagrammatic convention for macro-genres, genres and stages used throughout this chapter

The structure of macro-genres will be modelled as in Fig. 2.1. Down the left-most column we display the major steps in the YJC macro-genre (using block arrows), as they typically unfolded in the conferences we observed. Some of these steps are in fact themselves realized by other macro-genres and so we have inserted a second row of block arrows outlining the steps in this macro-genre where necessary. Finally, in the right-most column, we make room to display the canonical stages of each specific genre.

## 4 The Socio-legal Framing Genre in the YJC Macro-Genre

Youth justice conferences are an emergent, designed macro-genre reflecting the input of numerous governmental and non-governmental organizations, including institutions from the legal and welfare sectors

## 4 The Socio-legal Framing Genre in the YJC Macro-Genre

of NSW, international bodies such as the United Nations (in particular, through its Convention on the Rights of the Child) and grassroots community organizations such as Victims' support groups. Given that this is still a relatively new legal process for most members of our society, it makes sense that the opening of a conference needs to confirm that participants are ready to proceed with this novel way of doing justice. For this reason, in our analysis of the structure of conferencing, we describe the opening of each conference as a genre called *socio-legal framing* (Fig. 2.2).

If the overall function of the conference opening is to secure implicit and explicit agreement with respect to conduct of the conference, how then is this opening genre organized? Based on our analysis, the socio-legal framing typically unfolds through the staging suggested in Fig. 2.2 (Official Welcome, Legal Invocation, Role Declaration, Goal Affirmation, Consent Check, Confidentiality Reminder and Protocol Setting). Some of these stages can be very brief—even a single minor clause might suffice. Some are much longer and move through more than one sub-stage (technically speaking, more than one phase). To see this, let us look in detail at the Guide Dog YJC, highlighting as we go some of the linguistic and paralinguistic grounds on which we can argue for distinct stages of this genre and suggesting how they cumulatively support its overall function.

Every conference we attended began with a greeting.

**Fig. 2.2** The socio-legal framing genre

## Extract 2.2, Guide Dog YJC

**Convenor:**   Welcome everyone.

We will term this first stage the Official Welcome because on a number of occasions we observed participants who, as they started gathering in the room where the conference was held, would quietly introduce themselves to one another without the need for any prompting from the Convenor. The Official Welcome is cued by the shift in proxemic relations that occurs once everyone has settled into the seat the Convenor has designated for them. The Convenor, in this moment, always addresses the participants as a collective (it is 'Welcome *everyone*' not 'Welcome to you and you and you…'). The intonation with which these first words are uttered gives a strongly bounded sense to the welcome (there is no rising tone, for instance, that might prompt someone to reply 'Thanks, happy to be here!'). The welcome indicates that something formal is clearly about to begin. Having said this, it is possible for this formality to be softened. One of the Convenors we observed, particularly when the conference was a small gathering without a personal Victim present, had a habit of expressing gratitude that the participants have made an effort to attend. They did this while still implicitly signalling the importance of the conference as a special event.

## Extract 2.3, Shopping Trolley YJC

**Convenor:**   Welcome to the conference. Thank you very much for coming. Appreciate you giving up your time.

It should also be noted that there is scope for additional elements to be included in the Official Welcome (for instance, an acknowledgment of traditional custodians of the land, a prayer or other religious observances) if it is deemed culturally appropriate.

The next short stage we have labelled the Legal Invocation. Every Convenor makes a point of naming the Young Offenders Act 1997 straight after the Official Welcome, thereby reminding participants that, despite the relatively informal setting, the process in which they are engaged has a clear foundation in law. Where the Official Welcome, as in the example above, allows for the expression of some emotional language (known as AFFECT) on the part of the Convenor ('*Thank you very much* for coming'), the Legal Invocation stage stands out by virtue of the fact that there is no expression of evaluative language (AFFECT, APPRECIATION or JUDGEMENT) at all.[6] The Young Offenders Act is not appraised as a good, bad or indifferent piece of legislation; it is simply cited to indicate that the Convenor is taking responsibility in accordance with the Act.

**Extract 2.4, Guide Dog YJC**

**Convenor:** I'll be convening this youth justice conference in accordance with the provisions of the Young Offenders Act 1997.

The Role Declaration stage, which follows, is a much longer stage during which there is a transition to dialogue. This dialogue is heavily regulated by the Convenor. Other speakers are either directly asked to take a turn ('*Melanie, could you start it please?*') or else invited to speak by means of a nod or hand gesture. The brief moment of overlapping talk when Donna, the Victim of the Guide Dog YJC, checks that it is her turn to speak next is explained by a momentary lapse from the Convenor with respect to Donna's impaired vision; after having initially nodded in Donna's direction, the Convenor quickly remembered to give Donna a verbal cue. The Convenor also tends to mark the end of each individual speaker's turn in the Role Declaration with an explicit '*thank you*' before returning to a collective mode of address ('*OK well thanks all for making the effort to attend*') as the socio-legal framing moves into its next stage.

In the Role Declaration, there is the potential for slippage between the way participant roles are notionally defined (in legislation, conference-training materials, educational brochures or policy documents) and the way participants name themselves or are named by Convenors. For instance, the legislation and training materials consistently prefer the term 'Young Person' to the label 'Young Offender' used in the title of the relevant legislation (the influence of reintegrative shaming theory here is clear). In this regard, the Convenor in the Guide Dog YJC demonstrates exemplary practice, never referring to Nathan as an offender but always using his name. Yet the script the Convenor is following does explicitly call for admission of an 'offence'. So the 'Young Person' is associated, at least partly, with the label 'Young Offender'. In fact, this tension between a non-judgemental term and a potentially stigmatizing label seems necessary in conferencing insofar as it foregrounds straightaway the fact that identity—the conception that others may have of a boy like Nathan and his own self-concept—is always 'at risk' in conferencing. Not surprisingly, in our observation of conferences, we never heard a 'Young Person' introducing himself or herself with a formula such as 'I'm X and I'm the Young Person who did Y.' Even the obviously empathetic Convenors we were working with occasionally found themselves getting tangled up over the use of labels for the YP. The following example is definitely not what trainee Convenors were taught as best practice, despite the tone of this interaction being anything but stigmatizing.

**Extract 2.5, from Role Declaration in Shopping Trolley YJC**

| | |
|---|---|
| **YP**: | My name's Toby. I'm here because of what I did. |
| **Convenor**: | So you're the offender. |
| **YP**: | I'm the offender, yeah. |

We noticed a similar slippage between a participant's self-identification and their official role in the case of some Victims. Police officers who had been abused, spat upon or punched in the course of making an arrest never introduced themselves as a Victim even when this was their legal status in the matter ('*I suppose I am the Victim if you [the Convenor] say so*' was the closest we heard to an identification with this role). No doubt the pressure to project an in-control institutional persona as the guardian of law and order (not to mention the fact that these officers were attending in full uniform, including guns, handcuffs and capsicum spray) mitigated against police presenting themselves as Victims. Alternatively, participants who were comfortable about being introduced as Victims sometimes went on to subvert the expectations we might associate with this label (in

4  The Socio-legal Framing Genre in the YJC Macro-Genre

the case of the Guide Dog YJC, as we will see, Donna ends up talking more in the manner of a Support Person on behalf of Nathan, the youth who robbed her).

Following the Role Declaration, there is a stage of Goal Affirmation. This transition is associated with an emphasis on the 'here and now' of the conference, alongside constructions that use future tense and first-person plural pronouns to suggest the conference will involve a collective endeavour. Consider the following example.

**Extract 2.6, from Goal Affirmation in Shopping Trolley YJC**

| | |
|---|---|
| **Convenor:** | Your presence here will help us to deal with (this difficult matter). |
| **Convenor:** | So today we want to explore whether we can begin to repair the harm that's been done. |
| **Convenor:** | So as I said we will determine some positive actions. |

The Goal Affirmation can be a recurrent stage (i.e. a stage that occurs more than once) in the socio-legal framing genre. It is a task to which Convenors tend to return, tackling it in small chunks rather than a single, lengthy exhortation, and gently ramping up the expectation that something positive can come out of the conference gathering. As we will describe in more detail later, this is the start of a regular fluctuation of evaluative language (known as a 'prosody of attitude') that ebbs and flows over the course of a conference (like a musical motif characterizing a composition).

The Consent Check and Confidentiality Reminder stages are both required under the Young Offenders Act, and involve a highly formulaic style of talk. The brief dialogue between the Convenor and Nathan requires only a 'yes/no' response from him to questions about whether he is still admitting the offence with which he has been charged and whether he still consents for the matter to be dealt with via a conference. The Confidentiality Reminder in the Guide Dog YJC ('*Everything said at this conference should not be repeated outside this circle…*') is delivered as a monologue by the Convenor, a pattern that was repeated in other conferences (although one Convenor had a habit of adding a brief anecdote about an occasion where a police officer was fined and disciplined for not respecting this provision).

The stage of Protocol Setting is related to the Consent Check and Confidentiality Reminder. However, it differs in certain key features. Firstly, the emphasis in Protocol Setting is not so much on externalities (the legislation, the offence that happened at some other time and place) as it is on the mode of interaction that the Convenor wants people to 'buy into' here and now. In the Guide Dog YJC, for instance, one phase within this stage is explicitly about communication strategies.

**Extract 2.7, Guide Dog YJC**

Convenor:    You may see me referring to this sheet. It's just to ensure that everything is covered during the process.

**Extract 2.8, Guide Dog YJC**

Convenor:    In order to demonstrate respect, I ask that only one person speak at a time.

In addition to these explicit discussions of communication, this stage opens a place for the Convenor to do some 'housekeeping'—explaining things like where the toilets or exits are. The second distinguishing feature of the Protocol Setting is the use of modalized and conditional clauses ('*you may need to go to the toilet,*' '*if you need to go to the toilet,*' '*you may be feeling emotional*'), which often function as polite requests ('*If you can just turn your phones off that'd be great*', '*I would ask that during this conference that you treat everyone with respect*'). Analysis of our sample of conferences suggests that Protocol Setting, like Goal Affirmation, can be a recursive stage in the socio-legal framing and may have a greater degree of flexibility than other stages in terms of where they are placed in the genre.

Using a standard SFL form of genre notation (explained in Appendix B), we can now summarize the schematic structure of a typical socio-legal framing genre[7] as follows (where '^' signals sequence, '•' allows for variable order within the domain specified by the square brackets and the 'n' superscript indicates that a stage can occur more than once in the genre):

Official Welcome ^ Legal Invocation ^ Role Declaration ^ Goal Affirmation$^n$ ^ [Consent Check • Confidentiality Reminder • Conference Protocol$^n$][8]

We can unpack this formula as follows: Official Welcome stage, followed by Legal Invocation stage, followed by Role Declaration stage, followed by Goal Affirmation stage (which may occur more than once), followed by, in various sequences, a Consent Check stage, a Confidentiality Reminder stage and a Conference Protocol stage (which may occur more than once).

Before we move on to the organization of the rest of the conference, it is important to note how the socio-legal framing tends to involve frequent tacking back and forth between talk that emphasizes the formal legal status of proceedings (where participants have roles and obligations) and talk that seems more about 'knocking the sharp edges off the law'—intimating that participants have assembled with a common goal of achieving consensus regarding how the YP can make reparation for the harm caused by their actions. This is less evident in the Guide Dog YJC than in other conferences we observed since the Convenor here, at least initially, is sticking so closely to the scripted prompts. However, even in this case, there are sometimes abrupt shifts in tone. Compare, in the following extract from the Protocol Setting stage, the colloquial phrasing of *'it's a bit of disruption […] and stuff* to the more formal, impersonal *'it is acknowledged that.'*

### Extract 2.9, Guide Dog YJC

**Convenor:** If you can just turn your phones off that'd be great. It's a bit of a disruption when they ring and people talk on them and stuff. So it is acknowledged that you may be feeling very emotional at this time. However, I would ask that during this conference that you treat everyone with respect.

Thus, already in socio-legal framing, we can see that some aspects of the relationship between participants (in SFL terms, the 'tenor' of their interaction) will be gradually opened up for renegotiation. On the one hand, when it comes to social status—the 'vertical dimension of tenor' (Martin and Rose 2008: 12)—these relations are unequal. The Convenor and the attending police, for instance, clearly have greater authority in legal–judicial terms than the YP and this is reflected in the lack of reciprocity when it comes to turn-taking in the conferencing discourse. Turns are generally allocated by the Convenor and, on the rare occasions when speakers overlap, it is usually the Convenor who cuts in on someone else. However, if we think in terms of solidarity—the 'horizontal dimension of tenor' (Martin and Rose 2008: 13)—relationships can become quite close over the course of a conference as participants start to share a range of evaluative meanings in relation to the matters being discussed. An early example of this interplay between the vertical (status) dimension and horizontal (solidarity) dimension of tenor occurs in the socio-legal framing of the Guide Dog YJC when Jim, the Arresting Officer, introduces himself.

**Extract 2.10, Guide Dog YJC**

| | |
|---|---|
| **Arresting Officer:** | I'm Jim and I'm the one that arrested him and his worst nightmare. [Other participants laugh. Jim smiles and looks across to YP] Correct, Nathan? |
| **YP:** | [smiles and nods] |

On the one hand, Jim is asserting his status here as someone who has the power to arrest people and he does so in the form of a joke, a liberty that other participants do not take up during the socio-legal framing genre. On the other hand, to judge from the reaction of Nathan and his family/supporters, this was not a dig at Nathan, aimed to upset him, but rather a playful attempt to engage Nathan—to acknowledge there is a history to his relationship with Jim and that the conference might involve some re-evaluation of this relationship. Indeed, as the Guide Dog YJC unfolded, it became clear that Jim, unlike the Police YLO, had a highly sceptical attitude towards the potential efficacy of conferencing. His only reason for attending, he explained, was that he saw Nathan in a different light to most other young offenders.

**Extract 2.11, Guide Dog YJC**

**Arresting Officer:** I am generally I'm – because I'm a fairly senior officer in regards to time and service I have a generally poor view in all honesty of young offenders in regards to their attitude towards these things. A lot of them treat it as a joke. Melanie will back me up. But I don't think Nathan's treating this as a joke whatsoever. I think he's treating this as with the respect it deserves so that's the only reason I'm attending – besides Donna – that's the main reason I'm attending.

The opportunity for such negotiations of interpersonal meaning is a critical part of conferencing, for which the foundations are already, gently, being laid in the opening socio-legal framing genre.

# 5 From Genre to Macro-Genre: The Whole Conferencing Sequence

From the genre analysis that we have just introduced, it is apparent that some social purposes may be pursued through quite simple generic structures. For example, shifting to a different field for the purposes of explanation, a sales transaction might require no more than a 'Sales Request, Sales Compliance, Purchase, Payment and Purchase Closure' (Eggins 1994: 41). However, even in this case, there can be significant cultural variation—in Australia, a customer can immediately initiate a Sales Request; in France, it is very poor manners to request anything before having exchanged a Greeting. More complex purposes inevitably require more elaborate generic structures or, indeed, a 'macro-genre' in which a series of elemental genres are combined. In the field of education, for example, a suite of genre-based activities such as collecting consent forms for an excursion, handing back assignments, a reading activity, discussion

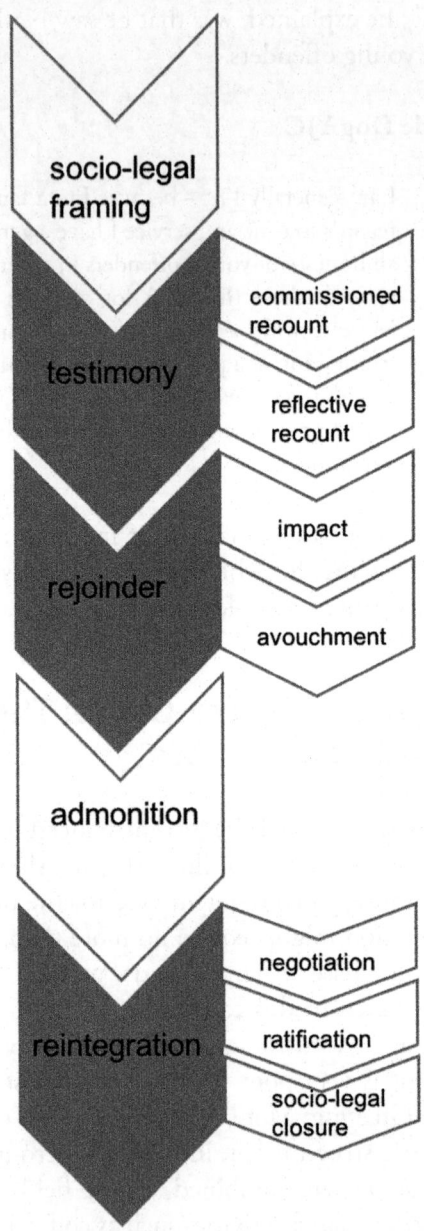

**Fig. 2.3** Canonical structure of the youth justice conferencing macro-genre

of the subject-specific content of that reading and assigning a homework task may work together to make up a discrete unit of study or what Christie would call a 'curriculum macro-genre' (Christie 1997). Alternatively, there are some situations where it becomes difficult, if not impossible, to analyse linguistic interaction in terms of a clearly segmented genre staging. In a casual conversation, for instance, there may be large chunks of talk that can be readily analysed as instantiations of various storytelling genres (narratives, anecdotes, recounts, etc.) but there are often equally large sections of 'chat' that are not so amenable to genre stage analysis (Eggins and Slade 1997: 269). As Eggins and Slade (1997: 238) point out, the concept of genre in SFL 'needs to be seen as a useful heuristic device for describing the globally structured moments in casual conversation and not as a rigid formula'. They go on to note how the fundamental characteristic of chat phases is that they foreground the negotiation of interpersonal meanings, above and beyond the ideational content of a conversation, and it is this privileging of the interpersonal which leads the speakers away from more obviously segmented structures.

Youth justice conferences can be seen as macro-genres which move through a series of elemental genres in order to ratify an outcome plan for the YP and enact some form of reconciliation. The emphasis on negotiating interpersonal meanings as part of this process means that there are some sections of the macro-genre where we need to look beyond the serial, segmented structures introduced above and consider other structuring principles, particularly where evaluative meanings are at stake (as we will see in Chap. 4). Nevertheless, as far as staging is concerned, Fig. 2.3 summarizes our present understanding of the overall macro-genre.[9]

## 6   The Commissioned Recount

At the end of the socio-legal framing genre, the Convenor will call upon the YP to offer an account of the circumstances leading up to their offending behaviour and its consequences. In labelling this part of the conference the commissioned recount genre (Fig. 2.4), we are drawing attention to the way in which it shares features with the kinds of recount we find in

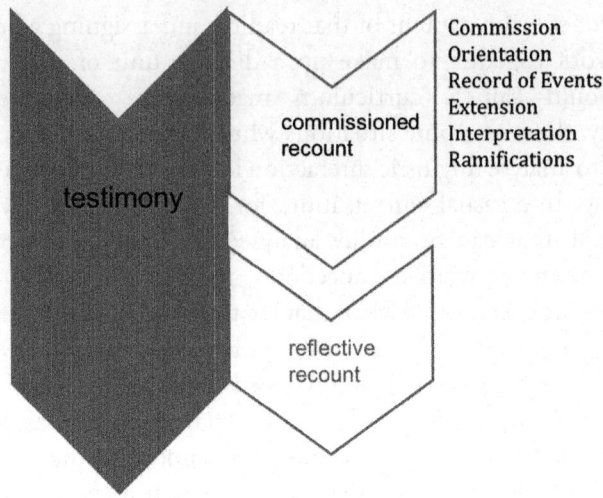

**Fig. 2.4** The commissioned recount genre (a step within the testimony macro-genre, itself a step in the YJC macro-genre)

casual conversation or classroom discourse (Christie 2002; Martin and Rose 2008); at the same time, it is clearly a recount supplied on demand (commissioned by the Convenor as it were). We will look in depth at the language features that help distinguish commissioned recounts from other storytelling genres in Chap. 4. For the moment, in order to preview that discussion, let us look at the story told by Nathan in the Guide Dog YJC and briefly consider how it is staged.

### Extract 2.12, Guide Dog YJC

**Convenor:** OK, Nathan, we'll get you to start by telling us exactly what happened on the day, telling the conference. Can you go back to what you were doing on the day, what you were thinking and when you planned to steal the wallet.

**YP:** Me and my friend Martin were walking down to Coles from the train station in Weathersbury. And I sat waiting for a shop to open. And I sat on the chair just outside Coles when the, when the lady come and I said 'hello' and I was talking to her and I asked her how, what she could see. And she gave me a

|             |                                                                                                                                                                                                                                                                                                                                                                                              |
|-------------|--------------------------------------------------------------------------------------------------------------------------------------------------------------------------------------------------------------------------------------------------------------------------------------------------------------------------------------------------------------------------------------------|
|             | pair of glasses and I put them on and I could see what she could see. Then she went, she got up and left and her wallet was sitting there and I grabbed it and then I waited there for a little while longer went and got my friend Martin and went out the other exit doors. Then we went we went down to the back of Hardacre had a look what was in the wallet and we put it in a tube. |
| **Convenor:** | What do you mean by that?                                                                                                                                                                                                                                                                                                                                                                  |
| **YP:**     | Like put it in a concrete tube, the wallet.                                                                                                                                                                                                                                                                                                                                                |
| **Convenor:** | Uhuh.                                                                                                                                                                                                                                                                                                                                                                                      |
| **YP:**     | Then we went to the pools and we went and got Barry. Then we went into Weathersbury. We went to Time Zone and McDonalds. Then we come back home.[10]                                                                                                                                                                                                                                       |

Note that the Convenor's move, at the beginning of the excerpt, constitutes a genre stage in its own right that we can refer to as the Commission. It suggests that the conference 'proper' will now proceed with the YP's acceptance of a key conversational turn (an offer not to be refused!). It also gives a starting point for the recount, which the YP takes up with a brief Orientation stage.

### Extract 2.13, Guide Dog YJC

Orientation
**YP:** Me and my friend Martin were walking down to Coles from the train station in Weathersbury.

The next stage in the commissioned recount is a Record of Events. The YP arranges the events in which he was involved as a simple activity sequence where one thing happens after another, serially, without any explicit causal connection between events.

Record of Events

**YP:** And I sat waiting for a shop to open. And I sat on the chair (...) and I said 'hello'. (...) Then she went (...) and her wallet was sitting there and I grabbed it. (...) Then we went to the pools and we went and got Barry.

Then we went into Weathersbury. We went to Time Zone and McDonalds. Then we come back home.

This genre staging recurs throughout our sample of recorded conferences, although the Record of Events is often minimal or hard to follow. It may involve quite a bit of prompting from the Convenor, as in the following excerpt from the Shopping Trolley YJC.

### Extract 2.14, Shopping Trolley YJC

| | |
|---|---|
| **Convenor:** | Alright, we're going to start with Toby. And basically Toby, you're going to, um, tell us all exactly what happened on that night. So, I need you to start from before you even got there, when you met your mates, what was going through your head, why you ==actually |
| **YP:** | ==(I can't remember) that much. |
| **Convenor:** | OK, well whatever you can remember will be great. |
| **YP:** | (I don't know. I was) going to there, to the place ==(…) (few drink). |
| **Convenor:** | ==So you met your mates.== |
| **YP:** | ==Yeah, met my mates there. |
| **Convenor:** | And what did you do when you met your mates. |
| **YP:** | Had a few drinks. |
| **Convenor:** | And how old are you? |
| **YP:** | Sixteen. |
| **Convenor:** | Right. OK. |
| **YP:** | And (then yeah) I, I don't know, I nearly had a fight with one of my mates. And then, yeah, so I was angry so I threw the trolley and then I was about to leave when, I don't know, ten, twenty people jumped out of the bushes, over the fence and s – yeah, I don't know, I was up the street and I got dragged back and my mates got bashed by them.== |
| **Convenor:** | ==Mm hm. |
| **YP:** | So yeah, that's pretty much what I remember. |

Given the brevity of the Record of Events in most commissioned recounts, Convenors will subsequently initiate a genre stage that we call the Extension. In the Guide Dog YJC, for instance, the Extension is part of the way in which the Convenor works with the YP to build up a fuller picture of his actions around the time of the offence.

### Extract 2.15, Extension Stage of Commissioned Recount, Guide Dog YJC

| | |
|---|---|
| **Convenor:** | Keep going with it as far as how you came under notice and how did — |
| **YP:** | Then we went back to my friend Tony's house. Then I went, after that, I went back to my Nan's house, no, then I went back to Barbara's house. Then Don and my Nan come and pick me up. Then that's when they said that we had to go in and talk about stuff that … Constable Kennedy. |
| **Convenor:** | Was that the same date? |
| **YP:** | Yes. |
| **Convenor:** | And what happened then? |
| **YP:** | Then — |
| **Convenor:** | And then what happened? |
| **YP:** | Yeah, then the next day we went to see – Constable Kennedy picked me up from my Nan's house and took us into the station. |
| **Convenor:** | And then you had an interview then or? |
| **YP:** | Yes. |
| **Convenor:** | And (…) |
| **YP:** | And I admitted to everything. |
| **Convenor:** | Rightee–o. |

A distinct shift in the unfolding of the commissioned recount genre comes when the Convenor starts to prompt the YP to share some thoughts and feelings about their behaviour, both at the time of the offence and subsequently. Here is how this Interpretation stage begins in the Guide Dog YJC.

### Extract 2.16, from Interpretation Stage of Commissioned Recount in Guide Dog YJC

| | |
|---|---|
| **Convenor:** | So … have you thought about this since then and –? |
| **YP:** | Yes== |

| | |
|---|---|
| **Convener:** | And what would you do differently now? And tell us about how you've – how you've been thinking about it and what's – |
| **Convenor:** | == (…) |
| **YP:** | Well I wouldn't done it and if she left the wallet there I would have got up and have it back to her. |
| **Convenor:** | And what's – what's changed – what's changed now than when you thought about it now than at the time? What made you steal it and –? == (…) |
| **YP:** | ==Don't know. It's just – It was just there and … and I thought it was some easy money so … |
| **Convenor:** | And how did – how did you get the money back to … to Donna? |
| **YP:** | Oh, I gave it back. |
| **Convenor:** | Did you spend some of the money or –? |
| **YP:** | I spent forty dollars of it … pretty sure … and then I gave the money back to Constable Kennedy (which he) I'm pretty sure gave it back to … the lady. |
| **Convenor:** | OK and there was a little bit outstanding is that right? |
| **YP:** | Yes. |
| **Convenor:** | ==Your mum's – your mum's loaned you that money for. |
| **YP:** | ==Forty dollars |
| **Convenor:** | ==for a short term |
| **YP:** | ==mm. Yes. |
| **Convenor:** | Alright. So have you spoken to Don and your mum and everything about this and –?== |
| **YP:** | ==Yes. Nan. |
| **Convenor:** | Um, how do you – how does that make you feel when you spoke to them? |
| **YP:** | It makes you feel pretty bad as is what it did … but (…) how much has it upset the – … |

One way of explaining the need for Extension and Interpretation stages in the commissioned recount would be to see it as a corollary of the YP being relatively unforthcoming in this unfamiliar YJC macro-genre. However, the Shopping Trolley YJC offers evidence to suggest that it is not as straightforward as this. At one point in the commissioned recount of this conference, the Convenor starts to explain to the other participants, on behalf of the YP, the circumstances around the bashing that was mentioned in Excerpt 13. Unbeknownst to this YP, just as he was angrily tossing an abandoned shopping trolley over the fence and onto State Rail property, a large group of police were lurking in nearby bushes, apparently in the hope of catching a group of graffiti vandals they had been targeting for some time. The shopping-trolley thrower and his friend were pounced upon and both young men claim that the police beat them quite severely. The Convenor explained that she had briefed the YP and his mother about the procedures for lodging a complaint about this matter and she proceeded to give the YP a chance to comment on the police's actions as part of extending his recount. Note that the YP is much more forthcoming here, compared with his response in the initial Record of Events quoted earlier.

## Extract 2.17, from Extension Stage of Commissioned Recount in Shopping Trolley YJC

**Convenor:** Toby, would you like to tell us how you felt when the police, um, came up to you?
**YP:** (Well), I wished they weren't police, I wished I could fight back.
**Convenor:** Right. So when they came up to you, what did they say to you?
**YP:** 'Come here'. (That same) police (officer) said 'Come here'. And I just kept walking and (…) with me, handcuffed me, kicked me in the face, and hit me in the back of the head.
**Convenor:** Mm hm.
**YP:** (Then) dragged me back to the house.
**Convenor:** OK, and what happened then?
**YP:** I don't know, got back there, and then, yeah, I don't know – they sat me down and they was bashing my mate, both my mates, (…), and then after that they – they took my cuffs off and said, 'You can go, soon as your mum gets here'. And then five minutes later they go, 'No, you can't go'. (…)==
**Convenor:** ==This is at the house? ==Or, back at the police station?
**YP:** == Yeah, at the house.
**Convenor:** OK. Yep.
**YP:** And, I don't know, I had to sit around for about an hour. I was talking to one of the (…) task force, and then, yeah, went to the police station.
**Convenor:** Did they put you in the paddy wagon?
**YP:** No. It was (…) an undercover car.

| | |
|---|---|
| **Convenor:** | Right, OK, and they drove you to Manduka police station? |
| **YP:** | Yeah. |
| **Convenor:** | OK. What happened at the police station? |
| **YP:** | I just sat in the cell for ages … Yeah. |
| **Convenor:** | And they rang mum? |
| **YP:** | Yeah, they already rang mum. Before I (even) got there. |
| **Convenor:** | So they rang mum back at the house. |
| **YP:** | (Yeah.) |
| **Convenor:** | OK. And how were you feeling with it – it all – you know, did they – did they put to you what had happened? Did they say to you, 'We saw you throw the trolley and that's why you're under arrest?'== |
| **YP:** | == (…) They said to me, 'If you say anything about us hitting ya'. He reckons I bit him. (…) (my mate) (…) bit him. He goes, 'See that scratch on my hand, if you say anything, (well) then you're in trouble== … for assault'. |
| **Convenor:** | ==OK. Right. |

As we will discuss at length in later chapters, the brevity of the YP's response to the Convenor's probes in the Extension stage appears as an attempt to position himself as a 'small target', deflecting potential criticism by saying as little as possible. This reflects the way he is positioning himself in relation to the macro-genre, and should not be interpreted as linguistic ineptitude. As we have just seen, the YP in the Shopping Trolley YJC can be forthcoming when he chooses to be.

Understandably, other participants are often alert to what is included or excluded in a YP's Record of Events. In particular, it should be noted that the Convenor and attending police have access to a written description of events that is produced by the police. In conferencing programmes in some other jurisdictions outside NSW, the police version of events is read out before the YP gives their gloss. Alternatively, as in several conferences we observed, the police have the official record on their lap and will use this to challenge or confirm what the YP is saying. For example, in the Running Shoes YJC, involving a YP who stole a pair of running shoes from a store in a large shopping centre, threatened other shoppers and fought with a security guard, the YP's initial Record of Events was very brief and barely coherent (the YP admitted to being highly intoxicated at the time of the offence). When he is unable or unwilling to participate more expansively in an Extension of the recount, the Convenor hands over to the Police YLO.

## Extract 2.18, from Extension Stage of Commissioned Recount in Running Shoes YJC

**Convenor:** [to YLO] Could you read out the report?
**YLO:** Well, in summary, it says you went to Bunderna and – Were you intoxicated when you went there or did you get drunk at Bunderna?
**YP:** I was intoxicated before I went there.
**YLO:** OK, you stayed there. You had a few verbal arguments with some other young people there, yeah?
**YP:** Yeah.
**YLO:** Yeah. And you produced a knife, is that right?
**YP:** Nup.
**YLO:** [looking down at the report] They say here that there was a knife located and you were seen to be holding it but that's –
**YP:** [laughs]
**YLO:** But that's not true?
**YP:** No. I didn't do nothing.
**YLO:** OK. Well that was one part that was mentioned to the police. The other part is where you went into Target and you take off your old shoes and put on some new ones. That right?
**YP:** Yeah.
**YLO:** Yep. And what happens after that?
**YP:** [pauses then sighs] I tried to walk out with 'em.
**YLO:** Mhm mhm. Yep.
**YP:** Security guard stopped me.
**YLO:** Yep. And so you sort of began to protest and you were threatening to assault the security and staff.
**YP:** He threatened us.
**YLO:** It says that you were threatening. That you made a lot of threats, that you were going to come back and stab people.
**YP:** [laughs in disbelief]
**YLO:** Yeah it's not saying **you** said that. It's saying 'each of them' meaning obviously your sister's boyfriend and yourself were making

|           |                                                                                                                                                                                                                                                                 |
|-----------|-----------------------------------------------------------------------------------------------------------------------------------------------------------------------------------------------------------------------------------------------------------------|
|           | threats that you were gonna find a load of mates, come back and do stuff. Do you remember that?                                                                                                                                                                 |
| **YP:**   | Yeah I remember him saying that.                                                                                                                                                                                                                                |
| **YLO:**  | Yeah. OK. It says – I think then the police attended. And then they conveyed you to Smallton, is that right? Yeah? [turns to Convenor] And then basically Brendan was interviewed with his sister and, yep, that's pretty much it.                              |

The extended recount that the YLO draws out via the police description of events is no doubt necessary. Without it, it was hard for outside observers like us to understand why this matter had come to a conference at all. Nevertheless, it is also clear that the above example is a long way from the 'ideal speech situation' that restorative justice theorists seem to have in mind when they refer to conferencing practice. In a manner similar to courtroom practice (and replete with the legalese that forensic linguists have often observed in this context such as 'you produced a knife'; 'there was a knife located and you were seen to be holding it'), the YP here is being tested on his ability to reproduce a narrative to which he apparently agreed in a police interview but now would rather contest.

The final stage of the commissioned recount genre, which we are calling Ramifications, comes as the Convenor invites the YP to reflect on who has been affected by his/her actions and how. Here, for instance, is a brief excerpt of this kind of talk in the Guide Dog YJC.

## Extract 2.19, from Ramifications Stage of Commissioned Recount in Guide Dog YJC

| **Convenor:** | And who else do you think's been affected by this?                                    |
|---------------|---------------------------------------------------------------------------------------|
| **YP:**       | Angela.                                                                               |
| **Convenor:** | Yep.                                                                                  |
| **YP:**       | The lady (…)                                                                          |
| **Convenor:** | Yep.                                                                                  |
| **YP:**       | And like the other people around.                                                     |
| **Convenor:** | How do you think it's affect Donna? Do you mind me calling you Donna? Is that OK?     |
| **Victim:**   | == That's fine                                                                        |

## 6 The Commissioned Recount

| | |
|---|---|
| **Convenor:** | ==That's fine? How do you think Donna's been affected by this? |
| **YP:** | Pretty bad. |
| **Convenor:** | Can you – Any ideas can you how she's been affected? |
| **YP:** | Like she wouldn't even be able to go out and have much confidence anymore and now she'll be afraid to walk outside and – |
| **Convenor:** | So how you – how do you know that now and you didn't think about it at the time? |
| **YP:** | I don't know. |
| **Convenor:** | You've just been thinking about it? Or? So you didn't think about how that was going to – how that was going to um affect Donna when you picked that wallet up? |
| **YP:** | No. |
| **Convenor:** | Were you affected by anything at the time that might have affected your judgement or your decision-making? Hadn't been drinking any alcohol or taking any drugs? |
| **YP:** | No. |
| **Convenor:** | Did your friend know you were going to take the wallet? |
| **YP:** | No. |
| **Convenor:** | Was it your idea? Completely yours? |
| **YP:** | Yep. |
| **Convenor:** | So it was only the fact that he (…) stole (…) he knew that Nathan stole the wallet is that why he got cautioned and he's received an official caution for this. Is that right, Melanie? |
| **YLO:** | Yep. |
| **Convenor:** | Alright. So we've got lack of confidence and obviously financial that would have been – you know – five hundred dollars is a lot of money for someone. I know she got it back but that's pretty – it's a lot of money for anyone so … I'm sure there's a lot more to the harm that's been caused to people here and I think it's important that we explore that so. I'd like it Donna if you could take us back (…) your movements on the day and (…) wallet and how you felt and that sort of stuff. You (…) |

The Ramifications stage thus typically serves as a point of transition into the rejoinder, with the Convenor explicitly suggesting that other participants will start developing complementary accounts of who has been harmed by the YP's actions and how.

## 7  The Reflective Recount

The second step in the testimony macro-genre involves the Victim recounting their version of what happened at the time of the offence (Fig. 2.5). Not surprisingly, this talk has structural features in common with the commissioned recount, but the sequence of events is viewed from the Victim's perspective.[11] In addition, there may be no need for a distinct Orientation stage, since the people involved in the offence, and where and when it took pace have already been established. Moreover, a Victim will often be more readily forthcoming than the YP will have been, so an Extension stage is not required. Beyond this, a Victim tends to provide much more than a simple 'yes' or 'no' response to any prompts from the Convenor; they introduce new topics of their own accord; and they use a wider range of evaluative language as part of their talk. So an evaluation of what went on does not have to be extracted by the Convenor through a distinct Interpretation stage.

A reflective recount may cover not just the events immediately surrounding an offence but also more distant events that help the other

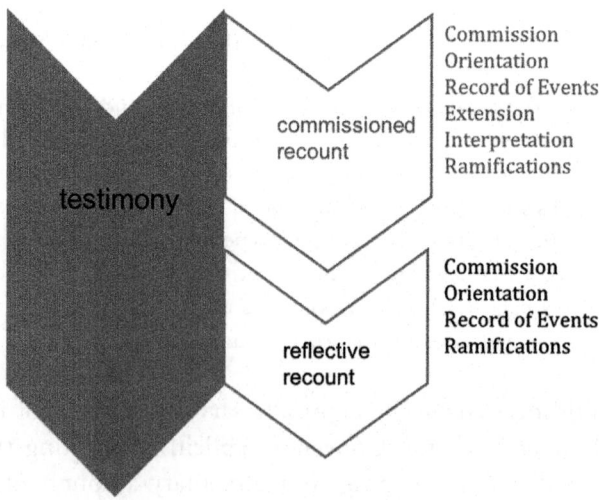

**Fig. 2.5**  The reflective recount genre

## 7 The Reflective Recount

participants to understand something of the Victim's general life circumstances, thereby pointing towards a wider range of ways in which the Victim may have been impacted on by what took place. In the Guide Dog YJC, for instance, the Convenor is clearly encouraging this movement from the specific to the general with a view to raising the emotional stakes of the conference. At the end of the commissioned recount, having heard the YP's thoughts about the likely impact of his actions on others, the Convenor initiates the reflective recount as follows.

**Extract 2.20, Guide Dog YJC**

| | |
|---|---|
| **Convenor:** | I'm sure there's a lot more to the harm that's been caused to people here and I think it's important that we explore that so. I'd like it Donna if you could take us back (…) your movements on the day and (…) wallet and how you felt and that sort of stuff. You (…) |
| **Victim:** | Yeah, I (…) I (…) in Weathersbury. I had a few bills to pay so I got my money out and I was actually on my way around to the baker and across Coles and out the side and we were walking around and something hit me in the leg and I bent down. I discovered it was Nathan's skateboard. And I didn't – if I said – I think I just said you know a hello or something like that and Nathan asked me how much could I see and I've got (…) glasses. You can have a look and see what I can see. We just had a little chat and I thought he was you know a nice friendly kid but I was thinking 'What's he not doing in school at 10 o'clock in the morning?', you know. |
| **Convenor:** | Can I just interrupt you for a minute? Have you got those glasses with you Donna? |
| **Victim:** | Oh yes. |
| **Convenor:** | Can we pass them around? And Michele (…) just opened that door just to let a bit of breeze in? Is that OK? Thanks. So these are the actual glasses that that Nathan put on? |
| **Victim:** | Yeah. |
| **Convenor:** | I might just pass them around so people can have a look at what your vision's like. Sorry, keep going. |

| | |
|---|---|
| Victim: | Ah, yeah, so we'd just (…) yeah I was thinking 'Why isn't he at school? It's 10 o'clock in the morning and' – and it was a Tuesday morning and on Monday I knew she had (…) the high school (…) mentoring program for high school students which would be around his age and so obviously he was playing truant from school. [laughs] I was just wondering how he was doing (…). |
| Convenor: | (…) |
| Victim: | So then I said goodbye and I went to stand up and go into the baker and I'm (…) at the door and I'm 'Ah' [clicks fingers] Can my purse be in my (…)? Agh (…) the seat and it was gone. Yes, so yeah. |

After responding to the Convenor's prompt for more details about her actions in the immediate aftermath of the theft (getting police help, having to block all her cards, get replacement ID, get locks changed, etc.), the Victim then continues, unprompted, and volunteers some further reflections on how she felt at the time.

### Extract 2.21, Guide Dog YJC

| | |
|---|---|
| Victim: | It was very – it was very stressful for me because I was thinking 'Oh, I've (…) my phone bill and rent and groceries' and, you know, like I had all accounted for it, you know. Normally I wouldn't carry that amount of money but – but I'd just been to the bank like minutes before then. Yeah. |

The Convenor latches onto this theme of the stress and anxiety caused by the offence and elicits a long recount of how the Victim came to be blind.

### Extract 2.22, Guide Dog YJC

| | |
|---|---|
| Convenor: | Do you mind sharing your story about when you lost your sight just so people can get a bit of a background so people realized |

## 7 The Reflective Recount

|  |  |
|---|---|
|  | how hard it's been for you to try and adapt and you know live by yourself and things like that?== |
| **Victim:** | ==oh yeah Yeah, um I lost my vision when I turned fifty. And what happened was I had an allergic reaction to a herbal medication I was taking for menopause and the – the reaction caused me to have a bleed in my brain and I had stroke-like symptoms. I thought I was having a stroke. Anyway, I ended up – I took the tablets on the Friday, ended up going into work and was very sick, came home and I had some (…) tea (…) I lay down (…) and (…) said 'Do you want a cup of tea?' and I said 'Why would you want a cup of tea when (…) you know' and it was actually still daylight so – I went to go to the bathroom and I just collapsed and (…) woke up in intensive care in (…) Doonbeg Hospital a few days later and my memory was vague and my hearing was very bad and I had no vision and (…) they first of all told me that I'd had a stroke and that – that hopefully things would resolve and come back but my hearing, memory and everything else came back over a couple of days but my vision didn't' return and I was (…) that I was allergic to a medication called quinine and quinine is used (…) it's also used for cramps and it's also used in – in alcohol as a preservative. It's (…) and (tank water) things like that. So if I had, you know, if I had been a social drinker earlier I – I would have gone blind earlier and what quinine did was it attacked the retina and dissolved the retina to the back of the eye and then shrank the optic nerve from my eye to my brain. So the damage is irreversible and there is no operation or anything they can do at the moment. So I am left permanently blind. |
| **Convenor:** | So you pretty well went blind overnight? |
| **Victim:** | Yeah. |
| **Convenor:** | Yeah. |
| **Victim:** | Yeah. |

The Convenor then highlights how community-minded the Victim is.

## Extract 2.23, Guide Dog YJC

| | |
|---|---|
| **Convenor:** | And you were a midwife before that? |
| **Victim:** | I was midwife for thirty years and (after thirty consecutive years) shift work and my area of expertize was neonatal intensive care (in) (…) and my speciality at that time was teenage pregnancy so … yeah. |
| **Convenor:** | So you're working up with the school as well as a volunteer in the mentoring program. |
| **Victim:** | Yeah volunteering at the school supporting – basically (…) supporting kids who just needed a bit of a hand through year 10 so they needed a hand at maths or science or whatever or they just wanted to talk or – or – |
| **Convenor:** | It's a bit ironic then for somebody of that age then comes and does that== |
| **Victim:** | ==Yeah a bit of a surprize yeah. |

Finally, the Convenor checks to see that the YP is attending to the Victim's talk (a move that recurs frequently across our sample whenever any participant's contribution to the reflective recount is drawing to a close).

## Extract 2.24, Guide Dog YJC

| | |
|---|---|
| **Convenor:** | What do you think about what Donna's just said Nathan? |
| **YP:** | I feel very bad (to what I am hearing). |

Donna's circumstances make her stand out as the obvious paradigmatic example of what restorative justice theorists might hope a personal Victim can bring to a youth justice conference. The impact of the offence on her life is strongly foregrounded and the YP is positioned to express remorse. However, in many conferences, we deal with either corporate or absent Victims. In these situations, it is clearly harder for the Convenor to create such a heightened sense of what is at stake. In the Shopping Trolley YJC, for instance, the Convenor and a Representative from State Rail collaborate on a reflective recount perhaps exaggerating the potential impact (the shopping trolley that YP tossed over the fence never went close to landing on the train tracks).

## Extract 2.25, Shopping Trolley YJC

| | |
|---|---|
| **Convenor:** | Michael, as the Victim Representative. |
| **Victim Representative:** | Just basically we've – it's a safety issue for you and other people because if you throw something on a track, someone's got to come and get that. You understand that, like, and there's got to be a railway worker then that has to risk himself to get down onto the tracks, go out, collect it – the trolley that you threw on there and he could be hit by a train. Any time you go onto the tracks it's dangerous. OK, apart from that, if it had've gone just enough to clip a train it could have been flung into a fence. If someone was leaning on the fence, yourself or your friends, or something like that, it could have hurt them too, so it's just basically a safety issue for you and other people, and, yeah, just lucky there was no damage incurred as – as a result of this, yeah. From our point of view, it's just, yeah, anything to with tracks is a – very unsafe. Yep. Pretty much all I can really think of (…). It's just a safety issue really, and, yeah. |
| **Convenor:** | And you've obviously seen the results of things, you know, whether it be someone's throwing a rock, or even stuff on the side of the track that's left there, like the trolley, for example, that somebody else can come along and throw, you know what I mean? |
| **Victim Representative:** | Yeah, if it's – if it's readily accessible it's – it's more likely to be put onto the tracks. And if it does get onto the tracks, then yeah, there's a – there's a likelihood of serious harm coming to someone even death so – and having seen someone that's been hit by a train it's not a pretty sight. No, it's not a real pretty sight at all. It's, yeah, pretty horrible, so. |

|  |  |
|---|---|
|  | And I'd hate for you to have to see that or any of your friends, or anyone for that matter, having to see that. It's not pretty. |
| **Convenor:** | OK, thanks Michael. |
| **Victim Representative:** | That's about it. |

Even more awkwardly, in the absence of any Victim or Victim's Representative, we see the Convenor in the Mobile Phone YJC having no other option than to suggest that anyone in the room could be a Victim.

**Extract 2.26, Mobile Phone YJC**

|  |  |
|---|---|
| **Convenor:** | This will be a fairly straightforward conference because you don't have a Victim here. So, what I want you to remember is that every single one of us in this room could be considered a victim of a crime. Is that correct? Yep? So, whether it's your mum, or Jane, Michele, Paul, or myself, even your== |
| **YP:** | ==Niece. |
| **Convenor:** | Niece – Just trying to work that out. We could all be victims of crime. As you could too. OK? So, even though we don't have a Victim, all of us here are going to play the Victims for today's purposes, of the conference, OK? Alright? OK. So, obviously we – we want to make sure that – doesn't reoffend. That's the whole desire of this conference. OK? |

We should note in passing that one of the reasons why Convenors sometimes find themselves in this awkward situation of having to artificially 'ramp up' the impact (actual or potential) of a YP's behaviour has to do with amendments to the NSW Young Offenders Act that were introduced in 2002. Under these amendments, if a YP has already received three cautions, the police must escalate any new matters to a conference, no matter how minor the offence. Several of the conferences in our sample would almost certainly have been dealt with by means of a caution had this option still been available to the police. This also helps to explain why (as we will see later) some of the rhetorical strategies of police cautions are becoming more prominent in conferencing practice.

# 8 The Rejoinder Macro-Genre

The conference script foreshadows a default order that participants will speak in after the commissioned recount, namely the Victim, followed by the Victim's Support Persons, followed by the YP's Support Persons and then any other participants ('third party' participants such as a teacher or welfare worker). However, in practice, we observed some deviations from this pattern. For instance, in cases where the Victim was a police officer or someone representing a corporation, one Convenor preferred to elicit comments from the YP's Support Persons before asking these Victims to speak. Nevertheless, regardless of the order of speaking, we can say that one way or another participants use the rejoinder (Fig. 2.6) is to *elaborate, extend* or *enhance* the meanings that have emerged during the commissioned recount. The terms 'elaboration', 'extension' and 'enhancement' are used here to describe how different genres can come together in a 'genre complex', based on an analogy with the way that Halliday and Matthiessen (2004) model logico-semantic relations between clauses that make up a clause complex. Elaboration involves re-stating a proposition in some way ('like', 'in other words', 'what I really want to say is…', etc.). Extension involves adding to the information (or subtracting from it), typically by means of simple coordinating structures ('and', 'also', 'too', 'moreover').

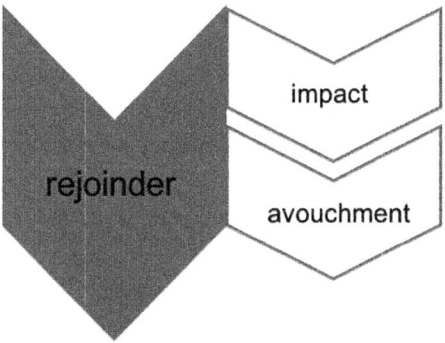

**Fig. 2.6** The rejoinder macro-genre

Enhancement involves subordinate structures to introduce dimensions of time, comparison, causality, conditionality or concession (see Martin and Rose [2008: 218–225] for further details). When we say that the rejoinder elaborates, extends or enhances the testimony step of the conference macro-genre, we mean that it restates, adds to or interprets that preceding step in the YJC.

The most important feature of the rejoinder is that the negotiation of interpersonal meanings—which are present but not strongly foregrounded in the socio-legal framing and commissioned recount—becomes more central. Given that this is a major focus in Chaps. 4, 5 and 6 where we explore the negotiation of interpersonal bonds and the kinds of identities that they enact, we will not go through the structure of the rejoinder here. Rather, we will simply illustrate some of the variety with which participants take up the opportunity afforded to them to respond to the YP's recount. As the following two sections detail, the impact is focused on feelings about how the YP's offence has affected the experience of the Victim as described by the Victim's supporters. Following this, the avouchment genre is focused on the feelings that the YP's supporters have about both the offence and the YP's openness to positive change.

## 9 The Impact Genre

Following the notional order of speakers set out in the conferencing script, after the Victim has spoken, the Convenor would normally turn to the Victim's Support Persons. Their role is usually to help broaden the Ramifications stage in the commissioned recount and/or to bear witness to the impact already described by the Victim in the reflective recount. The impact genre thus involves a focus on both the real and potential consequences of the offence (Fig. 2.7).

For instance, Greg's contribution to the impact within the rejoinder in the Guide Dog YJC draws attention to the effects that Nathan's actions could have not only for Donna but also for other vision-impaired people living in the local area.

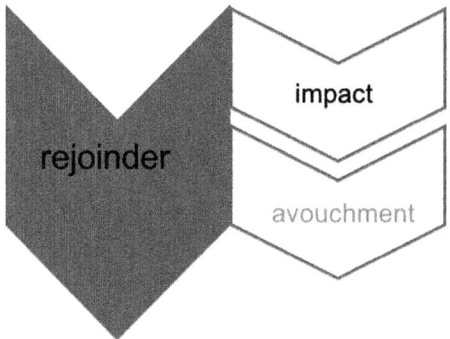

**Fig. 2.7** The impact genre in the rejoinder macro-genre

## Extract 2.27, Guide Dog YJC

**Victim's Support Person:** Yeah one of the issues we – we come across all the time with people who are losing their vision is the fact that they may have to use a long cane and they feel that that makes them a target. And in the past that has made them a target. People thinking that they're more vulnerable or won't be able to (…) them and things like that it's a big issue with us and it takes a lot of coercion and convincing them that perhaps it's better for them to be safer in terms of getting around, than to realize that you may be perhaps putting yourself in a vulnerable situation, you know, to– to that sort of element but – so it's one of the issues we do cover and, you know, it's always harmful. And it's a very very scary thing for people with lowered vision anyway. A lot of our clients are elderly and they feel vulnerable anyway because they are physically slower and older and whatever, so this sort of incident does send a fairly significant shockwave throughout the community in all – in all areas I suppose. You know, it's hard enough to have a vision loss and

| | go about your– your business and get through your daily concerns without having fears of your own safety other than that of just getting around without much vision. We can deal with the – with the people. We can teach people and give them tactics and skills to get around the community, but it's difficult to deal with the with the – that thought in the back of their minds that perhaps they could be robbed or mugged or assaulted or whatever. It's quite tough. It's a big – you know my clients are very brave people at the best of times and this sort of incident doesn't help this issue. |
|---|---|
| **Convenor:** | Absolutely. |

Once again, the Convenor checks in with the YP to see that they are taking in at least some of what they are hearing.

### Extract 2.28, Guide Dog YJC

| | |
|---|---|
| **Convenor:** | I think that's probably why this has gone to a conference Nathan rather than a caution because of the level of harm because (…) you know, Donna's blind but that's taken it up that extra level. I don't know whether it would have ended up as a (…) if you'd stolen a purse from a person like myself or someone else, so we need to be really mindful of that that it's not a very – not a very good thing. There's a lot of people feeling pretty sick in the stomach to think of it – that you even did consider stealing from Donna with her, you know, pretty defenseless – but how did – how did family find out about it and how did they react? |
| **YP:** | I don't know how my mum found out. (…) I knew you found out. |

We will return to the function of evaluative language targeted at the YP in Chap. 4.

## 10 The Avouchment Genre

Following the impact genre spoken by the Victim's Support Persons, the Convenor also gives the YP's Support Persons and any other third parties an opportunity to speak about their feelings in another genre that we term the avouchment (Fig. 2.8). This genre has the dual function of reporting the Support Person's feelings about what has happened and offering an account of the extent to which the YP is now open to positive change. Typically, these Support Persons are parents or primary carers, although some studies have questioned whether parents are such a natural fit for this role, given the often troubled dynamic of parent–child interaction (Prichard 2002; Hoyle and Noguera 2008; Bradt et al. 2007). Parents may feel that they are being held responsible for their child's behaviour (Hoyle and Noguera 2008; Prichard 2002) and some researchers have observed that parents may 'engage in apologising, neutralising, dominating, and punitive discourses, which seriously impinge upon the support they provide, and which also inevitably impact upon the dynamics of the process' (Hoyle and Noguera 2008: 83). Even where judgement is not explicitly targeted at these parties it is often invoked when issues such as poor academic performance or alcohol abuse are discussed as contextual factors influencing a YP's delinquent activity (Prichard 2002: 333).

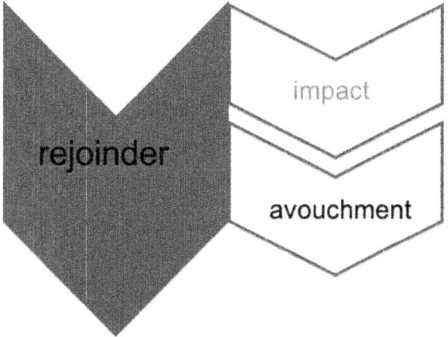

**Fig. 2.8** The avouchment in the rejoinder macro-genre

From our observations, the YP's parents and other Support Persons deal with this risk of losing social 'face' in a number of ways. First, they typically state how shocked, disappointed or angry they were upon learning of the YP's offending behaviour and, in so doing, voice their own respect for the moral and legal codes that have been infringed. Often this is accompanied by an expression of empathy for what the Victim has suffered. Here, for example, is Nathan's mother in the Guide Dog YJC.

**Extract 2.29, Guide Dog YJC**

| | |
|---|---|
| **YP's Mother:** | Yeah Constable Kennedy rang me up on the mobile phone asking if I knew where Nathan was and I said no and– and I just straight away I said 'well, what's he done?' and he said 'you wouldn't believe it. He's stolen a wallet off a blind lady'. And I went 'I beg your pardon'. And he said it repeated himself again (…) And then I rang my mum (…) and I said '(…) if you see him, grab hold of him because I need to speak to him' because I was going to take him straight to the police station up at Hardacre because I actually said to Jim, 'Well when you see him charge him'. I said 'It's disgusting'. I said 'I want him charged'. I said 'He's not learning any other way' and I said 'That poor lady', you know, I was actually disgusted. |

On several occasions, as parents or other Support Persons narrated, the circumstances in which they came to learn of a YP's transgression visibly upset them. Convenors were quick to check that these moments were hitting home with the YP, seizing the opportunity presented by the Support Person's distress, to go back and 'leverage' a level of affective response that was often absent during the YP's commissioned recount.

A second key contribution that the YP's Support Persons can make at this point in the conference is to provide some assurance that the YP has begun to understand the serious nature of their transgression. The Batteries YJC provides a clear example of a Convenor eliciting this type of talk:

### Extract 2.30, Batteries YJC

| | |
|---|---|
| **Convenor:** | So do you think he understands the consequences of what he did? |
| **YP's Stepfather:** | I think he understands now (…) I think he's sorry for what he did (…) I hope he's learnt a lesson. |

This is roughly comparable to what happens in a courtroom when witnesses may be called who can attest to the good character of the defendant. The YP must be shown to have redeeming qualities, as in the Batteries YJC where, again, the Convenor very explicitly prompts the avouchment.

### Extract 2.31, Batteries YJC

| | |
|---|---|
| **Convenor:** | So is he a good boy at heart? |
| **YP's Stepfather:** | He's really good. Never argues. Never rude. (…) For a teenager, he's really good. He does a fair bit of study (…) tutoring. |

We might think of a rough division of discursive labour in the rejoinder along the following lines: the Victim and Victim's Supporters enact the impact genre, and the YP's Supporters and third parties produce the avouchment. However, in actual conferencing practice, it is rarely as straightforward as this. Sometimes Victims will play down the impact of an offence or a YP's Support Person will focus straight away on producing an avouchment, and may even withhold an avouchment. A weak or absent avouchment from a YP's Support Persons can be compensated by the contributions of other participants, including the police or even, as in the Guide Dog YJC, the Victim.

### Extract 2.32, Guide Dog YJC

| | |
|---|---|
| **Convenor:** | Donna, is there anything you would like to ask Nathan more? |
| **Victim:** | I – I'd just, I think Nathan probably it was just something he did without even planning to do it. I think it was just an impulsive mistake and I've heard that Nathan's just lost his grandma |

and that would have been very disappointing for his grandma and his mother. I think Nathan might feel that he's let people who love him down, you know, and hopefully he'll – you know, this will be a one off thing and never happen again. Because it's a wonderful opportunity for you Nathan. I think you're very brave actually to have turned up today and I think it's a great opportunity for you to sort of you know look at what you're doing with your education and why you're skipping school and what's down the track for you in the future if you don't get some kind of education or training or – Because hanging around the shops, you know, there's no future in it really and I do believe you're a, you know, a good kid who just needs a little bit of help to get back on track again, you know.

Donna's magnanimous response to Nathan stands as an exemplary instance of the kind of reconciliation that many restorative justice advocates would hope to see realized in all conferences. However, it is worth noting how this contrasts with the notional roles ascribed to participants in early formulations of reintegrative shaming theory. Braithwaite and Daly (1998) have argued that the voice of the Victim's supporters 'structures shaming into the process' while the presence of the offender's supporters 'structures reintegration into the process' (1994: 226). However, Donna's contribution in the Guide Dog YJC cuts right across this discursive demarcation. Braithwaite himself has since acknowledged that his earlier model was too rigidly mechanistic (Ahmed et al. 2001). It is hard to predict sometimes who will do the work of recording the impact of an offence, vouching for the YP's good character, and highlighting their awareness of wrongdoing and any commitments they have made to reform. One thing is clear, however: experienced Convenors will keep going back around the circle until all three of these tasks have been achieved to some extent.

After the Victim's Support Persons and the YP's Support Persons have both had opportunities to talk, the Convenor will turn to any third parties who may be present, such as school teachers or representatives of welfare agencies, who may have some stake in the matter. These participants are generally careful not to align themselves too closely with either the Victim or the YP (indeed, the normal seating arrangements for a

10 The Avouchment Genre

conference would literally place them as 'cross-bench' players, sitting opposite the Convenor and between the other parties). From this position, they are able to add to the reflective recount or to any avouchment that other participants will have already offered. But their most useful contribution can be to extend upon any talk that has focused on the YP's consciousness of having done wrong. Thus, third parties will sometimes offer evidence of how the YP is committed to dealing with some of the causes and consequences of their behaviour.

An example of this is the following discourse by a Support Person of the YP in the Train Tracks YJC. This Support Person was a social welfare worker who had made a connection with the young woman.

**Extract 2.33, Train Tracks YJC**

| | |
|---|---|
| **Convenor:** | Kate, you've met Amy through a mutual friend or you've had dealings within your job (and you're) a friend of Amy's, and she's obviously built up a bit of a relationship with her over time. Can you just sort of give us a bit or a rundown on sort of where she's heading (whether) she's taken a few things on board? |
| **YP Support Person:** | Well first of all I just wanted to say that I think you [looking at YP] are doing fantastic. Well obviously in my line of work you see young kids kind of get to a point where (…) you can go one way or the other and it's that crucial kind of decision point which I'm hoping that you're at now, and with some changes and positive choices you can really just (…). When I first met you I was really impressed by the responsibility that you have shown for the things that have happened, and your maturity. I think I said to you (the other day), although we don't want kids coming into our system under a supervised order, I – you know – this is one Young Person who I would be excited with working with because a lot of kids that we deal with are quite resistant to making any kind of positive changes, but you have shown that you are at that point that you were willing to make a change. (…) So I think if you keep doing what you're doing now, you |

> have a bright future. It is about those choices that you make and, you know – you know that so – (…) It's very rewarding for me when I can see good things happen. Yeah.

Now that support persons and relevant third parties have had an opportunity to make their contributions, designers and proponents of the YJC macro-genre would have expected an apology from the YP to be forthcoming. But placement and enactment of an apology is a variable, which we will now explore.

## 11 The Apology

We have already seen, in Chap. 1, the importance that many restorative justice theorists place upon the role of apologies in conferencing. Indeed, the provision of a verbal apology (or the promise of a subsequent written apology in cases where a Victim is absent) is often explicitly recorded as part of the outcome plan of a youth justice conference. However, looking at our discourse sample, we were surprised at how much variation there can be in the way that apologies are proffered, if performed at all. The apology often occurs within the rejoinder genre, but may be found at other points in the conference macro-genre.

Some of this variation is to do with the presence or absence of a Victim. The two conferences we observed in which Victims were entirely absent were the only occasions when there was no apology offered at all, although in both these cases there were still stages where people discuss their feelings about what has taken place. Another factor is the nature of the Victim: young people were generally more committed to their apologies when they were addressing a personal (and 'civilian') Victim rather than a police officer or the Representative of a corporate Victim. By calling these apologies more *committed*, we mean that they tend to commit more appraisal resources—both verbal and non-verbal—not that they are necessarily or self-evidently more truly sincere.

As noted above, we observed considerable variation in the giving of apologies in terms of their placement within the macro-genre. In the conferencing script, it is clearly implied that the ideal placement of an apology would be *after* the rejoinder—that is, after all the other participants have had ample opportunity to evaluate, reframe and add to the matters initially canvassed in the YP's commissioned recount—and *before* the conference moves into the process of generating a formal outcome plan. This suggests that an apology, no matter how brief, functions as a crucial hinge between the first half of the conference, with its broad focus on assessing the YP's past actions and future potential, and the second half of the conference, with its focus on specific, immediate consequences. However, tellingly, the form of words that the conference script suggests Convenors might use to elicit an apology is, at best, a very indirect request.

[To YP_____]: Before we move on, is there anything you want to say to _____ [name of victim] or anyone else here?

This kind of pattern was seen in Guide Dog YJC.

**Extract 2.34, Guide Dog YJC**

| | |
|---|---|
| **Convenor:** | OK, before we move on is there anything you'd like to say to Donna or to anyone listening? |
| **YP:** | I'm sorry what I did, Donna. |
| **Victim:** | OK (...) |
| **Convenor:** | Why don't you go over and give her your hand and shake her and shake her hand? [hand shaking] (...). |

Note how much work the Convenor is doing as a broker here. It is always the Convenor who bids for the apology, never the person to whom the apology is addressed—although there were some cases where the apology was offered without prompting. The 'bid for apology' is very different to the explicit prompts the conference script offers for commissioning the recount, and, perhaps not surprisingly, on several occasions, we observed young people who did not respond at all to the bid for the apology. This brings to mind a sequence from the film *Educating Rita* (Gilbert 1983) where a working-class hairdresser named Rita attempts to better herself by studying literature with an Open University professor.

Their exchanges often feature Rita failing to recognize indirect moves such as the request for her name in the following.

**Tutor:** And you are …?
**Rita:** I'm a what?
**Tutor:** What is your name?
**Rita:** Me first name?
**Tutor:** Well that would at least constitute some sort of start.
**Rita:** Rita …

In this exchange, Rita appears unfamiliar with the telos and staging of the genre of first meeting with the tutor in Oxbridge, and hence does not give the appropriate reply to the tutor's first move.

Returning now to our youth justice conferences, we see a similar failure to give the expected reply, as in the following instance.

### Extract 2.35, Mobile Phone YJC

**Convenor:** Is there anything else you'd like to say about it?
**YP:** …
**Convenor:** Are you sorry for what you did?
**YP:** Yeah.
**Convenor:** Why are you sorry for what you did? Because you got caught or because it was wrong?

Rather than interpreting this young man's reluctance to apologize as a sign of recalcitrance, it seems more likely that he is genuinely confused about what is being asked of him at this point. This is likely because this was a conference without a Victim in attendance (despite the Convenor's suggestion that the YP could think of all the conference participants, including himself, as potential 'victims of society') and, more importantly, the YP included a good deal of talk regarding negative feelings about what happened as part of the Ramifications stage of his commissioned recount. Indeed, we often saw young people who volunteered negative judgement about their behaviour and sometimes an apology early on in the conference. Part of the reluctance of the YP in the Mobile Phone YJC to add to his earlier statements could simply be that he just had to sit through 30 minutes of rejoinder and admonition talk: why would you open your mouth again to speak if you feared that another round of rejoinder might ensue?

In other cases, however, it was clear that the YP(s) in the conferences we were observing is (were) genuinely ambivalent about the extent to which they needed to apologize for their behaviour.

### Extract 2.36, School Library YJC

| | |
|---|---|
| **Convenor:** | It's affected his life. |
| **YP1:** | Yeah I know it has. That's what I am saying. It's changed a lot. I – I do realize what we've done. |
| **Convenor:** | Well the snickering and the smiling doesn't make me think that – |

While the two YPs in this conference were particularly reluctant to apologize (with consequences that we will explore fully in the coming chapters), they were not atypical insofar as the grading of apologies is concerned. As we noted in Chap. 1, apologies are offered and accepted 'up to a point'. Hence, the final (often deferred) genre stage often involves what we might think of as 'apology check'.

### Extract 2.37, Guide Dog YJC

| | |
|---|---|
| **Convenor:** | So he's given a verbal apology to Donna today and you've accepted ==that apology Donna as genuine? |
| **Victim:** | == Yes I do, yes. |

### Extract 2.38, Shopping Trolley YJC

| | |
|---|---|
| **Convenor:** | Are you at all sorry for what you did? |
| **YP:** | Yeah. |
| **Convenor:** | Really? |
| **YP:** | Yeah. |
| **Convenor:** | Alright. You got anything else you want to say at this point? |
| **YP:** | No. That's it. |

Importantly, not only is there variation in the placement and status of an apology in a conference, the ideal apology that the conference script foresees is, on the basis of our analyses, optional. It may appear during different steps of the macro-genre, for instance during the rejoinder, and at different stages in the elemental genres. But it is not a deal-breaker, permitting or preventing the negotiation of an outcome plan. Nor is a 'good apology' necessarily a 'deal-sweetener' for the outcome plan. Some of the YPs who were most ready and willing to offer a fulsome apology were the ones who ended up with the toughest outcome plans.

## 12   The Admonition Genre

In our discourse samples, there was always a clearly distinguishable step in the conference in which—typically, though not exclusively—the YLO would outline some of the consequences that might befall a YP who failed to 'mend their ways' in a step in the macro-genre that we refer to as the admonition (Fig. 2.9). Significantly, this is not a step for which the notional conferencing script provides a template; nor is it referred to in the NSW Young Offenders Act. Most often it followed the rejoinder and worked to enhance the contributions of other participants who might already have touched upon the need for the YP to make changes in their life. Most likely, it represents a crossover into conferencing practice of the kind of talk that YLOs produce when giving an official Caution (hence the related term admonition).

The following excerpt from the admonition in the Guide Dog YJC is typical.

**Extract 2.39, Guide Dog YJC**

| | |
|---|---|
| **Convenor:** | Can you explain to everybody what would happen if Nathan did get charged and convicted at court? |
| **YLO:** | What would his future hold?== |
| **Convenor:** | ==Yep |
| **YLO:** | I guess to – at this point too that's – that's where you're at and you know that. You know what happens if you walk out the door. That you get charged for everything you do now. Everything you do, everything that happens is a step closer to Juvenile |

**Fig. 2.9** The admonition genre

Detention so you're not going to know which one's going to tip you over as well. Once you get charged and convicted of something, so it goes before the court and the magistrate will decide your penalty. You get charg – you get a criminal record. And that's going to affect your (things) in the future and then things like that. The magistrate can decide things like community service, a fine, or time in juvenile detention. There's lots of things that can happen. The other thing that your criminal record can affect is your visa, like travelling overseas. You won't be allowed into certain countries with that. OK? You're 15 years old. Who knows what you're going to do in the future. You might, you know, want to travel overseas or someone might win a holiday. 'Let's all go to America', and you're going to be sitting there going, 'well, I can't go because I've done these silly things when I was young'. And that's where you're at now. You're 15 and that's pretty scary. You've got to start to step up and make decisions for yourself; not worry about what these friends are doing. It's your responsibility; no one else's. You can be there and your friend may not have a caution before and you get in trouble together. He'll have the caution but you won't. OK? That's where you're at. So you really need to make some better decisions. I think probably in the last three weeks you've gone through a lot and you've probably grown up a lot. You've probably seen things and,

|          |  |
|----------|--|
|          | you know, that there's – I guess you've got to start to have a bit of respect for yourself, have a bit of respect for your family that are around you supporting you, and start to make the right decisions because this is, you know, from one extreme to the other. You've gone through sort of, you know, little things to – This is – this is quite disturbing and as a police officer it was very disturbing to get this kind of a crime from a Young Person and from you. You know, I had Dan ringing me up saying what can we do. What's the worst thing we can do to this person, because this is disgusting, and it's disturbing, and he doesn't belong on the streets, and you don't. |
| YP:      | Yeah. |
| YLO:     | You know, so, you know, you've got to really make some really serious decisions right now. Make some changes and it sounds like you have which is a credit to you, and you've got all these people here to support you and to try and make a difference for you. We can give you everything. We can give you all the programs. We can say all of this stuff, but at the end of the day it's up to you, and if you care about all these people in the room and you care about your Nan, well then you're – you're going to be OK. |
| Convenor:| Even Donna is here to support you. |
| Victim:  | mm. |
| Convenor:| You know, she's – she's OK. She's moved on and she's a very – very – one of the strongest ladies I've ever met, and she's here because she wants to help you get –, you know, come – come good and give you an opportunity to – to move from this and I want to mention one thing so your criminal record doesn't get wiped when you turn 18? |
| YLO:     | No. It stays with you forever. OK. |
| Convenor:| And a lot of people don't realize that. |
| YLO:     | Yeah. Some people think that it can be – yeah, that it goes after five years or something like that. It actually takes ten years. You can get it removed, but you actually have to physically apply for it to be removed, and for certain jobs it will never go away, and it doesn't just have to be like defence force, or fireries, or police, or ambulance. Things like teachers, real estate, most government jobs, your criminal record will never go away. OK. So you know – this is a huge turning point in your life, and you can go one way or you can go the other. And the way that you're going |

is a very hard and long and lonely road, because I'm sure that, you know, your family aren't going to put up with this anymore, and if you start to do the wrong thing it's going to make your relationships hard and things like that. Or you can start to do the right things and life will be a lot easier, and you'll feel better about yourself.

Two strategies stand out in this excerpt that help mark the admonition as a separate step in the macro-genre. First, there is a shift from a retrospective focus, building up an account of the YP's offending behaviour and evaluating its significance, to a prospective consideration of how the YP should behave in future. Second, there is the rhetorical trope of explaining to the YP that they have reached a limit or tipping point, often described as a 'line in the sand' or a 'fork in the road', the kind of threshold that theorists of ritual refer to as the *liminal* moment (see Chap. 7). As part of this rhetoric, YLOs will frequently appeal to the YPs to start taking responsibility for their actions. Obeying the law simply because the police might catch you is not enough. YPs are admonished to discipline themselves by thinking through how what they do might harm or negatively influence someone else, as in the following examples.

**Extract 2.40, Shopping Trolley YJC**

YLO: I just want to, (…) Bob is – you were saying before about how you were worried about committing an offence and, because it was illegal, OK. As Bob was saying, I'd really like you to start looking at it in the sense of the consequences, OK? Not so much the fact that there's that chance that the police may be hiding in the bushes to collect you, alright. I'd really like you to look at it in the sense, as Bob was saying, a train may be derailed, whatever may happen. And with any crime, you know, a lot of people, whether they're talking on their mobile phones while they're driving, they're, they've had six beers or whatever it may be and jump in their car, OK, a lot of that mentality may be, you know, OK, they advertize, every cop car can pull you over and breath test you and you may get caught, how about we look at it in the sense where, if we're on our phones, you have (momentary) trouble, lose our concentration, and we run over a poor lady that's crossing the road, OK. So I'd really like you to look at this, as far as, not getting caught, OK. Not because

they're illegal, but how about, 'I'm not going to throw that trolley because someone maybe lose a leg', or, whatever the case may be.
YP: Yep.
YLO: OK, I think that mentality more than anything would be – you know, something that would – in the future, you know.

**Extract 2.41, Mobile Phone YJC**

YLO: It also has consequences with your family. You have younger brothers and sisters?
YP: (…) (older brother)
Convenor: Older? Yeah? Have your older brothers and sisters, or older brothers been in trouble? No?
YP: (I don't know)
Convenor: Because what happens is, especially when you've got younger brothers and sisters, or little cousins, you – you set an example for them. And a lot of the times, because they idolize their big brother, or their cousin, or whatever, they look at them and they – they love them you know? And they tend to copy the behaviour and then they end up doing it. And we see it time and time again where the – where the older brothers have been in trouble and then the younger brothers just keep coming through and they do the same because they're influenced by the older people. Same as you could be influencing I mean your – your cousin. He's sitting here listening to this. You know, this influences them, they see what happens and – you know, in either a positive or a negative way, but it influences them.

This manner of drawing attention to negative consequences is complemented by talk that focuses on positive outcomes that a YP might experience if the right choices are made. YPs are encouraged to think of the 'big wide world out there', replete with opportunities that they wouldn't want to throw away.

**Extract 2.42, Mobile Phone YJC**

YLO: And as a Youth Liaison Officer, I want to see you do that – I want to see youse have – you know, have all the opportunities that you can to be the person that you want to be, you know. That's about all I wanted to – you probably – you've covered everything that I've said anyway, but as a mother I just had to nag that one in anyway. But, yeah, only you can choose which way you are going to be. Seriously look at your friends. Because you are at a really influential point now where you can go that way, or you can go that way. You know that don't you? Yep.

**Extract 2.43, Shopping Trolley YJC**

**YLO:** We're here to, you know, discuss what's happened and hopefully steer you on a path where you go 'Alright, I've learnt from this experience; I was only a kid', you know. Go ahead with your apprenticeship, you know, you never know, it may lead to bigger and better things. You get contacts, get to know people, get some numbers, go and work for, you know, you could – if (…) been a butcher, you could end up overseas mate and work. You know, you've got a whole lot ahead of you. You've got so much to experience and learn. You don't want to end up in Juvy and getting to know other kids who, don't have parents that you have, OK. (…) lucky (…) got support there. Alright, there's a lot of kids that don't have that support, and I think that has a lot to do with it also. You can see by their attitude (…), you don't want to end up down that path. Look it as, 'OK, as a kid, I made mistakes, everyone does. Unfortunately I got caught'. OK. But take away from this that, you know, you've got a job. Hopefully you've got new mates, you know. You've got a big opportunity now with this skill, you know. You can, even (…) interstate, you know. You might go to Perth, or, you know, (…) a butcher. It's one of those things that you can pretty much – well you can, take anywhere, you know. It's a big wide world out there, and it's not all about Manduka Railway Station, OK. So.

Significantly, the YLOs are not foregrounding direct proposals in their advice. They are rarely telling the YP what they should or shouldn't do. So there are very few imperatives (*Don't do this/do this*), modulated commands (*You shouldn't do this/you should do this*) or wishes (*I'd like you to do this/I'd prefer you not to do this*). Neither are the YLOs foregrounding rules; their counsel is not about spelling out the law as something to be obeyed.

Rather, as illustrated above, the YLOs are more concerned with propositions dealing with the consequences of an offence. Instead of explicit proposals they favour propositional contingency. So a potential proposal such as *'You should not take the wrong fork in the road'* is reconstrued as *'You can go this way or you can go this way'* or *'If you go X way then Y will happen.'* Here are some examples, relating to various outcomes:

— Adulthood

But what we're creating now, is your — we're creating a, what do you call it, a pattern of how you're going to be when you turn eighteen, and **if you continue this pattern now**, it will go on into your adult lifehood, and that will make a huge difference to you.

— Mates

If he's going to continue going down that track, do you want to go down that track too?
  **If he is doing stuff and you're with him**, you'll get into the same sort of trouble.
  So, **if he is one of your really good friends** and I'd really — you need to really start to question what you are going to do and how you are going to end up, because he will get you into some big trouble.

— Employment

**If you work for a bank**, and a lot of people now, even do it for retail, just working in being a checkout person. They will ask as part of their criteria to have a criminal history check, and you will have to provide that for them **if you want to go for that job**.
  **If you had a robbery offence on your record** and you went — do you think — how easy do you think you would get into a trade?

— Feelings

**If your mum or sister was on that train**, how would you feel, knowing that you were responsible for what had happened?

Because**, if you'd ever been robbed**, you would know, especially when somebody's made you give something over, you'd know how horrific that can be, and how– how largely that can affect that person that was robbed.

I can only imagine how I would feel **if somebody grabbed me and threw me in the back of the wagon**. But then I guess it depends whether you've done something wrong or not. **If you haven't done anything wrong**, then that would be even worse. But, when you know you've done something wrong, and you're in the back of the wagon and you think 'Oh (…)', cause, you know, well 'This is what I get for doing the wrong thing'. It's– It's how it goes.

Contingency is also explored in terms of what could have happened but didn't (the clear implication being that if the offence happens again, 'could haves' can become 'will haves'):

You must have known that there is the possibility it **could** have gone a bit further, god forbid.

I understand what you're saying. That you purposefully didn't throw it on the tracks, but somebody else **could**.

And, you **might** not of even known, thrown it over, **could** have hit somebody in the head. Somebody **could** have been drunk and stumbled over the train tracks.

… It's not one of the most serious offences we've ever seen, no way, (…) really huge, but at the end of the day it's what **could** happen, that's all I'm sort of saying, like– it's what **could** happen. It's not what did happen, it's what **can** happen.

The metalinguistic term YLOs use to focus on these contingent outcomes is *consequences*.

### Extract 2.44, Concordances lines from Mobile Phone YJC

I guess a lot of the things have already been spoken about, like the **consequences** and all that sort of thing.

You've already spoken about the **consequences** obviously, you know. This can have major **consequences** for you, let alone the rest of your family.

But now you'll start to learn about **consequences**, and if you choose to keep staying with him then you're choosing to be in the – in the eye of the police … and looking at trouble.

I'd really like you to start looking at it in the sense of the **consequences**, OK?

However, as I was getting back to, you've got those **consequences** there, where someone's life and their family and their friends are suffering, OK.

Balancing this bad consequences motif is the notion of possibilities later in life, referred to variously as *choices*, *options* and *opportunities*:

> The Young Offenders Act allows us to be able to deal with you alternatively, rather than just throwing you in the court system, OK, because the court system doesn't really solve any of the issues as to why you're here to start with. It just sets the punishment of what happens after. Once you turn eighteen you don't have those **options** anymore. You understand that?
>
> And as a Youth Liaison Officer, I want to see you do that – I want to see youse have – you know, have all the **opportunities** that you can to be the person that you want to be, you know.
>
> You don't have a good job, you have no money, you have … no **choices**. But you have money, you have **choices**.
>
> OK, but take away from this that, you know, you've got a job, hopefully you've got new mates, you know, you've got a big **opportunity** now with this skill.

The future is also explored through modalizations of possibility:

> Good things **may** happen in the future if you change your behaviour
> You **might** go to Perth …
> You know, you **could** if (…) been a butcher, you **could** end up overseas mate and work.

And also in terms of modulations of ability shading into inclination:

> And as a Youth Liaison Officer, I want to see you do that – I want to see youse have – you know, have all the opportunities that you **can** be the person that you want to be, you know …

Cause you are at a really influential point now where you **can** go that way, or you **can** go that way.

But, yeah, only you **can** choose which way you are going to be.

And only you **can** learn. You **can** – you **can** either ... go, you know, take what we're saying and take it on, or you **can** ignore it, but – and we'll see you again later. But it's up to you.

In short, the YP is characterized as being at a crossroads where they must weigh up alternatives: they can either become the future ('irrealis')[12] YP with jobs, options and potential to travel (Fig. 2.10), or become a despairing future ('irrealis') YP with no job and no options (Fig. 2.11).

The overall message is that YPs should avoid bad consequences and not foreclose choices. The YLOs' negative consequences are outlined in

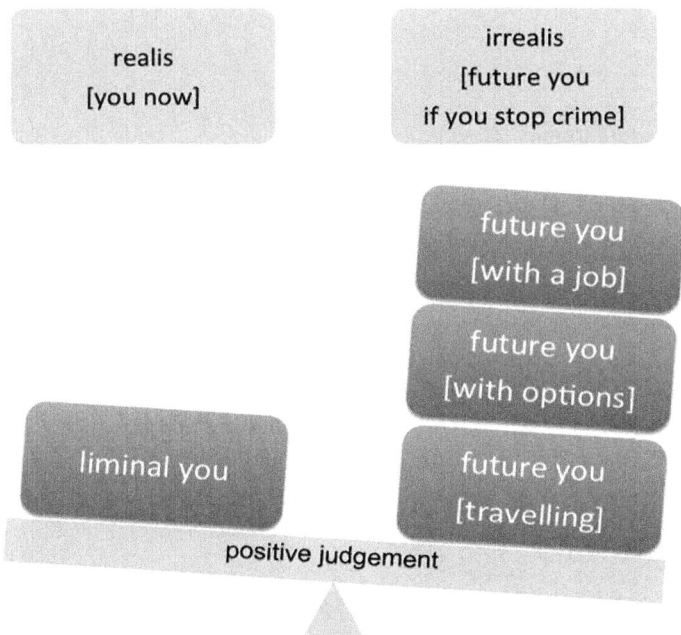

**Fig. 2.10** Future irrealis YP, positively judged

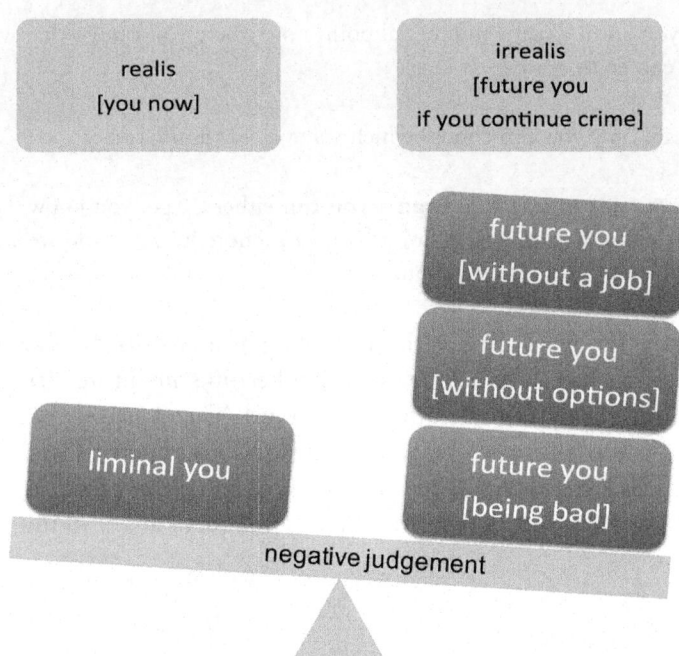

**Fig. 2.11** Future irrealis YP, negatively judged

Figs. 2.12 and 2.13, including possible problems relating to, for example, the following domains of experience:

– Detention:

You don't want to end up in Juvy.
  Or you can ignore it, but – and we'll see you again later.
  What's your feeling on being incarcerated and being putting to custody?

– Unemployment:

There's no way I would employ somebody who's had a record of that.

– Mates:

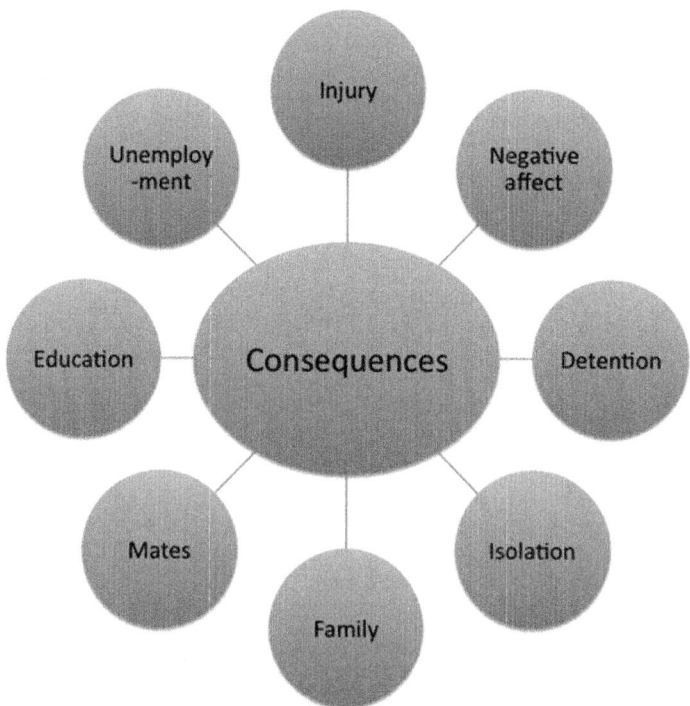

**Fig. 2.12** Domains of potentially negative outcomes

[You don't want to] getting to know other kids who, um, don't have parents that you have.

Mixing with the wrong people – there's only one place you'll end up, and usually that's big – big boys' goal.

You hang around with him, and they will target you too – just by being with him.

– Education:

Go ahead with your apprenticeship, you know, you never know, it may lead to bigger and better things.

– Family:

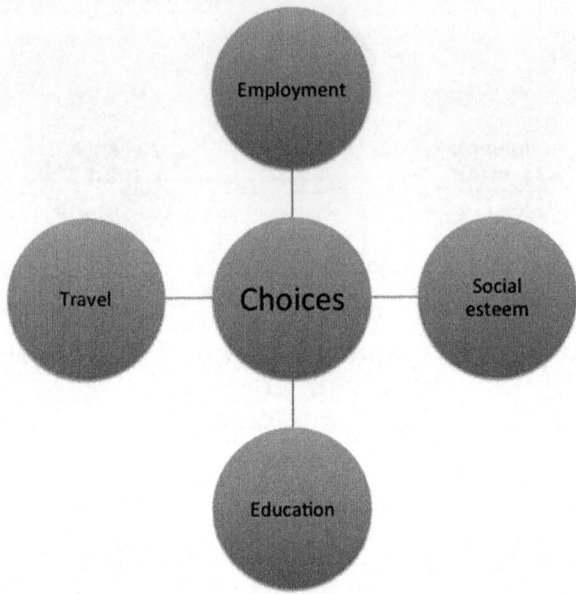

**Fig. 2.13** Domains of potentially positive outcomes

The older brothers have been in trouble and then the younger brothers just keep coming through and they do the same because they're influenced by the older people.

– Isolation:

They can stop you from getting a visa to travel.

– Negative affect:

How would you feel, knowing that you were responsible for what had happened?
    And their family and their friends are suffering.

– Injury:

A train may be derailed.
You could have been hit by a train.
Lose our concentration and we run over a poor lady that's crossing the road.

The YLOs' positive outcomes summarized in Fig. 2.13 include desirable outcomes for employment, education, travel and self-esteem.

The admonition may be thought of as a genre which is similar to the Christian church service genre of the homily in the sense that it shares the function of a moralizing lecture designed to steer the YP towards a better life. As we will see in Chap. 6, in the Youth Justice Conference, this better life involves the YP becoming a rational and re-affiliated youth. As part of this, there is a tendency for YLOs and Convenors to remind the YP that making mistakes is a common experience.

**Extract 2.45, Mobile Phone YJC**

**Convenor:** We all make mistakes. Adults make it as well. But kids, usually, because they're learning, they make a lot of mistakes when they don't know better.

This kind of talk appears to be part of enacting a kind of solidarity function (we've been through it/got over it and you can too) which we will explore later in the book. The YLO Caution is not always a 'folksy homily', however, and there were occasions such as in Running Shoes YJC where the discourse is closer to threat (emphasizing the possibility of imprisonment if the YP continues along a particular path) rather than admonition.

# 13 The Reintegration Macro-Genre

The final step in the Youth Justice Conference involves the participants coming to an agreement regarding an 'outcome plan' for the YP. This occurs as part of a final macro-genre that we will call the reintegration. Reintegration involves three steps (as shown in Fig. 2.14): a negotiation

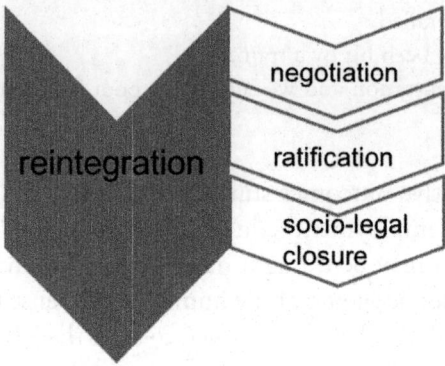

**Fig. 2.14** The reintegration macro-genre

of the outcome plan, a ratification of this plan and finally a closure that combines both formal legal protocols and more relaxed social interactions. In the first step, the YP commits to an outcome plan that involves certain tasks such as a formal apology, payment of some monetary compensation, volunteer work in a community organization and so on, as a way of 'putting things right'. Both the YP and the Victim (if they are present) must formally consent to the outcome plan in order for it to be ratified and implemented.

Following the discussion of the outcome plan, the Convenors will typically enquire whether conference participants more generally are 'happy with' its terms.

### Extract 2.46, School Library YJC

**Convenor:** OK. Alright, what we're going to do now is, we're gonna have a quick break and I'm going to write up the outcome plan, so, is everybody happy with the ten hours community service, and the apology letter?

As this and the following example show, in most conferences the Convenor draws up the written outcome plan during the break for refreshments after the verbal discussion of the plan has occurred.

## 13 The Reintegration Macro-Genre 119

### Extract 2.47, Mobile Phone YJC

**Convenor:** What we are going to do now is have a little break. OK? And I am going to write up the outcome plan, and that's the community service and the school issues, OK?

Following the break, the Convenor will usually formally read out this outcome plan to ensure that it represents the terms discussed.

### Extract 2.48, Train Tracks YJC

**Convenor:** OK, thanks guys. I'll just quickly read out the outcome plan so that everybody knows what it says before everyone signs it, OK. The Young Person will complete ten hours community service at Marie PCYC. The Young Person will write a letter of apology to the CEO of Sharp's and send it to Mr Glen Matthews at Marie. That's easy isn't it. OK? So there will be no doubt about where you got to send that letter, OK. Alright, her monitor is Murray Hartfeld and the start day will be the 21st of this month. There'll be a review date on the 4th of November and you'll finish it on the 18th of November, so that gives you plenty of time.

During the ratification genre the Convenor will explicitly ask whether the outcome plan is deemed satisfactory by those present and, by implication, that they consent to its implementation.

### Extract 2.49, Train Tracks YJC

**Convenor:** Does that sound fair enough to everybody? Okeydokey. So if I could please have you sign it, Amy, just there where it says 'Young Person', for me, and pass it over to mum and get mum to sign it where it says 'Carer', just over there un – above my signature there.==

**Mother:** ==(…)

**Convenor:** Car – carer. Thank you. And then just for you, thank you Michael, as the Victim, ta. Thanks Michael. Ah, you're gonna sign Victim, there. Excellent, thank you very much. OK, now (give) everyone their copies. There you go. That one's for you, that one's for you, and can you give that to YLO for me please? Thank you, alright. OK, well that wraps up the business end of the deal.

Parties will then sign the written document, codifying the accumulative consent that they have enacted throughout the conference. This oral presentation of the written plan echoes the tendency of Convenors to read aloud the opening of the socio-legal framing when invoking the Young Offenders Act at the beginning of the conference. The delivery suggests that participants are intended to perceive the agreement as legally binding.

The concluding part of the reintegration macro-genre is termed the socio-legal closure. It functions to bring the conference to a formal close and also to enact the re-affiliation of the YP with positively evaluated 'communities of concern' (Braithwaite 1989: 85) such as their family network. The Convenor will usually begin by thanking participants for their attendance.

**Extract 2.50, Mobile Phone YJC**

**Convenor:** OK, well that wraps that up. That's the end. I just want to say thank you very much for coming along.

They will often make special mention that they empathize with the YP, and positively evaluate them for choosing to attend.

**Convenor:** And, as I said before, we know how hard it has been for you, and hats off to you for making the effort to come along.

The Convenor and sometimes the YLO will take the opportunity to reinforce the importance of the conference and reaffirm the relationships that the YP should maintain (e.g. family) and those that they should avoid (e.g. negatively judged 'mates').

## 13 The Reintegration Macro-Genre 121

### Extract 2.51, Mobile Phone YJC

**Convenor:** Because it's important that we have this process and we got it dealt with, and you can move on now, can't you. Yep? Ah==
**YLO:** ==Seriously think about your mates. I mean really seriously.
**Convenor:** OK. You got to go away and think about that, alright? Do the right thing for yourself. Melanie's already told you, you're with them you're going to be targeted. So you can't blame the cops, == OK?
**YLO:** ==And let me tell what – what happens, most kids when you get into trouble, you think 'oh, they'd never dob you in'. They always fold. They always dob them in as quick as – [to Convenor] and you'd know that too from – from being a police officer yourself. They always dob you in, they fold. Cause if they think they can get out of trouble themselves. You don't think they do, but they do. ==All the time.
**Convenor:** ==Always dob your mates in. Cause it's – you know what it is? It's always about number one. You know who number one is Nathan? Yourself. … Look after number one. … That's what they do. Alright.
**YLO:** We have heaps that think – they never think that they're gonna dob them in. Every time.

The Convenor may also highlight offers of ongoing support aimed at helping the YP during the completion of the outcome plan.

### Extract 2.52, Mobile Phone YJC

**Convenor:** OK, thank you very much. Melanie's offered her help, you know, down the track, for the both of you, for the family. If you need it, she's here. That's her job, OK? You should use it. If you feel at any time you need to talk to, you know, a friendly cop, this is who you need to come and see alright?
**YLO:** (…)
**Convenor:** And your mates – your mates don't have to know. Alright.
**YP:** Yeah.
**Convenor:** OK? I'm sure Melanie will give you her number. … ==And,
**YLO:** ==I have it here. Can I put it on the back of your paper? Or just somewhere on there? Cause I haven't got a card with me.

The Convenor will in particular thank the Support Persons, acknowledging the difficulty of their role in their conference and suggesting their role in helping the re-affiliated YP remain on track.

### Extract 2.53, Mobile Phone YJC

| | |
|---|---|
| **Convenor:** | Alright? So thank you. Thank you Valerie, and thank you for contributing. I know how hard it was for you, OK, and we do – we really feel for you. OK? Hopefully he's going to be – be a good boy from now on? OK? Lead by example for your nieces and nephews. Yep. OK. |
| **YLO:** | You tell him he's got to be good. |
| **Convenor:** | Oh, [laughter]. OK, so thanks guys, OK, that's it. |
| **YLO:** | OK, thank you. ==(…). |
| **Convenor:** | ==Alright, good luck. Good luck==, |
| **YLO:** | ==That's my number there, so if you need (…) Good luck. |

At this point in the proceedings, the YP begins to pass out of a liminal phase where he is an offender who has admitted his offence but has not yet been sentenced and reintegrated into his community, into a new phase beyond the conference. Convenors will often use analogies such as drawing a line in the sand to convey this new status or, as in the following example, the shift in roles will be signalled by humour.

### Extract 2.54, Mobile Phone YJC

| | |
|---|---|
| **Convenor:** | And I hope if I see you round (…) cause you're doing something good. Alright? I never want to see you in here again. And I mean that in the nicest way. OK? If I meet you again, it's under better circumstances. Alright? Cause Melanie will be telling me what you've been up to== |
| **YLO:** | ==I'll be hassling you, all the time. Ringing up, seeing what you're doing, how you're going at school. |
| **Convenor:** | ==Aren't you lucky, hey? … That's right. OK, thanks guys. ==Thank you very much for your time. |
| **Mother:** | ==OK, thank you. |

### Extract 2.55, Guide Dog YJC

**Convenor:** So even though I don't have any involvement after I put the paperwork through, I'm still really interested in seeing how you go, and I'll contact Barbara and Dan just to make sure everything's good, and you're getting that support in the community that you need and Greg isn't giving you too much of a hard time [joking tone]. Alright so if you can just chuck your nametags on this desk there and ...

The close of the conference has a similar tone to the opening sociolegal framing with a blend of scripted sequences, and a fusion of legal discourse with banalities such as putting away the name tags.

### Extract 2.56, Guide Dog YJC

**Convenor:** So thanks for your time today. The agreement you've reached should go a long way to towards repairing the harm that's been done. The matter will be formally closed subject to the satisfactory completion of this agreement ...
... Alright so if you can just chuck your nametags on this desk there and ...

The overall function of the reintegration macro-genre is to re-affiliate the YP into the communities that have been harmed by the offence. This requires enacting, on the spot, some of the (re)integrative effects it is hoped the conference might be able to foster in the longer term. For example, a YP is made to talk and to listen but is also given, then and there, an opportunity to affiliate with his or her family, his or her ethnic group, the wider community (with the possible support of Police Liaison Officers) alongside, or in place of, his or her hitherto dominating affiliation with mates. As we have seen in this chapter, YPs are generally compliant in conferencing and we have not seen many instances where they actively or passively resist this kind of re-affiliation process. Seen in these terms, the opportunity for YPs, Victims, their families, friends and the police to affiliate during a conference is already a paradigm shift for criminal justice systems struggling to rehabilitate young offenders and reduce reoffending.

## 14  Genre and Macro-Genre

In this chapter, we have reviewed the way in which Convenors and participants enact conferencing as a staged goal-oriented social process. In doing so, we have highlighted the fact that there is a lot of different kinds of work to be done, entailing that a number of complementary elemental genres have to be brought together in a macro-genre involving steps, sub-steps alongside the recurrent staging within each elemental genre. We have also noted the ways in which conferences adhere to and depart from the script used to train Convenors, and flagged the evolution of the macro-genre in relation to the role taken up by YLOs in the admonition step of the interaction. From this point on in the book we will look more closely at various dimensions of verbal and non-verbal discourse that bear critically on the overall goals of YJCs.

## Notes

1. Under the NSW Crimes Act (Section 93C), the charge of 'affray' applies to a person 'who uses or threatens unlawful violence towards another and whose conduct is such as would cause a person of reasonable firmness present at the scene to fear for his or her safety'. The most serious cases of intimidatory and violent behaviour for which the charge of affray is proven can result in a custodial sentence of up to ten years.
2. There are a few exceptions to this rule, for instance with reference to an application to the armed services or police.
3. See, for instance, the findings of Snow and Powell (2008) with regard to what they refer to as undetected 'language deficits' in the population of male young offenders. Snow P. and Powell M. (2008) Oral language competence, social skills and high-risk boys: What are juvenile offenders trying to tell us? *Children and Society* 22: 16–28.
4. Greg did arrive not long after the conference had started, having been held up in traffic. He sat next to the victim, Donna, whose guide dog snarled somewhat as he did so. He remarked that this was unusual since he had worked with Donna's dog before as a trainer and he suggested that the dog's instincts to protect Donna were evidence of the fact that she had suffered more anxiety as a result of the robbery than she was letting on.

5. See Chap. 1 of Martin and Rose (2008) for a detailed account of how genre theory developed in SFL and for references to related work in the traditions of teaching English for Special Purposes (ESP) and the 'New Rhetoric'.
6. The terms AFFECT, APPRECIATION and JUDGEMENT have a technical meaning in SFL and constitute a major part of the APPRAISAL system that we will introduce in Chap. 3 when analysing the language of evaluation that occurs in conferencing talk.
7. Here we are intending to describe the most common patterning. It may be the case that particular iterations of conferences deviate from this pattern. Further quantitative follow-up studies are needed to verify the generalizability of the generic structures asserted throughout this chapter. Given the volume of transcription required and the sensitive nature of the data, this was beyond the scope of the current project.
8. The generic structure notation used here is explained in Appendix B. The superscript 'n' here indicates that the stage may occur more than once, interspersed prosodically throughout the socio-legal framing genre.
9. This modelling of the macro-genre structure differs somewhat from versions we have published elsewhere. While we regard it as an improvement, it is still not definitive.
10. The re-orientation that we find in other kinds of recounts is replaced here by Extension, Interpretation and Ramifications stages in the commissioned recount. In effect, it is not up to the YP to say when the genre is 'over'.
11. Indeed, in earlier publications, we referred to the commissioned recount and a 'Victim's rejoinder' as two components to a step within the conference's macro-generic structure that we called 'testimony'. We now see the commissioned recount as a strongly bounded 'chunk' of the conference to which all the participants who speak in the rejoinder are responding in complementary ways.
12. 'Irrealis' is a term used by linguists to refer to events that are not yet under way (signalled though a range of resources such as imperative mood, future tense, modality, conditional clauses or purpose clauses).

# References

Ahmed, E., Harris, N., Braithwaite, J., et al. (2001). *Shame management through reintegration*. Cambridge/Oakleigh: Cambridge University Press.

Bradt, V., Roose, L., & Nicole, R. (2007). Relevant others in restorative practices for minors: For what purposes? *Australian & New Zealand Journal of Criminology, 40*, 291–312.

Braithwaite, J. (1989). *Crime, shame and reintegration*. Cambridge/Sydney: Cambridge University Press.

Braithwaite, J., & Daly, K. (1998). Masculinities, violence and communitarian control. In D. Chappell & S. Egger (Eds.), *Australian violence: Contemporary perspective II* (pp. 221–252). Canberra: Australian Institute of Criminology.

Christie, F. (1997). Curriculum macrogenres as forms of initiation into a culture. In F. Christie & J. R. Martin (Eds.), *Genre and institutions: Social processes in the workplace and school* (pp. 134–160). London: Continuum.

Christie, F. (2002). *Classroom discourse analysis*. London: Continuum.

Clancey, G., Doran, S., & Maloney, E. (2005). The operation of warnings, cautions and youth justice conferences. In J. B. L. Chan (Ed.), *Reshaping juvenile justice: The NSW young offenders act 1997* (pp. 47–72). Sydney: Sydney Institute of Criminology.

Eggins, S. (1994). *An introduction to systemic functional grammar*. London: Pinter.

Eggins, S., & Slade, D. (1997). *Analysing casual conversation*. London/New York: Cassell.

Gilbert, L. (1983). *Educating Rita* [Film]. Burbank, California: Columbia Pictures.

Halliday, M. A. K., & Matthiessen, C. M. I. M. (2004). *An introduction to functional grammar*. London: Arnold.

Hoyle, C., & Noguera, S. (2008). Supporting young offenders through restorative justice: Parents as (in)appropriate adults. *British Journal of Community Justice, 6*, 67–85.

Labov, W., & Waletzky, J. (1967). Narrative analysis: Oral sessions of personal experience. In J. Helm (Ed.), *Essays on the verbal and visual arts* (pp. 12–44). Seattle: University of Washington Press.

Martin, J. R., & Rose, D. (2008). *Genre relations: Mapping culture*. London: Equinox.

Miller, D. R., & Bayley, P. (2016). *Hybridity in systemic functional linguistics: Grammar, text and discursive context*. London: Equinox.

NSW Department of Juvenile Justice. (1999). In Justice NDoJ (Ed.), *A guide to youth justice conferencing*. Sydney: NSW Department of Juvenile Justice.

NSW Department of Juvenile Justice. (2000). In Justice NDoJ (Ed.), *Youth justice conferencing policy and procedures manual*. Sydney: NSW Department of Juvenile Justice.

Prichard, J. (2002). Parent-child dynamics in community conferences: Some questions for reintegrative shaming, practice and restorative justice. *Australian & New Zealand Journal of Criminology, 35*, 330–346.

Snow, P., & Powell, M. (2008). Oral language competence, social skills and high-risk boys: What are juvenile offenders trying to tell us? *Children and Society, 22*, 16–28.

Taussig, I. (2012). Youth justice conferences: Participant profile and conference characteristics. *Crime and Justice Bulletin.*http://www.ntyan.com.au/images/uploads/news_docs/BB75.pdf

Van Stokkom, B. (2002). Moral emotions in restorative justice conferences: Managing shame, designing empathy. *Theoretical Criminology, 6*, 339–360.

Weijers, I. (2001). Family group conferencing. Kanttekeningen bij Herstelrecht voor Jeugdige Delinquenten. *Justitiële Verkenningen, 27*(3), 110–121.

# 3

# Conference Interaction: Exchange Structure

## 1  Regulative and Integrative Discourse

In the previous chapter, we have seen how actively the Convenors manage the macro-genre as they allocate roles, reaffirm the intended goals, decide when to move from one of the elemental genres of the whole conference sequence to the next, and so on. The analyses to be presented in this chapter move us down from the level of genre to focus more closely on discourse semantics. We will see how the Convenor's responsibilities also include managing the turn-taking between speakers and controlling many of the moves within the dialogic exchanges. This, in turn, allows Convenors to strongly influence the way the language of evaluation in a conference comes into play—how, in other words, participants go about sharing feelings and judgements.

Throughout this chapter, we will use the term 'regulative discourse' to refer to the many ways in which Convenors keep the macro-genre on track by managing and controlling the contributions of other conference participants. By highlighting that such regulation exists, we do not mean to suggest that Convenors are somehow manipulating the conference process to their own ends. On the contrary, given the fact that conferencing is a new genre for most participants and that some of them may be anxious about what it entails, it is quite likely that participants welcome the role of Convenor as chief regulator of the discourse. Furthermore, it is only through such regulative discourse that opportunities arise for participants to engage with the discourse of integration, which, as we will see in this chapter, also runs right through the exchanges that enact the conference.

This necessary interplay between regulative and integrative discourse can be seen in the legislative framework for conferencing. On the one hand, as the Young Offenders Act states, the purpose of a conference is to generate an outcome plan. On this score, the Convenor's job is to steer the process through to an agreement that can be written up and presented to the Children's Magistrate for approval. On the other hand, the Young Offenders Act also refers to broader principles that are meant to underpin conferences. These include promoting acceptance by the Young Person (YP) of 'responsibility for his or her own behaviour'; 'strengthening the [YP's] family or family group'; helping the YP to 'become a fully autonomous individual'; enhancing 'the rights and place of victims in the juvenile justice process', and so on (Section 34 (1)). Where we use the term 'integrative discourse' in the analyses, it is to describe language that is directed towards these harder-to-define but strongly aspirational goals. We could thus say that regulative discourse has to do with organizing social order within the conference, whereas integrative discourse has to do with negotiating how a YP may be re-affiliated with 'communities of concern' (Braithwaite and Daly 1998) such as their family or local groups (e.g. school, sporting groups etc.).

In order to explore the intersecting functions of regulative and integrative discourse, we will proceed as follows. We introduce a model for analysing the exchange structures in conferencing dialogue and use it to show how much of what the offender says during the commissioned recount can be considered a kind of 'linguistic service' (Ventola 1987), provided in response to requests from the Convenor. This allows us to draw some parallels between conferencing as a social practice and the kinds of interaction we find in classrooms or counselling sessions.

## 2 Analysing Exchange Structures

Youth justice conferences are a highly structured form of conversation. To analyse this dialogue, there are many relevant approaches such as conversation analysis (CA), interactional sociolinguistics, and speech act theory, among others (see Eggins and Slade 1997). For our purposes, the Systemic Functional Linguistics (SFL) model of exchange structure analysis—developed in the context of research into classroom interaction, quiz shows, service encounters and casual conversation—has proven particularly useful (Martin 1992; Berry 1981; Eggins and Slade 1997; Ventola 1987). With this kind of analysis, we are dealing with the NEGOTIATION system, which is concerned with 'interaction as an exchange between speakers: how speakers adopt and assign roles to each other in dialogue, and how moves are organized in relation to one another' (Martin and Rose 2007: 219). Through this system, speakers enact interpersonal meanings—negotiating not simply the turn-taking structure of their dialogue but also social relations of power and solidarity in a particular social context.

NEGOTIATION comprises a number of key oppositions. One relates to the nature of the commodity that is being exchanged between interlocutors. Is the exchange about knowledge or action? In other words, adopting the terms of Halliday and Matthiessen (2014), is it about giving or demanding information (a proposition), or is it about giving or demanding goods and services (a proposal)? The former is typically realized through statements and questions; the latter through offers and (direct or indirect) commands. This distinction between a knowledge exchange and an action exchange is illustrated in the following examples:

| 3.1 | Mobile Phone YJC<br>Knowledge exchange (negotiating a proposition):<br>Convenor: So did you commit the offences you are charged with?<br>YP: Yes. |
|---|---|
| 3.2 | Mobile Phone YJC<br>Action exchange (negotiating a proposal):<br>Convenor: I need you to speak a bit louder.<br>YP: OK. |

Each of these exchanges consists of two moves, comparable to the 'pair parts' of an adjacency pair in CA.

Another key dimension of exchange structure analysis relates to the roles that interlocutors take up as they are negotiating. For knowledge exchanges, the person with ultimate authority over the validity of the information exchanged is known as the primary knower (K1), while the person for whom that information is confirmed is known as the secondary knower (K2). Using the previous example, the distinction between K1 and K2 can be seen in the following:

| 3.3 | Mobile Phone YJC | | |
|---|---|---|---|
| | Convenor: | K2 | So did you commit the offences you are charged with? |
| | YP: | K1 | Yes. |

For action exchanges the primary actor (A1) is the person who hands over goods or performs a service (or promises to do so) and the secondary actor (A2) is the person who receives the goods or for whom the service is performed. This is illustrated in the following example (and a summary of this exchange structure notation is provided in Appendix B):

| 3.4 | Mobile Phone YJC | | |
|---|---|---|---|
| | Convenor: | A2 | I need you to speak a bit louder. |
| | YP: | A1 | OK. |

Next there is the question of who initiates the exchange. For knowledge exchanges, it is often the case that the secondary knower (K2) begins the exchange by seeking information from the primary knower (K1), as in the previous example. However, this is not always the case. A knowledge exchange may also be initiated by the primary knower asking a question about information for which they are in fact the ultimate authority. That is to say, the K1 primary knower may initiate an exchange by asking a question to which they already know the answer. This kind of exchange is familiar to most of us from quiz shows and classroom interactions, where the presenter or teacher will ask a question as a kind of test of the participant or student, and will end by evaluating the answer that is given. Exchanges of this kind thus require a third move by the primary knower. The primary knower's initiating move in these exchanges is annotated as Dk1, with 'D' for 'delay' (thus delayed primary knower), since the move which confirms the knowledge is in effect delayed while the person questioned offers a response. In the following extract, from the Affray YJC, for example, both parties in the exchange can see what the offender's mother is wearing on her head and thus know perfectly well the answer to the rhetorical question being asked as a Dk1 move (the acronym ECLO stands for police Ethnic Community Liaison Officer):

| 3.5 | Affray YJC | | |
|---|---|---|---|
| | ECLO: | Dk1 | Mate, what's your mum wearing on her head? |
| | YP: | K2 | Scarf. |
| | ECLO: | K1 | Yeah. |

Had the YP's mother been absent from the room, we can imagine the ECLO might have initiated a knowledge exchange in which he was the secondary knower (K2), asking a question to which he did not have the answer:

| 3.6 | | | |
|---|---|---|---|
| | ECLO: | K2 | Does your mum wear a scarf? |
| | YP: | K1 | Yeah. |

Or, alternatively, the YP as the primary knower might initiate an exchange by simply asserting information they control, such as in the following:

| 3.7 | | | |
|---|---|---|---|
| | YP: | K1 | My mum wears a scarf. |

Similarly, for action exchanges, there are comparable points of departure. The secondary actor, who does the action or provides the service, can delay handing over goods or performing a service by first checking if it is desired:

| 3.8 | | | |
|---|---|---|---|
| | Convenor: | Da1 | Would you like some water? |
| | YP: | A2 | Yes please. |
| | Convenor: | A1 | Here you go. |

Alternatively, the secondary actor (A2) can initiate the exchange by demanding goods or services:

| 3.9 | | | |
|---|---|---|---|
| | YP: | A2 | Can I have some water please? |
| | Convenor: | A1 | Here you go. |

Or the primary actor can initiate, by proffering goods or performing a service:

| 3.10 | | | |
|---|---|---|---|
| | Convenor: | A1 | Here's some water (handing it over). |

Note that in all cases the K1/A1 move is obligatory and nuclear. In contrast, the other moves are optional.

The K1/A1 move can be optionally followed up by the secondary knower/actor (A/K2) in a move known as the K2f (secondary knower follow-up) or A2f (secondary actor follow-up):

| 3.11 | Mobile Phone YJC | | |
|---|---|---|---|
| | ECLO: | K2 | How does that make our community look? |
| | YP: | K1 | Worse. |
| | ECLO: | K2f | It does, doesn't it? |

| 3.12 | Mobile Phone YJC | | |
|---|---|---|---|
| | Convenor: | A2 | I need you to speak a bit louder. |
| | YP: | A1 | OK. |
| | Convenor: | A2f | Thanks. |

Finally, this follow-up can be responded to again by the primary knower or actor:

| 3.13 | | | |
|---|---|---|---|
| | ECLO: | K2 | How does that make our community look? |
| | YP: | K1 | Worse. |
| | ECLO: | K2f | It does, doesn't it? |
| | YP: | K1f | Yes. |

| 3.14 | | | |
|---|---|---|---|
| | Convenor: | A2 | I need you to speak a bit louder. |
| | YP: | A1 | OK. |
| | Convenor: | A2f | Thanks. |
| | YP: | A1f | No problem. |

Putting all of these permutations together, we can now summarize the range of potential structures for knowledge exchanges and action exchanges. Using the notation we used for genre structure in Chap. 2 (where parentheses indicate optionality and ^ indicates sequencing), we have:

Knowledge exchanges:

$$((Dk1) \wedge K2) \wedge K1 \wedge (K2f \wedge (K1f))$$

Action exchanges:

$$((Da1) \wedge A2) \wedge A1 \wedge (A2f \wedge (A1f))$$

The structure potential can be generalized across knowledge and action as:
Knowledge or action exchanges:

$$((Dx1) \wedge X2) \wedge X1 \wedge (X2f \wedge (X1f))$$

This formula specifies that the nuclear move (X1) can be optionally preceded by an X2 move, and if it is, that X2 move can be optionally preceded by a Dx1 move; in addition, the nuclear X1 move can be optionally followed up with an X2f move, and if it is, that X2f move can be optionally followed up by an X1f move.

The model, then, allows for exchanges consisting of between 1 and 5 moves. These options are presented in Fig. 3.1 as a system network (following standard SFL notation, the curly brackets '{' in this figure mean 'and' while square brackets '[' mean 'or'; there are thus three sets of choices occurring for each move, each of which allows for a further, more specific, choice).

To round out this modelling of exchange structures, there are a few additional elements to add. First, we need to allow for multiple moves that repeat or rephrase one another (known as move complexes). Here the work of a single stage in the exchange is in a sense spread out over more than one clause, with the clauses in some sense elaborating one another.

# 3 Conference Interaction: Exchange Structure

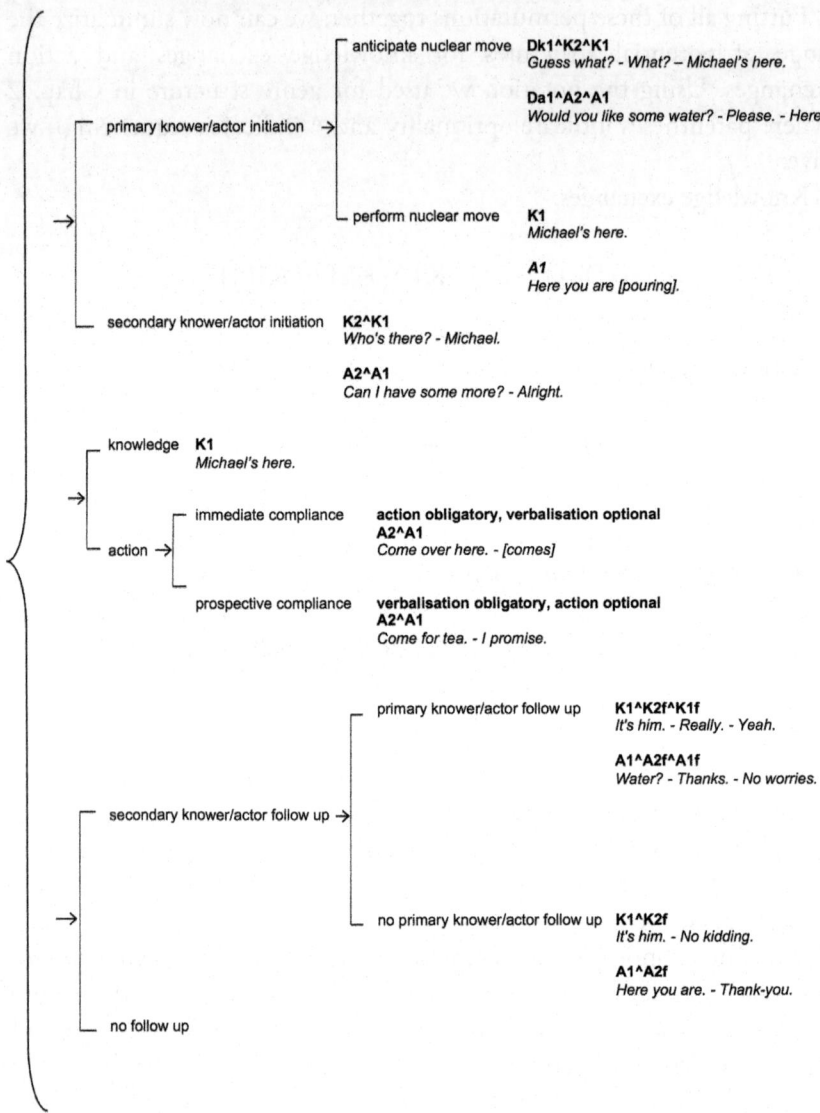

**Fig. 3.1** System network for knowledge and action exchanges (Martin 1992)

| 3.14 | An example of a K2 move complex | | |
|---|---|---|---|
| | ECLO: | K2 | Who went and visited you? |
| | | K2 | Who went and saw you there? |
| | YP: | K1 | -No-one. |

| 3.15 | An example of an A2 move complex | | |
|---|---|---|---|
| | ECLO: | A2 | You show me where in the Koran it says (...) |
| | | A2 | You show me where. |
| | | A2 | Tell me where. |
| | YP: | A1 | - Nowhere. |

In addition, we need to acknowledge moves that interrupt or block the culmination of the exchange, known as tracking and challenging moves. Tracking moves ('tr') and responses to tracking moves ('rtr') clarify experiential meaning (the content that is being negotiated):

| 3.16 | Affray YJC | | |
|---|---|---|---|
| | ECLO: | K2 | Any of your friends go? |
| | YP: | tr | At the police station? |
| | ECLO: | rtr | Yeah. |
| | YP: | K1 | No. |

Challenging moves function as resistance to the interpersonal trajectory of an exchange, frustrating, and at times derailing completely, the cooperative culmination of an exchange:

| 3.17 | Shopping Trolley YJC | | |
|---|---|---|---|
| | Convenor | K2 | And what were they doing? |
| | YP: | ch | I don't know. |

Another move type we need to consider is the back-channel move ('bch'), which signals to a speaker that the listener is attending to what they are saying; these moves do not predict a response, unlike the tracking and challenging moves we just reviewed.

### 3.18 Mobile Phone YJC

| | | |
|---|---|---|
| YP: | K1 | I was going to a mate's house... |
| Convenor: | bch | Yes. |
| YP: | K1 | ...and I was walking with him. |

We also need to consider check moves (check), which are used by speakers to make sure their interlocutor is following what they are saying; these moves may be followed by a verbal or non-verbal reassurance (rcheck).

### 3.19

| | | |
|---|---|---|
| YP: | K1 | I was going to a mate's house... |
| | check | Right. |
| Convenor: | rcheck | [nods] |
| YP: | K1 | ...and I was walking with him. |

Finally we will recognize invite moves, which function to encourage a response from the addressee:

### 3.20

| | | |
|---|---|---|
| Convenor: | A2 | So I want you to tell me everything that happened on that day that led to you being stopped by the police with the telephone |
| | Invite | OK? |
| YP: | A1 | [nods] |

## 3 Conferencing as a Pedagogical Practice

Before we start to apply this model of exchange structure to our discourse sample, there is one theoretical issue we need to address, namely the prominence of 'linguistic services' as a feature of conferencing talk. SFL theorists have coined this term as a way of describing exchanges that function semantically as a negotiation of both action and knowledge, all in the one exchange. In other words, these are exchanges where what is being proposed *as a service* is that *information* be given (Ventola 1987; Martin 1992). The most obvious situation in which we see this kind of exchange is in a classroom. For instance, a teacher might interact with a student as follows:

| 3.20 | An instance of pedagogic discourse | |
|---|---|---|
| | Teacher: | Give me an example of multiculturalism in Australia. |
| | Student: | One example of multiculturalism would be the programming of foreign language shows on the special broadcasting service. |
| | Teacher: | Right. |

On the face of it, the move made by the teacher can be interpreted as initiating an action exchange—it is after all an imperative, not a declarative clause; the student can preface the second move with something like *OK*; and the teacher could add a *thank-you* to the third move. However, the student's reply is predictably in line with what the teacher really wants, namely a statement in which some assessable information about multiculturalism is provided (presumably culled from a book or a previous lesson), rather than an actual transfer of physical goods or the performance of an embodied service. It would be a rare, albeit compelling, performance if the student were to take the teacher's question at face value and respond through a song, a dance or a call to prayer originating from a migrant or Indigenous community! It is thus an action move whereby the service being asked for is the telling of information—a knowledge move.

The preponderance of linguistic service exchanges in the classroom discourse reflects the fact that teachers are regularly engaged in the task of managing a lesson at the same time as they are teaching a specific subject area. Singing, dancing and praying may well have a place in a lesson about multiculturalism but the opportunity for such performances will typically be constrained by the teacher's professional obligations to maintain discipline and get through a certain amount of the curriculum in a certain time. The Convenor of a youth justice conference faces a broadly similar challenge: to make sure that the macro-genre unfolds in a relatively smooth and timely manner through each of its steps, while, at the same time, managing specific interactions within particular genres. Linguistic service exchanges appear throughout our discourse sample. The following example, in which the Convenor of the Mobile Phone YJC commissions the YP's recount, begins with an A2 move that requires a story be told (so, information is to be provided as a service), but it also specifies something about the manner of its telling (reinforcing the point that both action and knowledge are being exchanged here):

| 3.21 | Mobile Phone YJC | | |
|---|---|---|---|
| | Convenor: | A2 | What I want you to do now is, I need you to tell us in a really loud voice … what happened on that particular day. |

Equally typical is the way in which, as the YP proceeds to tell their story, the Convenor frequently acknowledges and retrospectively ratifies this linguistic service as an appropriate response to his or her initiating the A2 move. We see this happening when the Convenor adds an 'OK' (shown in bold) at several points during the Extension stage of the recount:

| 3.21 | Mobile Phone YJC | |
|---|---|---|
| | Convenor: | They found the phone and what did they say to you? |
| | YP: | They go this phone was stolen |
| | Convenor: | **OK.** What did you say? |
| | YP: | I go, you know, 'I swapped it' |
| | Convenor | Yeah |
| | YP: | And they just took me |
| | Convenor | Took you where? |
| | YP: | The police station |
| | Convenor: | **OK.** And who did they ring when they brought you to the police station? |
| | YP: | My dad |
| | Convenor: | **OK** |

These 'OK' comments are best considered as A2f moves by the Convenor, directed towards managing the local unfolding of the recount.

Looking at the parallels between linguistic servicing in classrooms and in conferences invites us to think more broadly about the relationship between what we are calling regulative discourse and integrative discourse in this chapter. Following Basil Bernstein, the British sociologist of education, we can now say that conferencing is, overall, a pedagogic discourse in which regulative and integrative discourses both play a part. By the term 'pedagogic discourse' Bernstein means 'the rule which embeds a discourse of competence (instructional discourse) into a discourse of social order (regulative discourse)' (Bernstein 1990: 183). What Bernstein explores in relation to classroom practices is the interplay we touched on earlier between the discourse of the subjects being taught in school (e.g. science, history, mathematics) and the discourse used to teach them (including control of student behaviour and the pacing, sequencing and evaluation of what is learned). Fundamental to his argument is the idea that 'the regulative discourse is the dominant discourse […] because it is the moral discourse that creates the criteria which give rise to character, manner, conduct, posture' (Bernstein 1996/2000: 48). As a consequence, the discourses of the subjects being taught are always re-contextualized discourses, taken out of the contexts in which knowledge is produced and subsequently reworked into the moral order of schools. In Bernstein's terms, the purpose of the 'pedagogic device', that is, the rules and social relationships that enable and regulate pedagogic communication, is 'to provide a symbolic ruler for consciousness' (Bernstein 1996/2000: 50).

Working from an SFL perspective, Christie develops these ideas in her analyses of classroom discourse, focusing on variables of register (and preferring Halliday's notion of 'projection' to Bernstein's 'embedding'): 'The first order or regulative register, it will be argued, "projects" a second order or instructional register' (Christie 2002: 25). She goes on to explain her metaphorical use of the grammatical term 'projection' as follows:

> A clause that projects in some sense takes something said or thought before and reinstates it. Hence the notion of projection is used metaphorically to refer to the relationship of the two registers in the pedagogic discourse. A field of knowledge and its associated activity is taken, relocated and in some sense therefore 'projected' for another purpose and another site. (Christie 2002: 25)

Other SFL scholars have followed Christie's lead and have applied Bernstein's notion of pedagogic discourse, as we have, to a range of practices outside the setting of school classrooms. Muntigl, for example, orients his study of relationship counselling discourse as follows:

> I shall argue that the narrative counselling discourse interview [...] includes both a regulative and instructional register. Regulation involves the degree to which the client's social actions are managed by the counsellor [...t]he instructional register [...] involves [...] the ways in which the clients are meant to construe experience. [...] [I]t is by regulating clients' verbal behaviour that a certain view of problems and their influences becomes possible. (Muntigl 2004: 124)

To summarize, then, we are suggesting that youth justice conferencing can be seen as a pedagogic discourse that is in part a regulative discourse. It is also what we are calling a discourse of integration, intended to realign the YP with the values of his or her family, ethnic group and community and diminish the relatively malign influence of peers. This duality is hardly surprising given that the design of this evolving macro-genre has its origins in the concerns of both the criminal justice and social work systems (Cuneen and White 2007). Note, however, as Bernstein and Christie would have it, that it is the regulative discourse which is dominant, 'projecting', and thereby re-contextualizing, the discourse of integration. A crude representation of this principle is outlined in Fig. 3.2.

Reconceived in these terms, it's not surprising that some exchanges in youth justice conferences can be interpreted from the perspectives of both knowledge and action. To show this process more clearly, and to tie

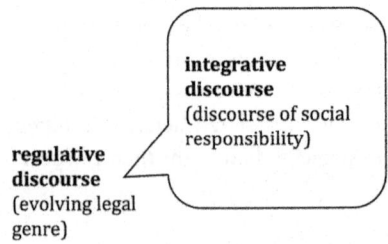

**Fig. 3.2** Regulative discourse projecting integrative discourse in youth justice conferencing

## 3 Conferencing as a Pedagogical Practice 143

Table 3.1 Adapted from transcript of Mobile Phone YJC—Version 1

| Speaker | Talk | Regulative |
|---|---|---|
| Convener | So what I need you to do is affirm you're here of your own free will | ↓ A2 |
| YP | OK. [nods] | A1 |

Table 3.2 Adapted from transcript of Mobile Phone YJC—Version 2

| Speaker | Talk | Integrative |
|---|---|---|
| Convenor | You're here of your own free will? | K2 |
| YP | Yep. [nods] | K1 |
| Convenor | Yep | K2f |

it in with the observations we have just made about conferencing as a pedagogic discourse, let us look at the way in which the Convenor checks for the YP's consent in the Mobile Phone YJC. In Tables 3.1 and 3.2, we have edited the transcript so as to artificially separate out, for a moment, the regulative moves from the integrative moves in the discourse (note also that, from this point on, we will start adding arrows to the notation of regulative moves in order to show whether they are explicitly prospective or retrospective). In the first version of this adapted transcript, where the Convenor demands a specific (verbal) action from the YP, the hierarchical relationship between them is very clear.

In the next version, the Convenor asks a question which, however formulaic, is at least premised on the notion that the YP has better knowledge of his or her 'own free will' than the Convenor does. To the extent that this exchange endows the YP with some sense of agency, it launches the process by which he can begin to establish himself as a candidate for reintegration into family and community networks.

Turning now to the actual transcript on which the two preceding examples are based, we can see how regulatory and integrative work can be happening at the same time (Table 3.3). In this example, the integrative moves in the discourse are 'projected' by the regulative moves, resulting in a jointly constructed admission of guilt. To do this, the Convenor prompts the YP and paraphrases his admission as 'you've already admitted your guilt…'. Thus, the A1 move complex spans both the Convenor's and YP's talk.

## 3 Conference Interaction: Exchange Structure

**Table 3.3** Simultaneity of regulatory and integrative moves

| Speaker | Regulative | Talk | Integrative |
|---|---|---|---|
| Convener | ↓ A2 | So what I need you to do is | |
| | A1 | You've already admitted your guilt to this offence | K2 |
| | | And you're here of your own free will? | =K2 |
| YP | | Yep. [nods] | K1 |
| Convener | | Yep | K2f |
| | ↑ A2f | OK | |

As noted above we use the downward and upward pointing arrows when there is an explicit signal the linguistic service nature of which is fundamentally an information exchange. So the downward-pointing arrow in Table 3.2 is based on the action-oriented *I need you to do*, and the upward-pointing arrow is based on the explicit action compliance markers *OK*.

Having established this point about how linguistic services operate in conferencing (interpreted as a pedagogic discourse), we will now proceed with an analysis of exchange structures from the commissioned recounts of two conferences from our sample: the Mobile Phone YJC (that we have already started looking at) and then the Affray YJC (where we will see the police ECLO taking over the regulative reins, as it were, from the Convenor). Throughout these analyses, we double-code many exchanges as negotiations of both action and knowledge. Linguistic servicing will only be recognized, however, when there is clear evidence of 'proposal' features in the initiation or follow-up moves in a regulatory exchange. For instance, in the example just considered, *what I need you to do* symbolizes a demand for service; it presents itself as an indirect speech act, involving what Halliday calls a MOOD metaphor (Halliday and Matthiessen 2004). We can test for this by checking that indexical markers of A2 moves such as *please* or *thank you* could be present (e.g. *what I need you to do **please**...*). Similarly, for follow-up moves, we can check for the presence or possibility of indexical proposal markers such as *OK, thanks, alright* and so on (one of which was present here). Finally, for greater clarity, in the following tables we will lay out any regulatory moves to the left of the transcript excerpts (column 3) and integrative knowledge moves to the right (column 6); each exchange will be numbered (regulative exchanges to the left, in column 2, and integrative exchanges to the right, in column 5); and speaker turns are designated in column 1.

… 3 Conferencing as a Pedagogical Practice 145

## 4   Guided Storytelling in the Commissioned Recount

As we described in Chap. 2, and as the preceding discussion of linguistic servicing elaborates, the term 'commissioned recount' is used to reflect the fact that the YP's story is supplied on demand. Typically, at least initially, it is sparse in terms of detail and emotional language. For example, Mobile Phone YJC, involving a quietly spoken young man of Pacific Islander background, is exemplary in this regard. To explore this further, we will continue the exchange analysis of the commissioned recount in this conference, carrying on from the linguistic service analysed earlier. In Table 3.4, we can see that the subsequent regulative discourse in this stage of the recount consists of a series of three action exchanges, all of which are initiated by the Convenor as A2 moves (Table 3.4). In two instances, these A2 moves are also backed up by what we can call an 'inviting move' (realized by an 'OK?' with rising intonation, the first of which in fact interrupts the

Table 3.4 Exchange structure of the commissioned recount genre in Mobile Phone YJC, extract 3.1

| Speaker | RE# | Regulative exchanges | Talk | IE# | Integrative exchanges |
|---|---|---|---|---|---|
| Convenor | 2 | ↓ A2… | What I want you to do now is I need you to tell us in a really loud voice, | | |
| | | ↓ invite | <<OK?>> | | |
| YP | | A1 | [nods] | | |
| Convenor | | …A2 | what happened on that particular day. | 2 | K2 |
| | | ↓ invite | Alright? | | |
| | 3 | ↓ A2 | So I want you to tell me everything that happened on that day that led to you being stopped by the police with the telephone. | 3 | K2 |
| | | ↓ invite | OK? | | |
| YP | | A1 | [nods] | | |
| Convenor | 4 | ↓ A2 | Can you do that for us? | | |
| YP | | A1 | [nods] | | |
| Convenor | | ↑ A2f | Thanks. | | |

initial A2 move); these inviting moves make explicit the Convenor's expectation of a response. The YP does respond, non-verbally, to each of these, giving a nod of the head to show that he is ready to perform the required linguistic service. Additionally, looking at this interaction from the perspective of integrative discourse, Table 3.4 codes two of the Convenor's statements as K2 moves on the basis that they specify the kind of detailed information that the Convenor is seeking in relation to the offending behaviour (the expected K1 reply from the YP is shown in Table 3.4).

Although the YP nods his head acquiescently, a brief, slightly awkward pause ensues after this interaction. Hence, as Table 3.5 shows, in the exchange that follows immediately from the previous ones, the Convenor has to make one more initiating A2 move ('Off you go') before the YP offers the first part of his recount as a linguistic service (acknowledged by the Convenor with an 'OK' follow-up move). At the same time, we can also view the YP's part in the following interaction from the perspective of the projected integrative discourse as a series of K1 moves, responding to the Convenor's K2 moves.

One technical problem that arises is the need to distinguish between what are new exchanges in the integrative discourse and what are, instead, repeated moves within a single exchange (constituting a move complex). To determine where the boundaries of an integrative exchange fall, we need a criterion to establish whether certain moves are best seen as initiating a new exchange or as a complex of K1 moves, one reformulating

Table 3.5 Exchange structure of the commissioned recount genre in Mobile Phone YJC, extract 3.2

| Speaker | RE# | Regulative | Talk | IE# | Integrative |
|---|---|---|---|---|---|
| Convenor | 5 | ↓ A2 | Off you go. | 3 | |
| YP | | A1 | I was – I was going to a mate's house. | | K1 |
| Convenor | | | Yep. [nods] | | bch |
| YP | | | And (…) | 4 | K1 |
| | | | And I was walking with him. | | K1 |
| | | | This guy just came up to me | 5 | K1 |
| | | | and he goes 'do you want to buy this phone?' | 6 | K1 |
| Convenor | | ↑ A2f | OK. | | |

another. We can do this by considering whether a K1 move is genuinely enacting a new proposition (giving new information) or whether it is elaborating an existing proposition that is essentially being rephrased or reformulated (see Martin (1992: 217) for discussion of reformulation categories or what Halliday and Matthiessen (2014: 461) call elaboration). All elaborating moves are treated as belonging to a move complex realizing a single functional slot in the exchange structure. Since the K1 moves in Table 3.4 extend the recount, rather than paraphrasing a single event, five distinct exchanges are recognized.

The next set of exchanges (Table 3.6, following straight on from the above) is purely regulatory in function: the Convenor interrupts the YP and encourages him to speak louder for the benefit of the police Youth Liaison Officer (YLO), and also, perhaps, to help ensure the soundtrack on our video recording would be audible.[1] In Table 3.6, there are two 'missing' verbalizations of A1 moves. One is in exchange 6, since the YP in fact stops talking as soon as he is interrupted by the Convenor and, having done so, does not need to agree verbally to this request (he enacts compliance with silence in other words); and the other is in exchange 11 where the Convenor simply assumes that the YP, having been asked, will agree to speak up. The interesting point to note about the following exchanges (Table 3.6) is that they involve a number of K1 moves within the regulative discourse (the Convenor gives information to justify her

Table 3.6 Exchange structure of the commissioned recount genre in Mobile Phone YJC, extract 3.3

| Speaker | RE# | Regulative | Talk | IE# | Integrative |
|---|---|---|---|---|---|
| Convenor | 6 | ↓ A2 | Can I just stop you for one second? | | |
| | 7 | K1 | I'm sorry. | | |
| | 8 | K1 | Jane has a problem with her hearing at the moment. | | |
| | 9 | K1 | Her ears are blocked | | |
| | 10 | K1 | so she can't (...) | | |
| | 11 | ↓ A2 | so she needs you to speak a bit louder. | | |
| | | ↓ invite | OK? | | |
| | | ↑ A2f | Thank you. | | |
| | | ↑ =A2f | Thanks Brody. | | |

request that the YP should try to speak louder). These are knowledge moves directed towards managing the conduct of the conference. So, as we can see, although most regulative exchanges are comprised of action moves, this is not always the case in pedagogic discourse.

The YP then resumes his story through a relatively monologic series of K1 moves (Table 3.7). These integrative moves are supported by two non-verbal back-channelling moves from the Convenor (she nods her head, encouraging him to continue) and finally a K2f move, at a moment where the YP has paused but the Convenor is clearly hoping for more detail. We can double-code this final move by the Convenor as a contribution to the regulative discourse—it's an invitation for the YP to continue—but it is challenged (not in an aggressive manner) by the YP's abrupt closure of the story: 'That's it.'.

Table 3.7 Exchange structure of the commissioned recount genre in Mobile Phone YJC, extract 3.1

| Speaker | RE# | Regulative | Talk | IE# | Integrative |
|---|---|---|---|---|---|
| YP | | | Yeah, I was, I was walking to a mate's house. | 7 | K1 |
| Convenor | | | [nods] | | bch |
| YP | | | This guy just came up to me | 8 | K1 |
| | | | and goes 'do you want to buy a phone?' | 9 | K1 |
| | | | and I go 'no'. | 10 | K1 |
| | | | And I go 'do you want to swap (...) want to swap with my phone?' | 11 | K1 |
| | | | And he looked at my phone | 12 | K1 |
| | | | and he goes 'Yeah' | 13 | K1 |
| | | | and we swap. | 14 | K1 |
| | | | And I went and stayed at – at my mate's house. | 15 | K1 |
| | | | And when it came to night time I was going back home, | 16 | K1 |
| | | | and we was walking, was walking me up the road | 17 | K1 |
| Convenor | | | [nods] | | bch |
| YP | | | and the police just came and got us. | 18 | K1 |
| Convenor | 12 | ↓ invite | Oh, OK. [nodding] | | K2f |
| YP | | ↑ ch | That's it. | | |

## 4 Guided Storytelling in the Commissioned Recount 149

As the preceding examples (and those following) show, we include as part of the regulative discourse any moves that are explicitly structuring the genre or controlling exchange structure, along with any moves that prospectively prompt, or retrospectively construe, other moves as a linguistic service. Challenging moves, such as the final move in the example in Table 3.7, can also be considered regulatory because they, too, are managing the exchange structure.

Let's turn now to the Extension stage of the Mobile Phone YJC commissioned recount where the exchanges are much more interactive than during the Record of Events (Table 3.8). Here the Convenor begins to assume a more explicit guiding role, initiating exchanges in relation to aspects of the offence and its aftermath that she wants tabled at this conference.

The Convenor continues to play a leading role in the exchanges that follow, moving from an Extension into an Interpretation stage and prompting some evaluation of the events that are being recounted. First, the Convenor explores the emotional reactions of those involved, including the YP's family (Table 3.9).

**Table 3.8** Extension in the commissioned recount genre, Mobile Phone YJC

| Speaker | RE# | Regulative | Talk | IE# | Integrative |
|---|---|---|---|---|---|
| Convenor | 13 | A1 | And then what – what happened? | 19 | K2 |
| YP | | | They found the phone. | | K1 |
| Convenor | | | They came and got you. | 20 | K1 |
| YP | | | Yeah. [nods] | | K2f |
| Convenor | | | They found the phone. | 21 | K1 |
| | | | And what did they say to you? | 22 | K2 |
| YP | | | They go that this phone was stolen. | | K1 |
| Convenor | | ↓A2f | OK. [nods] | | bch |
| | | | What did you say? | 23 | K2 |
| YP | | | I go, you know, [rubs face] 'I swapped it'. | | K1 |
| Convenor | | | Yeah. | | K2f |
| YP | | | And they just took me. | 24 | K1 |
| Convenor | 14 | A1 | Took you where? | | tr |
| YP | | | The police station. | | rtr |
| Convenor | | ↑A2f | OK. [nods] | | bch |

**Table 3.9** Interpretation in the commissioned recount genre, Mobile Phone YJC

| Speaker | RE# | Regulative | Talk | IE# | Integrative |
|---|---|---|---|---|---|
| Convenor | 15 | A1 | And who did they ring when they brought you to the police station? | 25 | K2 |
| YP | | | My dad. | | K1 |
| Convenor | | ↑ A2f | OK. | | |
| | | | And what did your dad say? | 26 | K2 |
| | 16 | A1 | Was he angry, happy? | 27 | K2 |
| YP | | | [nods] Angry. | | K1 |
| Convenor | | | Angry. [laughs] | | K2f |
| | | ↑ A2f | Yeah. | | =K2f |
| | | ↑= A2f | OK. | | |

**Table 3.10** Discussion of moral responsibility in the commissioned recount genre, Mobile Phone YJC

| Speaker | RE# | Regulative | Talk | IE# | Integrative |
|---|---|---|---|---|---|
| Convenor | | | Did you – did you realize that this phone was stolen? | 28 | K2 |
| YP | | | [nods] | | K1 |
| Convenor | | | You did. | | K2f |
| | | | So why did you take it if you realized it was stolen? | 29 | K2 |
| YP | | | (…) | | K1 |
| Convenor | 17 | ↓ A2 | You need to tell us why you took the phone. | 30 | K2 |
| YP | | A1 | Because it was new. | | K1 |
| Convenor | | | Because it was new. | | K2f |
| | | | Newer than yours? | 31 | K2 |
| YP | | | [nods] Yeah. | | K1 |
| Convenor | | | So you didn't care that it was somebody else's phone? | 32 | K1 |
| | 18 | | Is that right? | | Check |
| YP | | A1 | Yeah. | | K2f |
| Convenor | | ↑ A2f | OK. | | |

Next, the Convenor raises questions of moral responsibility (Table 3.10). As far as the Convenor is concerned, the general pattern is one in which she enacts a highly visible regulatory discourse, managing both global genre staging and local exchange structure. The Convenor initiates all knowledge exchanges, as a secondary knower (K2 moves); however, since she is familiar with the police report, these are rather calculated K2 moves, comparable to Dk1 moves in contexts where the secondary knower has less of an idea of what the answers to questions could be. Significantly, interpretation of the recount is jointly constructed with the Convenor in control; she introduces virtually all evaluation and the YP responds with a word or phrase at a time.

It is, of course, the case that the YP in the Mobile Phone YJC was very quiet, not just in the context of this conference but also—to judge from the Convenor's account of a pre-conference briefing session and from the mother's description of her son's general demeanour—in other situations as well. However, the intensive scaffolding of responses by the Convenor of the Mobile Phone YJC is not at all unusual in our discourse sample. For comparison, let us turn now to the Affray YJC where the YP was a good deal more talkative and, indeed, at certain moments, less compliant. In the following examples, we see the ECLO taking over from the Convenor much of the responsibility for extending and interpreting the YP's recount. To begin with, the ECLO draws attention to a visible sign of the YP's affiliation to the local Muslim community, namely the *hijab* (headscarf) worn by his mother (Table 3.11).

The ECLO continues, highlighting the fact that the YP's Mother has been placed in a highly embarrassing situation by having to attend this conference in the presence of three uniformed police officers (Table 3.12).

The presence of two members of our research team, who were attending the conference, is also referenced as a possible cause for embarrassment ('Where are these guys from?') as the ECLO starts to make explicit

Table 3.11 'What's your mum wearing on her head?', Affray YJC

| Speaker | RE# | Regulative | Talk | IE# | Integrative |
|---|---|---|---|---|---|
| ECLO | 1 | ↓ A2 | Listen, I want to take, with your permission, I wanna take a different angle. | | |
| ECLO | | ↓ invite | OK? | | |
| ECLO | 2 | A1 | Mate, what's your mum wearing on her head? | 1 | Dk1 |
| YP | | | Scarf. | | K2 |
| ECLO | | | Yeah. | | K1 |
| ECLO | | ↑ A2f | OK. | | |

Table 3.12 'Who's sitting here right now?', Affray YJC

| Speaker | RE# | Regulative | Talk | IE# | Integrative |
|---|---|---|---|---|---|
| ECLO | | | What a – where is she now? | 2 | Dk1 |
| ECLO | | | In the presence of who? | | =Dk1... |
| YP | | | = Me. | | K2 |
| ECLO | | | = Who – who's- | | ...Dk1... |
| ECLO | | | No. | | ch |
| ECLO | | | Who's sitting here? | 3 | Dk1 |
| ECLO | | | Who's sitting here right now? | | =Dk1 |
| ECLO | 3 | ↓ A2 | Have a look across. | | |
| YP | | A1 | Men. | | K2 |
| ECLO | 4 | ↓ A2 | Have a – but have a look across. | | |
| ECLO | | A1 | What uniform are they wearing? | 4 | Dk1 |
| YP | | | Police uniform. | | K2 |
| ECLO | | ↑ A2f | OK. | | [K1][a] |

[a]These instances where the K1 is shown in square brackets indicate that the K1 is 'implied' by the fact that the primary knower makes another Dk1 move right after this move.

Table 3.13 'What the perception going to be?', Affray YJC

| Speaker | RE# | Regulative | Talk | IE# | Integrative |
|---|---|---|---|---|---|
| ECLO | 5 | A1 | Where are these guys from? | 5 | Dk1 |
| ECLO | | | They're from a certain place. | | K1[a] |
| ECLO | | ↑ A2f | OK. | | |
| ECLO | | | What's the perception going to be? | 6 | Dk1 |
| YP | | | Think bad of me. | | K2 |
| ECLO | 6 | A1 | What are they gonna– | 7 | Dk1... |
| ECLO | | | when they see your mum wearing a scarf. | | ...Dk1... |
| ECLO | | | I'm Muslim background myself. | | <<K1>>[b] |
| ECLO | | | What are they going to think? | | ...Dk1 |
| YP | | | Bad | | K2 |
| ECLO | | ↑ A2f | OK | | [K1] |

[a]There is a missing K2 move here since the ECLO answers his own question
[b]The << >> here indicates an additional interrupting K1 move

his concern that the YP is creating a bad impression not only of himself but also of his family and the broader Muslim community (Table 3.13).

Next, the ECLO argues that there is a 'disconnect' between the reality of the YP's situation and his self-image. These exchanges are prefiguring the admonition genre that will unfold more fully later in the conference (Table 3.14).

**4 Guided Storytelling in the Commissioned Recount** 153

Table 3.14 Distancing the YP from his mates, Affray YJC

| Speaker | RE# | Regulative | Talk | IE# | Integrative |
|---|---|---|---|---|---|
| ECLO | 7 | ↓ A2 | I'm asking you Aatif. | | |
| ECLO | | ↓ invite | OK. | | |
| ECLO | 8 | A1 | Because I'm listening to you, man, | 9 | K1 |
| | | | and I don't see you as a leader at the moment. | | K1 |
| | | | I see you following your friends. | | K1 |
| | | | I see your friends say "Jump". | | K1 |
| | | | You say "How high?" | | K1 |
| | | | That's how I see you. | 10 | K1 |
| | | ↑ A2f | OK. | | |
| YP | | | Yeah. | | K2f |
| ECLO | | | You wanna be tough. | 11 | K1 |
| ECLO | | | But you just – you're not, number one. | 12 | K1 |

Table 3.15 Ethnic Community Liaison Officer's disgust, Affray YJC

| Speaker | RE# | Regulative | Talk | IE# | Integrative |
|---|---|---|---|---|---|
| ECLO | | | Number two, man, when I see someone of my own background bringing their mum in wearing a hijab, | 13 | K1… |
| | | | OK. | | check |
| | | | Honestly man inside I feel sick. | | …K1 |
| ECLO | 9 | K2 | You understand? | | |
| YP | | K1 | Yes. | | |

Rounding off this rapid-fire opening volley of exchanges, the ECLO registers his disgust at the possibility that the YP's actions will reinforce negative, anti-Muslim stereotypes (Table 3.15).

As with the Convenor in the Mobile Phone YJC, the regulative discourse is highly visible, with the ECLO in control of the interaction, including the projected integrative discourse. This is seen by the fact that he initiates all knowledge exchanges as Dk1 and K1 moves, which is not surprising given his 'insider' status as a member of the Muslim community. In this way, the ECLO positions himself as a primary knower, enacting Dk1 and K1 moves, unlike the Convenor who uses more K2 moves.

This analysis of exchange structure reveals the extent to which Convenors and YLOs take responsibility for scaffolding the verbal contributions of Young Offenders—playing the kind of directive mentoring role encouraged by the pedagogic nature of conferencing discourse.

## 5 Conferencing as Pedagogic Discourse

This chapter has explored how the Convenor manages the conferencing macro-genre as a communicative interaction featuring multiple participants. We have surveyed how exchange structures operate in the conference, in particular focusing on the joint construction of the YP's commissioned recount. The focus on exchange structure reveals that conferencing is best interpreted as a pedagogic discourse in which the Convenor plays the important role of scaffolding the YP so that he or she may produce a full and productive account of the offence, paving the way for the possibility of reintegration into relevant communities of concern. In other words, what we have seen is a regulative discourse projecting an integrative discourse, supported by Convenors who attempt to open up the possibilities of taking responsibility for their behaviour.

This survey of exchange structure naturally raises questions about what exactly is being exchanged in the kinds of interaction we have sampled. All of the analyses presented in this section have underlined the fact that the Convenor, along with other experienced, institutionally powerful participants like the ECLO, is not simply allocating turns or managing major transitions across the macro-genre. The Convenor is in control of the regulative discourse and, through this, is able to shape many of the knowledge exchanges that make up the integrative discourse as well. These knowledge exchanges, of course, often touch on moral judgements and emotional reactions; and, as we saw in Chaps. 1 and 2, moral judgements and reactions are posited as central to the efficacy of conferencing in almost all versions of restorative justice theory. Certainly, there are many places in the New South Wales youth justice conferencing script where the Convenor is instructed to directly question the YP, or a Support Person, probing for their emotional reaction to the offence (and we have seen examples of this in the exchange structure analysis provided earlier).

Contrary to the impression that some restorative justice theorists have evoked in their characterizations of conferencing—where a YP is supposed to be suddenly overcome and transformed by 'an avalanche of shame' (Nathanson 1997)—what we are looking at here is a careful, deliberative process whereby the Convenor, and other well-positioned conference participants, map out the territory within which 'emotion talk' and interpersonal bonding is possible. In the next chapter, we will re-examine our set of conferences using the tools of APPRAISAL, a framework for analysing the patterning and rhetorical function of the evaluative language that is negotiated through the various steps and stages of the conference macro-genre.

## Notes

1. This is one of the rare occasions in which our presence has arguably affected the interaction.

## References

Bernstein, B. (1990). *Class, codes and control 4: The structuring of pedagogic discourse.* London: Routledge.
Bernstein, B. (1996/2000). *Pedagogy, symbolic control and identity: Theory, research, critique.* London: Taylor and Francis.
Berry, M. (1981). Systemic linguistics and discourse analysis: A multi- layered approach to exchange structure. In M. Coulthard & M. Montgomery (Eds.), *Studies in discourse analysis* (pp. 120–145). London: Routledge.
Braithwaite, J., & Daly, K. (1998). Masculinities, violence and communitarian control. In S. L. Miller (Ed.), *Crime control and women: Feminist implications of criminal justice policy* (pp. 151–180). Thousand Oaks: Sage.
Christie, F. (2002). *Classroom discourse analysis.* London: Continuum.
Cuneen, C., & White, R. (2007). *Juvenile justice: Youth and crime in Australia.* Oxford: Oxford University Press.
Eggins, S., & Slade, D. (1997). *Analysing casual conversation.* London/New York: Cassell.
Halliday, M. A. K., & Matthiessen, C. M. I. M. (2004). *An introduction to functional grammar.* London: Arnold.

Halliday, M., & Matthiessen, C. M. (2014). *An introduction to functional grammar*. London: Routledge.

Martin, J. R. (1992). *English text: System and structure*. Philadelphia: John Benjamins Pub.

Martin, J. R., & Rose, D. (2007). *Genre relations: Mapping culture*. London: Equinox.

Muntigl, P. (2004). *Narrative counselling: Social and linguistic processes of change*. Amsterdam/Philadelphia: John Benjamins Pub.

Nathanson, D. L. (1997). From empathy to community. *The Annual of Psychoanalysis, 25*, 125–143.

Ventola, E. (1987). *The structure of social interaction: A systemic approach to the semiotics of service encounters*. London: Pinter (Open Linguistics Series).

# 4

# Expressing Feeling: Appraisal Systems

## 1   Introduction

Having explored the structure of the interactive exchanges that constitute a conference, we now consider what is primarily at stake in those exchanges—namely feelings. One of the most important aspects of the interpersonal meanings we negotiate through language has to do with how we evaluate the things we are talking about, the attitudes we express as we talk about them, the strength of these attitudes, the sources to which we attribute them, and (as we will see more clearly in Chap. 5) whether or not we find ourselves bonding with someone through a sense of shared values. The analysis of evaluative meanings used in language is captured through the system of APPRAISAL. The premise underpinning appraisal analysis is that, as we are socialized into a culture, the emotional reactions to the world with which we were all born become codified in various ways (Martin and White 2005: 45). In one direction, emotion is re-socialized as judgements about our character and behaviour; in the other, emotion is re-socialized as appreciations of natural and human-made phenomena (including goods, services, texts, performances, ceremonies, etc.). Later on, we adjust to judgements that have been institutionalized as rules and regulations constraining our behaviour, in a

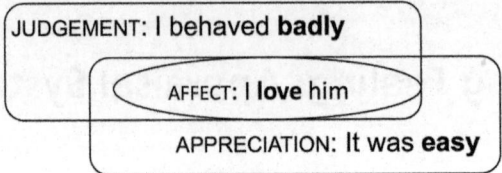

**Fig. 4.1** Dimensions of evaluation (Adapted from Martin and White (2005: 45))

system of penalties and rewards designed by church and state; and we adjust to appreciations that have been institutionalized as demarcated values, in an often digitalized system designed by adjudicators (e.g. the price we pay for goods and services, the payment we receive for our labour, or the mark we get for assessment tasks). Figure 4.1 offers a schematic representation of these dimensions of evaluation.

In short, AFFECT refers to the language choices we use to express emotion; JUDGEMENT has to do with assessing behaviour; and APPRECIATION is about estimating value.

## 2     Introducing Appraisal

Together, the choices available to us for expressing the types of evaluative meaning identified from the system of ATTITUDE. This is one of three main systems that the APPRAISAL system as a whole involves. Operating in concert with ATTITUDE are the systems of ENGAGEMENT and GRADUATION. Figure 4.2 provides examples of each region of meaning, formalized in a system network. While the network may be further specified to greater levels of delicacy depending on the kind of analysis for which it is being used, the examples displayed in the boxes of Fig. 4.2 (all taken from our sample of conferencing discourse) offer a guide to the main types of appraisal. In summary, ATTITUDE is concerned with *types* of feeling,

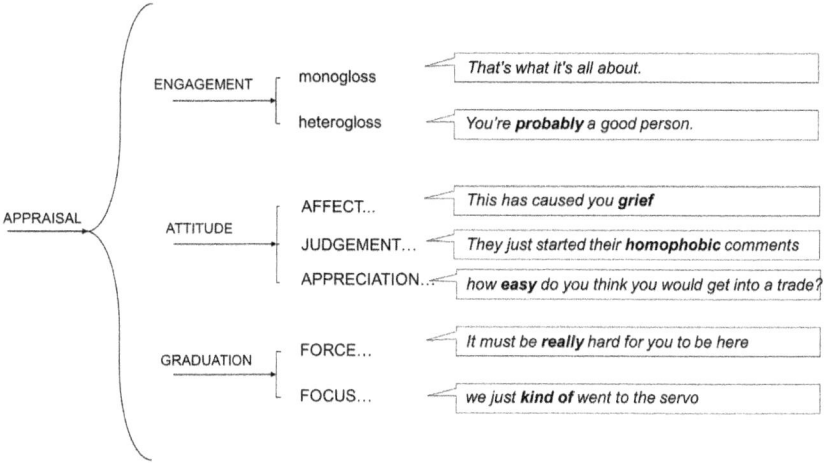

**Fig. 4.2** APPRAISAL systems (After Martin and White (2005))

GRADUATION with their *strength* and *boundedness*, and ENGAGEMENT with their *sourcing* and the *acknowledgement* of alternative voices in relation to the feeling being negotiated.

To elaborate briefly on the negotiation of interpersonal meaning afforded by these APPRAISAL systems, we begin with ENGAGEMENT. The key issue here is the kind of stance one adopts towards the attitudes being expressed. On the one hand, we can assert the independence of our views, presenting them as monologic, standalone propositions (monogloss) as in the following example:

### Extract 4.1, Shopping Trolley YJC

I was under the influence of drugs at the time.

In this instance, the Young Person's (YP) intoxication is presented as a bare fact that is not open for negotiation. On the other hand, we will often reference other voices (heterogloss) when we produce a text. In the example in Fig. 4.2, this is enacted through the use of modality (*probably* in 'you're *probably* a good person'). This implies something like 'other people might well say this, although I am not yet fully committed to the idea'. Another common form of heteroglossic appraisal is to attribute opinion through a projecting clause:

### Extract 4.2, Affray YJC

**ECLO:** We're not saying, 'Aatif, you're a this or you're a that'.

Clearly, such means of managing other voices within the text you are producing can do a lot to finesse the legitimacy of your stance and/or to mitigate or forestall criticism.

Turning back to the ATTITUDE system, we should emphasize that while the main resources are lexical, the same lexical item can be used to perform different kinds of appraisal work. For instance, depending on the target and source of the evaluation, a word such as *good* can work with any of the ATTITUDE systems. Consider the difference between JUDGEMENT in the following:

**Convenor:** So he's a **good** boy?

and affect:

**Convenor:** Does that make you feel **good**?

or appreciation:

**YP:** I got offered the job. So I will (...) see if it's **good** or not.

Finally, it is through the system of GRADUATION that attitudes may be scaled up or down in intensity. For example, we might upscale using FORCE:

**Convenor:** So he's a **really** good boy?

Or scale down:

**Arresting Officer:** Doesn't matter how many times I've caught him, he's always been **fairly** truthful, **fairly** respectful.

Similarly GRADUATION can be used to sharpen or soften categories using FOCUS. For example, sharpening (scaling up):

**Convenor:** ... as a result of his actions on that **particular** evening

Or softening (scaling down), a frequent tendency, as we have seen, of YPs in the commissioned recount:

**YP:** And so I **kind of** shut the door.

Sometimes 'the selection of ideational meanings is enough to invoke evaluation, even in the absence of attitudinal lexis that tells us directly how to feel' (Martin and White 2005: 62). Thus, alongside considering the type of attitude, we need to account for its explicitness—that is, whether or not the attitude is inscribed in specific evaluative lexis that can be identified in the text, such as the examples shown earlier, or whether it is implied or indirect. Where attitude is implied or indirect, relying on connotation, we refer to it as 'invoked'. An example of invoked attitude is seen in the following exchange from the ABC Radio Eye conference (Davis 2002) introduced in Chap. 1, where the Convenor asks the YP how the offence has impacted those around him:

**Convenor:** Who do you think has been affected by this?
**YP:** Everyone. Everyone here today. I was living with my dad at the time, now I live with mum because of that. Yeah.

While the YP's response does not contain any inscribed negative attitude, it implies that the YP incurred the judgement of his father and was sent away to his mother, hence 'invoking' negative attitude.

Most of the analyses in this chapter dealt with instances of inscribed attitude. In the following excerpts, for example, the Ethnic Community Liaison Officer (ECLO) explicitly queries the YP who committed the affray about his reactions, (through affect such as *upset, pissed off*),

**162**   **4 Expressing Feeling: Appraisal Systems**

challenges him to remake his character (through judgement such as *wrong*), and comments on how easy it is to break the law (through appreciation such as *so easy*).

**Extract 4.3, Affray YJC**

*affect*:
ECLO:   Hey. You think I'm talking to you now I'm – I'm **upset** with ya? Do you think I'm **pissed off** with ya? I don't know you but do you think I'm **upset** with ya?

*judgement*:
ECLO:   You find out how much of a man it takes, hey, to stay out of trouble. You tell me which one takes more of a man to do. How – does it take more of a man to listen to your friends or to say to your friends, 'No, what you're doing is **wrong**'.

*appreciation:*
ECLO:   Do you know **how easy** it is to break the law? It's **so easy**. [clicks fingers] It's **so easy**. [clicks fingers] It is **so easy**.

In the analyses we will present, our main concern is to show how the Convenor (in the Mobile Phone YJC) and the ECLO (in the Affray YJC) are using the system of ATTITUDE to add evaluation to the YP's recount. In the following tables we break these attitudes down into clusters realizing AFFECT (emotional reactions), JUDGEMENT (the way we evaluate people's character and behaviour) and APPRECIATION (the value we place on things).

## 3   Adding Evaluative Language to the Commissioned Recount

At the point where we left the discussion of exchange structure in the Mobile Phone YJC, the Convenor was just starting to explore the emotional reactions of the YP and his family to the news that he had been

### 3 Adding Evaluative Language to the Commissioned Recount

arrested for stealing a phone. The Convenor starts by asking about the father's reaction, offering the YP a pretty obvious choice between the binary opposition of 'angry' and 'happy':

**Extract 4.4, Mobile Phone YJC**

| | |
|---|---|
| **Convenor:** | And who did they ring when they brought you to the police station? |
| **YP:** | My dad. |
| **Convenor:** | OK. And what did your dad say? Was he angry, happy? |
| **YP:** | [nods] Angry. |
| **Convenor:** | Angry. [laughs] Yeah.¹ OK. |

Next, the Convenor asks after the mother's reaction (note that 'Mum' was in the room as a Support Person during this conference; the father was absent):

**Extract 4.5, Mobile Phone YJC**

| | |
|---|---|
| **Convenor:** | What did mum say when you got home? |
| **YP:** | She was sleeping. [nodding] |
| **Convenor:** | She was sleeping. Was Mum angry? |
| **YP:** | [nods] Yeah. |
| **Convenor:** | Did she get upset? |
| **YP:** | [half nod/raises eyes] |

Later, the feelings of the YP, were he to find himself in a comparable situation to the victim, are explored:

**Extract 4.6, Mobile Phone YJC**

| | |
|---|---|
| **Convenor:** | So if that was your phone, how would you feel if somebody stole your phone and then, you know, I decided I wanted to swap it with mine because mine was older. How would you feel about that? |

| | |
|---|---|
| **YP:** | Pretty angry. |
| **Convenor:** | Yeah. |

Turning from the language of affect to expressions of judgement, we can observe how the Convenor probes for some understanding that the YP has behaved badly, out of self-interest:

### Extract 4.7, Mobile Phone YJC

| | |
|---|---|
| **Convenor:** | [bobs head] You need to tell us why you took the phone. |
| **YP:** | Because it was new. |
| **Convenor:** | Because it was new. Newer than yours. |
| **YP:** | [nods] Yeah. |
| **Convenor:** | So you didn't care² that it was somebody else's phone? Is that right? |
| **YP:** | Yeah. |
| **Convenor:** | OK. |

The Convenor then checks to make sure that the YP, with the benefit of hindsight, is ready to share his father's condemnation of the offending behaviour:

### Extract 4.8, Mobile Phone YJC

| | |
|---|---|
| **Convenor:** | Did he say anything to you? ... |
| **YP:** | Don't go anywhere. |
| **Convenor:** | Don't go anywhere. As in when you get home you've got to stay at home? |
| **YP:** | [raises eyes in a half-nod] |
| **Convenor:** | Do you think your father was disappointed³ in you? |
| **YP:** | [nods] Yep. |
| **Convenor:** | So you know you did the wrong thing. |

This line of questioning is then expanded to include an acknowledgement that the mother's condemnation is equally valid:

## 3 Adding Evaluative Language to the Commissioned Recount

**Extract 4.9, Mobile Phone YJC**

| | |
|---|---|
| **Convenor:** | Tell me what happened when mum found out what you did. [tilts head] … Did she <u>cry</u>? |
| **YP:** | St-(…) Lecture. |
| **Convenor:** | You got a lecture. [nodding] |
| **YP:** | [nods] |
| **Convenor:** | Do you think you deserved a lecture? |
| **YP:** | [looks down] |
| **Convenor:** | Why did you deserve the lecture? |
| **YP:** | Because I did something <u>wrong</u>. |
| **Convenor:** | <u>Yep</u>. [nods] |

The Convenor invites the YP to confirm that his parents have acted reasonably in 'grounding' him:

**Extract 4.10, Mobile Phone YJC**

| | |
|---|---|
| **Convenor:** | So it's quite limiting in terms of what you can do, in terms of what you can do. And that's- Do you understand that that was the consequence of what you did? |
| **YP:** | [nods] Yeah. |
| **Convenor:** | Yeah? Do you think that was <u>reasonable</u> what mum and dad did grounding you? |
| **YP:** | [<u>nods</u>] |
| **Convenor:** | <u>Yeah?</u> |
| **YP:** | [<u>nods</u>] |

The Convenor also checks twice that the YP has apologized to his victim (who was not attending the conference):

**Extract 4.11, Mobile Phone YJC**

| | |
|---|---|
| **Convenor:** | Right and what did you- Did you say anything to him [shaking head] when you found out that it was his phone? |
| **YP:** | [shakes head] Nah. |

| | |
|---|---|
| **Convenor:** | So you didn't say <u>sorry</u>[4] to him? [shaking head] |
| **YP:** | (Nah), I said <u>sorry</u> and he goes 'you don't have to say <u>sorry</u>, it wasn't you that did it'. |
| **Convenor:** | Right. [half nodding] OK. ... |
| **Convenor:** | Hey? So you've <u>apologized</u> to Tuvale already. |
| **YP:** | Yeah. |
| **Convenor:** | OK. |

Finally, the Convenor also guides the YP towards an expression of remorse:

### Extract 4.12, Mobile Phone YJC

| | |
|---|---|
| **Convenor:** | Do you think that mum and dad were <u>disappointed</u> in you? |
| **YP:** | [nods] |
| **Convenor:** | [nods] Were you <u>disappointed</u> in yourself? Or Not? Or you don't care? |
| **YP:** | [nods] <u>Yeah</u>. |
| **Convenor:** | Yeah or you don't care? [nodding] |
| **YP:** | <u>Disappointed</u> in myself. |
| **Convenor:** | [tilts head] <u>You are</u>. |
| **YP:** | [nods] |

The full range of inscribed expressions of AFFECT and JUDGEMENT during the Interpretation stage[5] of the Mobile Phone YJC, predominantly introduced into the discourse by the Convenor, appears below in Tables 4.1 and 4.2 (as footnoted earlier, *disappointed*, *sorry* and *apologise* have been double-coded for AFFECT and JUDGEMENT and so appear in both tables partially bolded). The tables reveal the way in which the YP is being invited to re-script his identity (recalling Braithwaite's notion of conferencing as 'restorative storytelling' to which we referred in Chap. 1). In terms of AFFECT (including the two inscriptions of happiness, which are tendered ironically by the Convenor), the YP's family is understood to experience only negative emotions as a result of his behaviour.

The moral judgements associated with the YP and his friend's behaviour are also largely negative.

### 3 Adding Evaluative Language to the Commissioned Recount

**Table 4.1** Inscriptions of affect in the Interpretation stage of the Mobile Phone commissioned recount

| Speaker | Appraising item | Attitude | Polarity | Emoter | Trigger |
|---|---|---|---|---|---|
| Convenor | Angry | Dis/satisfaction | Negative | Father of YP | YP at police station |
|  | Happy | Un/happiness | Positive (ironic) | Father of YP | YP at police station |
| YP | Angry | Dis/satisfaction | Negative | Father of YP | YP at police station |
| Convenor | Angry | Dis/satisfaction | Negative | Father of YP | YP at police station |
|  | Happy | Un/happiness | Positive (ironic) | Father of YP | YP at police station |
|  | **Disap**pointed | Dis/satisfaction | Negative | Father of YP | YP |
|  | **Sorry** | Un/happiness | Negative | YP | Receiving phone |
| YP | **Sorry** | Un/happiness | Negative | YP | Receiving phone |
| Convenor | Angry | Dis/satisfaction | Negative | Mother of YP | YP receiving phone |
|  | Upset | Un/happiness | Negative | Mother of YP | YP receiving phone |
|  | Cry | Un/happiness | Negative | Mother of YP | YP receiving phone |
| YP | Angry | Dis/satisfaction | Negative | YP | Hypothetically having own phone stolen |
| Convenor | **Apo**logized | Un/happiness | Negative | YP | Receiving phone |
|  | **Disap**pointed | Dis/satisfaction | Negative | YP's parents | YP |
|  | **Disap**pointed | Dis/satisfaction | Negative | YP | YP |
| YP | **Disap**pointed | Dis/satisfaction | Negative | YP | YP |

Bearing in mind the results of our earlier exchange structure analysis—namely, that the Convenor almost always initiates, with the YP briefly and compliantly responding—we can conclude that the Interpretation of this recount stems primarily from the Convenor. It's the Convenor, not the YP, who in effect controls what the YP's story means.

## 4 Expressing Feeling: Appraisal Systems

**Table 4.2** Inscriptions of judgement in the Interpretation stage of the Mobile Phone commissioned recount

| Speaker | Appraising item | Attitude | Polarity | Appraiser | Appraised |
|---|---|---|---|---|---|
| YP | Stolen | Propriety | Negative | Police | Person stealing phone |
| Convenor | Stolen | Propriety | Negative | YP | Person stealing phone |
|  | Stolen | Propriety | Negative | YP | Person stealing phone |
|  | Disap**pointed** | Propriety | Negative | Father of YP | YP |
|  | **Wrong** | Propriety | Negative | Convenor | YP receiving phone |
|  | **Sorry** | Propriety | Negative | YP | YP receiving phone |
| YP | **Sorry** | Propriety | Negative | YP | YP receiving phone |
|  | **Wrong** | Propriety | Negative | Convenor | YP receiving phone |
| Convenor | Stole[a] | Propriety | Negative | Convenor | Hypothetical thief |
|  | Stolen | Propriety | Negative | Convenor | Hypothetical thief |
| YP | Stolen | Propriety | Negative | Convenor | Hypothetical thief |
| Convenor | Good | Propriety | <u>Positive</u> | Convenor | YP agreeing |
|  | Reasonable | Propriety | <u>Positive</u> | Convenor | Mum/dad grounding YP |
|  | Apologized | Propriety | Negative | YP | YP receiving phone |
|  | Disap**pointed** | Propriety | Negative | YP's parents | YP |
|  | Disap**pointed** | Propriety | Negative | YP | YP |
| YP | Disap**pointed** | Propriety | Negative | YP | YP |

[a] We have taken the lexical item *steal* as inscribing negative judgement because it means <u>wrongfully</u> taking something one doesn't own

## 3 Adding Evaluative Language to the Commissioned Recount

Such a conclusion perhaps raises the spectre of a manipulative Convenor, abusing the conferencing process. As noted in Chap. 1, this is a matter of ongoing concern to critics of restorative justice, particularly with regard to the involvement of police as Convenors. But we do not think this is a fair characterization of what was happening in the conferences we observed. Rather, it seems to us that the Convenor—along with others who are participating in a professional capacity and who have previous experience of conferencing—are using the extensions and interpretations of the commissioned recount genre as a way of leading the YP to the point where the conferencing macro-genre needs them to go (by guiding the YPs through unfamiliar generic terrain and helping them achieve the goals of the overall process).

For example, as we look at the appraisal analyses for the Affray YJC where the Police ECLO takes over from the Convenor, we can see this guiding process being played out through a tension between the rhetoric of inclusion and the rhetoric of exclusion. At the start of the transcript we considered earlier, the ECLO immediately focuses upon the Muslim cultural background that he shares with the YP—repositioning himself in relation to the police and other cultural outsiders in the room. He raises the risk that the YP's actions will bring shame on himself, his family *and* his community—in effect, questioning the YP's right to claim his heritage and be a leader in this community.

### Extract 4.13, Affray YJC

| | |
|---|---|
| **ECLO:** | Listen, [looking to the Convenor] I want to take, with your permission, I wanna take a different angle. OK? Mate, what's your mum wearing on her head? |
| **YP:** | Scarf. |
| **ECLO:** | Yeah. OK. What a- where is she now? In the presence of who? |
| **YP:** | Me. |
| **ECLO:** | Who- who's- No. Who's sitting here? Who's sitting here right now? Have a look across. |
| **YP:** | Men. |
| **ECLO:** | Have a- but have a look across. What uniform are they wearing? |
| **YP:** | Police uniform. |

| | |
|---|---|
| **ECLO:** | OK. [pointing to the university researchers] Where are these guys from? They're from a certain place. OK. What's the perception going to be? |
| **YP:** | Think <u>bad</u> of me. |
| **Convenor:** | What are they gonna- when they see your mum wearing a scarf, I'm Muslim background myself. What are they going to think? |
| **YP:** | <u>Bad</u>. |
| **ECLO:** | OK. I'm asking you Aatif. OK. Because I'm listening to you man and I don't see you as a <u>leader</u> at the moment. I see you following your friends. I see your friends say jump, you say how high. That's how I see you. OK. |
| **YP:** | Yeah. |
| **ECLO:** | You wanta be <u>tough</u>. But you just- you're not-, number one. Number two, man, when I see someone of my own background bringing their mum in wearing a Hijab, OK, honestly man inside I feel <u>sick</u>. You understand? |
| **YP:** | Yes. |

The ECLO sets the tone here for what is to follow in the rest of the Interpretation. Through this stage, the evaluative language is almost all about judgements of the YP—such as the need for honesty and sincerity (see Table 4.3).

Because of the importance of judgement in this interaction, Tables 4.3, 4.4, 4.5, 4.6 and 4.7 follow Martin and White (2005) in distinguishing judgements of social esteem (normality, capacity, tenacity) from

Table 4.3 Inscriptions of honesty in the ECLO's Interpretation stage of the affray commissioned recount

| Speaker | Appraising item | Social sanction |
|---|---|---|
| ECLO | I honestly don't think you do | Veracity |
| ECLO | I'm being honest with you | Veracity |
| ECLO | Honest | Veracity |
| YP | Honest | Veracity |
| ECLO | Swear | Veracity |
| YP | Swear | Veracity |
| ECLO | Honest | Veracity |
| YP | Yeah [honest] | Veracity |
| ECLO | Honest | Veracity |

3  Adding Evaluative Language to the Commissioned Recount    171

Table 4.4  Inscriptions of capacity in the ECLO's Interpretation stage of the affray recount

| Speaker | Appraising item | Social sanction |
|---|---|---|
| ECLO | Don't see you as a leader | Capacity |
|  | Tough … you're not | Capacity |
|  | (You think…) hard criminal | Capacity |
| ECLO | I've got half a brain | Capacity[a] |
|  | *How much* of a man[b] | Capacity |
|  | *More* of a man | Capacity |
|  | *More* of a man | Capacity |
| ECLO | You can control[c] yourself | Capacity |
| YP | I can control myself | Capacity |
|  | I can't [control myself] | Capacity |
|  | Just can't [control myself] | Capacity |
| ECLO | Temper | Capacity |
| YP | Yeah [temper] | Capacity |
| ECLO | (If…) smart | Capacity |

[a]The judgement is 'provoked' by the metaphor.
[b]The grading here shows that *man* is being used as an inscription of CAPACITY.
[c]This refers to the YP's control of his emotions. For this reason, we have coded this instance as inscribing capacity.

Table 4.5  Inscriptions of propriety in the ECLO's Interpretation stage of the affray commissioned recount

| Speaker | Appraising item | Social sanction |
|---|---|---|
| YP | Bad | Propriety |
|  | Bad | Propriety |
| ECLO | Put down (our community) | Propriety |
|  | Put down (our religion) | Propriety |
|  | Put down (the Hijab) | Propriety |
|  | Contradicting our religion | Propriety |
|  | Respect your mum | Propriety |
| YP | Yes [respect] | Propriety |
| ECLO | No you don't [respect] | Propriety |
|  | You don't respect your mum | Propriety |
|  | You have no respect for your mum | Propriety |
|  | You have no respect for your mum *whatsoever* | Propriety |
|  | You have no respect for what your mum's got on her head | Propriety |
|  | You have no respect for our community | Propriety |
|  | You have no respect | Propriety |
|  | Trying to impress | Propriety |
|  | The right to go and hurt other people | Propriety |

(*continued*)

**Table 4.5** (continued)

| Speaker | Appraising item | Social sanction |
|---|---|---|
| YP | No right [hurt] | Propriety |
| ECLO | (If you get a job) you'll be out of trouble | Propriety |
| | (If you don't get a job) you'll get into trouble | Propriety |
| | Responsibility | Propriety |
| | Break the law[a] | Propriety |
| | Break the law | Propriety |
| | Breaking the law | Propriety |
| | Try staying out of trouble | Propriety |
| | Stay out of trouble | Propriety |
| | Wrong | Propriety |
| | Disrespecting | Propriety |
| | Disrespect | Propriety |
| | No respect | Propriety |
| | Laugh at your face | Propriety |
| | Pretend that they care | Propriety |
| | Wrong | Propriety |
| | Trouble | Propriety |
| | Getting your mum into this crap | Propriety |
| | Getting your family into this crap | Propriety |
| | Not right | Propriety |
| | No good | Propriety |
| | Good person | Propriety |
| | Not good | Propriety |
| | Trouble | Propriety |
| | Hurting | Propriety |
| | Hurting | Propriety |
| | Don't care | Propriety |
| | Alright | Propriety |
| | Alright | Propriety |

[a]We include items about contravening the law (e.g. *break the law*, *steal*, etc.) since they clearly involve wrongful behaviour (i.e. impropriety); they are in fact judgements which have been technicalized as part of a legal system (as axiologically loaded technicality, legal definitions of the these terms and debates around their application make their inscription of judgement clear)

judgements of social sanction (veracity and propriety). Judgements of social esteem have to do with how special, how capable, or how dependable someone is; these are judgements we tend to negotiate through chat, gossip, jokes, texts, tweets, posts and stories of various kinds—often

## 3 Adding Evaluative Language to the Commissioned Recount 173

**Table 4.6** Inscriptions of impropriety by the YP in relation to his mother

| Speaker | Appraising item | Social sanction |
|---|---|---|
| ECLO | Bad | Propriety |
|  | Respect your mum | Propriety |
| YP | Yes [respect] | Propriety |
| ECLO | No you don't [respect] | Propriety |
|  | You don't respect your mum | Propriety |
|  | You have no respect for your mum | Propriety |
|  | You have no respect for your mum *whatsoever* | Propriety |
|  | Disrespecting | Propriety |
|  | Disrespect | Propriety |
|  | No respect | Propriety |
|  | Hurting | Propriety |
|  | Hurting | Propriety |
|  | Don't care | Propriety |

**Table 4.7** Inscriptions of impropriety by the YP in relation to the Muslim community

| Speaker | Appraising item | Social sanction |
|---|---|---|
|  | Bad | Propriety |
| ECLO | Put down (our community) | Propriety |
|  | Put down (our religion) | Propriety |
|  | Put down (the Hijab) | Propriety |
|  | Contradicting our religion | Propriety |
|  | You have no respect for what your mum's got on her head | Propriety |
|  | You have no respect for our community | Propriety |
|  | You have no respect | Propriety |
|  | Don't care | Propriety |

involving humour. Judgements of social esteem are in a sense more serious, since they have to do with how truthful or how ethical someone is; these are judgements which may have institutional or legal implications if religious or governmental institutions codify them as edicts, decrees, codes of conduct, rules, regulations and laws about how to behave—with penalties and punishments for those not complying with the code. Both sets of values obviously bear critically on formal and informal processes of reintegration.

The YP's capacities were also explored, including his lack of leadership, manhood and ability to control his temper (see Table 4.4).

But the majority of the explicit judgements dealt with the impropriety of the YP's behaviour (Table 4.5).

As noted, at the heart of this impropriety, is the ECLO's concern about the lack of respect being shown by the YP, first in relation to his family (see Table 4.6).

And, second, there is the lack of respect being shown in relation to the Muslim community (Table 4.7).

Just like the Convenor in the Mobile Phone YJC, the ECLO in this conference is controlling the Interpretation of the YP's recount. This Interpretation contains few expressions of affect, but is dominated by judgements, nearly all of them introduced by the ECLO.

On the one hand, the sheer volume of these judgements could be read as evidence that the YP is simply being harangued. On the other hand, taking a more generous view, the tempo and rhythm of the ECLO's speech, along with his frequent use of in-group vocatives (*brother, man, mate*) and his code-switching between English and Arabic, suggest the ECLO is enacting a degree of solidarity in this interaction (which will be further explored in Chap. 5). We should bear in mind that the conference was taking place against the backdrop of widespread anti-Muslim prejudice, regularly fostered by conservative government ministers and right-wing media commentators as part of the nationalistic rhetoric that legitimated Australia's involvement in the 'War on Terror' and its ongoing demonization and incarceration of asylum-seekers. For the ECLO, it is thus no small matter that the YP in the Affray YJC is bringing his Muslim community into disrepute. Therefore, rather than reading the ECLO's Interpretation of the YP's commissioned recount as simply a tirade, we can see it as supporting the YP to better meet the demands of the genre.

Further to this, the ECLO takes pains to spell out that his judgements relate to the YP's offending behaviour, not to his overall character as a person:

### 3 Adding Evaluative Language to the Commissioned Recount

**Extract 4.14, Affray YJC**

ECLO: Why don't you look at why we're here today? Are we here because of me?
YP: No.
ECLO: Are we- who are we here for?
YP: Because of me.
ECLO: Not because of you as a person because of something you're doing that's not <u>right</u>. You're probably a <u>good</u> person. What you're doing is not <u>good</u>. You understand the difference?
YP: Yes.
ECLO: We're not saying, 'Aatif, you're a this and you're a that'. What we're saying is your behavior is getting you into <u>trouble</u>, man. You're <u>hurting</u> your family, brother. You're <u>hurting</u> your [Arabic], brother. You understand?
YP: Yes.
ECLO: If I didn't <u>care</u> about you, man, I didn't <u>care</u> about your mum I didn't <u>care</u> about, you know, the Den and everything, I wouldn't even be here. I mean, I've finished my work. But if we- if everyone here today could help you just to sorta think to yourself, 'What am I doing to my family? What am I doing to myself?', man, Salaam. That's what it's all about. That's is what today is all about. It's about you sitting down and having a look- ...

It would be difficult to find a more emphatic instantiation of the basic idea behind reintegrative shaming (i.e. 'communicating disapproval of an *act* with respect' (Braithwaite in Ahmed et al. 2001: 39)) than these words from the ECLO. However, as the analyses in Chap. 3 showed, this approach does not necessarily entail the YP having control of the way the genre unfolds.

The work on appraisal that we have considered thus far, as well as the analysis of exchange structure undertaken in the previous chapter, has allowed us to reconsider the dynamics of reintegration in the conference macro-genre. As for the analysis of exchange structure, the guiding role of the Convenor and Police Youth Liaison Officer is clear. We will now focus on how feelings are shared and negotiated in two key steps in the macro-genre: the commissioned recount and the rejoinder.

## 4   The Commissioned Recount as a Storytelling Genre

Thus far we have approached the stories told in conferencing from the perspective of discourse semantics, looking at patterns of exchange structure (NEGOTIATION) and patterns of evaluative language (APPRAISAL). In this section, the focus of our analysis shifts back up to the level of genre as we consider these commissioned recounts in relation to the larger family of story genres (Martin and Rose 2008).

We have seen how the Convenor and ECLO very actively introduce attitudinal lexis in the Extension and Interpretation stages of the commissioned recount, and implicitly or explicitly invite the YP to subscribe to these expressions of AFFECT, APPRECIATION or JUDGEMENT. The function of these manoeuvres appears to be to position the YP as an amenable candidate for reintegration. If we go back to the start of the commissioned recount in the Affray YJC, we can see more clearly how this need can arise. The YP offers quite a detailed account of how he went to back up a mate who had arranged to fight someone one-on-one. In this incident, the 'duel' gets out of hand with someone being stabbed and a chase ensuing.

**Extract 4.15, Affray YJC, YP's Commissioned Recount**

> It was up there –
> It was – (…) on a Tuesday yeah. (…)
> and I got a call from my friend, Tahseen, (…) to come down to Falconswood Park.
> Something going on;
> but when I went down with them to Paulberg station
> and jumped on the train (…)
> and the train we got it straight to Falconswood Park,
> we got off at Falconswood Park.
> (…) Misbah and other – his other two friends.
> And they had a one on one
> and I jumped in
> and I turn around.

## 4 The Commissioned Recount as a Storytelling Genre

I was having a go with his friends
and the [one] next to me got stabbed
and he (…) goes 'Chase him!'
and I went and chased him,
started chucking stuff at him,
hitting him.
I couldn't stop him.
He still had the knife in his hand
and after that I walked back to the station to see Tahseen
and I see the policeman coming as I walked away
and (…) happened to him
and I said to the two officers 'Assault me, search me'.
They took out all my stuff
and they found out I was involved
and they took me back to the police station.
And my (…)
and I had an interview
and they took my pants, my hat, my jacket
and I was released.

The genre-staging here matches the other recounts we looked at in Chap. 2, beginning with an Orientation and continuing with a Record of Events; however, there is no formal closing (i.e. Reorientation).

Orientation
It was up there –
It was – (…) on a Tuesday yeah. (…)

Record of Events
and I got a call from my friend, Tahseen, (…) to come down to Falconswood Park. Something going on;
but when I went down with them to Paulberg Station …
and they found out I was involved
and they took me back to the police station
…
and I had an interview
and they took my pants, my hat, my jacket
and I was released.

The Convenor then initiates the Extension stage of this commissioned recount, probing for more details, asking why the YP went to back up his mate, and establishing that he was charged with possession of a knife:

### Extract 4.16, Affray YJC, YP's Commissioned Recount

| | |
|---|---|
| **Convenor:** | And when you- when you decided you would go down and help your friend, what did he actually say to you? |
| **YP:** | He was going to see Misbah. |
| **Convenor:** | And why was he going to see Misbah? |
| **YP:** | Because Misbah offered him out.[6] |
| **Convenor:** | Offered what? |
| **YP:** | Nah (…) two of us have a go like one on one. |
| **Convenor:** | To fight? |
| **YP:** | Yeah. |
| **Convenor:** | And so why did he need you there if he was going to fight him one on one? |
| **YP:** | Because I'm closer. (…) He trusts me like in case anything happens because I've known him since primary. |
| **Convenor:** | And why did he think something would happen? |
| **YP:** | … In case. |
| **Convenor:** | And when you went to this location you had something on your person. You had something with you. What was that? |
| **YP:** | The knife. |
| **Convenor:** | So you want to tell us about the knife? |
| **YP:** | (…) Didn't know I even had it on me. Forgot I had it on me the whole time and then I couldn't remember I had it until they (…) and pulled it out and showed them. It doesn't even work. You can't even use it. |
| **Convenor:** | But it's not actually a knife. |
| **YP:** | No. |
| **Convenor:** | A knife is included in it isn't it? |
| **YP:** | Yes. |
| **Convenor:** | What else is it? |
| **YP:** | A can opener, screwdriver |
| **Convenor:** | And so when the police searched you and found the- what are they a Leatherman? Is that what they're called? |

## 4 The Commissioned Recount as a Storytelling Genre

| | |
|---|---|
| **Arresting Officer:** | A Leatherman sort of tool. |
| **Convenor:** | When they found that what did you say to them? |
| **YP:** | Said it's for work. |
| **Convenor:** | Tell everybody what you did for work back then. |
| **YP:** | Panel beater. |
| **Convenor:** | So, as I explained to you the other day, why do you think the police charged you with having that weapon in your possession? |
| **YP:** | (…) They thought I got ready for a fight … to use it. |
| **Convenor:** | And what else did they say to you? Do you remember? |
| **YP:** | Nup. |
| **Convenor:** | Did they say anything to you about the fact that it, you know, as a panel beater you probably don't need a knife? |
| **YP:** | Yes. |
| **Convenor:** | Is that- do you think that's reasonable? |
| **YP:** | Yes. |
| **Convenor:** | So you accept the fact that you got charged with the possession of the knife. |
| **YP:** | Yes. |
| **Convenor:** | Alright and then when you chased after Niyaz what were you going to do when you caught him? |
| **YP:** | Wasn't going to fuck with him. Was going to bring him back. |
| **Convenor:** | Bring him back to where? |
| **YP:** | The station. … Well I couldn't, he had the knife in his hand still. |
| **Convenor:** | What did you think when you saw Niyaz with the knife? |
| **YP:** | I didn't want to get – I didn't want to get (next to him) in case I got stabbed. If I only had the knife I would have pulled it out on him too but I didn't have it. I forgot I had it on me. |
| **Convenor:** | So what did he say to you when you- when you caught up with him? |
| **YP:** | He just goes 'What did I do? I didn't do nothing'. |
| **Convenor:** | And then what did you do to him? |
| **YP:** | I chased him until he went in – inside a shop. |
| **Convenor:** | Yeah. And then what did you do? |
| **YP:** | I went back to the station and I went back down and that's when I got stopped. |

Notwithstanding the YP's defensive responses to the questions about why he was in possession of a knife, it is clear that he is willing to provide a lot of detail about the incident and to respond to further questions. Detailed information is not lacking. However, the YP's recounting of events is so heavily focused on ideational meaning that it creates a 'flat' and rather institutional tone. In this respect, commissioned recounts contrast markedly with the text features that we see in *personal* recounts deployed to sustain solidarity with partners, friends and family. For instance, we can compare the previous transcript to the following excerpt, a written text that was gathered during fieldwork for previous research on language and literacy in schools. The writer is a female Year 8 student (so, about 14 years of age) of Aboriginal Australian background.

> Fucken Hell man, who the hell told you I liked doing this kind of shit. On Saturday I saw Brian and Brendon and his Girlfriend at Waterloo, I was waiting to catch the bloody bus, anyway they started talking to me so that killed a lot of time. Anyway I had to go to the Laundromat Yesterday and I saw my ex-boyfriend man he looks fucken ugly god knows what I went out with him, he looks like a fucken dickhead
>
> ANY WAYS HE WAS
> so ugly only a blind woman would go out with him. I ran into this elderly man that lived down one of my old streets and because I had a bag of clothes the stupid cunt said to us are you running away from home which is bullshit because the sooner that I got home the happier I would have been. Then my ex-boyfriend comes up which makes it even worse and he starts calling this old cunt a cradle snatching little ass-hole. I mean as if it's any of his business, and like this is totally humiliating cause I mean everybody and I mean everybody tried to see who the hell was making all the fucken noise and yes there I was trying to hide my face as soon as possible …

This young woman's story is told with an ongoing prosody of evaluation—almost every piece of information is accompanied by forceful, sharply focused attitudinal lexis and, of course, slang and taboo language designed to generate rapport, laughter and empathy among members of the writer's in-group. Even less colourful personal recounts, among friends from very different demographic backgrounds, tend to have this kind of ongoing evaluation, woven richly through the Record of Events. The absence of such evaluation in the Record of Events of a commissioned recount shows very clearly how YPs in a conference strive to adjust their everyday storytelling strategies to a very different context. The downside to this absence of evaluative language, however, is that it can create an impression that something is missing—a sense of feeling, commitment and honesty—from the YP's story. After all, evaluation is an essential part of all storytelling even if its distribution varies from one story to another. In fact, it is partly by tracking this variation that we can construct a system network for some of the most typical story genres.

A brief review of this story genre family provides further insight into how commissioned recounts function in relation to cultural context. Following Martin and Rose (2008), we can compare commissioned recounts not just to personal recounts but also to the genres of exemplum, anecdote and narrative (see Eggins and Slade 1997; Jordens and Little 2004; Jordens 2003; Martin and Plum 1997; Muntigl 2004; Plum 1988 for related work on story genres).

Let's start with another example of a personal recount, showing again the ongoing prosody of evaluation that typifies this genre. The following text comes from a work of non-fiction by the Aboriginal author, Sally Morgan. Her mother Gladdie (Talahue) was taken from Sally's grandmother (who had herself been taken from her mother a generation earlier) as part of the Stolen Generations in Australia.[7] Sally tells the story of her mother's removal using the voice of her grandmother, Daisy Corunna:

> When Gladdie was 'bout three years old, they took her from me. I'd been 'spectin' it. Alice told me Gladdie needed an education, so they put her in Parkerville Children's Home. What could I do? I was too <u>frightened</u> to say anythin'. I <u>wanted</u> to keep her with me, she was all I had, but they didn't <u>want</u> her there. Alice said she cost too much to feed, said I was <u>ungrateful</u>. She was <u>wantin'</u> me to give up my own flesh and blood and still feel <u>grateful</u>. Aren't black people allowed to have feelings?
>
>   I <u>cried</u> and <u>cried</u> when Alice took her away. Gladdie was too young to understand, she thought she was comin' back. She thought it was a picnic she was goin' on. I ran down to the wild bamboo near the river and I hid

and <u>cried</u> and <u>cried</u> and <u>cried</u>. How can a mother lose a child like that? How could she do that to me? I thought of my <u>poor</u> old mother then, they took her Arthur from her, and then they took me. She was <u>broken-hearted</u>, <u>God bless her</u>. (Morgan 1987: 340–341)

Negative AFFECT runs iteratively through this heart-rending tale, colouring everything that happens with the sadness of those involved. This is a very common feature of personal recounts and indeed can be seen to be one their overarching purposes.

Turning from the genre of personal recounts to anecdotes, we can look at a text by another Aboriginal writer, Elaine Russell, to see how an anecdote makes its point by culminating in an emotional reaction to be shared. This particular anecdote concerns a young Aboriginal girl growing up in La Perouse, Sydney, and her experience of Christmas:

One Christmas eve, my parents took me and my brothers and sisters to nearby Matraville, where a charity was giving away toys to Aboriginal children. It was a very hot day, and the queue was so long. I watched lots of kids going home, happy with their dolls and bikes and scooters and toy cars. My heart was set on a doll that said 'Mama, Mama'. When we finally reached the head of the queue, the people told my parents that they'd run out of toys. I <u>cried</u> and <u>cried</u>. (Russell 2004)

Another story genre, the exemplum, builds up to its point in a similar way to an anecdote. The evaluation in which it culminates, however, and the purpose for which this particular kind of story is being told involves judgement rather than affect. The point of the exemplum in some sense is to judge someone's behaviour or moral compass. The following exemplum shows this by illustrating the kindness of Aboriginal people as a counterpoint to the fears of the mother of the narrator, Miss F. May Nevell:

When my parents were married in 1863, they lived across the creek at Butheroe, from the original home, where the Joseph Nevells lived then. My mother was always nervous of the Aborigines – one dark night, my parents had been at tea at the Joseph Nevells' home and as they were going home, some Aborigines were sitting around a fire, about half way between the house and the old well, going down to the creek. Father said, 'don't be afraid, they will not hurt us', and he spoke to one of the group as they passed by. A few minutes later, boomerangs were lighted at one end, came overhead and of course, went back to the Aborigines, then came a series of these lighted boomerangs showing a light to father and mother until they reached the front door – it was a <u>kindly</u> action from the natives. (Johnson 2002: iii)

Personal recounts, anecdotes and exempla all contrast with narratives of the kind introduced in Labov and Waletzky (1967). Narratives of this type involve a stage of Evaluation following the events that disturb the status quo, as well as a Resolution when order is re-established (shown through the Complication ^ Evaluation ^ Resolution staging). Here's another of Russell's stories, which resolves the predicament in which the heroine finds herself on the first day of school:

My School
**Complication**
My sister Violet walked me to school on my first day, saying 'Hurry up! We'll be late!' When we got to the school gate, she just left me there – she went to a different building because she was older.
**Evaluation**
I was <u>scared</u>!
**Resolution**
I felt a lot <u>better</u> when we lined up to go to our classes. I soon made some new friends and we played games in the schoolyard. The next day I wasn't <u>scared</u> at all! (Russell 2004)

Had this experience been told as an anecdote, it would have built up to the little girl's fear and ended there; had it been told as an exemplum it would have culminated with criticism of her sister's behaviour (or perhaps the school's)—and in neither case would the problem have been resolved (just as we don't learn what happened, for better or worse, when the toys ran out in the earlier story). Told as a personal recount, the fear felt by the little girl at being left alone would have been downplayed, perhaps by being spread as a prosody of anxiety throughout the day, and the sequence of events would have been treated as relatively unproblematic (as just an eventful day at school).

# 4 Expressing Feeling: Appraisal Systems

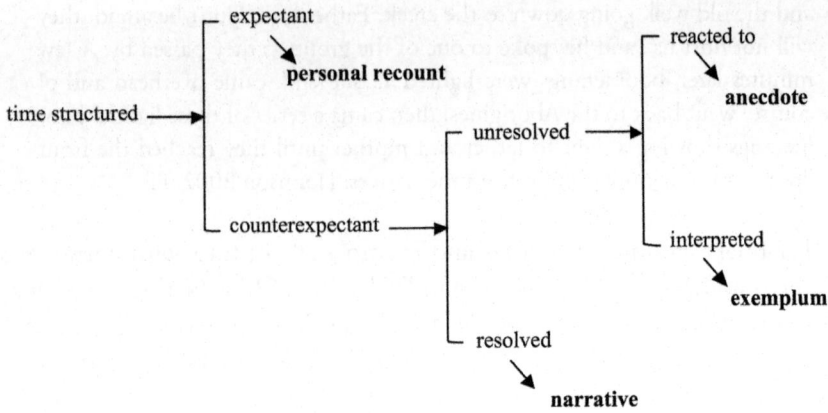

**Fig. 4.3** Some story genres (After Martin and Rose (2008))

Relations among these genres are presented as a system of choices in Fig. 4.3 all unfold chronologically through time (as opposed to news stories; see Martin and Rose 2008)—recounts unfold expectantly, without major disruptions, whereas anecdotes, exempla and narratives deal with problematic events. Narratives are resolved, but for anecdotes and exempla the outcome is not the point (we usually don't find out how equilibrium is restored). Finally, anecdotes culminate by sharing emotional affect, whereas exempla share judgements of character and behaviour.

Compared with the story genres we have just reviewed, commissioned recounts resemble anecdotes and exempla in building up to a culminating evaluation following the event sequence, which contrasts with the prosody of ongoing comments in personal recounts and some narratives.[8] The Interpretation stage of the commissioned recount may resemble the structure of an anecdote in those moments when it is oriented towards affect or it may resemble an exemplum whenever the orientation is more towards judgement. However, commissioned recounts differ from both anecdotes and exempla in that evaluation is 'directed' by the 'audience' (that is, the Convenor or other participants) rather than the narrator. Finally, commissioned recounts differ from narratives proper in the sense that the ultimate resolution of the offence lies beyond the commissioned recount itself (arguably in the outcome plan and its successful implementation). From a typological perspective, we can thus classify commissioned recounts as expectant, alongside personal recounts, but still distinct from personal recounts by opposing their culminative interpretative stage to the prosodic evaluation of recounts. This typology is networked in Fig. 4.4.

Alternatively, we can look at the relations between this family of story genres from a topological perspective by setting up two vectors, as in Fig. 4.5. Here, the vertical axis represents a cline with culminative evaluation at one end and prosodic evaluation at the other; in contrast, the horizontal axis is a cline with an inscribed interpretation at one end and a prescribed interpretation at the other. By 'inscribed interpretation' we mean evaluation encoded by the speaker or writer of the story; by 'prescribed evaluation' we mean evaluation that comes from a listener or reader, for example, the Convenor and Liaison Officers in the case of

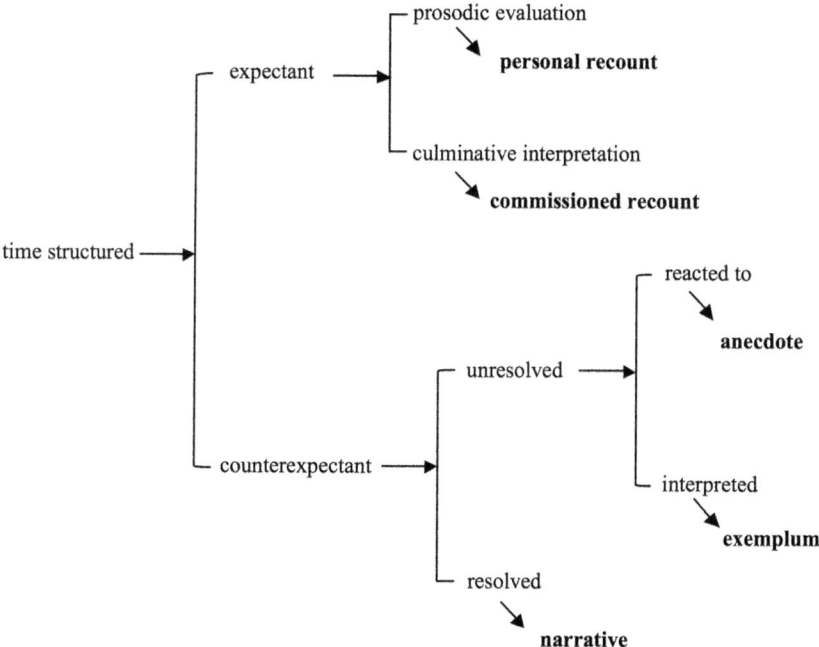

**Fig. 4.4** Commissioned recount as a story genre (After Martin and Rose (2008))

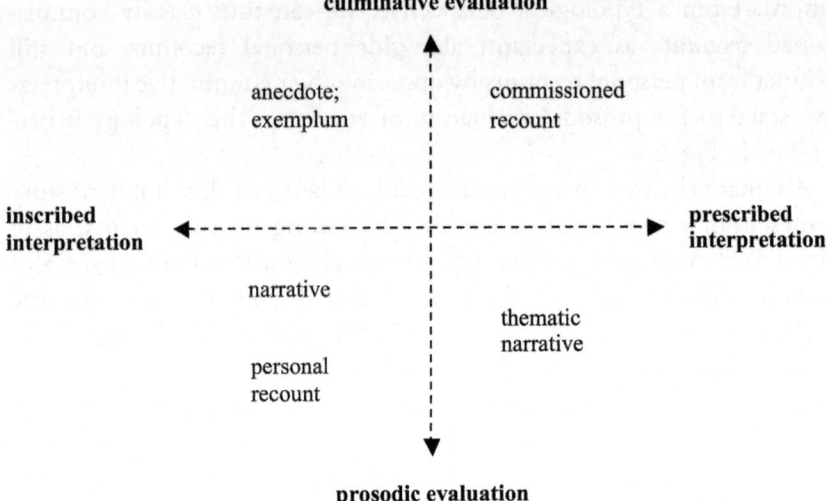

**Fig. 4.5** Some story genres—a topological perspective

commissioned recounts, or a critic as far as thematic narratives (literary narratives) are concerned (see Martin and Rose 2008; Rothery 1994; Rothery and Stenglin 1997, 2000). This style of representation is useful for mapping a contextual space into which genres (or the text instantiating them) can be arranged as having more or less prosodic/culminative evaluation and more or less inscribed/prescribed interpretation.[9] Viewed in these terms, anecdotes, exempla, narratives and personal recounts all tend to have more inscribed interpretation, whereas commissioned recounts and thematic narratives[10] tend to have their interpretation more prescribed (Martin 1996). Along the vertical axis, anecdotes, exempla and commissioned recounts tend to have a more culminative evaluation whereas evaluation in narratives, thematic narratives and personal recounts tends to be more prosodic.

The critical point to sum up with here is that the commissioned recount tends to position the YP as responsible for the ideational meaning of the genre (what happened), but the YP does not take responsibility for its evaluation (the point of what went on). As far as evaluation is concerned the commissioned recount in effect hands the responsibility over to the Convenor or at times other strongly positioned participants in the conference. Recalling Bernstein's work on pedagogic discourse, we can see that the distinctive nature of the commissioned recount, as a very ideationally focused 'flat' kind of story genre, stems from the way in which it is circumscribed by the overall design of the conferencing macro-genre. The macro-genre does require that feelings eventually 'get into' these stories but the YP has limited control over how this will happen. By way of contrast, the reflective recounts[11] offered by the Victim do not feature the kind of 'extraction' of evaluation seen in the YP's commissioned recount. As we noted in Chap. 2, in the reflective recount the Victim is more likely to proffer evaluation on their own, which means that a distinct Interpretation stage is not required. To conclude our focus on evaluative meanings, we now turn to the evaluation that is offered in the rejoinder step of the macro-genre.

## 5   The Rejoinder: 'Outsourcing' Evaluation to Support Persons and Carers

We have already looked at how Convenors (and other key participants such as the ECLO) can use the Extension and Interpretation stages of the commissioned recount as opportunities to add evaluation to the YP's story. Another strategy is to draw other participants into this task of appraising the facts of the story, particularly the YP's supporters. This commonly occurs during the rejoinder macro-genre in the conference, a point we touched on in Chap. 2. As part of the rejoinder, there is a strong expectation that the YP's parents or carers will respond emotionally not only insofar as their own feelings are concerned but also, in a sense, as a proxy for feelings that the YP may have been unable or unwilling to express appropriately. This expectation can be seen, for instance, in the way that Convenors will often make a meta-comment about the Support Person's emotional state (e.g. 'it must be very hard for you to listen to all this') before asking them to speak, or comment in similar terms as a brief aside while the YP is still speaking. In almost every conference we attended, the burden of this emotional labour fell upon the mother of the YP. The following are examples from our conferences that suggest a rhetorical pattern whereby the Convenor appeals to the YP to have regard for the negative affect (shown in bold) that the YP's mother is feeling:

> And she [mother] got <u>upset</u>?
> Was she [mother] <u>crying</u>?
> She <u>cry</u>?
> How do you <u>feel</u> about the fact that, you know, mum is still getting <u>upset</u> about this?
> Not good to <u>see</u> mum <u>upset</u> is it?
> Mums <u>don't like</u> getting <u>upset</u>, trust me.
> When our kids do something wrong, it really <u>hurts</u> us deep down, here.
> He [YP] gets to <u>see</u> how <u>upset</u> it makes your [mother] still.
> Do you <u>feel</u> OK about the fact that mum gets <u>upset</u>?
> And she's [mother] got a lot of <u>sadness</u> in her life at the moment but she still here to support you.
> And what about- did you <u>see</u> mum <u>upset</u>? Was mum <u>upset</u>?
> Do you <u>feel bad</u> about letting mum down?

On the one hand, the 'coupling'[12] of negative affect and 'mother' (with her being the 'emoter', the person experiencing unhappiness) invites an empathetic response from other conference participants who see the mother's vulnerability. On the other hand, the proliferation of mental processes and states in this kind of talk (i.e. clauses that are about conscious sensing, underlined in the examples) positions the YP as 'Senser' of the 'Phenomenon' that is the mother's pain. The clear implication is that the YP can better position himself or herself as a 'redeemable' subject by bearing witness to the emotional distress the mother is experiencing.

For example, consider the moves made by the Convenor in the following Shopping Trolley YJC where she prompts the YP to express his feelings about waking his mother in the middle of the night and invites him to imagine how she felt:

### Extract 4.17, Shopping Trolley YJC

| | |
|---|---|
| **Convenor:** | Do you – did you feel anything about, having to get mum out at four o'clock in the morning. Did you feel <u>bad</u> about that? |
| **YP:** | Yeah. |

## 5  The Rejoinder: 'Outsourcing' Evaluation to Support Persons...    189

| | |
|---|---|
| **Convenor:** | You did. And what about, um, did you see mum <u>upset</u>? Was mum <u>upset</u>? |
| **YP:** | She was angry |
| **Convenor:** | Yeah== |
| **YP:** | ==Yeah |
| **Convenor:** | How'd that make you feel? |

This pattern continues in the same conference when the Convenor later suggests the YP consider the negative affect engendered by disappointing his mother:

### Extract 4.18, Shopping Trolley YJC

| | |
|---|---|
| **Convenor:** | So, you got to set an example for them then, Toby. Like mum obviously tries to do for you. OK. And not let her down. Do you <u>feel bad</u> about letting mum down? |
| **YP:** | Yeah. |
| **Convenor:** | Yeah? Cause she's pretty good to you isn't she. |
| **YP:** | Yeah. |

Once again, the function of these emotional probes is to realign the YP into his family unit by considering the damage being done to his kin. The appropriate attitudinal response to the probes is intended to guide the YP towards taking on the morally reformed, emotionally expressive persona that the macro-genre of conferencing expects.

Of course, the figure of the suffering mother has such a long and rich history in many cultures (the hymn *Stabat mater dolorosa* comes to mind as a paradigmatic example in the Western tradition) that we should not be surprised if Convenors are drawing on this rhetorical trope and viewing it as critical to the efficacy of conferencing. The Convenor in the Mobile Phone YJC is quite explicit in this regard:

### Extract 4.19, Mobile Phone YJC

| | |
|---|---|
| **Convenor:** | This is a good thing for Brody, to come here and do this, alright, rather than going before the magistrate at court. |
| **Mother:** | Mm |

| | |
|---|---|
| **Convenor:** | Because he gets to talk about it, you get to hear about it, you get to – **he gets to see how upset it makes you still**. Yeah? And, we then get to move on, alright? Draw the line in the sand, ok? |

Nor should we be surprised when the same rhetorical trope is deployed in the Affray YJC in the context of the YP's failure to respect his mother and, by extension, the wider Muslim community. In the following exchange, the ECLO has asked the YP to move chairs so that he is now sitting directly opposite his mother:

**Extract 4.20, Affray YJC**

| | |
|---|---|
| **ECLO:** | **Look at your mum,** man. Give – honestly we can sit around and none of – none of – none of us say a word. **Look at your mum.** If you **look at your mum,** man, you understand exactly what every – every – the message is we're trying to tell you is, if you're, you know, this smart, man, when you **look at your mum** you'll understand without us talking what we're trying to say to you. |

Empathy toward the mother's pain is again marshalled with the aim of achieving the reintegrative purposes of the macro-genre. The concentration of evaluative language in relation to mothers means that we will need to return in Chap. 7 to consider the ceremonial power of leveraging the mother as a bonding icon in the service of reintegration.

# 6 Scaffolding Evaluation

The main focus of Chap. 3 and this chapter has been to problematize the notion that asking the YP to tell their story automatically gives them agency and that, from this point, the Convenor can start to sit back and let things take their course. On the contrary, as we have seen, the value of the YP's recount in terms of the integrative discourse of conferencing is very carefully and actively supported. We have noted how the YPs are for the most part very reserved when it comes to self-appraisal of their offending behaviour. However, there are exceptions to this general pattern. To see this, we can return to the youth justice conference broadcast on the Australian Broadcasting Corporation Radio National's Radio Eye programme that we touched on in Chap. 1, but here consider the discourse of the more forthcoming YP in the conference (Davis 2002)[13]:

> Well David and I, we'd skipped school and we were walking around and doing things, just walking around, and we ended up at the house, and we walked in there, the doors were open, we walked in and looked around and there was <u>damage</u> done to the place so we thought it was like ready to be demolished and one thing led to another and we started to kick in the walls and dismantle the place.

This YP reveals his feelings about the offence and its potential impact:

> And at the time I wasn't thinking of what we were doing. I wasn't thinking of how it would affect the other people and the people who owned the place, but once the police had turned up I was <u>shocked</u> to find that we had been caught and that we had to now go through a lot of <u>hassle</u> to work it out and find out what had to be done and it affected my family a lot, because it wasn't something that was <u>expected</u> of me to do, and it wasn't something I <u>expected</u> myself to do either, it just, it had happened, and I wasn't thinking <u>right</u> at the time and I don't know why I done it and, like, I look back now and I wish I had never done it, and it made quite a bit of <u>damage</u>, and it wasn't really a <u>good</u> thing that I done.

Clearly, as the highlighted attitudinal inscriptions this example illustrates, YPs are capable of expressing plenty of feeling in relation to their actions and the consequences of those actions. Nevertheless, it takes a kid with a certain amount of emotional maturity to pitch this performance of remorse correctly. Compare the YP in the previous example to his co-offender, whose recount we considered briefly in Chap. 1:

**Convenor:** And David, what about you, what happened for you on that day?
**YP:** Same sort of thing. We were just walking around, and walked up the path that the house was on and the door was just a bit

open. We went in there. It was all dark and the windows were boarded up and so there was a few holes in the walls. We just started running around the place, punching and kicking holes in the walls … there's one wall that just kept getting <u>damaged</u>. We just seemed to be getting more into it as it went on and then before we knew it the police had arrived out the front. We tried to get out but we couldn't.

**Convenor:** How did you feel then?
**YP:** <u>Scared</u>, <u>worried</u>, what me dad would think and that.
**Convenor:** And when you look back on it now, how do you feel about it?
**YP:** I wish – I wish I just went to school. It's not <u>worth</u> all this <u>trouble</u>.
**Convenor:** Who do you think has been affected by this?
**YP:** Everyone. Everyone here today. I was living with my dad at the time, now I live with mum because of that. Yeah.

For this second offender, as with most of the YPs we observed in conferences, the kind of affective responses that the genre expects require some scaffolding from the Convenor (or perhaps a Liaison Officer), as well as the contributions of Support Persons and other participants (including the Victim, as we saw in the Guide Dog YJC in the previous chapter). If we forget this and start to imagine that asking a YP to 'tell the story of what happened' is a straightforward invitation, then we are playing into some possibly unhelpful assumptions that, to use Bernstein's terminology, are all the more likely due to the way conferencing operates as a kind of invisible pedagogical practice (Bernstein 1975).

We have stressed that the participation of YPs in conferencing is heavily scaffolded by Conveners and other powerful participants, to the point where YPs can find it difficult to comply with expectations regarding both the genre and their identity (which we will explore further in Chap. 6). It is not so easy for YPs to present themselves as forthcoming, sincere and remorseful when they have little control over the genre. That said, we do not mean to suggest that scaffolding is necessarily a bad thing. On the contrary, given that youth justice conferencing is still an emerging macro-genre and a novel, typically one-off experience for most participants (not to mention the low levels of literacy and fluency in English of some YPs), some form of scaffolding is clearly essential. Furthermore, while the regulative discourse in conferencing inscribes hierarchical power relations among participants, this is often paired with close and certainly negotiable relations of solidarity with respect to the values of family, ethnicity, religion or other community affiliations invoked as part of the integrative discourse of conferencing. Indeed, many times in our fieldwork observations, we have been impressed by the sensitivity with which Conveners and, in particular, Indigenous Liaison Officers or ECLOs have steered YPs through the demands of the macro-genre.

It remains a concern for us, however, that there is widespread misrecognition among theorists and advocates of restorative justice of the extent to which regulative discourse drives conferencing. To ignore this is to ignore how relations of power are masked while YPs and other 'lay' participants are loaded up with responsibility for the success of the process. It is also to understate, as various critics have argued in relation to disenfranchised indigenous youth in particular (Daly 2001; Cuneen 2002; Dickson-Gilmore and La Prairie 2005; Blagg 2008), the extent to which the experience an individual has of conferencing will relate to the wider social struggles of communities that are frequently subjected to racial discrimination and aggressive over-policing. While conferencing can be practised in ways that are 'flexible and accommodating toward cultural differences', as Daly (2001: 65) acknowledges, it would be naive to think that the relative informality of conferencing talk could be, in and of itself, sufficient to persuade 'at-risk' YPs from 'targeted' communities, that they can (or would want to) have a voice.

The ability to perform well in this complex macro-genre seems, in many respects, a product of what Bourdieu (1991) would define as 'habitus': the whole gamut of habitual thoughts, actions, and ways of being in the world to which social agents become heavily predisposed through family upbringing, schooling, and other formative life experiences, and which, while not class-determined, are definitely class-related. In the case of YJCs we have observed and documented, it is clear that some YPs are much better equipped to deal with the genre than others. They 'just seem to know' (in other words, they learnt long ago) when to look down, when to look at the person who's talking, how to speak with a deferential tone and, most importantly, how to put across a metanarrative that suggests they've learned from the past. The genre suits them. We don't see these more gifted performers as necessarily insincere, but to argue that such a gift comes naturally is to perpetuate a form of additional 'symbolic violence' (Bourdieu 1991) against those for whom the genre is less straightforward and for whom conferencing has often been most zealously promoted as a less alienating, more rehabilitative framework than formal court proceedings.

One key issue that has been raised in this chapter is the question of preferred genre identities, for the YP and for Support Persons. Obviously negotiating feeling is fundamental as far as performing identity is concerned. To this point we've concentrated on how feeling is negotiated verbally. In the next chapter, we bring another crucial dimension of this negotiation into the picture, namely the body language that works in tandem with verbal recourses as conference participants exchange feeling.

# Notes

1. In these examples, we have underlined elliptical responses that would have made the attitude explicit in non-elliptical form (e.g. *Was Mum angry?* – *Yeah* implying <u>Yeah, she was angry</u>); similarly, an anaphoric reference to feelings is underlined (e.g. <u>*you didn't care*</u> ... is <u>*that*</u> right?).
2. This instance, in fact, explicitly inscribes affect; it describes the YP's emotions or lack thereof. However, on top of this, it also invokes a negative judgement of the YP. That is to say, the fact that the YP didn't care reflects poorly on his behaviour or moral compass.
3. *Disappointed* is coded as judgement here, since the father is construed as feeling sad about something his son has done wrong (*disappoint* is one of a small set of lexical item that inscribes both affect and judgement).
4. *Sorry* and *apologized* are also double-coded for affect and judgement, since these words entail the speaker feeling sad about something they've done wrong. It seems that the victim was prepared to excuse the YP on the basis that the latter received the phone as stolen goods but it was the YP's friend who actually stole the phone.
5. The inscriptions in the analysis tables cover the whole Interpretation stage, not just Extracts 4.4–4.12.
6. Colloquial expression referring to the offer of a one-on-one fight.
7. For documentation of the genocidal 'Stolen Generations' policy by the Human Rights and Equal Opportunity Commission of Australia, see

*Wilkie M. (1997) Bringing them home: Report of the national inquiry into the separation of Aboriginal and Torres Strait Islander children from their families: Human Rights and Equal Opportunity Commission.*

8. For comments on the sprawling realization of evaluation in narrative, see Labov W. (1972) *Language in the inner city: Studies in the Black English vernacular*, US: University of Pennsylvania Press; Labov W. (1982) Speech actions and reactions in personal narrative. *Analyzing discourse: Text and talk*: 219–247; Labov W. (1984) Intensity. In: Schiffrin D. (ed) *Meaning, form, and use in context: Linguistic applications*. Washington, DC: Georgetown University Press, 43–70.
9. In other words, the advantage of a topological perspective is that it allows individual texts to be placed *regionally* according to how prototypically they instantiate one or another genre, thus allowing for the possibility of more and less ideal, or even generic hybrids.
10. The term thematic narrative refers to literary narrative genres symbolizing an underlying message (or 'theme' in the sense of Hasan R. (1985) *Linguistics, Language and Verbal Art*, Geelong: Deakin UP [republished by OUP 1989]; see Martin 1996 for discussion.
11. Reflective recounts have not been included in the story genre typology and topology formalised in this chapter; they are most closely related to personal recounts.
12. We use the term 'coupling' to indicate an association of ideational and evaluative meaning. The role of coupling in proposing social bonds will be discussed in Chap. 5.
13. For more detailed analysis of this conference, see Zappavigna M., Dwyer P. and Martin J.R. (2007) 'Just like sort of guilty kind of': The rhetoric of tempered admission in Youth Justice Conferencing. In: Zappavigna M. and Cloran C. (eds) *Proceedings of Australian Systemic Functional Linguistics Congress*. Woollongong, http://www.asfla.org.au/category/asfla2007/

# References

Ahmed, E., Harris, N., Braithwaite, J., et al. (2001). *Shame management through reintegration*. Cambridge/Oakleigh: Cambridge University Press.

Bernstein, B. (1975). Class and pedagogies: Visible and invisible. *Educational Studies, 1*, 23–41.

Blagg, H. (2008). *Crime, aboriginality and the decolonisation of justice*. Sydney: Hawkins Press.

Bourdieu, P. (1991). *Language and symbolic power*. Cambridge, UK: Polity Press.

Cuneen, C. (2002). Restorative justice and the politics of decolonization. In E. Weitekamp & H. J. Kerner (Eds.), *Restorative justice: Theoretical foundations* (pp. 32–49). Cullompton: Willan Publishing.

Daly, K. (2001). Conferencing in Australia and New Zealand: Variations, research findings, and prospects. In A. Morris & G. Maxwell (Eds.), *Restorative justice for juveniles: Conferencing, mediation and circles* (pp. 59–83). Oxford/Portland: Hart Publishing.

Davis, S. (2002). *"Offending behaviour": Episode four of "crime and punishment"*. Documentary broadcast on the program Radio Eye, Australian Broadcasting Commission.

Dickson-Gilmore, E. J., & La Prairie, C. (2005). *Will the circle be unbroken?: Aboriginal communities, restorative justice, and the challenges of conflict and change*. Toronto: University of Toronto Press.

Eggins, S., & Slade, D. (1997). *Analysing casual conversation*. London/New York: Cassell.

Hasan, R. (1985). *Linguistics, language and verbal art*. Geelong: Deakin University Press. [Republished by Oxford University Press 1989].

Johnson, D. (2002). *Lighting the way: Reconciliation stories*. Sydney: The Federation Press.

Jordens, C. F. (2003). *Reading spoken stories for values: A discursive study of cancer survivors and their professional carers*. [Doctoral dissertation]. Sydney: School of Public Health, Faculty of Medicine, University of Sydney.

Jordens, C. F., & Little, M. (2004). 'In this scenario, I do this, for these reasons': Narrative, genre and ethical reasoning in the clinic. *Social Science & Medicine, 58*, 1635–1645.

Labov, W. (1972). *Language in the inner city: Studies in the Black English vernacular*. Philadelphia: University of Pennsylvania Press.

Labov, W. (1982). Speech actions and reactions in personal narrative. In *Analyzing discourse: Text and talk* (pp. 219–247). Washington, DC: Georgetown University Press.

Labov, W. (1984). Intensity. In D. Schiffrin (Ed.), *Meaning, form, and use in context: Linguistic applications* (pp. 43–70). Washington, DC: Georgetown University Press.

Labov, W., & Waletzky, J. (1967). Narrative analysis: Oral sessions of personal experience. In J. Helm (Ed.), *Essays on the verbal and visual arts* (pp. 12–44). Seattle: University of Washington Press.

Martin, J. R. (1996). Evaluating disruption: Symbolising theme in junior secondary narrative. In *Literacy in society* (pp. 124–171). London: Longman. [Reprinted in Text Analysis 2012. 213-248].

Martin, J. R., & Plum, G. A. (1997). Construing experience: Some story genres. *Journal of Narrative and Life History, 7*, 299–308.

Martin, J. R., & Rose, D. (2008). *Genre relations: Mapping culture*. London: Equinox.

Martin, J. R., & White, P. R. R. (2005). *The language of evaluation: Appraisal in English*. New York: Palgrave Macmillan.

Morgan, S. (1987). *My place*. Fremantle: Fremantle Arts Centre Press.

Muntigl, P. (2004). *Narrative counselling: Social and linguistic processes of change*. Amsterdam/Philadelphia: John Benjamins Pub.

Plum, G. A. (1988). *Text and contextual conditioning in spoken English: A genre approach*. Linguistics, University of Sydney.

Rothery, J. (1994). *Exploring literacy in school English (write it right resources for literacy and learning)*. Sydney: Metropolitan East Disadvantaged Schools Program.

Rothery, J., & Stenglin, M. (1997). Entertaining and instructing: Exploring experience through story. In F. Christie & J. R. Martin (Eds.), *Genre and institutions: Social processes in the workplace and school, Open linguistics series* (pp. 231–263). London: Pinter.

Rothery, J., & Stenglin, M. (2000). Interpreting literature: The role of appraisal. In L. Unsworth (Ed.), *Researching language in schools and communities* (pp. 222–244). London: Cassell.

Russell, E. (2004). *The shack that dad built*. Surry Hills: Little Hare Books.

Wilkie, M. (1997). *Bringing them home: Report of the national inquiry into the separation of aboriginal and Torres Strait islander children from their families*. Sydney: Human Rights and Equal Opportunity Commission.

Zappavigna, M., Dwyer, P., & Martin, J. R. (2007). "Just like sort of guilty kind of": The rhetoric of tempered admission in Youth Justice conferencing. In M. Zappavigna & C. Cloran (Eds.), *Proceedings of Australian systemic functional linguistics Congress*. Woollongong. http://www.asfla.org.au/category/asfla2007/

# 5

# Negotiating Feeling: The Role of Body Language

## 1 Introduction

The previous chapter explored the kinds of feelings that are expressed in a youth justice conference, drawing on the appraisal framework (Martin and White 2005) to interpret the function of evaluative language in different steps of the macro-genre. This chapter extends this analysis to consider how those feelings are negotiated in interactions between conference participants. This means accounting for how feelings become associated with particular ideas in these interactions—i.e. how participants construe different kinds of values as 'couplings' of evaluation and ideation (as evaluations of things). It also means exploring the critical role that body language plays in the way these couplings are negotiated, since sharing or contesting values in the conferences is a multimodal endeavour—it inevitably involves incorporating spoken discourse and other modes of meaning-making in the service of forging, contesting and maintaining social bonds.

The multimodal nature of the performance enacted by the Young Person (YP) is regularly noted in work on conferencing. Non-verbal

© The Author(s) 2018
M. Zappavigna, JR. Martin, *Discourse and Diversionary Justice*,
DOI 10.1007/978-3-319-63763-1_5

meaning, for example, is cited as key to the YP's ability to appear appropriately remorseful for their behaviour:

> A complex sequence of actions, words, body language, and symbolic exchanges occurs in the course of a YP's 'taking responsibility for an offence', 'showing remorse', and wishing to 'repair the harm', and the victim's ability to explain the impact of the offence and to 'read' the YP's sense of contrition and the genuineness of an apology. (Daly 2003: 223)

Important here is the question of how the multimodal repertoire of a YP, conditioned by the demands of the macro-genre and mediated by the interpersonal pressure of the circle configuration of a conference, can construe a suitably remorseful persona. What kind of body language should a 'redeemed' YP persona produce? Equally significant is the related issue of how the YP uses these multimodal resources to create alignments with other participants. We will begin by considering the kinds of social bonds that the YPs construe from a monomodal perspective, looking at the values that unfold in discourse through couplings of ideational and evaluative meanings (in the following section); we then move on to consider the role of body language in relation to how these values are negotiated as social bonds.

## 2 From Feeling to Belonging: The Role of 'Coupling' in Affiliation

Thus far in this book we have considered the language used by participants in conferencing by looking at how participants are positioned within the conferencing macro-genre, and how they use the linguistic resources available to them. This, however, is an incomplete picture if we consider conference interaction from the perspective of social affiliation and attempt to answer the difficult question of how, by expressing feelings, we negotiate values that bind us into different kinds of communities. In order to explore this further we need to consider how values are negotiated in discourse.

## 2 From Feeling to Belonging: The Role of 'Coupling' in Affiliation

Following Knight (2010: 43) we treat the bonds negotiated when personae interact as shared 'couplings' of ideation and attitude (couplings of the 'reference' of what we are saying with its evaluation)—the communion of epistemology with axiology if you will. Knight's theory of affiliation, developed through analysis of conversational humour, describes how communal identities are discursively negotiated in texts as personae rally around, defer or reject different ideation–attitude couplings (Knight 2008, 2010, 2013):

> Specifically, couplings realize bonds of value with experience linguistically, as bonds are on a higher order of abstraction in the socio-cultural context. We discursively negotiate our communal identities through bonds that we can share, and these bonds make up the value sets of our communities and culture, but they are not stable and fixed. (Knight 2010: 43)

For example, consider an extract from the Mobile Phone YJC where the Convenor probes the YP for his reaction to his parents hearing about the offence:

### Extract 5.1, Mobile Phone YJC

| | |
|---|---|
| **Convenor:** | And what did dad say when he got here? |
| **YP:** | He (was) just asking why am I here? And the police told him. |
| **Convenor:** | And was he happy? Did he say anything to you? |
| **YP:** | Don't go anywhere. |
| **Convenor:** | As in when you get home you've got to stay home? Do you think your father was disappointed in you? |
| **YP:** | Yep. |
| | …. |
| **Convenor:** | Do you think you deserved the lecture? Why did you deserve the lecture? |
| **YP:** | Because I did something wrong. |
| | … |
| **Convenor:** | Do you think that mum and dad were disappointed in you? Were you disappointed in yourself? Or Not? Or you don't care? |
| **YP:** | Yeah. |
| **Convenor:** | Yeah or you don't care? |
| **YP:** | Disappointed in myself. |

In this extract, the Convenor puts forward for negotiation three couplings by asking (i) whether the YP's father was happy when he arrived at the police station, (ii) whether he was disappointed in the YP and (iii) whether the YP's mother and father together were disappointed in him. She also instigates the proposal of two couplings by the YP—namely that he did something wrong and that he is disappointed in himself. In all, five potential bonds are proposed (couplings of ideation and attitude are presented in square brackets, with the trigger or target of the attitude before the slash and the attitude after):

| | |
|---|---|
| Convenor asks | [ideation: *father*/attitude: *happy*] |
| Convenor asks | [ideation: *father*/attitude: *disappointed*] |
| YP proposes | [ideation: *Young Person*/attitude: *wrong*] |
| Convenor asks | [ideation: *Mum & Dad*/attitude: *disappointed*] |
| YP proposes | [ideation: *Young Person*/attitude: *disappointed*] |

Each of these couplings of ideation and attitude is negotiated as shared feelings in this text, and so, in Knight's (2010) terms, they enact social bonds. As mentioned earlier, these bonds are negotiated not just through spoken language but also through the body language used by the conference participants. Thus, in order to explore the role of postural and gestural semiosis in negotiating the bonds associated with the kinds of coupling that we have introduced, it is first necessary to outline the Systemic Functional Linguistics (SFL) model of body language in which our work is grounded.

## 3 A Metafunctionally Organized Model of Body Language

During our preliminary field observations of Convenor-training workshops, the important role of body language in conferencing was noted by both trainers and practitioners. Prominent in this training were animated discussions about the interpretability of 'body language', advice about seating arrangements and dress choices, anecdotal wisdom about the

## 3  A Metafunctionally Organized Model of Body Language

emotional dynamics of an ideal-typical conference and other performance-related behaviours. Apart from an early article by Retzinger and Scheff (1996) which notes the importance of facial expression, gestures and physical posture in conferencing for the communication of emotions and negotiation of social bonds, there is little in the youth justice conferencing research literature which matches up specifically to these conference Convenor concerns.

We undertake the analysis of body language presented here not only because the meanings negotiated in a conference cannot be fully interpreted on the basis of one modality alone, but because body language gives us an important insight into the bonding process flagged by Knight (2010). The model of body language that we have used in this study arose out of previous work investigating the co-patterning of gesture and phonological structure, viewed as sibling systems on language's expression plane (Zappavigna et al. 2009). Analysis of body language is a new region in SFL-based multimodal discourse analysis, although it is relatively well established in other disciplines such as anthropology and cognitive science (Efron 1941; Morris 1979; McNeill 1992; Goldin-Meadow and Singer 2003; Kendon 2004). SFL-oriented work has included exploration of gesture realizing experiential process types and interpersonal meaning (Martinec 2000, 2001), an article on face-to-face teaching in classrooms (Hood 2011) and a case study of the nonverbal communication of a child with an intellectual disability (Dreyfus 2011). These perspectives arise out of Halliday's (1985) initial framing of gesture as paralinguistic—as a resource functioning to support language systems. Gestures are, in Halliday's model, 'not part of the grammar, but rather additional variations by which the speaker *signals the import* of what he is saying' (Halliday 1985: 30). As a mode of expression, gesture has a prosodic structure which we might think of as akin to an intonation contour because of its tendency to range over a number of grammatical units.

Our model of body language shares with Kendon (2004: 125) the notion that gesture is 'fully integrated' into the expression of meaning as an 'ensemble' and as 'a partner with speech in the utterance as finally constructed' (Kendon 2004: 111). Cléirigh (2011) further specifies this partnership by factoring body language as three distinct semiotic systems: *protolanguage*, *language* and *epilanguage*. In brief, as a protolinguistic system, body language sustains the kinds of meanings a small child can make with infant protolanguage (Painter 1998; Halliday 1977); as a linguistic system it functions in sync with, and as a reinforcement of, speech rhythm and intonation; and as an epilinguistic system it works to illustrate verbal meanings (drawing in the air as it were). Each of these systems of body language is introduced in more detail below, beginning with linguistic body language and then moving on to the epilinguistic and protolinguistic systems.

In exploring intermodal co-patterning of this kind we used ELAN (Max Planck Institute for Psycholinguistics, 2008), a software tool that allowed us to track multiple data series while concurrently tracking the time series of the video text. These data series took the form of different 'annotation tiers'. For example, the layers shown at the bottom of Fig. 5.1 correspond to a number of types of annotation (e.g. tone groups) that were applied to the video shown in the upper left side of the screen. The analysis also appears on the transcript shown to the right of the image.

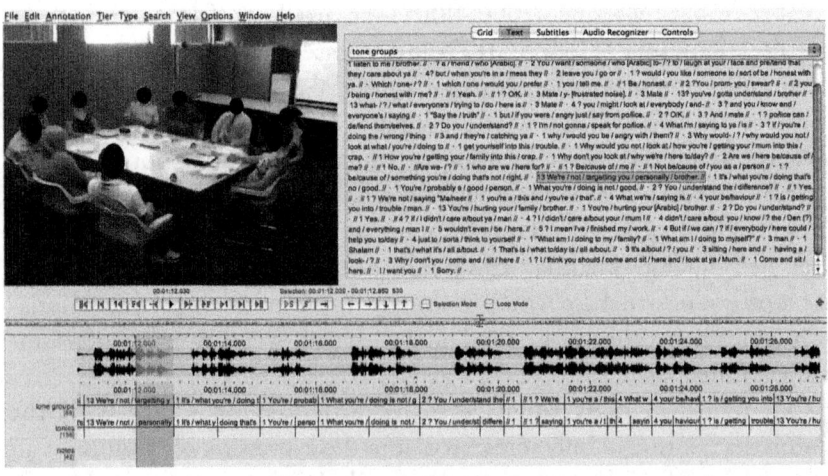

**Fig. 5.1** An example of tone group analysis performed using ELAN

Below this can be seen the waveform of the audio track and the time series. The ability to link the properties of the audio track and the video track with the time series in relation to the various annotation tiers meant that we had a powerful tool for doing intermodal analysis. We were able to consider how posture, gesture and speech all worked together in an interaction, as we will see in the examples of body language analysis shown later in this chapter.

# 4 Linguistic Body Language

As a *linguistic* system, body language works in tandem with language. For example, it is produced (relatively) synchronously with the rhythm of the spoken language or in tune with its major pitch movement. As Table 5.1 specifies, the meanings realized may be textual or interpersonal, but they are not ideational.

The Ethnic Community Liaison Officer (ECLO) in the Affray YJC produced many examples of linguistic body language used to realize salience. For example, he devoted a large amount of semiotic energy to emphasize his message in an attempt to hold the YP's attention so as to influence his behaviour. In so doing, he made use of different beat-

Table 5.1 Linguistic body language (Cléirigh 2011)

|  | Lexicogrammatical systems | Prosodic expression | |
| --- | --- | --- | --- |
|  |  | Phonology | Kinetic |
| **Textual** | Potential focus of new information | Salience | Gestural beat (*hand*, *head*) in *sync* with the speech rhythm |
|  | Focus of new information | Tonicity | Gestural beat (*hand*, *head*) in *sync* with the tonic placement |
|  | Information distribution | Tonality | Gestural beat (*hand*, *head*) *co-extensive* with tone group |
| **Interpersonal** | Key | Tone | Gestural beat (*eyebrow*, *hand*) in *tune* with the tone choice |

ing gestures where we he would repetitively beat one part or another of his body (e.g. his hand), either in the air, against his body or on the tabletop, increasing the frequency of the beat on salient syllables in his talk. This kind of body language often occurred at moments when he was attempting to emphasize the reintegrative aim of the conference to the YP:

**Extract 5.2, School Library YJC**

**ECLO:** If I didn't care about you, man, I didn't care about your mum, I didn't care about, you know, the Den and everything, I wouldn't even be here. I mean, I've finished my work. But if we – if everyone here today could help you just to sort of think to yourself, 'What am I doing to my family? What am I doing to myself?', man, Salaam. That's what it's all about. That's what today is all about. It's about you sitting down and having a look –

When the ECLO calls attention to the function of the conference in his verbiage, saying '*That's what today is all about*', he raises the frequency with which he beats his clasped hand (shown in the second bottom row of Table 5.2). This gesture involves clasping his hands together and beating the chest on salient syllables, with a beat afforded to the tonic segment (the unit of rhythm featuring the main pitch movement in a tone group) realizing the culmination of 'new' information (Halliday and Greaves 2008).

Increasing salience by using linguistic body language can also function to increase the intensity of evaluations (graduation in Martin and White 2005)) that the ECLO makes about the YP's behaviour. Again, increased frequency of a beating gesture supported the increase in salience. By beating on (interpersonal) evaluative meanings, and thus giving them (textual) salience, the gestures also served to upscale those attitudes in terms of graduation. For example, the ECLO says '*Your behavior is getting you into trouble, man*', while adopting an arched hand position with fingers fanned and beating his fingers on the table in front of him (Table 5.3). The beats fall on 'get-' and every subsequent syllable in the tone group, highlighting the negative JUDGEMENT.

## 4 Linguistic Body Language   207

**Table 5.2** Increased salience realized as increased frequency of gestural beats[a]

| Tone type | | | Tone 1 | | | | |
|---|---|---|---|---|---|---|---|
| Tone group | *Pretonic segment* | | | | | *Tonic segment* | |
| Feet | that's is | what to | day is | all a | **bout** | | |
| Gesture | Clasp beats towards chest on salient syllable, with extra beat on 'a(bout)' | | | | | | |
| Gestural beats | ◇ | ◇ | ◇ | ◇ | ◇ ◇ | | |

[a]The diamonds in the bottom row of the tables represent gestural beats

**Table 5.3** Increased salience scaling up evaluation[a]

| Tone type | Tone 1 | | |
|---|---|---|---|
| Tone group | *Pretonic segment* | *Tonic segment* | |
| Feet | ^ is | getting you into | **trouble** man |
| Gesture | Finger-fanned right hand arches right beating the desk on salient 'get-' and beats on every following syllable | | |
| Gestural beats | ◇ ◇ ◇ ◇ ◇ | ◇ ◇ | ◇ |

[a]The caret (^) in the rhythm analysis (feet row in tables) signifies a silent beat at the beginning of a foot

## 5 Epilinguistic Body Language

As *epilanguage*, body language realizes textual, interpersonal and ideational meaning (Table 5.4). Epilinguistic body language includes gestures such as those that involve drawing in the air. In the absence of speech, these epilinguistic gestures are thought of as mime.

An example of epilinguistic body language that contributes to the realization of meaning iconically (Martinec 2000) is the reference that the ECLO in the Affray YJC makes to police during the Interpretation in Extract 5.3.

**Extract 5.3, Affray YJC**

ECLO: And, mate, police can defend themselves. Do you understand? I'm not going to speak for police.

In this instance, the ECLO slaps one hand on another when he talks of police being able to 'defend' themselves, a gesture iconic to the action of fending off an attacker (Table 5.5).

Table 5.4 Epilinguistic body language (Cléirigh 2011)[a]

|   | Meaning | Kinetic Expression |
|---|---|---|
| Ideational | PHENOMENA: elemental (and configurational) | Drawing shapes; mimicking movements with hands |
| Textual | E.g. IDENTIFICATION: exophoric vs endophoric; personal vs demonstrative (near speaker, near addressee, near both, near neither) | Pointing with hands, eyes, head: (exophoric: pointing to material and semiotic phenomena in the field of perception; endophoric: pointing to regions of gesturing space) |
| Interpersonal | E.g. MODALITY; POLARITY | E.g. oscillating hand (MODALITY); nodding head (POLARITY) |

[a]For explanation of the technical SFL terms in this table, see Halliday and Mattheissen (2014), Martin and Rose (2003/2007)

## 5 Epilinguistic Body Language

Table 5.5 Gesture representing a process

| Tone type | | Tone 1 | |
|---|---|---|---|
| Tone group | Pretonic segment | | Tonic segment |
| Feet | ^ po      lice can de | fend them | **selves** |
| | Left hand moves left on 'police', then claps right hand on 'defend' into clasp | | |
| Gestural beat | | | |

Another example of epilinguistic body language in this conference involves gesture used to realize deixis, identifying persons in the exchange (cf. Kendon 2004) on deictic gestures). For instance, when the ECLO says the following (Extract 5.4), he identifies two types of participants with pointing gestures: the people seated around the table and the YP.

**Extract 5.4, School Library YJC**

**ECLO:** But if we – if everyone here today could help you just to sorta think to yourself, 'What am I doing to my family? What am I doing to myself?', man, Salaam. That's what it's all about. That's what today is all about. It's about you sitting down and having a look –

He also makes a circular gesture to refer to everyone at the table and points at the YP to identify him (Table 5.6). His gestural expression thus varies with the meaning being distinguished: circular for plural 1st person 'we all', pointed for singular 2nd person 'you'. He also couples the Deictic 'here' with a downward pointing gesture.

## 5 Negotiating Feeling: The Role of Body Language

Table 5.6 Gesture realizing deixis

| Tone type | | Tone 4 | | |
|---|---|---|---|---|
| Tone group | *Pretonic segment* | | | *Tonic segment* |
| Feet | but if we can ^ if | everybody | here could | **help** you to | day |
| Gesture | | Right hand moves out and left and around table for 'everybody' (simultaneously mimicked by head swivel) | Points down at table for 'here' | and points to YP for 'you' (personal reference) | reclasping at 'today' |
| Gestural beat | | | | | |

## 6  Protolinguistic Body Language

As a *protolinguistic* system, body language develops in individuals out of infant protolanguage with its kinological expression organized microfunctionally. Cléirigh (2011), following Halliday (1975), defines protolinguistic body language as follows:

> 'Protolinguistic' body language systems are those 'left behind' in the transition to the mother tongue (i.e. not incorporated into language), but nevertheless expanded from the pre-linguistic systems and contextually different, since it is not used instead of language by non-language users, but can be deployed by language users with or without speech. Whereas prosodic and mimetic body language are used with speech, and their meanings are those of language, protolinguistic body language occurs with both speech or silence, and their meanings are not those of language, but protolanguage. (Cléirigh 2011: 6)

Cléirigh's (2011) model draws directly upon Halliday's (1975) analysis of the microfunctions that emerge during the protolinguistic phase of language development (). In infant protolanguage, meaning making is microfunctional (since it is a simple system of signs, with no combinatorial potential), rather than metafunctional (and so involving the complementary ideational, interpersonal and textual dimensions of the adult language). There are four possible microfunctions which may be expressed in the body language of a speaker who has developed language:

- The **regulatory** ('do as I tell you'), e.g. a mother raising her finger at her child while giving an instruction
- The **interactional** ('me and you'), e.g. a mother and child looking lovingly at one another
- The **instrumental** ('I want'), e.g. a friend extending their hand toward you so that you pass something to them
- The **personal** ('here I come'), e.g. a friend sobbing while telling you something negative that has happened to them

Halliday groups the meanings that can be made with these microfunctions according to whether they involve an active or reflective mode of consciousness, as shown in Table 5.7.

**Table 5.7** Protolinguistic body language (Cléirigh 2011)

|  |  | Meaning | Kinetic expression |
|---|---|---|---|
| Action | Regulatory | I want, refuse, threaten | E.g. raised fist, glower |
|  | Instrumental | Give me, I invite you | E.g. extended hand |
| Reflection | Personal | Emotions | E.g. smiling face |
|  | Interactional | Togetherness, bonding | E.g. mutual eye gaze |

Taking note of protolinguistic body language is crucial for understanding the multimodal meaning being made in an interaction. For example, the YP in the Mobile Phone YJC mainly offered monosyllabic responses to the Convenor's questions; based on a transcript of the verbiage alone, this gives an impression of a YP who is not engaging with the process. However, if we inspect his body language, we see that he maintains mutual eye gaze with the Convenor throughout her Extension of his recount, indicating that he is indeed paying attention.

We have introduced the three semiotic systems of body language separately (for explanatory purposes); however, it is important to note that they work in tandem with one another in real discourse. For example, consider a teacher in a classroom leaning forward (protolinguistic body language), pointing at three students (epilinguistic body language: textual deictic) while saying 'you and you and you, outside now!', tapping the air with her index finger each time she says 'you' (linguistic body language). The teacher enacts this protolinguistic, epilinguistic and linguistic semiosis with her body as a single performance, together with the meanings made in her spoken discourse. From the perspective of the language user, the performance is seamless, but by modelling the body language as three distinct systems we can see the different strands of meaning at play.

## 7 Body Language and the Small Target Young Person Identity

As noted throughout this volume, the YPs in our sample tend to adopt what can be thought of as a 'small target' persona, attempting to minimize the extent to which they come under negative scrutiny in the commissioned recount. They correspondingly adopt postures that support

# 7 Body Language and the Small Target Young Person Identity

**Fig. 5.2** YP body language during the commissioned recount, Mobile Phone YJC

this kind of identity: slouching inwards in their chairs (Fig. 5.2) or with hands in their laps or arms crossed (Fig. 5.3). Some YPs sit with their ankles crossed and legs extending into the circle (Figs. 5.3 and 5.4).

The YP in the Mobile Phone YJC is an example of a YP who maintains this kind of small target identity throughout the conference. During all exchanges with the Convenor during the commissioned recount he remains a compliant subject, responding to the Convenor's Dk1 moves with short responses that sometimes consist simply of epilinguistic interpersonal body language such as shaking or nodding his head. Throughout the Extension and Interpretation stages of this genre he maintains frequent eye contact with the Convenor, always looking at her directly when he responds. The following exchange is an example of this pattern (the body language analysis shown in Table 5.8):

### Extract 5.5, Mobile Phone YJC

**Convenor:** Do you think your father was disappointed in you?
**YP:** Yep.

## 214   5 Negotiating Feeling: The Role of Body Language

**Fig. 5.3** YP body language during the commissioned recount, Guide Dog YJC

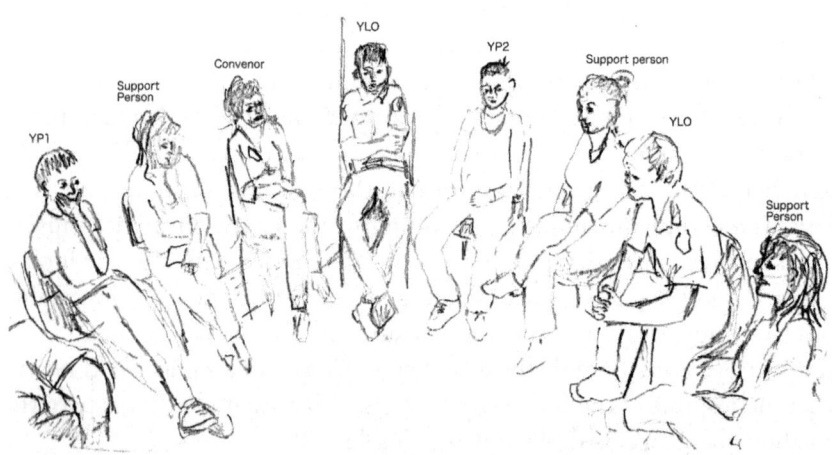

**Fig. 5.4** YP body language during the commissioned recount, School Library YJC

**Table 5.8** YP's body language during the commissioned recount, Mobile Phone YJC—'Do you think your father was disappointed in you?'

| Body language system | Description | Screen capture |
|---|---|---|
| Protolinguistic | eye contact while answering, hands clasped in lap, shoulders slightly slouched | |
| Epilinguistic interpersonal | nods | |

This exchange centres on negotiation of the following coupling:

[ideation: *father*/attitude: *affect* + *judgement* (hybrid[1])]

The YP compliantly accepts the bond proposed by the Convenor through this coupling, which was designed to prompt the YP to evaluate his behaviour.

# 8 The Role of Body Language in Negotiating Coupling: A 'Bond by Bond' Analysis

Thus far we have introduced the notion that body language plays a role in supporting the types of interaction we have seen in conferences and have suggested a metafunctional model of body language that can be used to illuminate the role it plays in negotiating feelings in these interactions. We will now attempt to work 'bond by bond' through a particular interaction in a conference by way of illustrating how this type of analysis explains how body language functions in the exchanges.

By way of contrast to the small target persona considered briefly (which we will return to in Chap. 6 in further discussion of identity), the School Library YJC is an interesting conference in our sample because it involved two YPs who did not take up this typical identity, and who were instead quite resistant to the readings of their behaviour promoted by the Convenor and Youth Liaison Officers in the conference. The body language of these YPs supported this resistance. This section will explore the role this body language plays as these Young Offenders propose various controversial bonds to the other participants, resulting in the YLO intervening with his description of the boys as 'fluffed-up roosters'.

We will begin this analysis at the beginning of a phase of a School Library YJC where one of the YPs (YP1) rejects the label that he imagines the Convenor has ascribed to him—namely that he is a rat from Bridgeton. Indeed, the two YPs in this conference resist many of the comments made about them. For example, consider their reaction to the Convenor's comment that the offence has had a negative impact on the Victim.

**Extract 5.6, School Library YJC**

| | |
|---|---|
| **Convenor:** | It's affected his life. |
| **YP1:** | Yeah I know it has. That's what I am saying. It's changed a lot. I – I do realize what we've done== |
| **Convenor:** | ==Well the snickering and the smiling doesn't make me think that== |
| **YP1:** | ==(…) Yeah well I'm not a rat from Bridgeton. |
| **Convenor:** | W – I know that. |
| **YP1:** | I'm not one of those friggin' retarded people that just say 'oh yeah I done that. I w – I'll do it again'. (…) I'll do everything that I can to change everything that's happened. Seriously. Walk the streets, mate. Go have fun. Go get drunk. Do whatever. Party on. (…) |

It is the body language of YP1 here that the Convenor flags as transgressive conference behaviour when she comments on his smiling and snickering. The smirking demonstrates to her that YP1 has not been taking the discourse of the Victim seriously and that body language of this kind is undermining the redressive power of the conference macro-genre.

The YP1's reply to the Convenor, 'Yeah I know it has. ... I do realize what we've done', with contradictory stress on *do* (phonologically//1 ^ /**do**/realize/what we've/done//), is the first verbal move in this conference where the 'angry boy' persona clearly emerges. The full impact of this shift in the conference discourse can only be appreciated by looking beyond the verbal transcript alone. Here we see this YP leaning forward, engaged in the circle, but relatively self-contained with his hands clasped and his feet crossed; he does not make eye contact with the Convenor until the end of his turn, when he looks up to his left at her to check on the impact of his rebuttal (Table 5.9).

YP1 then looks away again, protesting that he is not a 'retarded' person; this coupling of ideation and attitude is supported by linguistic body language (falling gesture with right arm on *retarded*). Epilinguistically the key feature during this gesture is the palms-down prone position of his hands (see screen capture in Table 5.10). Following Hood (2011) we interpret this gesture, in terms of appraisal theory (Martin and White's 2005) ENGAGEMENT system in particular), as contracting the dialogic space as YP1 further dismisses the Convenor's accusation.

Table 5.9 YP1's body language—'I'm not a rat from Bridgeton'

| Body language system | Description | Screen capture |
|---|---|---|
| Protolinguistic | no eye contact while speaking, leaning forward, hands clasped, feet crossed; eye contact with Convenor at end of turn | |

Table 5.10 YP1's body language—'I'm not one of those friggin' retarded people'

| Body language system | Description | Screen capture |
| --- | --- | --- |
| Protolinguistic | no eye contact while speaking, leaning forward, feet crossed, hands clasped (except for gesture); eye contact with Convenor at end of turn | |
| Linguistic interpersonal | right arm rises and falls in tune with tone (tone 1 high falling) | |
| Linguistic textual | right arm falls in sync with major pitch movement (tonic syllable re*tar*ded) | |
| Epilinguistic interpersonal | palm down prone hand during linguistic gesture | |

Table 5.11 YP1's body language—'I'll do everything that I can to…'

| Body language system | Description |
| --- | --- |
| Protolinguistic | No eye contact, leaning forward, feet crossed, hands clasped (except for gestures); eye contact with Victim at end of turn |
| Linguistic textual | Raises arms, opens hands for four of his five tone groups |
| Epilinguistic interpersonal | Palm-up supine hand position during linguistic gestures |

[ideation:   *YP1*/attitude: *not retarded*]
**YP1:**   I'm not one of those friggin' retarded people…

The main shifts in body language as YP1 continues his rejection of the charge of insincerity is to raise one or both arms with hands in supine palms-up position. This supine hand position contrasts to the prone palms-down position in terms of how it interplays with engagement in the verbiage. Supine hands tend to support a meaning of 'opening-up' the conversational space to include other voices, while prone hands tend to 'close off' other positions (Hood 2011) (Table 5.11). He does this in support of four of his five tone groups in the corresponding spoken discourse, as he quotes what a 'friggin' retarded' person might say and pro-

# 8 The Role of Body Language in Negotiating Coupling: A 'Bond... 219

poses how he will otherwise behave. This expands the play of voices in the conference—YP1's voice among others. Of interest here as far as sincerity is concerned is the reaction of the Victim's mother, who holds her face in her hands, shaking her head in disbelief.

**Extract 5.7, School Library YJC**

YP1:   … that just say 'oh yeah I done that. I w – I'll do it again'. … I'll do everything that I can to change everything that's happened. Seriously.

YP1 then proposes a bond to his Victim, assuring him that he has nothing more to fear when he goes out and possibly 'parties on'. The offer of security is welcome in the YJC macro-genre, but the categorization of the Victim as someone (presumably like YP1 and YP2) who likes to go out, have fun, get drunk and party on is a generically inappropriate construal (and acknowledged as such through YP1's half smile and full smiles from his sister and YP2). The 'party boy/no worries' coupling at stake here is parleyed protolinguistically through eye contact with the Victim as YP1 continues to lean forward (Table 5.12). Epilinguistically, YP1 uses hand motions to mime a heading-off movement illustrating 'Walk the streets, mate'. He culminates this turn with open palm-supine hand gestures both before and after 'Party on', nodding in reinforcement of his offer. These supine gestures appear to function to support a meaning of 'offering' the coupling for negotiation in the interaction.

[ideation:   *Victim partying*/attitude: *secure*][2]
YP1:   Walk the streets, mate. Go have fun. Go get drunk. Do whatever. Party on. (…)

YP1's transgressive categorization of his Victim as a party boy in fact precipitates an arguably intemperate intervention by the Youth Liaison Officer (YLO), who denigrates YP1 and YP2 as barnyard roosters, lording over their flock. The YLO uses eye contact and a deictic hand gesture to address both YP1 and YP2. He supports 'No one's going to stop me' with two downward beats of his right arm, and most significantly, mimes

**Table 5.12** YP1's body language—'Walk the streets, mate'

| Body language system | Description | Screen capture |
|---|---|---|
| Protolinguistic | eye contact with Victim, leaning forward, feet crossed, hands clasped (except for epilinguistic gestures); half-smile after 'party on' | |
| Linguistic textual | motion gesture in sync with 'walk the streets'; nodding in rhythm with 'party on' | |
| Epilinguistic ideational | right arm gesture miming moving with 'walk the streets' | |
| Epilinguistic interpersonal | nodding in affirmation of 'party on' offer; supine hands gesture before and after 'party on' | |

## 8 The Role of Body Language in Negotiating Coupling: A 'Bond...

**Table 5.13** YLO's body language—'See you two guys are a bit like the old farmyard rooster'

| Body language system | Description | Screen capture |
|---|---|---|
| Protolinguistic | eye contact with YP1 (initial and final glance at YP2), leaning forward, arm muscle tension | |
| Linguistic interpersonal | falling right arm in tune with tone 1 //no one's /going to /**stop** me// | |
| Linguistic textual | bouncing fluffing gesture in sync the rhythm (x3); right arm beats in sync with 'stop me' | |
| Epilinguistic ideational | arm motion/position miming fluffed up rooster, clenched fist | |

the fluffed-up rooster three times (while saying 'all fluffed up', 'all fluffed up' and 'I'm here') (Table 5.13).

[ideation: YP1 & YP2 *barge through*/attitude: arrogant pride (hubris)]
**YLO:** See you two guys are a bit like the old farmyard rooster.
**YP1:** The what?
**YLO:** All farmyard roosters are all fluffed up and want to impress people. So you go into the school grounds all fluffed up ready to go and then you want to impress people so you barge through and just 'I'm here. I'm here to do what I like. No one's going to stop me'==
**YP1:** ==No.
**YP2:** ==(…) [shakes head then folds arms]

YP1 verbally rejects this coupling proposed by the YLO, and YP2 refuses to bond by withdrawing eye contact, shaking his head folding his arms and leaning back (Table 5.14).

YP1 doesn't simply withdraw in exasperation from the bond proposed but mocks it, flippantly imitating the YLO's rooster mime. He can also be seen to laugh snidely under his breath at the YLO (Table 5.15). This is an insolent challenge to the YLO's authority, with both YP1 and the YLO now interacting well outside the normal bounds of the conferencing genre.

**Table 5.14** YP2's body language—rejecting YLO's bond

| Body language system | Description |
|---|---|
| Protolinguistic | No eye contact, leaning back, shakes head |
| Epilinguistic interpersonal | Folds arms |

**Table 5.15** YP1's body language—imitating YLO's 'fluffed-up rooster' gesture

| Body language system | Description | Screen capture |
|---|---|---|
| Protolinguistic | feet crossed, eye contact, leaning forward, open mouth, shaking head, laughs snidely; then looks away and down | |
| Epilinguistic ideational | arms mimic YLO's miming of fluffed up rooster; shakes head | |

As the YLO continues, YP1 makes three embodied moves (Table 5.16). To begin he disengages protolinguistically, lowering his gaze to the floor, leaning back and scratching the back of his head with his left arm. He then resumes eye contact, re-crosses his feet and half-smiles; epilinguistically he places his left hand on his chin, as if considering the YLO's charge. Finally, he disengages again, with a full smile and slight laugh, interrupting his epilinguistic gesture as he scratches his left cheek. The YLO continues:

**Extract 5.8, School Library YJC**

YLO:    … and then you want to impress people so you barge through and just 'I'm here. I'm here to do what I like. No one's going to stop me'.

Matters soon get worse as YP1's sister breaks down, tearing up while attempting to defend him from the fluffed-up rooster charge and has to

# 8 The Role of Body Language in Negotiating Coupling: A 'Bond...

**Table 5.16** YP1's body language in response to YLO

| Body language system | Description | Screen capture |
|---|---|---|
| Protolinguistic | [1] eye contact, feet re-crossing, half smile<br>[2] no eye contact, gaze to floor, feet uncrossing leans back, scratching back of head with left arm<br>[3] no eye contact, gaze to floor feet crossed full smile slight laugh | [1]   [2]   [3] |
| Epilinguistic ideational | [1] hand on chin (as if reflecting)<br>[2] -<br>[3] hand scratches cheek (dissolving reflection) | |

leave the conference. YP1 accuses the YLO of having engineered his sister's collapse and of enjoying the result, affirming his proposal by nodding his head up and down (Table 5.17).

| [ideation: | YLO/attitude: *happy*] |
|---|---|
| **YP1:** | Happy now? |
| **YLO:** | Pardon? |
| **YP1:** | Happy now? |

Rejecting this bond the YLO replies that people have different sides to them, with the implication that while YP1's sister might see one persona, his behaviour with his mates is another story. Both YPs withdraw protolinguistically from this accusation. YP2 has his arms and feet crossed, slouching back, with his gaze to the ceiling and then down to the floor; YP1 meanwhile lowers his head and slumps forward (Table 5.18).

## 5 Negotiating Feeling: The Role of Body Language

**Table 5.17** YP1's body language—'Happy now?'

| Body language system | Description | Screen capture |
|---|---|---|
| Protolinguistic | leans forward in direction of YLO, uncrossed feet, eye contact with YLO, eyes wide | |
| Linguistic textual | head nod in sync with rhythm | |
| Epilinguistic interpersonal | nodding head | |

**Table 5.18** YP1's & YP2's body language—rejecting YLO's bond

| Body language system | Description | Screen capture |
|---|---|---|
| Protolinguistic | YP2 arms/feet crossed, slouching back, gaze to ceiling then down to floor; YP1 leaning forward, eye contact then head down, slumping forward | |
| Epilinguistic interpersonal | YP1 supine hands before slumping forward | |

[ideation:   YP1 & YP2 *behavior in family*/attitude: not arrogant pride (hubris)]

[ideation:   YP1 & YP2 *behavior with mates*/attitude: arrogant pride (hubris)]

## 8 The Role of Body Language in Negotiating Coupling: A 'Bond... 225

YLO: Mate, I've been doing the job for 22 years and there's people that have different sides to them. There's the side you portray to your family, there's the side you portray by yourself, and then when you get together as a group, there's another side that comes out again.

YP2 sarcastically repeats the YLO's accusation (*a fluffed-up rooster*) and rejects that bond by proposing another one appreciating it as wrong (*a bad way to describe me*).

[[ideation: YP2/attitude: *arrogant pride (hubris)*]/attitude: *incorrect*]]
**YP2**: A fluffed-up rooster.
<<…>> **YP2**: A bad way to describe me.

YP1's reaction overlaps YP2's, as he accuses the YLO himself of being the fluffed-up rooster—leaning back again and pointing at the YLO with his index finger as he does so (Table 5.19). YP1's bent arm as he points and the fact that he tilts his head left to peek around his accusing finger gesturally mitigates the coupling by indicating its irreverence.

[ideation: YLO behavior/attitude: *arrogant pride (hubris)*]
**YP1**: ==Yeah. Maybe you're the fluffed-up rooster. (…)

Table 5.19 YP1's body language—accusing YLO

| Body language system | Description | Screen capture |
|---|---|---|
| Protolinguistic | leaning back, eye contact with YLO, tilted head looking round hand | |
| Epilinguistic interpersonal | bent arm for pointing gesture | |
| Epilinguistic textual | pointing at YLO with index finger | |

This degree of disrespect for authority is unique in our corpus, and has no doubt been afforded in part by the YLO himself stepping out of line. The YLO attempts to recover from this by commenting metalinguistically on what is going on, suggesting that he was not intending to insult the YPs by proposing the fluffed-up rooster bond, but simply drawing an analogy. In relation to this bond, YP2 contradicts the YLO verbally ('You slinged one') while YP1 slouches back, with his hand on his chin as he skeptically considers the retort and replies sarcastically 'Yeah. I see. I see, mate' (Table 5.20).

**Table 5.20** YLO's & YP1's body language—'Well, we're not here to sling comments at you'

| Body language system | Description | Screen capture |
|---|---|---|
| Protolinguistic | YLO leans forward with elbows resting on knees, eye contact with YP1<br>YP1 slouching back, feet crossed | |
| Linguistic<br>Epilinguistic ideational<br>Epilinguistic interpersonal | YP1 nodding in sync with YLO<br>YP1 hand on chin (as if reflecting)<br>YLO hands supine<br>YP1 nodding | |

| | |
|---|---|
| [ideation: | *YP1 & YP2* /attitude: *not bad*] |
| YLO: | Well, we're not here to sling comments at you. |
| YP2: | You slinged one.== |
| YP1: | ==(...) |
| YLO: | It was an analogy – an analogy I drew – that's all – to try and portray what it looks like. |
| YP1: | Yeah. I see. I see, mate. |

In this section, we have highlighted the important role body language plays in negotiating couplings of ideation and attitude as bonds. We now turn to the question of bonds and communities.

# 9  Belonging and Community

As flagged in Sect. 2, our interest with the ways in which couplings of attitude and ideation are negotiated as bonds is based on Knight's (2008, 2010, 2013) concern with the ways in which bonds enact membership in one or another community. In order to explore this perspective on belonging further, we need to consider what we mean by community. Our work here draws upon Tann's (2010b) research into identity and membership categorization (to which we will return in Chap. 7 in order to explore the ceremonial dimensions of the re-affiliation practices suggested here). Tann (2010a, 2013) borrows the concept of 'Gemeinschaft' from the sociologist Ferdinand Tönnies who used it to refer to the kinds of social associations, based on common geography and values, that form in religious and kinship communities. Figure 5.5 shows the three kinds of Gemeinschaft that contribute to construing a 'sense of belonging' proposed by Tann (2010b, p. 81): Categorization (classifying a persona as being of a particular type, e.g. Muslim, Indigenous, feminist, disabled, middle-class, generation X, etc.); Collectivization (setting up an opposition between a particular collectivity and an imagined or real other, e.g. Australians vs refugees, loggers vs greenies, straight vs LGBT, etc.); and Spatialization (classifying a type of persona based on place, e.g. Westies, Yankees, Newfies, Kiwis, etc.). Each type of Gemeinschaft is exemplified from our data.

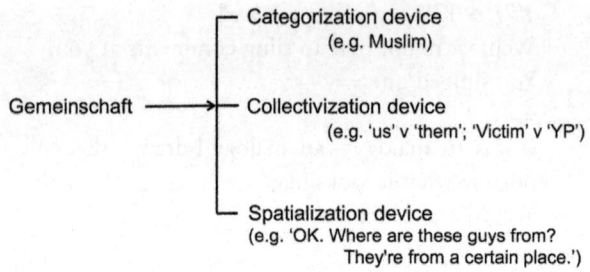

**Fig. 5.5** Three kinds of Gemeinschaft (Adapted from Tann 2010b: 96)

In the conferences, potential fellowships for the YP are named, and the YP is instructed to move from one classification to another. As we will see in the following examples, categorization and spatialization work to identify this shift in classification that the YP is required to make (from a transgressive to a reintegrated persona). Whereas categorization and spatialization identify types of persona, collectivization discourse on the other hand interpersonally enacts the memberships required by the macro-genre and is frequently used by the Liaison Officers. The most frequently used collectivizing discourse that we will explore in this section is the Liaison Officers' use of vocatives (e.g. *mate, man, brother*), which are interpersonally inclusive rather than ideationally categorizing and call upon the YP to adopt a particular membership.

Tann's concept of categorization was inspired by Membership Categorization Analysis (MCA) (Schegloff 2007) and Sack's concept of 'membership categorization devices', which holds that categories exist as collections that consist of sets of corresponding roles (mother/child; man/woman, etc.) as part of a particular society's resources for interpreting talk (see e.g. Schegloff 2006; Sacks 1995). Tann (2010b) reinterprets this framework from the perspective of SFL by drawing on Martin's (1992) linguistic concept of taxonomic relations and his approach to discourse analysis more generally (see Martin 1992; Martin and Rose 2003/2007). Where MCA categories are posited as 'inference-rich', which means that each category is already associated with certain attributes, activities and values, Tann addresses couplings of ideational and interpersonal meaning (which we have used earlier in this chapter). Working along these lines Tann defines categories in terms of entities coupled with events and attitudes at the level of discourse semantics. The main difference between the two approaches is the focus of analysis. For MCA the main analytical unit appears to be the word, while for Tann Categorization involves stretches of discourse (discourse phases) that take into account all three metafunctions—interpersonal, ideational and textual—in order to illuminate different dimensions of the meanings being made.

Consider, for example, a phase of discourse where the Convenor in the Affray YJC is warning the YP that his transgressive behaviour encourages the wider community to categorize his ethnic community in negative ways:

**Extract 5.9, Affray YJC**

**Convenor:** Yep. So people's perceptions, Aatif, that's what Amir's getting at. Because the rest of us sitting around this table may have a perception and you are holding that perception up. You are allowing us to keep thinking that. Aren't you? Because of your behavior. Some people may think, 'Well, Muslims are this'. Just like they might think Asians are this or Australians are this. But if you keep doing it and you keep behaving that way, the people will think that way. Some people, won't they?

The ECLO in the same conference, concerned with this bad image of his ethnic community, categorizes himself as a member (shown in bold), in order to invoke the moral authority to speak on its behalf:

**Extract 5.10, Affray YJC**

**ECLO:** What are they – when they see your mum wearing a scarf, I'm **Muslim** background myself. What are they going to think?

Here, the ECLO's specification of his ethnic background, together with a prosody of negative JUDGEMENT of behaviours that go against the notion of a 'good Muslim' and a textual pattern featuring repetition of rhetorical questions (e.g. 'You show me where in the Koran it says we can do things like that') all contribute to the construal of a Categorization device that aims at aligning the ECLO and the YP in terms of ethnic community.

At times, Categorization sets up tensions as far as negotiating the appropriate membership in YJCs is concerned. For example, the YP in the extract from the following Affray YJC identifies himself as the Victim when positioned to nominate himself as the Offender during the Mandate (see Extract 5.11). This is likely because his offence involved another Offender who had an altercation with the YP. When the YP went to 'back up' his mate at a fight he traded punches with this other offender and started chasing him. The other offender pulled a knife out and the YP took evasive action, which included throwing bricks at him across a street. What happened subsequently was that both YPs were charged by the police and both referred to a conference. They were invited to attend the same conference—where both of them would have been present as Offenders. However, the second YP withdrew from the conference on the advice of a lawyer. The YP who did attend the conference, however, obviously still bore ill feelings towards the YP with whom he had had this skirmish and, in his own common-sense way of explaining things, felt that he was as much a Victim as a perpetrator:

**Extract 5.11, Affray YJC**

| | |
|---|---|
| **Convenor:** | What we are going to do is go quickly around the table and introduce ourselves and say what our respective roles are in the conference. |
| | …[translation into Arabic for Mother] |
| **Convenor:** | Thanks, Translator. OK, my name is Jude and I'm the Convenor. Aatif? |
| **YP:** | My name's Aatif. |
| **Convenor:** | And you are the? |
| **YP:** | The Victim. |
| **Convenor:** | No, you're the Offender. |
| **YP:** | Oh, OK. |
| **Convenor:** | Yep. |

## 9 Belonging and Community   231

In addition to Categorization devices, different kinds of personae were also classified in the conferences though Spatialization devices. We can see this in the episode discussed earlier in this chapter where YP1 in the School Library YJC reacts to the Convenor's suggestion that his snickering shows he is not taking the conference seriously:

**Extract 5.12, School Library YJC**

| | |
|---|---|
| **YP1:** | (…) Yeah well I'm not a rat **from Bridgeton**. |
| **Convenor:** | W– I know that. |
| **YP1:** | I'm not one of those friggin' retarded people that just say 'oh yeah I done that. I w- I'll do it again'. … I'll do everything that I can to change everything that's happened. Seriously. Walk the streets, mate. Go have fun. Go get drunk. Do whatever. Party on. (…) |

In this extract, the YP uses a Spatialization device to dispel the implication that he's 'a rat' associated with a particular place (shown in bold), using a phrase presumably common when complaining about the negative behaviour of this type of persona. Another example where Spatialization is deployed is when the ECLO in the Affray YJC (during a phase of the conference where he attempts to shame the YP for bringing his mother into the presence of police) refers to our presence as researchers documenting the conference by indicating that we have come there from another place (the university):

**Extract 5.13, Affray YJC**

| | |
|---|---|
| **ECLO:** | OK. **Where** are these guys from? They're **from a certain place**. OK. What's the perception going to be? |
| **YP:** | Think bad of me. |

The spatial references to these outsiders to the community (police, researchers, etc.) are used pedagogically by the ECLO to show the YP that his behaviour will result in a membership classification ('the perception') amongst these outsiders that negatively appraises his community.

While Categorization and Spatialization devices classify the kind of persona involved in the liminal shift in identity the conference is working towards, Collectivization devices play an important role in conferences of inviting the YP back into their communities of concern. Collectivization devices, according to Tann's model, are relational concepts that contrast an identity with a perceived other (e.g. Victim vs Offender). Consider, for example, the distinction between 'us' as law-abiding citizens (shown in bold) and an implied criminal other:

### Extract 5.14, Mobile Phone YJC

**Convenor:** So, what I want you to remember is that every single one of **us** in this room could be considered a **victim** of a crime.

This example illustrates a frequent pattern in conferencing whereby the Convenor attempts to invoke a collective sense of belonging to an imagined community of ethical citizens into which the YP needs to be realigned. This device, supported by coupling of the YP persona with negative JUDGEMENT of their behaviour (contrasted with an imagined Victim persona associated with ethical behaviour), is often deployed when there is no tangible 'Victim' of the crime or particular sub-community who has been harmed, sometimes referred to as 'victimless crimes' (e.g. stealing from a supermarket). We will return to further explore the nature of this imagined community in the next chapter.

Because we are focusing on reintegration, Collectivization phases are the most important for our discussion. Having established Tann's focus, we will now examine how interactive Collectivization resources are used to negotiate the borders of communities into which the YP might be reintegrated. We are asking how the YP is being positioned to realign himself or herself with particular communities framed in certain ways. Our concern here is mainly with the naming of collectivities (working in tandem with other resources) used as part of the transformative rhetoric of the conference. The significance of Collectivization is, in fact, flagged in the Convenor-training guidelines, which instruct the Convenors to avoid referring to the YP as an 'offender'—for fear of labelling the YP as a deviant and aligning him or her with an imagined community of 'criminals'. Instead the YP is named as the more neutral, 'Young Person', an identity open to being re-affiliated with the right kinds of associates.

Within our sample, it is in the interaction of the YP with the Liaison Officers that Collectivization devices play the most pronounced role in negotiating realignment. For example, the ECLO draws heavily on Collectivization devices (shown in bold in the following example) to suggest that the YP has contravened the social boundaries of their shared ethnic community:

**Extract 5.15, Affray YJC**

ECLO: You have no respect for your mum whatsoever, brother. You have no respect for what your mum's got on her head. You have no respect for **our community**. You have no respect. You tell me, brother, how it's a part of **our culture** or **our religion** or **our tradition** to do things like that. You tell me when.

Critical in many of these interactions between YPs and Liaison Officers is what we might think of as 'inviting/warning' Collectivization. In other words, these interactions involve Collectivizations that suggest that the YP can align himself or herself with a particular community or 'lose out'. These resources invite the YP to commune and negotiate the borders of positively valued communities, while at the same time warning the YP of the consequences of failing to re-affiliate. An important resource contributing to this kind of inviting/warning Collectivization is the use of vocatives directed at the YP. Our analysis of vocatives draws on the work on Poynton (1990a, b) who addresses the way in which their usage is sensitive to and constructive of gender, ethnicity, generation and social class. Our interpretation of vocation in the following extracts is based on our reading of the Australian variables in play in the conference on hand.

Three kinds of vocatives were seen in our sample of Liaison Officer–YP interaction, which we interpret as contributing to the enactment of three kinds of collectivization: generational (e.g. 'man'), ethnic (e.g. 'brother') and gendered (e.g. 'mate'). The following extract shows examples of vocatives such as these in bold:

**Extract 5.16, Affray YJC**

**ECLO:** That's what I'm saying to you, **man**. I say – I'm talking to you **man**, look at me as your older brother. Do you understand what I'm saying to you?
**YP:** Yeah.

Note that most of the vocatives in our sample that occurred beyond Mandate (in which participants are being identified for the first time in the conference) were not used because there was ambiguity in the exchange regarding the identity of the next speaker. Rather they functioned to establish a specific relationship with the addressee; they functioned as collectivization devices, not simply as turn-assigning address.

When used in this way by the YLO, the vocatives occurred in the initial, medial and final positions in the clause, as shown in Extract 5.16. In contrast, when used by the Convenor, vocatives tended to be both a proper name and in initial position:

**Extract 5.17, Affray YJC**

**Convenor:** OK, Aatif, one of the conditions of a juvenile conference is that you admit to the offence in front of all of us here today and that you tell us that you are here of your own free will. So did you commit the offences you were charged with?

Poynton notes, working with a corpus of written Australian texts, that in adult conversation a vocative is most likely to occur in the final position in a clause, whereas in adult to child talk it is more likely to occur in the initial position (Poynton 1990a). The greater tendency towards initial position usage of a proper name vocative is suggestive of a greater power distance between the Convenor and the YP. This relates in part to the Convenor's role of managing who is to speak and when, and to the control the Convenor has over the exchange structure (see Chap. 3).

While collectivizing vocatives were frequently used by the Liaison Officers in our sample, they were never used by the Convenors or the YPs themselves. A possible reason for their proliferation in the discourse of the Liaison Officers is the special role that these officers play in the process of re-affiliating the YP during and potentially after the conference—hence the concern they show in the Caution with the YP's future identity as a law-abiding citizen (which we explored earlier in this chapter) and with de-affiliating them from their 'mates'. These conference participants tend to favour vocatives of 'solidarity' (Poynton 1990b: 212) acting as forms of 'in-group address' (Brown and Levinson 1978). As we will see, these vocatives align the interactants with different kinds of communities. 'Mate', 'man' and 'brother' (enacting in turn what we interpret as the gendered, generational and ethnic collectivities mentioned earlier) were particularly common in the discourse of the ECLO in the Affray YJC (shown in Tables 5.21, 5.22 and 5.23).

Before we turn to consider the kinds of communities being referenced, let us first reflect on the regulative function of these vocatives. These vocatives work in the service of the macro-genre in the sense that they relate to the overall concern for 'warning' the YP that they have adopted the wrong kind of affiliation (e.g. with mates who are a bad influence). In other words, they have a dual function of both the inviting and warning Collectivizations mentioned earlier. For example, in many instances of

Table 5.21 Examples of 'mate' in initial position with Tone 3

|  |  |  |
|---|---|---|
|  | Mate, | you've got to understand what you do doesn't just affect you, doesn't just affect your mum, it affects the whole community, it affects the perception, it affects our culture, it affects everything |
|  | Mate, | First of all when I talk to you, man, I'm not talking to you so you can be my friend |
|  | Mate, | Ya- your mate didn't have to go down there did he? |
| So, | Mate, | In here I think there's nothing |
|  | Mate, | If you- if there's a fire do you walk straight into it or do you walk around it? |
|  | Mate, | You've gotta understand brother, what- what everyone's trying to do here is… |
| And, | Mate, | Police can defend themselves |

**Table 5.22** Instances of the use of 'man' by ECLO

| Because I'm listening to you, | man | and I don't see you as a leader |
|---|---|---|
| You tell me- you tell me if I'm speaking- if my English is too hard for you | man, | I'll go down a couple of steps [sarcastic tone] |
| I've got three kids, | man. | |
| I honestly don't think you do, | man. | |
| That's what I'm saying to ya, | man. | |
| I'm talking to you | man, | Look at me as your older brother |
| I'm thirty six, | man. | |
| Be upfront, | man. | |
| What we're saying is your behavior is getting you into trouble, | man. | |
| Look at your mum, | man. | |

**Table 5.23** Examples of the use of 'brother' by the ECLO

| I'm telling you, | brother, | you don't respect your mum |
|---|---|---|
| You have no respect for your mum whatsoever, | brother. | |
| You tell me, | brother, | how it's a part of our culture or our religion or our tradition to do things like that? |
| Why aren't they with you, supporting you, | brother? | |
| How many times- how old are you now, | brother? | |
| After it's too late, | brother. | |
| We're not targetting you personally, | brother. | |
| You're hurting your family, | brother. | |

the ECLO's interaction with the YP in the Affray YJC, vocatives functioned to issue a warning at the same time as construing camaraderie:

### Extract 5.18, Affray YJC

ECLO: **Mate**, you've got to understand what you do doesn't just affect you, doesn't just affect your mum, it affects the whole community, it affects the perception, it affects our culture, it affects everything.

In this example, 'Mate' contributes to a collectivization phase designed to motivate the YP to accept the coupling of his offending behaviour with negative JUDGEMENT. In other words, the ECLO is effectively saying 'if we are mates, then you agree that what you are doing is wrong'.

Further examples of this kind of pattern are shown in Table 5.21 where 'mate' is realized with an intonation pattern that typically indicates a warning (tone 3 in Halliday and Greaves (2008)). The ECLO's usage seems quite marked since, although vocatives can occupy the initial position in a clause as a single tone group, it is usually done with a less threatening tone (tone 1, with the pitch movement going down generally indicating a statement, or tone 2, with the pitch movement rising indicating a question (Halliday 1967: 47)). It is part of an ongoing prosody of warning that occurs at the end of the commissioned recount in the Affray YJC. This kind of patterning was less apparent with the other YLOs in our sample, although there were examples such as the following (in the intonation analysis '//' marks a tone group boundary, '/' a foot boundary and 'Δ' a silent beat; see Appendix B for details):

**YLO:** //3 Δ A/**tif**//1 Δ he's not/joking/when he/says you'll/ go to/**gaol**. //

We can also think of 'mate' as construing a gendered in-group of Australian men. In Australian spoken discourse, 'mate' is most commonly used among males:

> In Australia, one finds the considerably less formal *mate* used between males in many kinds of service encounter, especially when the transaction involves a 'male' product such as petrol, auto parts, hardware, paint, and particularly alcohol (either in the bar or the bottle-shop). *Mate* is also used in more neutral contexts such as post offices, milk bars or delis and the local paper shop. Such public male usage is often reciprocal and is best seen as a conventionalized marker of Australian egalitarian ideology, which historically has been constructed as exclusively male (Ward 1958). (Poynton 1990b: 241)

However, the gendered nature of this vocative may have dissipated somewhat since Poynton's study in the 1980s (Formentelli 2007); in fact, the other participant who used 'mate' most frequently was the young female YLO in the Shopping Trolley YJC:

**Extract 5.19, Shopping Trolley YJC**

| | |
|---|---|
| **YLO:** | You get contacts, get to know people, get some numbers, go and work for, you know you could – if (…) been a butcher, you could end up overseas **mate** and work … |
| **YLO:** | When you turn eighteen, if you get something small like this on your record, that's there forever **mate**. |

'Man' appears to be associated with a more generational affiliation, invoking the sense that the YP and Liaison Officers are both of the same generation; as the ECLO explicitly states, the YP can think of him as an 'older brother' (Table 5.22, example 6).

The vocative 'brother' is used by the ECLO to mark the YP and ECLO as members of the same ethnic community (Table 5.23). This vocative is part of the Collectivization device drawn on by the ECLO in various phases in the conference, particularly during the extension of the commissioned recount. The collectivization is marked by the use of the pronoun 'we' in the thematic position and a prosody of negative JUDGEMENT (both invoked and inscribed) about activities and stances contravening what it means to be a good Muslim (e.g. 'do things like that', 'no respect for your mum', etc.).

**Extract 5.20, Affray YJC**

| | |
|---|---|
| **ECLO:** | You show me where in the Koran it says **we** can do things like that. |

This phase of discourse also includes explicit reference to the collectivities ('our culture', 'our religion', 'our tradition') who hold particular value orientations:

## Extract 5.21, Affray YJC

ECLO: What are you doing- you tell me what you're doing does that help our community at the moment or does it make our community look worse?
YP: Looks worse.
ECLO: It does, doesn't it.
YP: Yes.
ECLO: What are you going to do to fix that image because, you know what, brother, I'm going to tell you straight out, I get sick and tired, man, of people like you, OK, that put down our community, put down our religion, put down the Hijab, it makes me sick. I've got three kids, man. I want to make sure that when my kids grow up they have it good.

By using the vocatives 'man', 'brother' and 'mate' the ECLO invokes the authority to speak as a 'young Muslim male' (collectivized via generation, ethnicity, gender). The tone 3 warning recurrently coupled with these vocatives functions to 'caution' the YP that he is transgressing the boundaries of the community of young Muslim males. However, these vocatives do not function alone to enact or negotiate membership of particular communities but contribute to phases of discourse construing the kinds of collectivities that have been touched upon here. For instance, the patterns of appraisal that we see in phases of discourse where the vocatives occur begin to give us a picture of the axiological loading of these subject positions (which we will explore in the next chapter). For instance, in the following phase, the ECLO draws on a syndrome of features (**vocatives**, familial taxonomic relations and NEGATIVE JUDGEMENT) to make explicit to the YP how his behaviour is de-aligning him from the collectivity which he should be embracing:

## Extract 5.22, Affray YJC

ECLO: But you – don't you have anything in your head? You've got a younger brother, **man**, and a sister. If you're DISRESPECTING your family like that, that means you're saying to me and

> everybody here we can DISRESPECT your mother. That's what you're doing. Because you have NO RESPECT for your mother. You only thought after you were locked up not before you got locked up. Maybe you've got to start thinking before not after. After it's too late, **brother**. It's too late.

This section has shown how the YP is prompted to make a shift in classification as part of the rhetoric of reintegration enacted by the YJC macro-genre. This recategorizing involves Categorization and Spatialization devices that classify the kinds of personae available to the YP, and Collectivization devices that invite the YP back into particular positively valued memberships. We have seen the special role that vocatives play in this collectivizing over other potential resources such as pronouns (e.g. *we*). The main membership that might be expressed in a collectivized way for the YP would be their transgressive 'mates' and it is this membership that the Liaison Officers are trying to disintegrate.

# 10   Conclusion

The focus of this chapter has been the relation of feelings to the community. Inspired by Knight (2008, 2010, 2013), we have explored the idea that belonging involves enacting bonds, with a bond defined as a shared 'attitude plus ideation' coupling. This means that looking at how couplings are negotiated as bonds is crucial for understanding the reintegrative practice of conferencing. Accordingly, we looked carefully at the interaction of language and body language as far as negotiating bonds was concerned. This in turn raises the question of how to address the communities engendered by these bonding processes. For this we turned to the work of Tann, illustrating the operation of Categorization, Collectivization and Spatialization devices in conferencing, and attending to the use of vocatives to flag relevant communities of feeling.

As we have seen, however, YPs may be less than forthcoming as far as reintegration is concerned, and occasionally resistant. In the next chapter, we consider the negotiation of identity in conferencing in more detail, developing models of the different kinds of belonging in play—for both ideal and less ideal YPs and Support Persons.

## Notes

1. The attitude in this example is classified as hybrid since 'disappointed' inscribes both affect and judgement—the father is sad (affect) about what the YP did wrong (judgement).
2. For examples in which the attitude is invoked rather than inscribed, we have made explicit the kind of feeling involved in the coupling.

## References

Brown, P., & Levinson, S. (1978). Universals in language usage: Politeness phenomena. In E. Goody (Ed.), *Questions and politeness* (pp. 56–289). Cambridge: Cambridge University Press.

Cléirigh, C. (2011). *Gestural and postural semiosis a systemic-functional linguistic approach to 'body language'*. Unpublished manuscript.

Daly, K. (2003). Mind the gap: Restorative justice in theory and practice. In A. von Hirsch, J. V. Roberts, A. E. Bottoms, et al. (Eds.), *Restorative justice and criminal justice: Competing or reconcilable paradigms* (pp. 219–236). London: Bloomsbury.

Dreyfus, S. (2011). Grappling with a non-speech language: Describing and theorising the nonverbal multimodal communication of a child with an intellectual disability. In S. Dreyfus, S. Hood, & M. Stenglin (Eds.), *Semiotic margins: Meaning in multimodalities* (pp. 53–72). London: Continuum.

Efron, D. (1941). *Gesture and environment: A tentative study of some of the spatio-temporal and "linguistic" aspects of the gestural behavior of eastern Jews and southern Italians in New York city, living under similar as well as different environmental conditions*. New York: King's Crown Press.

Formentelli, M. (2007). The vocative mate in contemporary English: A corpus based study. In A. Sansò (Ed.), *Language resources and linguistic theory* (pp. 180–199). Milano: Franco Angeli.

Goldin-Meadow, S., & Singer, M. A. (2003). From children's hands to adults' ears: Gesture's role in the learning process. *Developmental Psychology, 39*, 509–520.

Halliday, M. A. K. (1967). *Intonation and grammar in British English*. The Hague/Paris: Mouton.
Halliday, M. A. K. (1975). *Learning how to mean – Explorations in the development of language*. London: Arnold.
Halliday, M. A. K. (1977). *Learning how to mean: Explorations in the development of language*. New York: Elsevier.
Halliday, M. A. K. (1985). *Spoken and written language.* Geelong: Deakin University Press. [Republished Oxford University Press 1989].
Halliday, M. A. K., & Greaves, W. S. (2008). *Intonation in the grammar of English*. London/Oakville: Equinox Pub.
Halliday, M., & Matthiessen, C. M. (2014). *An introduction to functional grammar*. London: Routledge.
Hood, S. (2011). Body language in face-to-face teaching: A focus on textual and interpersonal meaning. In S. Dreyfus, S. Hood, & M. Stenglin (Eds.), *Semiotic margins: Meaning in multimodalities* (pp. 31–52). London: Continuum.
Kendon, A. (2004). *Gesture: Visible action as utterance*. Cambridge: Cambridge University Press.
Knight, N. K. (2008). Still cool… and American too!': An SFL analysis of deferred bonds in internet messaging humour. Systemic Functional Linguistics in Use, Odense Working Papers in Language and Communication 29: 481–502.
Knight, N. K. (2010). Wrinkling complexity: Concepts of identity and affiliation in humour. In M. Bednarek & J. R. Martin (Eds.), *New discourse on language: Functional perspectives on multimodality, identity, and affiliation.* London: Continuum.
Knight, N. K. (2013). Evaluating experience in funny ways: How friends bond through conversational hum. *Text & Talk, 33,* 553–574.
Martin, J. R. (1992). *English text: System and structure*. Philadelphia: John Benjamins Pub..
Martin, J. R., & Rose, D. (2003/2007). *Working with discourse: Meaning beyond the clause*. London/New York: Continuum.
Martin, J. R., & White, P. R. R. (2005). *The language of evaluation: Appraisal in English*. New York: Palgrave Macmillan.
Martinec, R. (2000). Types of process in action. *Semiotica, 130,* 243–268.
Martinec, R. (2001). Interpersonal resources in action. *Semiotica, 135,* 117–145.
Max Planck Institute for Psycholinguistics. (2008). *ELAN*. Nijmegen: The Language Archive.

McNeill, D. (1992). *Hand and mind: What gestures reveal about thought*. Chicago: University of Chicago press.
Morris, D. (1979). *Gestures, their origins and distribution*. New York: Stein & Day Pub.
Painter, C. (1998). *Learning through language in early childhood*. London: Cassell.
Poynton, C. (1990a). *Address and the semiotics of social relations: A systemic-functional account of address forms and practices in Australian English*. University of Sydney, 1991, xii, 277 leaves.
Poynton, C. (1990b). *Address and the semiotics of social relations: A systemic-functional account of address forms and practices in Australian English*. Department of Linguistics, Faculty of Arts, University of Sydney, Sydney, 284.
Retzinger, S., & Scheff, T. (1996). Strategy for community conferences: Emotions and social bonds. In B. Galaway & J. Hudson (Eds.), *Restorative justice: International perspectives* (pp. 315–336). Monsey: Criminal Justice Press.
Sacks, H. (1995). *Lectures on conversation*. Oxford: Blackwell Publishing.
Schegloff, E. A. (2006). Interaction: The infrastructure for social institutions, the natural ecological niche for language, and the arena in which culture is enacted. In N. J. Enfield & S. C. Levinson (Eds.), *Roots of human sociality: Culture, cognition and interaction* (pp. 70–96). Oxford: Berg.
Schegloff, E. A. (2007). A tutorial on membership categorization. *Journal of Pragmatics, 39*, 462–482.
Tann, K. (2010a). Imagining communities: A multifunctional approach to identity management in texts. In M. Bednarek & J. R. Martin (Eds.), *New discourse on language: Functional perspectives on multimodality, identity, and affiliation* (pp. 163–194). London: Continuum.
Tann, K. (2010b). *Semogenesis of a nation: An iconography of Japanese identity*. Sydney: Department of Linguistics, University of Sydney.
Tann, K. (2013). The language of identity discourse: Introducing a systemic functional framework for iconography. *Linguistics & The Human Sciences, 8*, 361–391.
Zappavigna, M., Cléirigh, C., Dwyer, P., et al. (2009). The coupling of gesture and phonology. In M. Bednarek & J. R. Martin (Eds.), *New discourse on language: Functional perspectives on multimodality, identity, and affiliation* (pp. 237–266). London: Continuum.

# 6

# Performing Identity: A Topological Perspective

## 1 Introduction: Users in Uses of Language

Thus far we have considered youth justice conferencing from the point of view of *uses* of language, looking at the kinds of meanings that are made as the macro-genre unfolds. We now shift perspective to think about *users* of language and the kinds of identities that can be played out across the 'different discursive environments in which *identity work* is being done' (Benwell and Stokoe 2007: 5) within a youth justice conference. In other words, we are concerned with how conference participants enact different 'personae' through their communicative choices.

Language-based perspectives on identity consider how users of language vary in the way in which they project different kinds of social identities through choices in their linguistic style (Coupland 2007). Approaches include variationist sociolinguistics, which explores linguistic variables that correlate with predetermined social categories (Labov 2006; Trudgill 1974), interactionist and ethnomethodological perspectives (Zimmerman and Weider 1970; Berger and Luckmann 1966; Antaki and Widdicombe 1998) such as Membership Categorization Analysis, which considers the common-sense identity categorizations that organize our social world (Sacks 1992; Jayyursi 1984), positioning theories that focus on how people take up various social roles in discourse (Davies and Harré 1990) and a range of post-structuralist perspectives such as those that view identity as a performance (Bauman 2004; Butler 1990). Hasan's (2005, 2009) work on semantic variation is also very relevant; her programme attends to the ways in which semiotic resources are differentially distributed amongst users—both in terms of which options are available and, among those available, which are likely to be taken up in specific contexts of instantiation.

Our perspective, drawing on Firth (1957), is grounded in the idea that users of language perform their identity within uses of language. In other words, to understand how identities are performed in context, we need to understand not just how the systems of language are used (*langue* and *parole* in Saussure's terms), but also how resources are allocated to users of language and how they are used to affiliate. In this way we hope to better address Firth's user-focused goals:

> The unique object of Saussurian linguistics is '*la langue*', which exists only in the *collectivité*. Now at this point I wish to stress the importance of the study of persons, even one at a time, and of introducing the notions of personality and language as in some sense vectors of the continuity of repetitions in the social process, and the persistence of personal forces. (Firth 1957: 183)

This user-oriented perspective also considers two important dimensions of meaning-making which impact on the kinds of meaning a user, or in more Firthian terms a 'persona', can construe in a particular interaction within a youth justice conference:

- The influence of the conferencing macro-genre on the range of meanings open to a persona at different points in the unfolding discourse
- The patterns of meaning that characterize the different 'roles' a persona takes up at these points in the macro-genre, which is inflected by the linguistic repertoire the language user has accrued in their lifetime

The latter perspective is particularly focused on a kind of pattern relevant to how social bonds are forged and maintained through combinations of ideation and evaluation. In other words, it considers evaluations about things, which we referred to as 'couplings' (Martin 2008) in the previous chapter.

## 2   How Can Young Persons Enact a 'Sincere' Persona in YJCs?

Young offenders are in a challenging semiotic position in a YJC in terms of enacting identity: they need to convince the other participants in attendance that they are being sincerely contrite and, in addition, have the potential to be reformed. At the same time, there are many factors leading Young Persons (YPs) to assume a 'small target' identity, admitting only what is necessary in the Record of Events in the commissioned recount (as we have seen in Chap. 3). Hayes (2006), among others (Retzinger and Scheff 1996; Van Stokkom 2002; Harris et al. 2004), has raised the problem of sincerity in relation to remorse, apology, shaming and forgiveness in conferencing. While the sincerity of the YP is obviously important to Victims, Convenors, Police/Liaison Officers and other participants, it is not at all clear what behaviours are 'read' as sincere given that the macro-genre makes it difficult for the YP to speak as young people are often imagined to speak when 'being themselves'.

Dissatisfaction in relation to sincerity can in fact erupt in later stages of the macro-genre, as it does on several occasions following the Interpretation of the recount in the Affray YJC. The following are some selected examples:

### Extract 6.1, Affray YJC

| | |
|---|---|
| **Convenor:** | So do you think that this whole process is a waste of time? Do you really care about what comes out of this? Seriously, honestly. |
| **YP:** | Yeah, I do. |
| **Convenor:** | Ah, no, honestly? You can say it. |
| **YP:** | No. I do. |

| | |
|---|---|
| Arresting Officer: | Be upfront, man. |
| YLO: | Be honest. OK. Because it's no use sitting here saying, 'I'm gonna change, blah, blah, blah, lies, oh, I'm not really saying what I'm thinking' because I know this isn't you. OK. Because I've spoken to you before. If someone had a go at you like this, just react how you would normally. Say what you think. |
| YP: | Yeah. |
| | ... |
| ECLO: | You got a temper? |
| YP: | (yeah) |
| ECLO: | OK. At least you're being honest now. It's alright, man. It's alright to say how you feel. That's what, mate – That's what this lady's trying to get you to do, to be honest. |

In effect, the macro-genre leads to a possible conundrum: How can YPs sound sincere when they can't be themselves (or at least not the selves that adults may expect them to be based on their interactions with them in social processes of other kinds)? How can a YP employ, for instance, the kind of talk conference participants might associate with teenagers, when this discourse is at odds with the heavily scaffolded nature of the interaction?

We can reinforce this point by drawing on a commissioned recount from a mock conference improvised on our behalf by staff and students of the Performance Studies Department at the University of Sydney (from a period when we were trialing our recording procedures). The professional actor cum research student playing the young offender role produced the following text, with explicit markers of adolescent identity strongly foregrounded through numerous instances of slang, swearing and colloquial phrasing which the actor uses to perform his 'part' in the mock drama:

> [colloquial phrasing in bold, <u>swearing bold underlined</u> below]
> [A]nd so, so it's a Sunday night and **me, me and Trav** were out and just, you know, **hanging around** and **mucking about**. (...) We'd run out of

## 2 How Can Young Persons Enact a 'Sincere' Persona in YJCs?

cigs so we just kind of, we just kind of (…) went to the **servo** and stuff and, and (…) the car door was open and the key was in the ignition and my **mate was like** 'Yeah, do you want– Yeah, we should **jump in** the car and, you know, and **jump in** and kind of–' and I **was like** 'Oh, I think, you know, are you sure about it?' And so he, then we kind of, we kind of, **yeah**, we just **jumped in** it and – I was in it for a while and, and, and then, you know, then he starts screaming at me, you know, '<u>**Shit**</u>, she's coming!' You know, 'Just **burn** it, **burn** it mate! Go, just get out!' And so I kind of shut the door and don't think, and **I'm just out of there**, you know, just round the corner and then kind of on the road and stuff and then I realized like 'Oh <u>**shit**</u>, I've taken the car' and then we, and then we kind of feel like 'Oh OK, we can't do much now'. So we kind of drive around for a while. We didn't **fang** it or anything and, you know, we each **had a go** and yeah, then, a bit later, after we kind of drove around for a while, yeah, I kind of **took a corner** too, too, sort of quickly and, and just sort of, you know, didn't– before I knew it, I was just (…) and (…) in Mr Hemford's umm front yard and in his fence and, and then again, you know, just, I just didn't know what was going on and just <u>**shit**</u>-**bolted** out of there and […] you know, and I was a bit, kind of, **weirded** out, like, so I was just kind of, kind of, just sitting at the bus stop and stuff (…) till the **cops** came and saw us. **Yeah**, they just came and got us.

In terms of the highlighted phrasing, the mock recount is absolutely untypical of recounts by YPs in our data. In addition, the actor deploys a great deal of soft focus (hedging phrases such as *kind of* and *and stuff*) and draws heavily on the adverb *just* to minimize his actions, intensify them or make them precipitous.

[*softened focus* in bold italics; minimizing **just** in bold; intensifying/precipitating <u>**just**</u> in bold underlined]

[A]nd so, so it's a Sunday night and me, me and Trav were out and **just**, you know, hanging around and mucking about. (…) We'd run out of cigs so we **just** *kind of*, we **just** *kind of* (…) went to the servo *and stuff* and, and (…) the car door was open and the key was in the ignition and my mate was like 'Yeah, do you want– Yeah, we should jump in the car and, you know, and jump in and *kind of*–' and I was like 'Oh, I think, you know, are you sure about it?' And so he, then we *kind of*, we *kind of*, yeah, we **just** jumped in it and– I was in it for a while and, and, and then, you know, then he starts screaming at me, you know, 'Shit, she's coming!' You know, '**Just** burn it, burn it mate! Go, **just** get out!' And so I *kind of* shut the door and don't think, and I'm **just** out of there, you know, **just** round the corner and then *kind of* on the road *and stuff* and then I realized like 'Oh shit, I've taken the car' and then we, and then we *kind of* feel like 'Oh OK, we can't do much now'. So we *kind of* drive around for a while. We didn't fang it *or anything* and, you know, we each had a go and yeah, then, a bit later, after we *kind of* drove around for a while, yeah, I *kind of* took a corner too, too, *sort of* quickly and, and **just** *sort of*, you know, didn't-before I knew it, I was **just** (…) and (…) in Mr Hemford's umm front yard and in his fence and, and then again, you know, **just**, I **just** didn't know what was going on and **just** shit-bolted out of there and […] you know, and I was a bit, *kind of*, weirded out, like, so I was **just** *kind of*, *kind of*, **just** sitting at the bus stop *and* **stuff** (…) till the cops came and saw us. Yeah, they **just** came and got us.

Although these tempering features are found in our data, they are much less frequent than in the recount cited above (Zappavigna et al. 2007, 2008). It is clear that in order to project an adolescent identity the actor in question draws on lexical resources which are almost never taken up by YPs in YJCs (e.g. slang, swearing) and vastly overplays grammatical resources which are less frequently found. The result is a caricature of adolescent speech—dramatically effective perhaps as an instance of 'method acting', but uncharacteristic of YPs' behaviour in our data.

What this divergence underlines is the sense in which identity is shaped by genre. The commissioned recount assigns YPs a role to play, and they recognize and accommodate the formal institutional setting in which they are expected to provide an account of their offence. Adjusting to the genre in this way, they are no different from any other participants in the conference process. At the same time, adult participants in the process may have expectations about adolescent discourse comparable to those of the actor caricaturing this discourse and these expectations may bear critically on how they judge the sincerity of YPs. Recognition of the difficult task the YP has in construing any kind of contrite, apologetic persona led us to the task of mapping out just what are the personae that are available to YPs in the conference and how we can model the identities that the YPs draw upon at different steps in the conference.

## 3   Modelling Identity: A Topological Perspective

In order to address this question of how to model identity, we have drawn on Maton's Legitimation Code Theory (LCT) (Maton 2007, 2009, 2014), specifically the dimension of Specialization. Maton explores how social fields of practice represent fields of struggle for legitimacy. These struggles involve both the knowledge that constitutes fields of practice and the people who have that knowledge—the knowers.

The LCT dimension of Specialization conceptualizes practices and actors' dispositions within these fields in terms of two independent sets of relations: (i) *epistemic relations* between sociocultural practices and the part of the world they are oriented to (that is, the relations between a practice or field and the knowledge involved in understanding its object of study); and (ii) *social relations* between sociocultural practices and their actors or authors (the relations between a practice or field and the people that are involved in it). The strengths of epistemic relations (ER) and of social relations (SR) can vary independently from stronger (+) to weaker (−), generating four principal modalities or *specialization codes*.

These specialization codes involve different principles upon which the legitimacy of a social practice may depend. Knowledge codes (ER+, SR−) are codes for which legitimacy depends on what you know and how (your legitimacy is based on your knowledge); knower codes (ER−, SR+) are codes where what matters is who you are (your position in a hierarchy of knowers and/or your dispositions and values); elite codes (ER+, SR+) are codes where both specialist knowledge and dispositions underpin legitimacy (your knowledge and your position as a knower); and relativist codes (ER−, SR−) are codes where 'anything goes' (you don't need any specialist knowledge, nor do you need to be a particular knower). These

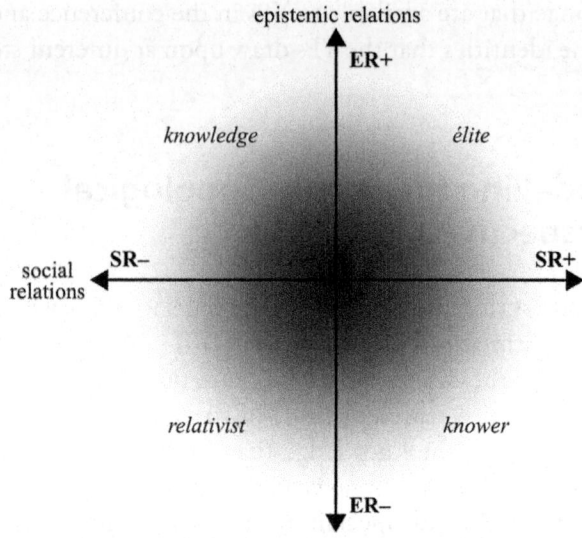

**Fig. 6.1** The Specialization plane (Maton 2007: 97)

four codes and the epistemic and social relations that give rise to them are illustrated in Fig. 6.1.

These concepts are being widely used to explore social practices and actors' dispositions across a range of fields, most notably in education. They enable analysis of the organizing principles underlying *both* the social field of practice (such as Youth Justice Conferencing) *and* the dispositions actors bring to those social situations (as illustrated by their practices within the conferencing). Such an analysis highlights contestations over the ways in which legitimacy is defined and the degrees to which the specialization codes characterizing different social groups may 'code clash' or 'code match' with those dominant within the context being studied. In other words, specialization codes provide a means for exploring why specific actors may adopt specific subject positions within specific social contexts.

To illustrate these codes, we might consider the historical debate over evolution: we can consider Wallace, whose scientific expertise (knowledge code) underwrote his vision of evolution; Darwin, whose expertise and gentlemanly social status *together* (elite code) afforded both this vision *and* its promotion; Bishop Wilberforce, whose Church of England faith and values (knower code) led him to challenge scientific opinion; and contemporary bloggers who opine freely on the Web without privileging specialist knowledge or specialized dispositions (relativist code). Differences in Specialization can have profound effects on people's lives. In the English-speaking world, for example, appointment to an academic position ideally depends more on a scholar's record of teaching, research and administrative service than on the university granting their PhD (a knowledge code); in China, on the other hand, the standing of a scholar's undergraduate university may also be a key factor, with some top universities reluctant to appoint applicants with an undergraduate degree from a middle- or low-ranking university no matter how much they have achieved in academic life since that time (an elite code).

As Maton (2014) emphasizes, the form and strengths of epistemic relations and social relations may differ according to the specific object of study. This means that the salient features that characterize the differing strengths of epistemic and social relations in one field or practice may be very different from those in another field. In order to see how these relations play out in a specific field, then, they require what has been termed an 'external language of description' or 'translation device' (Bernstein 1996/2000; Bernstein 2000) for, as it were, translating between the concepts and the concrete particularities of the research focus (Maton and Chen 2016; Maton and Doran 2017). Such a device allows analysis that can highlight the form taken by ER+/−, SR+/− within the specific study. For our specific purposes of exploring identity construction in YJC, this process of enactment comprises two stages. First, we recontextualize, from a Systemic Functional Linguistics (SFL) perspective, epistemic relations as an ideational dimension (concerned with what is being talked about) and social relations as an interpersonal axiological dimension (concerned with social values), as shown in Fig. 6.2. This is *not* to suggest that epistemic relations equate to the ideational and social relations equate to the axiological; it is to highlight how these concepts are being enacted from a linguistic perspective within the context of our specific research focus.

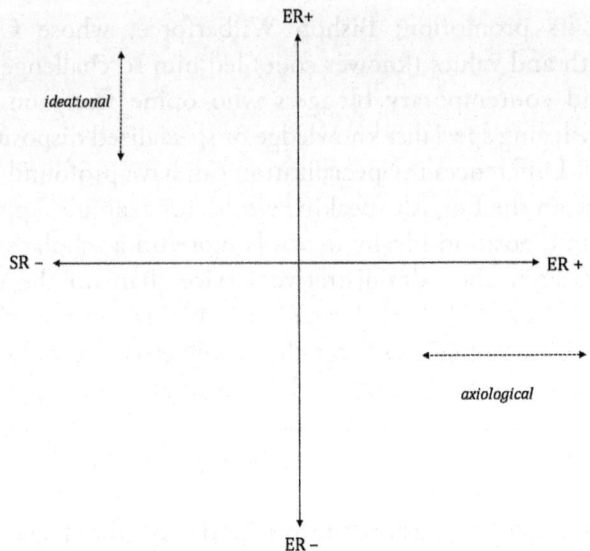

**Fig. 6.2** Enacting Maton's 'specialization plane' to analyse identities in YJC

We will now specify how the dimensions outlined earlier play out within our data, beginning with the commissioned recount.

## 4  YP Identities in the Commissioned Recount

As mentioned at the beginning of this chapter, designers and advocates of conferencing seem to have in mind an ideal YP persona who provides a detailed recount of the offence and is convincingly remorseful about what went on. However, as we have seen, it is far more common for YPs to enact a 'small target' persona who construes a minimalist account of the offence with details 'extracted' by the Convenor (as we have seen in Chap. 3), and who enacts next to no evaluation of what went on so that regret has to be 'promoted' by the Convenor (as we have seen in Chap. 4). On this basis, the ideational dimension (epistemic relations) of our topology traces an axis of 'forthcomingness' depending on how detailed the

## 4 YP Identities in the Commissioned Recount 255

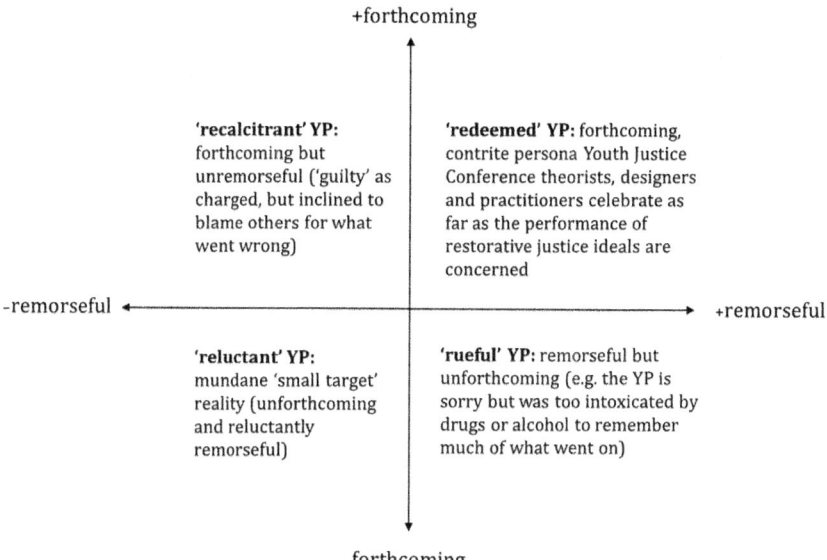

**Fig. 6.3** YP personae topology for commissioned recount and rejoinder steps in the YJC macro-genre (retrospective)

YP's recount of the offence is, and the axiological dimension (social relations) traces an axis of 'remorsefulness' depending on how contrite the YP's attitude to what occurred is (Fig. 6.3). Thus, in our data, epistemic relations are recontextualized (via a focus on the ideational) as degrees of 'forthcomingness', and social relations are recontextualized (via a focus on the axiological) as degrees of 'remorsefulness'. This language of enactment establishes a topology of possible personae, including four principal types: a redeemed persona that is both highly forthcoming and remorseful (+forthcoming, +remorseful), a reluctant persona that is neither forthcoming nor remorseful (−forthcoming, −remorseful), a recalcitrant persona that is forthcoming but not remorseful (+forthcoming, −remorseful) and a rueful persona that is not forthcoming but is remorseful (−forthcoming, +remorseful) (Fig. 6.3).

For example, the 'angry boy' identity enacted in the School Library YJC is an instance of the 'guilty' YP persona (upper left quadrant). This persona is characterized by a fulsome disclosure of the offence but without the corresponding lack of remorse:

### Extract 6.2, School Library YJC

**YP1:** When it all comes down to it I know I wouldn't change anything I've done for anything. Like I still feel like – like a girl's getting picked on and that. It's not right for a guy to pick on a girl and I've just been brought up to stand up for girls and guys shouldn't do it. If a guy's got a problem do something to a guy not to a girl.

This persona contrasts sharply with the significant degree of remorse shown in the recount provided by the 'redeemed' YP (upper right quadrant) in the Train Tracks YJC:

### Extract 6.3, Traintracks YJC

**Convenor:** So what have you thought about since, um, since this incident?
**YP:** How stupid I was. I was just, you know, I dunno, I was just stupid, I think, at that time. I'll think twice next time before I do something like that again.
**Convenor:** So how long after the incident did you have a chance to sort of reflect back on it and think about what happened.
**YP:** Pretty much that day. I called home and I was describing to my mum doing that stupid incident that night because that day I (wanted to) go back and apologize cause (…) I always go there and I felt so bad cause they're always nice to us and we went and done stupid things. (…) Yeah, I was stupid.

Both of these personae produce forthcoming recounts and thus reside in the upper quadrants of the topology, based on their relation to the ideational axis. However, they differ along the axiological axis in terms of the degree of self-reflection and regret which they enact in the conference.

The two other possible personae proposed by our topology are less forthcoming in their recounts. As we have seen in the previous two chapters, the small target 'accused' persona (lower left quadrant) is the most frequent identity enacted by YPs in our sample of conferences; we have already given examples of unforthcoming commissioned recounts where the details have been extracted by the Convenor, virtually a word or short phrase at a time from reluctant YPs. Equally unforthcoming, but more remorseful, is the 'ashamed' YP (lower right quadrant), who typically offers drugs or alcohol as the reason why he or she cannot remember details of the offence. They may also claim to not have knowledge of facts relating to the offence as a way of excusing their behaviour; for example, the YP in the Affray YJC claims that he forgot he was carrying a knife in his pocket at the time of the offence:

**Extract 6.4, Affray YJC**

| | |
|---|---|
| **YP:** | (I) didn't know I even had it on me. |
| **Convenor:** | Ahum. |
| **YP:** | Forgot I had it on me the whole time and then I couldn't remember I had it until they (…) and pulled it out and showed them. It doesn't even work. You can't even use it. |

The major distinction between these two unforthcoming personae is the degree of remorse shown regarding the offence, represented topologically as the distinction between the two lower quadrants.

## 5   YP Identities and the Admonition

A further crucial step in understanding YP identities at stake in the macro-genre is during the admonition. We saw in the examples of Youth Liaison Officer (YLO) discourses provided Chap. 2 that, during the admonition, YLOs often encourage the YP to think about the 'choices' that they make in terms of potential 'consequences'. The YLO's admonition is a future-oriented genre, where the YLOs implore the YPs to think about how their behaviour will impact on their ability to make the most of future opportunities, particularly in relation to employment:

### Extract 6.5, Running Shoes YJC

**YLO:** That's why you need to grow up now and start proving to people you are not the little boy that acts like an idiot. You need to grow up. If you kept behaving this way, you know, your reputation will still follow you. You need to grow out of it. And you know hopefully you can get another job. Your mum says you are a better person when you are working. Maybe that's something you should throw your energy into is finding a job. Put your name out there. That's the things I like to remind you.

The YLOs typically stress the importance of the YPs not reoffending for fear of creating a permanent criminal record that will limit their future prospects:

### Extract 6.6, School Library YJC

**YLO:** If they can do that sort of thing again, they won't get a youth conference. (I'll) refer for a charge. And when they get criminal conviction out of that, they won't get a passport to go to America or New Zealand or European states. They won't be able to apply to go into the defence forces simply because they've got a criminal conviction and a criminal conviction involving offence of violence against a person. If they want to apply for truck drivers job, or whatever laboring job, that employer will do pre-employment check based on the criminal record. So they fill in the application to gain an apprenticeship or whatever they want to do, that employer then does a check through the criminal record section of the NSW Police Department. It comes back, they've got criminal record. That employer then gets that application of theirs and throws it in the shredder. Because they then go through their other applications, they have no adverse history. So that's the idea of Young Offenders' Act, that's why we refer to a conference. So that we sit down and discuss the issues. Get it all out in the open and then they can move on. Everyone can move on.

The YLOs will also often attempt to undo the YPs' alignment with mates who may be pressuring them into criminal behaviour:

## 5 YP Identities and the Admonition 259

**Extract 6.7, Mobile Phone YJC**

YLO: It's a tough time in – in your life when you're getting peer pressure from everybody, and you want to look cool. We understand you want to look cool and hang out with different people, but there's cool and then there's cool, really in trouble, and it's – let me tell you it's not cool. Where you'll end up from getting into all the – all these problems and mixing with the wrong people – there's only one place you'll end up, and usually that's big – big boys' gaol, and there's always somebody tougher than you there, and if they're not tougher, they've just got many more of them to be tough. So, you know, you can't win with it. It – you – it's pointless trying to even – even match up with them.

YLOs may also suggest the personal responsibility that the YP has in governing the unfolding of their future and taking on the advice they have been given in the conference:

**Extract 6.8, Mobile Phone YJC**

YLO: You know, just – and only you can learn. You can – you can either go, you know, take what we're saying and take it on, or you can ignore it, but – and we'll see you again later. But it's up to you. I don't want you to – to do that.

The YLOs will also emphasize the importance of education in being able to enact the right kind of persona:

**Extract 6.9, Mobile Phone YJC**

YLO: But your education is, you're right, it is the biggest thing now, because it depends whether you get into your trade, and most trades – and I know I've got a son the same age and he's just left year eleven and doing a pre-apprenticeship course, and they have to sit tests. They have to sit tests to even get into all these things. Same with the army to do trades, all that sort of stuff. It's no longer just 'Yeah, I'll take you on for a trade', you got to pass tests, and –

and the only way you can pass those tests is by learning. You don't have an education and you're really limited as to what you can do. And you have good job, good money, you have good life. You don't have a good job, you have no money, you have no choices. But you have money, you have choices. But you know, you do it honestly so and so you can feel good about yourself. Be someone that that everybody's proud of, you know.

As we proposed in relation to the commissioned recount, we can also think about the persona being valorized in the admonition genre topologically. The YLOs seem to be promoting an ideal YP who makes rational decisions about their future and who decides to reintegrate with family and community. Here again we are recontextualizing the LCT specialization plane of epistemic relations and social relations as ideational and axiological axes. The ideational axis now involves reasoning about possible effects (how rational will the YP become) and the axiological axis now involves a moral orientation to possible futures (how reintegrated will the YP become). The identities imagined can be glossed as those that are reintegrated (the rational, re-affiliating ideal), delinquent (neither rational nor re-affiliating—YPs who get inadvertently caught up in offending behaviour because they continue to hang with mates), criminal (rational but not re-affiliating—YPs who choose to hang with their mates and purposefully pursue a life of crime) and law-abiding (re-affiliating but not rational—YPs who steer clear of their mates and stay out of trouble for fear of being caught). These personae that the YP might adopt following the conference are outlined in Fig. 6.4. In this model, the ideal prospective YP persona is re-affiliated into key fellowships, including his family and ethnic community, and chooses, through rational deliberation, to avoid the negative influence of other groups, especially 'mates' with a propensity for delinquent behaviour.

We can contrast this identity profile with the profile generated for the commissioned recount and rejoinder steps in the YJC macro-genre that were introduced earlier. As outlined in Fig. 6.5, these unfold during the conference from a past-oriented logic of redemption to a future-oriented logic of reintegration (from retrospective personae to prospective personae).

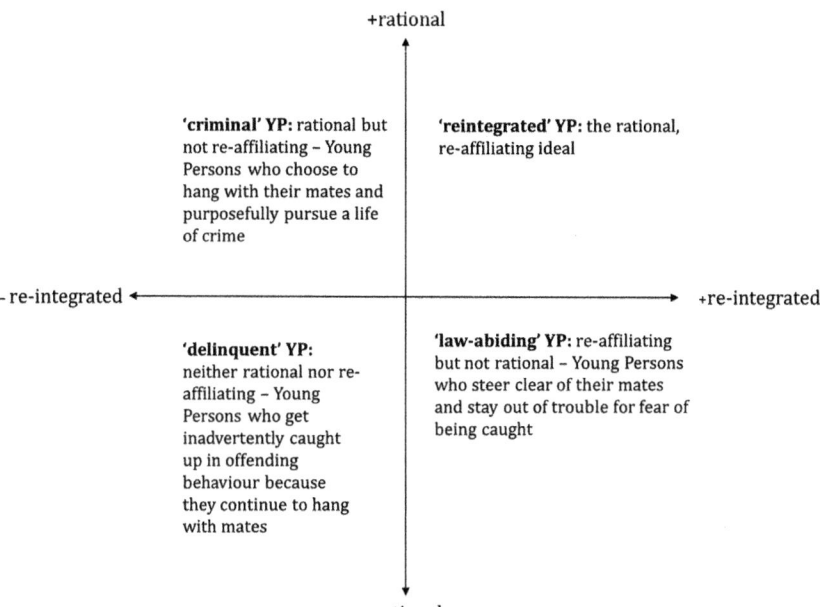

**Fig. 6.4** YP personae topology for admonition step in the YJC macro-genre (prospective)

The main point we are making here is that the personae YPs are expected to construe ideationally, enact interpersonally and compose textually are sensitive to the staging of the macro-genre as it unfolds. The ideal retrospective identity is not constructed out of the same semiotic resources as their prospective one. As ever, the choices we make as users of language depend on their use—or, to put this more technically, coding orientations (i.e. predispositions to meaning) interact with genre.

As Maton has pointed out to us (personal communication), the ideal retrospective YP for the Convenor in the commissioned recount and rejoinder steps in a YJC and the ideal prospective YP for the YLO in the admonition step (Fig. 6.5) perform comparable personae—both embody an identity capable of displaying publicly that they are self-disciplining social subjects who have internalized the power that will ensure they maintain ways of acting, thinking and being appro-

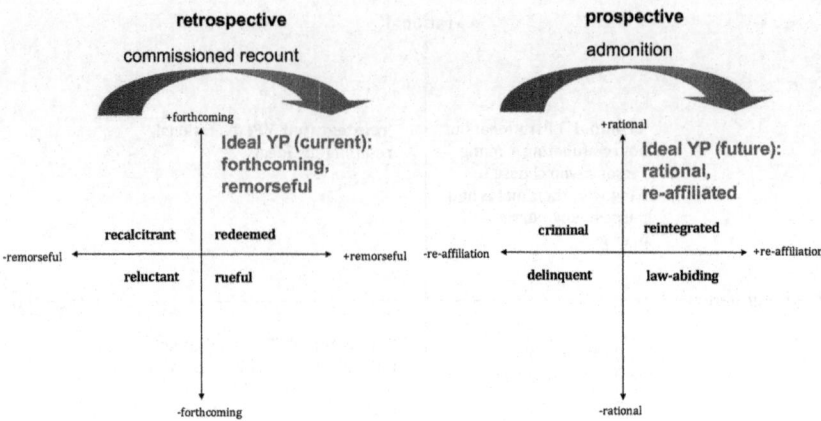

**Fig. 6.5** Retrospective and prospective identity profiles for the commissioned recount and admonition genres

priate to a citizen (after Foucault 1977). These YP personae can be further generalized to the personae celebrated by constructivist discovery learning educators in student-centred classrooms, where the same kind of social subject is facilitated to learn via osmosis—to the exclusion of social subjects of other kinds (Rose and Martin 2012). Generalizations of this kind across personae show how we might eventually conceptualize affiliation, seen in terms of how personae negotiate feeling, as a hierarchy of bond complexes—of shared values at ever-higher levels of abstraction, configuring subcultures—and eventually master identities organized by gender, ethnicity, class, generation and dis/ability.

As Maton further notes (personal communication), we can 'translate' from the 'external languages' used to describe the retrospective and the prospective personae in the two stages of the macro-genre back into the internal language of description of ER/SR (the specialization plane outlined in Fig. 6.1). This enables us to see the two personae as instantiations of the same organizing principles: they are the ways that specific modalities of ER and SR play out in those stages. While they may appear different empirically, they are both underpinned by the same organizing principles, as shown by Specialization codes.

# 6  Support Person Identities

It is of course not only the YP who is positioned to produce particular identity performances in the macro-genre. For example, the identities enacted in the avouchment by Support Persons are less future-oriented than those proposed for YPs in the Caution; they have more of a focus on vouching for a YP's current capacity to behave appropriately. Two dimensions are important in relation to Support Person personae in this genre:

(i) Change, an epistemic relation between current and future behaviour (how far under way), where the epistemic relation involves ideational management of transformation
(ii) Faith, a social relation between the Support Person and the YP (how good inside), where the social relation involves an axiological orientation to the YP's true character (Fig. 6.6)

The idealized Support Person in conferencing is the 'guarantor' (upper right quadrant, Fig. 6.6) who has faith in the YP's character and the possibility for transformation. This persona is usually enacted by a parent who expresses negative emotions about how the offence has impacted on them but praises the virtues of the YP and his or her capacity to change. It is possible for this kind of Support Person to apologize on behalf of the YP:

**Extract 6.10, School Library YJC**

**Support Person:** I don't condone his actions at all and I'm really sorry to everyone for what he did to everyone

Guarantors, in our sample of conferences, are usually mothers who are positioned by the macro-genre and used by the Convenor (and sometimes an Ethnic Community Liaison Officer (ECLO) or YLO) to foster shame and contrition in the YP (as we will see later). By way of contrast, the 'disowner' divests themselves of responsibility for the YP. For example, in the following extract, the Support Person wants her son to be dealt with by authorities in a non-diversionary legal process:

## 6 Performing Identity: A Topological Perspective

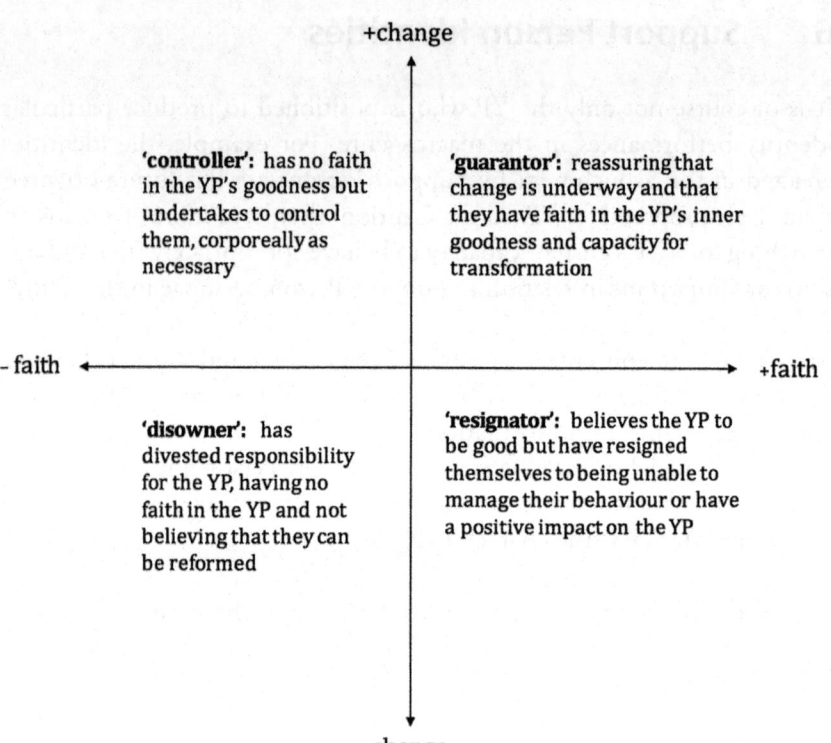

**Fig. 6.6** Support person personae topology for the avouchment step in the YJC macro-genre (retrospective)

### Extract 6.11, Guidedog YJC

**Convenor:** Sharon, what – how did you find out? Were you the first one of the family to find out?

**Support Person:** Yeah Constable Kennedy rang me up on the mobile phone asking if I knew where Nathan was and I said no and and I just straight away I said 'well, what's he done?' and he said 'you wouldn't believe it. He's stolen a wallet off a blind lady'. And I went 'I beg your pardon'. And he said it, repeated himself again and I (…) he goes 'Do you know where he is?'. I went 'No' but I said 'Oh'. Me and my older daughter go straight in the car and went down to Morwood because I thought if he's got money that's – they usually – where the kids go and so yeah that's how I found out. And then I rang my mum later on that afternoon and said 'Nathan's stolen a wallet from a blind lady'. And my mum's a bit naive when it comes to Nathan. She seems to look for the best in Nathan and I (…) and she goes 'oh, he wouldn't have done that' and I said 'Well, he has and so if you see him, grab hold of him because I need to speak to him' because I was going to take him straight to the police station up at Hardacre because I actually said to Constable Kennedy 'Well when you see him charge him'. I said 'It's disgusting'. I said 'I want him charged'. I said 'He's not learning any other way' and I said 'That poor lady', you know, I was actually disgusted.

As we can see, ideal support persons (so positioned in Fig. 6.6) are closely aligned with the ideal YP (so positioned in Fig. 6.4). They believe in the YP's potential for reintegration.

# 7 Conclusion

In this chapter we have considered the range of identities made available for YPs and Support Persons at critical stages of conferencing (testimony, rejoinder and admonition), adapting Maton's work on specialization codes. This meant recontextualizing his ER and SR axes from the perspective of ideational and axiological meaning in SFL, selecting dimensions sensitive to the goals of YJCs and mapping identities accordingly. This mapping highlights some of the key values underpinning the design of conferences, with ideal YPs and Support Persons positioned to publicly confirm that YPs have the confidence and self-discipline to behave as responsible citizens. The way in which conferences foster these ideals, through a process of ritual redress, will be the focus of the next and final chapter of this volume.

# References

Antaki, C., & Widdicombe, S. (1998). Identity as an achievement and as a tool. In C. Antaki & S. Widdicombe (Eds.), *Identities in talk* (pp. 1–14). London: Sage.

Bauman, Z. (2004). *Identity: Conversations with Benedetto Vecchi*. Cambridge: Polity Press.

Benwell, B., & Stokoe, E. (2007). *Discourse and identity*. Edinburgh: Edinburgh University Press.

Berger, P. L., & Luckmann, T. (1966). *The social construction of reality: A treatise in the sociology of knowledge*. Garden City/New York: Anchor Books.

Bernstein, B. (1996/2000). *Pedagogy, symbolic control and identity: Theory, research, critique*. London: Taylor and Francis.

Bernstein, B. (2000). *Pedagogy, symbolic control and identity: Theory, research, critique*. London: Taylor & Francis. [Revised Edition].

Butler, J. (1990). *Gender trouble and the subversion of identity*. London: Routledge.

Coupland, N. (2007). *Style: Language variation and identity*. London: Cambridge University Press.

Davies, B., & Harré, R. (1990). Positioning: The discursive production of selves. *Journal for the Theory of Social Behaviour, 20*, 43–63.

Firth, J. R. (1957). *Papers in linguistics, 1934–1951*. London: Oxford University Press.

Foucault, M. (1977). *Discipline and punish: The birth of the prison*. New York: Vintage.

Harris, N., Walgrave, L., & Braithwaite, J. (2004). Emotional dynamics in restorative conferences. *Theoretical Criminology an International Journal, 8*, 191–210.

Hasan, R. (2005). *Language, society and consciousness*. London: Equinox. (The collected works of Ruqaiya Hasan, edited by J. Webster, Vol. 1).

Hasan, R. (2009). *Semantic variation: Meaning in society and sociolinguistics*. London: Equinox. (The collected works of Ruqaiya Hasan, edited by J. Webster, Vol. 2).

Hayes, H. (2006). Apologies & accounts in youth justice conferencing. *Contemporary Justice Review, 9*, 369–385.

Jayyursi, L. (1984). *Categorization and the moral order*. Boston/London: Routledge and Kegan Paul.

Labov, W. (2006). *The social stratification of English in New York City* (2nd ed.). Cambridge: Cambridge University Press.

Martin, J. R. (2008). Innocence: Realisation, instantiation and individuation in a Botswanan town. In K. Knight & A. Mahboob (Eds.), *Questioning linguistics* (pp. 27–54). Cambridge: Cambridge Scholars Publishing.

Maton, K. (2007). Knowledge-knower structures in intellectual and educational fields. In F. Christie & J. R. Martin (Eds.), *Language, knowledge and pedagogy* (pp. 87–108). London: Continuum.

Maton, K. (2009). Progress and canons in the arts and humanities: Knowers and gazes. In K. Maton & R. Moore (Eds.), *Social realism, knowledge and the sociology of education: Coalitions of the mind* (pp. 154–178). London: Continuum.

Maton, K. (2014). *Knowledge and knowers: Towards a realist sociology of education*. London: Routledge.

Maton, K., & Chen, R. T. (2016). LCT in qualitative research: Creating a translation device for studying constructivist pedagogy. In K. Maton, S. Hood, & S. Shay (Eds.), *Knowledge building: Educational studies in legitimation code theory* (pp. 27–48). London: Routledge.

Maton, K., Doran, Y. (2017). Semantic density: A translation device for revealing complexity of knowledge practices in discourse, part 1-wording. Onomazein, Special Issue SFL(1), 46–76.

Retzinger, S., & Scheff, T. (1996). Strategy for community conferences: Emotions and social bonds. In B. Galaway & J. Hudson (Eds.), *Restorative justice: International perspectives* (pp. 315–336). Monsey: Criminal Justice Press.

Rose, D., & Martin, J. R. (2012). *Learning to write, reading to learn: Genre, knowledge and pedagogy in the Sydney school*. London: Equinox.

Sacks, H. (1992). In G. Jefferson (Ed.), *Lectures on conversation. Volumes I and II*. Oxford: Blackwell.

Trudgill, P. (1974). *The social differentiation of English in Norwich*. Cambridge: Cambridge University Press.

Van Stokkom, B. (2002). Moral emotions in restorative justice conferences: Managing shame, designing empathy. *Theoretical Criminology*, 6, 339–360.

Zappavigna, M., Dwyer, P., & Martin, J. R. (2007). "Just like sort of guilty kind of": The rhetoric of tempered admission in Youth Justice conferencing. In M. Zappavigna & C. Cloran (Eds.), *Proceedings of Australian systemic functional linguistics Congress*. Woollongong. http://www.asfla.org.au/category/asfla2007/

Zappavigna, M., Dwyer, P., & Martin, J. R. (2008). Syndromes of meaning: Exploring patterned coupling in a NSW youth justice conference. In A. Mahboob & K. Knight (Eds.), *Questioning linguistics* (pp. 03–117). Newcastle upon Tyne: Cambridge Scholars Publishing.

Zimmerman, D., & Weider, L. (1970). Ethnomethodology and the problem of order. In J. Douglas (Ed.), *Understanding everyday life* (pp. 285–295). Chicago: Aldine.

# 7

# Ceremonial Redress: How Conferencing in Fact Achieves Its Goals

## 1 Introduction

Our first exposure to New South Wales (NSW) Youth Justice Conferences (YJCs), observing and recording these events while sitting in the circle among other participants, was surprising to us as linguists. Having surveyed the restorative justice literature and theories of reintegrative shaming and emotional transformation, we were puzzled by the relative absence of sustained emotional language and behaviour in the conferences. Why didn't the Young Person (YP) cry? Why was the apology often prompted by the Convenor rather than fervently offered by a visibly contrite offender? Where was the 'passion play'? In fact, what we observed seemed fairly procedural. Despite this, the social significance of these proceedings was also very apparent, and we were aware of research suggesting that participants reported high rates of satisfaction with the process (Palk et al. 1998; Trimboli 2000; Strang et al. 1999; Hayes and Daly 2003).

As this chapter suggests, we came to suspect that theorists may have been looking in the wrong place when trying to find a way of explaining the transformation that occurs in a conference. Instead of a theory of transformation based on personal internal emotional states, we came to prefer a social semiotic approach that accounted for the interactive power of the macro-genre—an approach that dealt with the way it drew on shared cultural resources to realign the YP with the positive values of particular communities. What was needed, in other words, was a secular theory of ritual and attendant iconization.

## 2   Discourse Iconography

Tann's (2010a, b, 2013) work was introduced in relation to membership categorization and vocatives in Chap. 5 in order to investigate how the different communities into which the YP might be reintegrated are referenced in conferences. His work on Gemeinschaft is part of his more general model of what he calls discourse iconography. Tann's basic approach involves a tripartite model, comprising the concepts of 'Gemeinschaft' (drawing on Tönnies 1887/1974), 'Doxa' (drawing on Bourdieu, and Thompson 1991) and Oracle (drawing on Systemic Functional Linguistic SFL) perspectives on bonding icons (Stenglin 2008b)] (Fig. 7.1)). As we have seen, Gemeinschaft is concerned with the ways in which discourse enacts communities as fellowships that both include and exclude; Doxa attends to the communal values around which fellowships rally—their 'core values' if you will; and Oracle deals with iconic artefacts, images and texts radiating these values.

Tann (2010b) illustrates this perspective with respect to Obama's rise to power in the USA. During this period, there were a range of discourses that construed 'Americans' as a distinct fellowship (as opposed to say Iraqis or Chinese), collectivized as 'we' and with a homeland 'in America', not elsewhere (not, for example, in Bush's 'axis of evil'). These characteristics of the discourse surrounding Obama's rise are captured in terms of Gemeinschaft. Bonding this American fellowship were values such as 'freedom' and 'democracy', and the 'we can do it if we just try hard enough and believe deeply enough' mythology immortalized in the campaign adage 'yes we can'. These values are captured as Doxa. In addition, campaign posters and TV ads drew heavily on Obama as an icon, including

## 2 Discourse Iconography

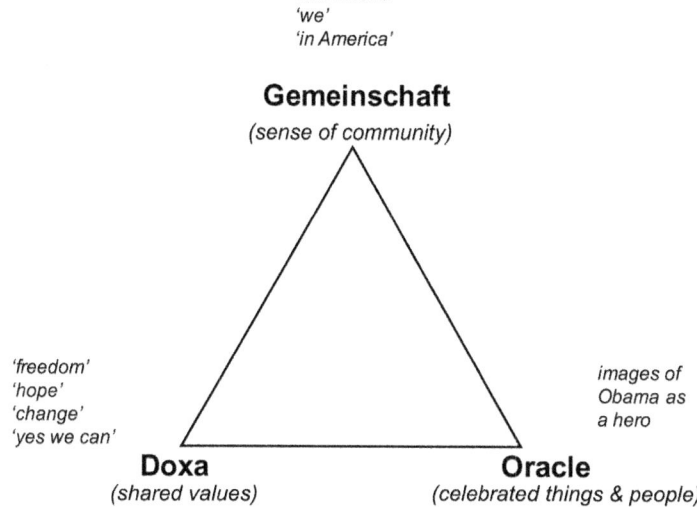

Fig. 7.1 Tann's topological perspective on discourse iconography (Adapted from Tann 2010b)

images of Obama construed as a 'hero', the multicultural story of his life and the star-spangled banner. These artefacts are captured as Oracle. The resources at play here are exemplified in Fig. 7.2.

In our work on discourse iconography in YJCs we have adopted Tann's three basic dimensions, although renaming Gemeinschaft as Communitas—in part paying homage to Turner's concern with the intensity of communion experienced by those participating in a rite of passage and in part with respect to reservations we have about opposing Gemeinschaft to Gesellschaft (opposing 'community and society' in Tönnies' (1887/2001) terms). Tann's Oracle category has also been provisionally adjusted to make room for our interest in ceremony. As outlined in Fig. 7.3, the current model opposes icon to creed, with icons distinguished as heroes (e.g. Obama) and relics (e.g. the American flag). Creed is divided into rituals (e.g. presidential inaugurations), parables (e.g. generalized exemplary 'stories' such as those invoking the Horatio Alger 'rags to riches' myth) and scripture (phases of discourse preserved in writing or collective memory, typically sourced, which distil the essence of a particular set of values that bond a community).

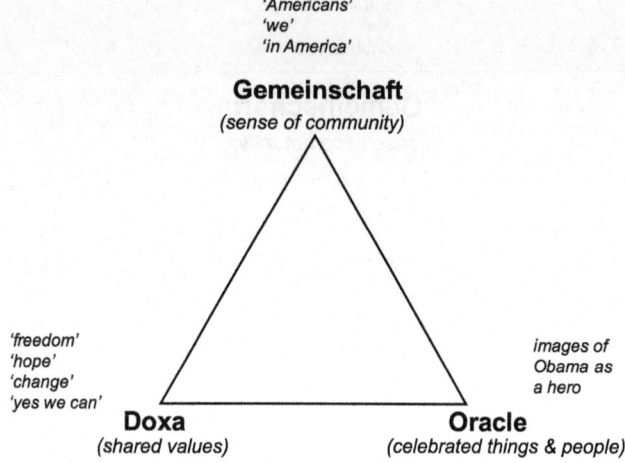

**Fig. 7.2** Obama iconography (Based on Tann 2010b)

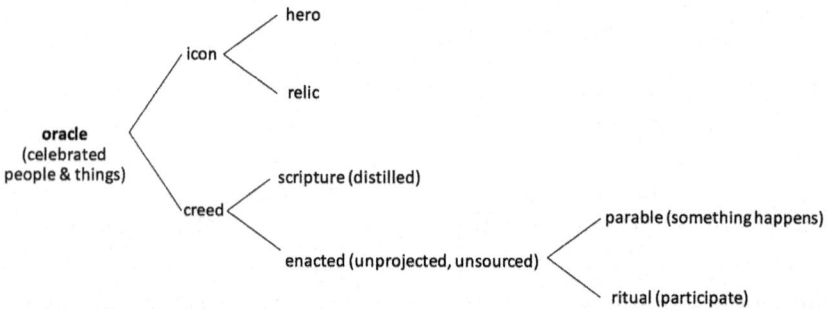

**Fig. 7.3** Extended Oracle dimension of discourse iconography resources in discourse

## 3 Iconization

From the perspective of functional linguistics, we are interested in how iconography is realized in discourse. Specifically, we are concerned with the realization of Oracle via processes of what we call iconization. In general terms, within SFL work on affiliation, iconization refers to the process whereby the everyday meaning of an event or an entity is backgrounded while its emotional significance to members of a group is foregrounded (or vice versa). Technically speaking, iconization involves ideational meaning being discharged and interpersonal meaning being charged (or vice versa). This is a familiar process in language, which we all recognize in relation to idioms and metaphors. An idiom such as *cool as a cucumber*, for example, invokes a judgement of someone's imperturbable character, and doesn't normally call the salad vegetable to mind; similarly, if we describe the toilet paper in a pristine lavatory as hidden in its cover and peeping through its slit (as Bernstein does when using types of lavatory to illustrate his concept of classification (Bernstein 1975: 153)), then we are commenting on the prophylactic character of the householder, not the toilet paper's sneaky 'peeping Tom' ogling of people in the loo (see Martin and White (2005) on lexical metaphor and provoked attitude).

The same iconization process is at work with interpersonal grammatical metaphors (Halliday and Matthiessen 2014). An indirect speech act like *Would you like to do the washing up now?* is pragmatically a request for a service, not just an inquiry about what you'd like to do; the expected response is compliant action (*OK, I'll do it*), not an expression of feeling (*No, I'd hate it*). Similarly, with explicitly subjective metaphors of modality (e.g. *I think they'll win*), we're mainly assessing the probability of a proposition ('maybe they'll win'), not telling someone about our mental processes of cognition ('what I'm thinking').

Significantly, iconization is a matter of degree; ideational meaning may be more or less fully discharged, inversely in relation to the interpersonal charge. This enables Sherlock's smug repartee in the following exchange from 'The Great Game' episode of the TV series *Sherlock*; Watson is modalizing (*Has it occurred to you…*) but Sherlock cuts him off by treating the metaphorical modality literally as a question about what Sherlock is thinking:

**Watson:** You realize we've only stopped for breath since this thing started. *Has it occurred to you–*
**Sherlock:** *Probably.*

This forces Watson to repeat his move, in order to table the proposition he is actually trying to negotiate (i.e. the fact that the bomber is playing a game with Sherlock):

**Watson:** No, has it occurred to you that the bomber's playing a game with you. The envelope. Breaking into the other flat. The dead kid's shoes. It's all meant for you.
**Sherlock:** Yes, I know.[1]

Iconized expressions of this kind (including highly iconized items like idioms) can be ideationally recharged, as Caple's (2008, 2013) work on image nuclear news stories has shown. This happens frequently in this news genre as editors select an image which draws attention to ideational meaning that has at some point been discharged from the headline in order to charge the attitudinal meaning of a phrase. For example, in one of Caple's examples, the idiom *getting the cold shoulder*, attitudinally charged as 'being rudely brushed off', is recharged ideationally in an image of men tipping buckets of water over their heads in the snow.

Work on iconization was initially inspired by Stenglin's work on bonding in museum exhibitions, where bonding is concerned with constructing the attitudinal disposition of visitors in relation to exhibits. Its basic function is to align people into groups with shared dispositions. Stenglin concentrated on artefacts which have been super-charged, axiologically speaking, giving as examples symbolic icons such as flags, logos, colours, memorabilia and so on, which rally visitors around communal ideals. These bonding icons, termed bondicons for short, are explored in a Te Papa museum exhibition in Martin and Stenglin (2007), and in relation to Olympian ideals in Stenglin (2008b) (see also Stenglin 2004, 2008a, 2009, 2012; Stenglin and Djonov 2010).

Familiar bondicons for peace, which anchor communities of protest against war, are exemplified in Fig. 7.4. Symbols of this kind illustrate the way in which values can be materialized as images. But iconization can also involve people, including well-known embodiments of peaceful protest, such as Gandhi, and of liberation, such as Mandela. Further examples of iconization would include ceremonies, proverbs, slogans,

## 3 Iconization

**Fig. 7.4** Well-known bondicons for peace

memorable quotations, flags, team colours, coats of arms, mascots and so on—all of which radiate values for specific communities of people to rally around.

What about iconization in YJCs? Taken at face value, YJCs are spartan events when compared with formal court proceedings, in the sense that they are stripped bare of the symbolic regalia iconizing the authority of the state (coat of arms, gowns and robes, wigs, gavel, bible, elevated seating, crafted wooden joinery, designer furnishings, legal tomes and so on). This absence of regalia, however, can be seen as creating opportunities for iconization of other kinds. The circle seating arrangement (Fig. 1.1, Chap. 1) prescribed for conferences itself symbolizes the consultative reintegrating processes designers had in mind. In addition, in our data, both the hijab (Muslim head scarf) and police uniform were leveraged as iconizing identities of different kinds (see later examples). And, arguably, even the modest, often shabby room in a Police Citizens Youth Club is itself a kind of bondicon—its bareness, relying as it does on minimal resources from the state and the unremunerated goodwill of most involved, standing against the richly appointed courtroom alternatives which iconize the retributive power of the state.

Consider at this point a phase from the Affray YJC. The YP is from a Muslim background and his mother is acting as his Support Person with an Ethnic Community Liaison Officer (ECLO) from the Muslim community also present. Here, out of apparent frustration that the exchanges aimed at eliciting remorse from the YP may have failed, the ECLO invokes relevant bondicons as a means of getting through to the YP. As we have seen, the first bondicon he introduces is the hijab (which brings to bear the Islamic cultural background that the YP and the ECLO share):

### Extract 7.1, Affray YJC

**ECLO:** Listen, [looking to the Convenor] I want to take, with your permission, I want to take a different angle. OK? Mate, what's your mum wearing on her head?
**YP:** Scarf.
**ECLO:** Yeah. OK.

Here the ECLO is presuming that the YP shares his respect for this Islamic symbol, and that it will thus provoke an emotional response that might inspire him to talk more candidly about his offending behaviour.

Following this, the next bondicon is the police uniform, symbolizing the regulatory power of the state and thereby drawing attention to the YP's transgression. The uniform is leveraged here to condemn the YP's behaviour and to shame him in front of his mother:

### Extract 7.2, Affray YJC

**ECLO:** What a – where is she now? In the presence of who?
**YP:** Me.
**ECLO:** Who – who's – No. Who's sitting here? Who's sitting here right now? Have a look across.
**YP:** Men.
**ECLO:** Have a – but have a look across. What uniform are they wearing?
**YP:** Police uniform.
**ECLO:** OK.

From these examples we can see that iconization can play a pivotal role in shaming discourse processes aimed at reintegrating YPs into relevant communities. The hijab has been used to align the YP, his mother and the ECLO into a religious cum ethnic community whose ideal values would not position them in opposition to police, and the values of the wider community they represent.

One of the most highly significant bonding icons in youth justice conferencing appears to be the figure of the Mother.[2] If there are moments when the conferences do approach what is envisioned in the restorative justice literature in terms of an imagined passion play of remorse, apology and forgiveness, then it is the iconized figure of the Mother that is the pivot. Mothers acting as Support Persons for the YP are regularly subjected to a number of questions about the pain that they might feel about their child's offence. The overdetermined frequency of these questions positions the mothers as iconized 'heroes' enduring this pain ('heroes' in the sense of Fig. 7.3)—a kind of 'Mater Dolorosa' icon, to draw on a Catholic perspective, who endures maternal pain as part of conference proceedings.

This patterning of repeated emphasis on the mother's experiences surrounding the offence has a particular role in the iconization processes at work in the conferences. As an icon of maternal pain, the mother is positioned to ignite shame in the YP in order to prompt the remorse needed for the hoped-for passion play. Her presence also functions to suggest the possibility of forgiveness through maternal love. In almost every conference in our sample, the Convenor repeatedly calls on the YP to reflect on the distress that their offending behaviour has caused their mother through direct references to the mother's emotional AFFECT. For example, consider again the probing moves made by Convenors in the extension stage of the commissioned recount. These moves are designed to leverage the mother's negative affect as a catalyst invoking shame in the YP (**affect shown in bold**):

### Extract 7.3, Shopping Trolley YJC

**Convenor:** You did. And what about, um, did you see mum **upset**? Was mum **upset**?

### Extract 7.4, Affray YJC

**Convenor:** So Aatif, how do you **feel** about the fact that, you know, mum is still getting **upset** about this? How does that make you **feel**?

In YJCs we suggest that the YP is asked to connect with their own mother's pain as a means of achieving secular renewal via 'reintegrative shaming' (Braithwaite). Central to the probing moves made by the Convenor to prompt the YPs to reflect on this maternal pain is Braithwaite's concern with reintegration in the presence of the YP's 'community of concern' (Braithwaite 1989: 85). As we have seen, by drawing attention to the shared values central to different Communitas (Tann's Gemeinschaft) invoked in the conferences, this involves a reintegration of the YP both into a putative community of ethical citizens and into more particular networks such as family. The mother in the avouchment can thus be seen to represent both the mother–child dyad and the family as a network of concern into which the YP should be realigned.

As far as family relationships are concerned, Convenors will sometimes make an explicit meta-comment on familial roles, as in the following example:

### Extract 7.5, Mobile Phone YJC

| | |
|---|---|
| **Convenor:** | So Brody, how do you feel about the fact that, you know, mum is still getting upset about this? How does that make you feel? |
| **YP:** | (Sad) |
| **Convenor:** | Do you feel OK about the fact that mum gets upset? |
| **YP:** | [shakes head] |
| **Convenor:** | Nup? How does it make you feel? |
| **YP:** | Sad. |
| **Convenor:** | Sad. … Not good to see mum upset is it? |
| **YP:** | Mm. |
| **Convenor:** | Mums don't like getting upset. Trust me. Stephanie and I will tell you that. When our kids do something wrong, it really hurts us. Deep down, here. OK. Because you think you are doing the right thing for your kids and you're teaching them and educating them and giving them a roof over their head. Remember I spoke to you about that the other day? How lucky you are? And yeah, all all par – every parent wants is the best for their kid. Don't they, you can imagine that. You've got nieces and nephews, yeah? You don't want them to get into trouble do you? So you can |

|        | understand how mum's feeling and dad's feeling? Does that make you stop and think about whether or not you may do something like that again? What does it make you feel? What does it make you think? |
|--------|---|
| YP:    | Think before you do something. |

The offending behaviour of the YPs has obviously brought them into conflict with shared values associated with the Doxa of the parent–child dyad. The YPs have broken the value of respecting their mother and have, as far as affiliation is concerned, broken the parent–child bond. The radiating iconography at play is outlined in Fig. 7.5 (using our term Communitas in place of Tann's Gemeinschaft, as previously noted).

The tears shed by the mothers during the avouchment, which we discussed in Chap. 4, appear to be a result of this liminal disintegration. Convenors and Youth Liaison Officers (YLOs) draw on the emotional power of this disintegration when they call the YPs to observe their mothers' pain, a powerful rhetorical move that can be seen to be an important device in the passion play more globally. The maternal tears themselves act as a super-charged icon (a bondicon). Making the mother cry in this way is thus a 'special' form of crying; the mother is positioned by the conference as more than sad—her crying is a demonstration to the YPs of the painful consequences of their behaviour, not just to the Victim, but to all concerned.

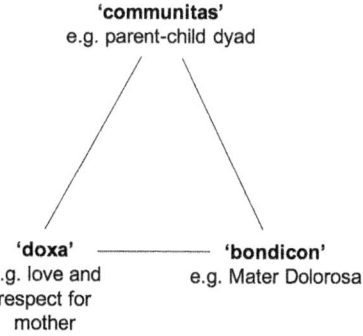

**Fig. 7.5** The parent–child dyad as Communitas

Let us now consider some significant examples of the Oracle dimension of Tann's model that is associated with artefacts and texts in our YJC data. The most obvious example of sourced scripture is the New South Wales Young Offender's Act 1997. In the Mandate step of conferences, this act is invoked as the relevant encompassing legal framework for the meeting. Its invocation enacts the conference, performatively, as a legal proceeding.

**Extract 7.6, Mobile Phone YJC**

**Convenor:** … and the conference has been convened under the Young Offender's Act, OK, and Brody has admitted to his offence. Yes?
**YP:** [nods]

In our next example, the Convenor invokes a 'decisive moment' parable by way of impressing on the YP that it is time to turn his life around. The parable is introduced through the expression 'draw a line in the sand', a piece of distilled creed[3] which names the generalized story line to follow. The story is then unpacked as the sequence of events an ideal YP should be proceeding through. This idiom and the generalized story surrounding it are here enacting a ceremonial transition, creating a boundary between an unreformed YP persona and the reintegrated YP persona, which the YP is expected to assume.

**Extract 7.7, Mobile Phone YJC**

**Convenor:** Draw the line in the sand, OK? Have you heard that expression before? You draw a line in the sand. Yesterday was on this side of the line, everything we did, everything we did wrong, decisions we made, are forgotten, and we step over that line to tomorrow, to the future, where we learn to make the right decisions and where we think about what we do before we do it. Yep? So this is it, today's the line in the sand, Brody, alright? Tomorrow you move on. You go back to school, you work hard, you get your school certificate, you stay out of trouble, you make yourself proud and you make your family proud, by not getting into trouble. Alright?

The Convenor uses the parable to invite the YP to realign with the Communitas at risk, the family ('you make your family proud'), and to assume the attendant shared values of self-respect and pride. This iconized reintegration process is interpreted in relation to Communitas, Doxa and the relevant bondicon in Fig. 7.6.

Shared values are also negotiated in the previous example where the ECLO invokes the hijab and police uniform bondicons in order to associate with the Muslim community. The evaluative charge of these iconization manoeuvres is further intensified as the ECLO reintroduces the icon as 'your mum wearing a scarf', with its attendant iconized religious and cultural meanings in relation to the presence of outsiders (we researchers) at the conference.

**Extract 7.8, Affray YJC**

**ECLO:** [pointing to the university researchers] Where are these guys from? They're from a certain place. OK. What's the perception going to be?
**YP:** Think bad of me.
**ECLO:** What are they going to – when they see your mum wearing a scarf, I'm Muslim background myself. What are they going to think?
**YP:** Bad.
**ECLO:** OK.

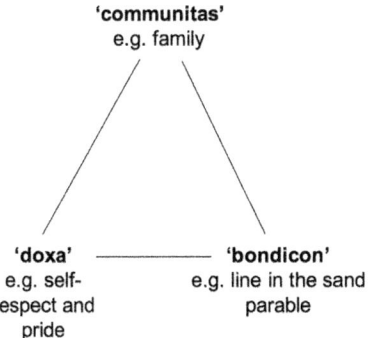

**Fig. 7.6** Reintegration iconography (family, self-respect and pride, 'line in the sand' parable)

These values are even more explicitly inscribed by the ECLO in the following exchange:

### Extract 7.9, Affray YJC

| | |
|---|---|
| **ECLO:** | You respect your mum? |
| **YP:** | Yes. |
| **ECLO:** | No you don't. I'm telling you, brother, you don't respect your mum. Do you understand? You have no respect for your mum. |
| **ECLO:** | You have no respect for your mum whatsoever, brother. You have no respect for what your mum's got on her head. You have no respect for our community. You have no respect. You tell me, brother, how it's a part of our culture or our religion or our tradition to do things like that. You tell me when. |

This iconized reintegration process is interpreted in relation to Communitas (Muslim community), Doxa (respect for mother) and the relevant bondicon (hijab) in Fig. 7.7.

Even where there is no directly apparent sub-community of particular values to call upon, such as those we have seen earlier leveraged by the ECLO, the Convenor will draw upon the idea of an imagined community of ethical citizens. This is an imagined community who self-regulate their behaviour (as opposed to being regulated by a particular world view

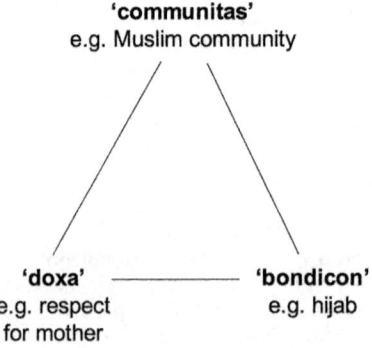

**Fig. 7.7** Reintegration iconography (Muslim community, respect for mother, hijab bondicon)

such as a religious creed) and obey the law. The rhetoric will often involve invoking an iconized 'Victim', particularly in conferences where the actual Victim of the crime is absent, as in the following example:

**Extract 7.10, Mobile Phone YJC**

| | |
|---|---|
| **Convenor:** | Have you ever been a victim of crime? |
| **YP:** | No. |
| **Convenor:** | You are very fortunate, very, very fortunate. Because most people, on average, have had something happen to them in the course of their life, OK. Whether it – whether they had have had their car stolen, or their bag snatched, or their house broken into, or they've been assaulted. Like Stephanie and myself, you know, in the police, you get assaulted. Lots of bad things happen. I'm sure David and Margaret have had things happen to them. So, everybody, usually has had something happen to them, and I hope touch wood you don't ever have anything happen to you. OK? Because it's not a good – it's not a good feeling, to have something taken away from you, as you could imagine. Can you imagine if someone came into your home, when you weren't there, and just took everything? How would you feel? |

The iconization of an imagined Victim here reinforces a Doxa demanding empathy for other citizens and a corresponding logic of obeying the law. These are the values shared by an imagined Communitas of ethical citizens (Fig. 7.8).

Perhaps the most strongly iconized Victim that we encountered with our data was a vision-impaired woman who had her wallet stolen after chatting with the YP in a shopping centre. The YP's mother explains that she could scarcely believe it when she received the news that her son had stolen from a 'blind lady'.

**Extract 7.11, Guide Dog YJC**

| | |
|---|---|
| **Mother:** | I said 'well, what's he done?' and he said 'you wouldn't believe it. He's stolen a wallet off a blind lady'. And I went 'I beg your pardon'. And he said it, repeated himself again… |

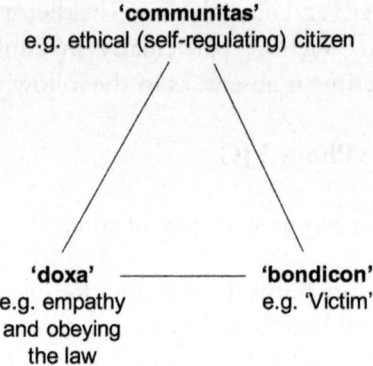

**Fig. 7.8** Reintegration iconography (ethical citizen, empathy and obeying the law, 'Victim')

The importance of the subject position of a vision-impaired person in the iconization processes of this conference is further evidenced by the way the Convenor interrupts the Victim's recount of the offence to allow the members of the conference circle to try on glasses that give the wearer an impression of what it is like to have a comparable vision impairment:

### 7.12, Guide Dog YJC

| | |
|---|---|
| **Convenor:** | Can I just interrupt you for a minute? Have you got those glasses with you Donna? |
| **Victim:** | Oh yes. |
| **Convenor:** | Can we pass them around? And Pat just open that door just to let a bit of breeze in? Is that OK? Thanks. So these are the actual glasses that that Nathan put on. |
| **Victim:** | Yes. |
| **Convenor:** | I might just pass them around so people can have a look at what your vision's like. Sorry, keep going. |

The Convenor also invites this Victim to give a moving personal recount of how she lost her vision:

## Extract 7.12, Guide Dog YJC

**Convenor:** Do you mind sharing your story about when you lost your sight just so people can get a bit of a background so people realize how hard it's been for you to try and adapt and, you know, live by yourself and things like that.

**Victim:** Yes – yes, I lost my vision when I turned fifty. And what happened was I had an allergic reaction to a herbal medication I was taking for menopause and the – the reaction caused me to have a bleed in my brain and I had stroke-like symptoms.

In effect what is going on here is that the Victim is being canonized as a hyper-victimized Victim. And she is being super-charged by the Convenor in this way to maximize the impact of the crime and a concomitant feeling of shame in the YP and empathic Support Persons.

Further examples of iconization occurred where YPs were advised to distance themselves from an inappropriate group. In this case, iconization was being used not for alignment into a community, but rather to achieve disalignment of the YP with certain groups. Most conferences involved phases where the Convenor or YLO counselled the YP to discontinue associating with a negatively iconized group of 'mates':

## Extract 7.13, Mobile Phone YJC

**Convenor:** Seriously think about your **mates**. I mean really seriously. That's the big – that's the big I think message today, Brody, OK. You got to go away and think about that, alright? Do the right thing for yourself. Stephanie's already told you. You're with them, you're going to be targeted. So you can't blame the cops, OK?

The idea of the 'mateship' is widely celebrated in Australian male culture, with mateship iconized as radiating masculine camaraderie, loyalty and bravado. In this phase, we see the Convenor drawing on the figure of the 'mate' as a bondicon (associated with an imagined Communitas of 'mates'), not as a rallying icon, but as a 'condemning' icon to warn the YP that they are engaging in inappropriate bonding. Along the same lines, in the following phase, the ECLO draws on Spatialization devices (Fig. 5.5, Chap. 4), distinguishing those people who are present in the conference (family) from those who are not present (mates). He points out that the YP's mates did not accompany him to the police station, quickly shooting down the YP's attempt to suggest that an adult friend could be used as an example of a mate who came to support him ('How old's he?'):

**Extract 7.14, Affray YJC**

| | |
|---|---|
| **ECLO:** | Where's your **mates** now? |
| **YP:** | They're at home. |
| **ECLO:** | At home. Why aren't they with you, supporting you, brother? |
| **YP:** | I didn't tell them to come. |
| **ECLO:** | You didn't tell them to come. |
| **YP:** | No. |
| **ECLO:** | Or they can't be here anyway. Do you think they'll come for you if you get locked up? |
| **YP:** | Yes. |
| **ECLO:** | Who went and visited you? Who went to see you there? Any of your friends go? |
| **YP:** | At the police station? |
| **ECLO:** | No. Wherever you were. Any of your friends go? |
| **YP:** | My **mate's** brother did. |
| **ECLO:** | Yeah. |

The ECLO draws on 'alternating' evaluative prosody, which has a 'to-and-fro' structure, moving back and forth between positive and negative evaluative polarities throughout his interaction with the YP in order to contrast behaviours that are socially sanctioned by their shared community and those that are not. This general rhetorical tendency is a prosodic enactment that actively undermines a key Doxa of the mates Communitas, namely loyalty amongst friends.

As we can see through these iconization processes, doing a conference requires enacting, on the spot, some of the reintegrative effects it is hoped the conference might be able to foster in the longer term: a YP is made to talk and to listen, but is also given, then and there, an opportunity to affiliate with his family, his ethnic group and the wider community, often in place of his hitherto dominating affiliation with his mates. It is an open question as to which affiliations will remain. But the opportunity for YPs, Victims, their families, friends and police to affiliate in the course of a conference is a paradigm shift for the criminal justice system that offers a potential avenue away from the consistent failure to rehabilitate offenders and to meet the needs of Victims.

## 4 Conferencing as Ritual: The Power of Ceremonial Redress

If conferences are not 'passion plays' governed by outpourings of emotion, from where then do they derive their restorative power? And what does iconization have to do with their success? Here, we suggest, conferences gain their power from their position as a ritual—a rite of passage that ideally transforms a delinquent YP into an acceptably self-regulating social subject.

However dismissive we may feel at times about the social value of ceremonies and ritual (or, conversely, however much we might wish to leave their ineffable mysteries intact), in common-sense terms we can all appreciate the difference between winning a race and the medal/trophy presentation, between passing exams and the graduation ceremony, between a casual prayer and a religious service or, in the case of youth crime, between getting caught by the police and being sentenced. In social semiotic theory, questions about the power of such genres are only beginning to be explored (cf. Bednarek and Martin 2010). However, as a starting point, we can look at how scholars in anthropology and performance studies have thought about these 'special events' (a category that includes ritual) as 'intensifications of some of the tendencies inherent in an ordinary event, sometimes tendencies that are latent or subliminally present' (Lewis 2013: 68).

Following Turner (1982), for instance, we can consider the problem of youth crime (and the attendant failure of institutions like the Children's Court and juvenile detention centres to deter and/or rehabilitate young offenders) as a form of 'social drama'—a breach in the social order which has reached a point of crisis and now requires redressive action if an eroding schism in the community is to be avoided. Turner uses the concept of 'social drama' to characterize periods of social disorder resulting from transgression of the normative order, viewing them as 'units of aharmonic or disharmonic process' that typically unfold in four phases: breach, crisis, redressive action and reintegration (Turner 1974: 37). He identifies legal-judicial processes and ritual performances as the two most important mechanisms of redress, though clearly these are not mutually exclusive negotiations of meaning. Some elements of ritual have always existed in courtroom proceedings. At the same time, an emergent genre such as conferencing may be understood as a ritualization of alternative social processes (police cautions, family counselling, parent/teacher interviews, carer/child admonitions, etc.) which function as adjuncts to conventional legal-judicial remedies.

Lewis (2008: 50, 2013), drawing on Tillich (1963), argues that we can usefully consider events as more or less 'ritual-like' based on whether or not they constitute matters of 'ultimate concern' for a particular group. The kind of transgression dealt with in conferencing is typically relatively minor, since offences that can legally be addressed by a conference are at the less serious end of the offence spectrum and they do not result in a permanent criminal record for the YP as the process is envisioned as 'diversionary'. The aim is to avoid the YP having further contact with the criminal justice system or coming to see themselves as a 'criminal'. Since passage through the conference cannot be seen as a ritual in which life and death hang in the balance, following Lewis we suggest that conferences are 'ritual-like', having some of the features of a full-blown ritual—but not meeting all of the criteria.

Lewis's criteria for determining whether an event is a ritual or ritual-like are summarized in Table 7.1 across five dimensions: importance (is the event of ultimate concern?), social consensus (which parts of society are involved?), mode of participation (how do we engage in the event?), past orientation (what relation does the event have to the past?) and encompassment (what is the scope of the event?). Lewis suggests that by better defining the criteria for determining whether an event is sufficiently special and elaborated to be considered a ritual we can preserve the essential insight which Turner has made. Rather than diluting Turner's theory so that every kind of performance is seen as a ritual, we can

# 4 Conferencing as Ritual: The Power of Ceremonial Redress

**Table 7.1** Criteria for distinguishing types of events on a continuum of ritual, ritual-like, not ritual-like (Adapted from Lewis 2013)

|  | Ritual | Ritual-like | Not ritual |
|---|---|---|---|
| 1. Importance | Most important events/types | Of secondary or subsidiary importance | Mere entertainment |
|  | Matters of ultimate concern | Matters of concern, but not fundamental concern | Elective or optional events |
| 2. Social consensus | Concerns entire society | Concerns subsections of society | Concerns individuals primarily |
|  | Minimal variation in interpretation | Consensus within subsections, variation between them | Maximum variation of interpretation |
|  | Most prominent in small-scale societies |  | Prominent in large-scale societies |
| 3. Mode of participation | Personal or social transformation | Engaged participation by believers | Passive spectators or audience |
|  | Active engagement by most | Possibility of detached observation by others | Maximum distance between performers and spectators |
| 4. Past orientation | Events seen as continuous with past | Events re-created as they may have been | Emphasis on creativity and innovation |
|  | Strong degree of repetition | Imagined tradition | Artistic genius |
| 5. Encompassment | Establish relations between human society and environing powers | Events linked to more encompassing frameworks, but not integral to them | Events trivial or of passing interest |
|  | Events cannot be encompassed by greater concerns | Important events, but secondary to more fundamental concerns (see criterion 1) | Fads and fashionable events |

improve our ability to determine the key characteristics of ritual play in the development of other genres, as we are arguing here for youth justice conferencing.

We use the term 'ritualization' here to highlight some 'logical entailments' (Rappaport 1999: 26) of the conferencing macro-genre. To begin, conferencing practice frequently involves an appeal to tradition and various kinds of authority.[4] In New Zealand, conferences involving Maori YPs typically take place on the *marae*[5] and begin with a communal prayer; in other jurisdictions, they may begin with a Bible reading. In NSW, though it is a legally constituted process, YJC certainly allows for, and often seems to encourage, participants to reframe the matter they are dealing with as an infringement of family, religious or cultural values, and not simply as a legal violation. In terms of Lewis's dimension of 'encompassment', conferences do appear to link themselves to more encompassing frameworks and fundamental concerns since family, religion and culture are no doubt greater sources of moral authority for many citizens than the state. Thus, because they can be encompassed by greater concerns, they are unlike Lewis's rituals which attend to concerns too important to be circumscribed.

Commensurate with such a sense of moral purpose, conferencing also involves a high degree of repetition and formality. While restorative justice advocates are probably right when they describe the protocols of conferencing as less alienating for some participants than those of courtroom practice, the genre nevertheless involves its own strongly classified procedures (Bernstein 1975; Douglas 1973). This is reflected in the care taken to train Convenors in the appropriate use of script/prompts, the attention given to briefing participants before the conference, the highly deliberate turn-taking structures within the conference and so on. Based on our observations, we would expect each youth justice conference to exhibit a comparable controlled and repetitive macro-generic unfolding.

To participate in a conference is also, in a ritual-like manner, to respond to a demand for performance. Participants will frequently talk of 'facing up to the challenge' of meeting the other participants, of 'getting through' the conference process in order to be able to 'draw a line in the sand' and

## 4 Conferencing as Ritual: The Power of Ceremonial Redress

'move on' with their lives. As Catherine Bell writes, a 'fundamental dimension of ritualization' is 'the simple imperative to do something in such a way that the doing itself gives the acts a special or privileged status' (Bell 1997: 166). Indeed, much of what is commonly thought to be 'symbolic communication' in ritual, or ritual-like processes, might be better understood in terms of the cultivation of embodied dispositions: 'the act of kneeling does not so much communicate a message about subordination as it generates a body identified with subordination' (Bell 1992: 99–100). While the physical spaces in which YJCs are held, as noted earlier, rarely feature obvious rallying symbols or bondicons such as those of a courtroom (the national flag, the coat of arms, etc.) (Martin 2008; Martin and Stenglin 2007; Stenglin 2004), the enactment of the conference itself does involve a hyper-charged axiological process through which participants re-affiliate in relation to restorative justice ideals.

In order to explore what it might mean for a social subject to be transformed through ritual-like experiences in the way that is celebrated in the restorative justice literature, we will again draw on Turner, who has argued that the 'liminal phase' is critical in making such transformations possible. As a result of their transgressive behaviour, YPs in YJCs are in a transitional phase, where, as we have discussed a number of times, in order for the macro-genre to come to a successful completion, they must be reintegrated back into their 'community of concern' (Braithwaite 1989: 85). The conferencing literature casts this reintegration as the product of 'transformative' processes during the conference with some arguing that this term be favoured over reintegration 'since it emphasizes not restoration of the status quo ante, but transformation of individuals and social networks' (Moore et al. 1995). The transformation is presented as occurring at different orders of experience, including both a personal emotional transformation of the YP and a more abstract transformation of the personal apology into a kind of 'public drama' of restoration (Hayes 2006: 379).

Liminality is central to the concepts of 'transformation' and 'reintegration'. It is a state which Turner viewed as arising out of social disruption (here, the offending behaviour of the YP). Turner viewed liminality as an 'in-between' position:

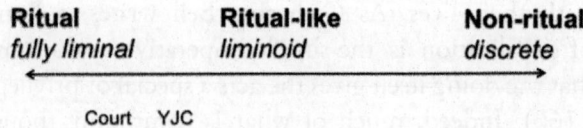

Fig. 7.9 Youth justice conferencing and court as a level of liminality

[L]iminality occurs in the middle phase of the rites of passage which mark changes in a group's or individual's social status. Such rites characteristically begin with the subject's being symbolically killed or separated from ordinary secular or profane relationships, and conclude with a symbolic birth or reincorporation into society. The intervening liminal period or phase is thus betwixt and between the categories of ordinary social life. (Turner 1974: 53)

Conferences seem closer to what Turner terms 'liminoid genres' (which Lewis (2013) has argued should be termed 'ritual-like' rather than rituals involving true liminality). Turner argues that 'liminal genres put much stress on social frames, plural reflexivity, and mass flow, shared flow, while liminoid genres emphasize idiosyncratic framing, individual reflexivity, subjective flow, and see the social as problem not datum' (Turner 1979: 117). We would thus, for example, consider a YJC closer to the liminoid than a more formal court proceeding.

Our interpretation of the ceremonial nature of YJC and courtroom in relation to Turner's and Lewis's discussion of ritual and liminality is outlined in Fig. 7.9.

## 5 Ceremonial Redress

Up to this point we have drawn on work by Turner, Lewis and Braithwaite to suggest that conferencing is a form of ritual-like redress with the aim of reintegrating the YP 'back into the community of responsible citizens' (Braithwaite 1989: 4). In Lewis's terms, it is clear that they are special events—that participants are carefully prepared for by Convenors, and have the opportunity to remember and reflect upon their experience for years to come. As noted earlier, according to Turner (e.g. Turner 1982) the problem of youth crime (and the attendant failure of institutions like the children's court and juvenile detention centres to deter and/or rehabilitate young offenders) is a form of social drama—a breach in the social order that requires redressive action if an eroding schism in the community is to be avoided. And following Van Gennep (1960), we can read the YJC form of redressive action as a rite of passage, which participants talk about in terms of 'facing up to the challenge' of meeting the other participants, and of 'getting through' the conference process in order to be able to 'draw a line in the sand' and 'move on' with their lives. The parallels we are noting between the van Ganeep and Turner perspectives and the macro-generic structure of YJCs is outlined in Fig. 7.10.

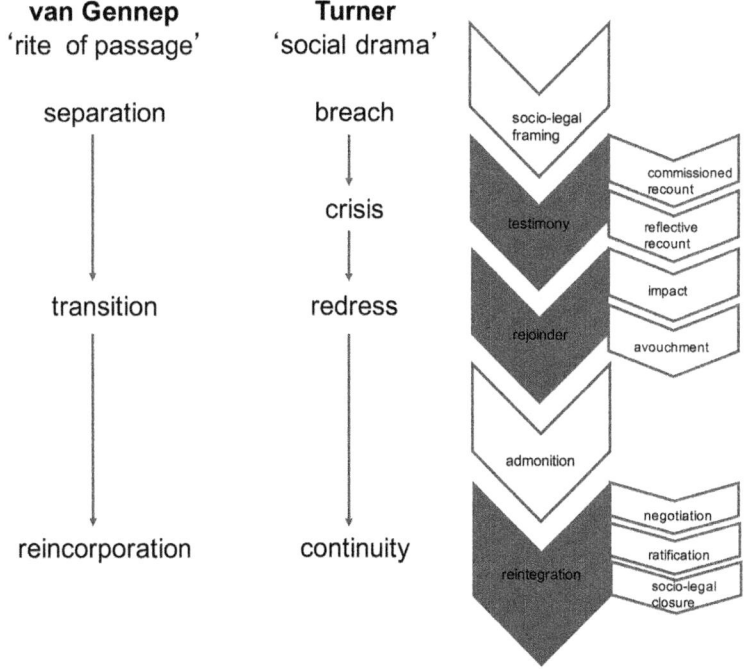

**Fig. 7.10** Youth justice conferencing as a form of ritual redress

We suggest that it is the iconization processes, employed to communally align participants during the macro-genre, that allow 'reintegrative shaming' to have its impact. Our basic point is that instead of attributing the restorative power of conferencing to an outpouring of emotion (a passion play), it is the ceremonial impact of iconization processes and possibilities that achieves transformation. Compared with the court, conferences look at first blush like a legal process stripped bare: where, we might wonder, has all the ritual gone? But from a discourse perspective, conferences create an orderly convocation which affords a range of iconizing processes that invite, enact and hopefully enable reintegration of the YP into the appropriate 'communities of concern' (Braithwaite 1989).

The re-bonding of the YP into their community of concern is engendered by the ritual-like unfolding of the macro-genre. The iconization foregrounded throughout this macro-genre offers a path back to the community of mutual dependency which Braithwaite positions as necessary for a truly communitarian society:

> [I]ts heavily enmeshed fabric of interdependencies therefore must have a special kind of symbolic significance to the populace. Interdependencies must be attachments which invoke personal obligation to others within a community of concern. They are not perceived as isolated exchange relationships of convenience but as matters of profound group obligation. Thus, a communitarian society combines a dense network of individual interdependencies with strong cultural commitments to mutuality of obligation. Individual interdependencies are interpreted within the framework of group loyalties – father-son interdependencies are symbolically part of family obligation, employer-employee interdependencies part of company loyalty. (Braithwaite 1989: 85–86)

In invoking these symbolic obligations, both the activity sequence of conferencing itself and the entities involved are iconized. For example, the crying mother, the police uniform, the 'line in the sand' parable and the hijab are leveraged to motivate the YPs to re-commit themselves to the values that are associated with the family and ethnic community, while the fellowship of 'mates' (Communitas) and their accompanying transgressive values (Doxa) are iconized in a way that pushes the YP to dissociate from them. Importantly, the ideational meaning associated with these bondicons is backgrounded: the hijab has no real hat function, the police uniform (e.g. badge) does not have a weather-oriented clothing function and the parables told to the YP have lost the specificity of individual people, places and events. The loss of specificity foregrounds their iconic evaluative function.

If sharing feeling is about aligning into communities, the iconization process at the heart of a ceremony involves the enactment of a kind of 'super' or 'hyper' feeling. The core of iconization is a sense of communion or social 'fusion' construed interactively by social actors. This type of experience might be described as sublime (foregrounding transcendence, as in award ceremonies) or unifying (foregrounding affinity, as in youth justice conferences). Although our capacity to explain the axiological semantics in play is still in its infancy, it is possible for us to map out the stages through which a ceremony unfolds (Chaps. 2 and 3), the values that are negotiated (Chap. 4), the role of body language in this negotiation (Chap. 5) and the identities enacted (Chap. 6), all the while considering the interpersonal and social functions of these dimensions, as we have done in this book.

We began this chapter by reminding readers that they have probably all experienced the difference between everyday activity and ritual—whether this has involved the difference between birth and baptism, between falling in love and marriage, between dying and the funeral and so on. But outside of religious life, this difference is not something many of us are used to talking about. We experience it, but the sublime transcendent impact of ceremony is hard to verbalize; and very few of us are gifted enough to compose the song or write the poetry that captures the momentous emotion—the Communitas in Turner's terms. As we have found, theorizing this impact is no easier. But as theorists our job is to face up to what we'd have rather left unsaid, especially where something as important as restorative justice is concerned in a world where diversionary processes for offenders continue to be a controversial dimension of redressive action. One important challenge for forensic linguistics is thus to develop an ever-improving secular theory of ceremony which can be drawn on to inform and possibly reform truly reintegrative performances of ritualized redress. We hope to have scattered a few seeds in this direction here.

The typical conference that we have documented, carried out in a modest, often shabby room in a Police Citizens Youth Club and relying on minimal resources from the state, can have all the ceremonial impact in the life of a YP that much grander occasions might have. We have argued that this is due to the unique power that iconization holds in its ability to motivate social realignment, even where at first it might seem that no grand emotions have been displayed. The impact of conferencing on the lives of YPs, and the attendant power of iconization to encourage the YP's reintegration into 'communities of concern' (Braithwaite and Daly 1998: 228), should be motivation enough for governments to address the under-funding of youth justice conferencing in NSW (and the lack of resources for comparable processes around the world). Imagine what might be gained if the ceremonial power of semiosis and the material power of proper financing were to converge.

## 6    Envoi

In this book we have drawn on functional linguistics and semiotics to explore the enactment of restorative justice in NSW YJC. We contextualised this work in Chap. 1, drawing on our ethnographic research that included observation of conferences and Convenor training, and interviews with Convenors. Chapter 2 presented our analysis of YJCs as a designed and evolving macro-genre, which provided a platform for us to drill down into the interpersonal meanings exchanged in conference dialogue in Chaps. 3 and 4. This highlighted the instrumental role played by Convenors as far as scaffolding the negotiation of feelings was concerned, especially in relation to the commissioned recount story genre. Chapter 5 took this micro-analysis a step further by bringing body language into the picture, emphasizing that in conferencing, as in any negotiation of meaning, non-verbal semiosis plays a key role. In Chap. 6 we stepped back to interpret the patterns of meaning enacted by conference participants in terms of the identities performed, distinguishing ideal from less ideal YP and Support Person roles. Finally, in this chapter we have consolidated this work by interpreting conferencing as a secular ceremony involving ritual redress—an interpretation which fits our data far more closely than the 'passion play' envisioned by conference designers and proponents.

In doing so, we bring conferencing into the descriptive and theoretical ambit of functional linguistics and semiotics for the first time. The power of this approach, which Halliday (2008) has referred to as appliable linguistics, lies in its ability to move from the micro-analyses of conference interaction to the synthesis of multiple strands of meaning in terms of the identities enacted in genres. As far as appliable linguistics is concerned, the major contribution of this synthesis has been to draw attention to the ceremonial power of the YJC genre, opening up a new iconization-oriented dimension of analysis complementing previous studies in educational, clinical and forensic linguistics and beyond.

Although we have looked critically at the explanations offered by conference designers and advocates concerning how and why conferencing works, we do not wish this criticism to deflect readers in any way from our endorsement of their restorative justice ideals. Our research has only strengthened our conviction that YJCs and comparable modes of diversionary justice make the world a better place to live in. Many have professed restorative justice ideals far more ably than we can. So we leave you with some words from one of its most articulate advocates, Desmond Tutu (1999a, b), writing in his inspirational monograph *No Future without Forgiveness*, and speaking at the University of Sydney, where he was awarded the Sydney Peace Prize, just four years before our project began. YJCs enact the spirit of Tutu's 'ubuntu' on our shores.

> I contend that there is another kind of justice, restorative justice, which is characteristic of traditional African jurisprudence. Here the central concern is not retribution or punishment but, in the spirit of ubuntu, the healing of breaches, the redressing of imbalances, the restoration of broken relationships. This kind of justice seeks to rehabilitate both the victim and the perpetrator, who should be given the opportunity to be reintegrated into the community he or she has injured by his or her offence. This is a far more personal approach, which sees the offence as something that has happened to people and whose consequence is a rupture in relationships. Thus

we would claim that justice, restorative justice, is being served when efforts are being made to work for healing, for forgiveness and for reconciliation (Tutu 1999a: 52).

But you see our country was saying retributive justice is not the only kind of justice. There is another kind of justice – restorative justice – based on something that we find difficult to put into English. Ubuntu is the essence of being human; it speaks of compassion and generosity, of gentleness and hospitality and sharing because it says: 'my humanity is caught up in your humanity'. I am because you are. A person is a person through other persons. An offence breaks a relationship, ruptures an interconnectedness, a harmony so essential for a full human existence. Ubuntu does not give up on the perpetrator but sees his capacity to change for the better and so Ubuntu seeks to heal a breach, to restore relationships, to forgive and to reconcile (Tutu 1999b).

# Notes

1. Source: http://www.planetclaire.org/quotes/sherlock/series-one/the-great-game/; downloaded 19/2/2013.
2. This role may in fact be played by a de facto parent, for example an older sister, stepmother or grandmother.
3. We are treating the expression as oral 'scripture', distilling in collective memory the 'decisive moment' parable, just as the Young Offender's Act distils in writing the conferencing rituals we are exploring here.
4. Many restorative justice advocates invoke as precedents for these innovations in Western legal systems the example of dispute resolution customs in Melanesian, Indigenous Australian or other 'traditional' cultures. While, as Cuneen has pointed out, these comparisons can be very misleading (Cuneen C. (2002) Restorative justice and the politics of decolonization. In: Weitekamp E and Kerner HJ (eds) *Restorative Justice: Theoretical Foundations*. Cullompton, UK: Willan Publishing, 32–49), conferencing, as a 'fragmented' form of justice has at least proved 'flexible and accommodating toward cultural differences' (Daly K. (2001a) Conferencing in Australia and New Zealand: Variations, research findings, and prospects. In: Morris A and Maxwell G (eds) *Restorative Justice for Juveniles: Conferencing, Mediation and Circles*. London: Bloomsbury

Publishing, 59–84), and its early development in New Zealand was certainly seen as part of a wider political response to the over-representation of young Maori and Pacific Islander people in the criminal justice system.
5. In Maori culture a marae is a meeting place where a range of ceremonial activities are enacted.

# References

Bednarek, M., & Martin, J. R. (2010). *New discourse on language: Functional perspectives on multimodality, identity, and affiliation*. London: Continuum.

Bell, C. (1992). *Ritual theory, ritual practice*. New York/Oxford: Oxford University Press.

Bell, C. (1997). *Ritual: Perspectives and dimensions*. New york/London: Oxford University Press.

Bernstein, B. (1975). *Class, codes and control, volume 3: Towards a theory of educational transmissions*. London: Routledge & Kegan Paul.

Bourdieu, P., & Thompson, J. B. (1991). *Language and symbolic power*. Cambridge, MA: Harvard University Press.

Braithwaite, J. (1989). *Crime, shame and reintegration*. Cambridge/Sydney: Cambridge University Press.

Braithwaite, J., & Daly, K. (1998). Masculinities, violence and communitarian control. In D. Chappell & S. Egger (Eds.), *Australian violence: Contemporary perspective II* (pp. 221–252). Canberra: Australian Institute of Criminology.

Caple, H. (2008). Intermodal relations in image nuclear news stories. In L. Unsworth (Ed.), *Multimodal semiotics: Functional analysis in contexts of education* (pp. 123–138). London: Continuum.

Caple, H. (2013). *Photojournalism: A social semiotic approach*. London: Palgrave Macmillan.

Douglas, M. (1973). *Natural symbols*. New York: Random House.

Halliday, M. A. K. (2008). *Complementarities in language*. Beijing: The Commercial Press.

Halliday, M., & Matthiessen, C. M. (2014). *An introduction to functional grammar*. London: Routledge.

Hayes, H. (2006). Apologies and accounts in youth justice conferencing. *Contemporary Justice Review, 9*, 369–385.

Hayes, H., & Daly, K. (2003). Youth justice conferencing and re-offending. *Justice Quarterly, 20*, 725–763.

Lewis, J. L. (2008). Toward a unified theory of cultural performance: A reconstructive introduction to Victor Turner. In G. St John (Ed.), *Victor Turner and contemporary cultural performance* (pp. 41–58). New York: Berghahn.

Lewis, J. L. (2013). *The anthropology of cultural performance.* New York: Palgrave Macmillan.

Martin, J. R. (2008). Intermodal reconciliation: Mates in arms. In *New literacies and the English curriculum: Multimodal perspectives* (pp. 112–148). London: Continuum.

Martin, J. R., & Stenglin, M. (2007). New directions in the analysis of multimodal discourse. In T. Royce & W. Bowcher (Eds.), *Materialising reconciliation: Negotiating difference in a post-colonial exhibition* (pp. 215–238). Mahwah: Lawrence Erlbaum Associates.

Martin, J. R., & White, P. R. R. (2005). *The language of evaluation: Appraisal in English.* New York: Palgrave Macmillan.

Moore, D., Forsythe, L., & O'Connell, T. (1995). *A new approach to juvenile justice: An evaluation of family conferencing in Wagga Wagga.* Criminology Research Council grant.http://www.criminologyresearchcouncil.gov.au/reports/moore/

Palk, G., Hayes, H., & Prenzler, T. (1998). Restorative justice and community conferencing: Summary of findings from a pilot study. *Current Issues in Criminal Justice, 10,* 125–137.

Rappaport, R. (1999). *Ritual and religion in the making of humanity.* Cambridge, UK: Cambridge University Press.

Stenglin, M. (2004). *Packaging curiosities: Towards a grammar of three-dimensional space.* Department of Linguistics, University of Sydney, Sydney.

Stenglin, M. (2008a). Binding: A resource for exploring interpersonal meaning in three-dimensional space. *Social Semiotics, 18,* 425–447.

Stenglin, M. (2008b). Interpersonal meaning in 3D space: How a bonding icon gets its 'charge'. In L. Unsworth (Ed.), *Multimodal semiotics: Functional analysis in contexts of education* (pp. 50–66). London: Continuum.

Stenglin, M. (2009). Space odyssey: Towards a social semiotic model of three-dimensional space. *Visual Communication, 8,* 35–64.

Stenglin, M. (2012). *Transformation and transcendence: Bonding through ritual.* Paper presented at the International Systemic Functional Congress, University of Technology, Sydney, 16–20 July 2012.

Stenglin, M., & Djonov, E. (2010). Unpacking narrative in a hypermedia 'artedventure' for children. In C. R. Hoffman (Ed.), *Narrative revisited: Telling a story in the age of new media.* Amsterdam: John Benjamins.

Strang, H., Barnes, G., Braithwaite, J., et al. (1999). *Experiments in restorative policing: A progress report on the Canberra reintegrative shaming experiments*

(RISE). Canberra: Research School of Social Sciences, Australian National University.

Tann, K. (2010a). Imagining communities: A multifunctional approach to identity management in texts. In M. Bednarek & J. R. Martin (Eds.), *New discourse on language: Functional perspectives on multimodality, identity, and affiliation* (pp. 163–194). London: Continuum.

Tann K. (2010b). *Semogenesis of a nation: An iconography of Japanese identity*. [Doctoral dissertation]. Sydney: Department of Linguistics, University of Sydney.

Tann, K. (2013). The language of identity discourse: Introducing a systemic functional framework for iconography. *Linguistics & The Human Sciences, 8*, 361–391.

Tillich, P. (1963). *Christianity and the encounter of the world religions*. New York: Colombia University Press.

Tönnies, F. (1887). *Community and society: Gemeinschaft und Gesellschaft* (C. P. Loomis, Ed., & Trans.). East Lansing: The Michigan State University Press, 1957.

Trimboli, L. (2000). *An evaluation of the NSW youth justice conferencing scheme*. Sydney: NSW Bureau of Crime Statistics and Research.

Turner, V. W. (1974). *Dramas, fields, and metaphors: Symbolic action in human society*. Ithaca: Cornell University Press.

Turner, V. W. (1979). *Process, performance, and pilgrimage: A study in comparative symbology*. New Delhi: Concept Publishing Company.

Turner, V. W. (1982). *From ritual to theatre: The human seriousness of play*. New York: Performing Arts Journal Publications.

Tutu, D. (1999a). *No future without forgiveness*. London: Rider.

Tutu, D. (1999b). *Peace through reconciliation. 1999 Sydney Peace Prize lecture* (CPACS Occasional Paper 1). Sydney: The Centre for Peace and Conflict Studies.

Van Gennep, A. (1960). *The rites of passage*. Chicago: University of Chicago Press.

Weijers, I. (2001). Family group conferencing. Kanttekeningen bij Herstelrecht voor Jeugdige Delinquenten. *Justitiële Verkenningen, 27*(3), 110–121.

# Appendix A: Anonymized Cast of Characters and Youth Justice Conference Locations

## Video-Recorded Youth Justice Conferences

### Guide Dog YJC

| Role | Name |
|---|---|
| Convenor | Louise Horton |
| Police YLO | Melanie |
| Victim's support person (Guide Dog Association rep) | Greg |
| Victim | Donna O'Neill |
| Researcher | Paul, Michele |
| Mother of YP's girlfriend | Julie |
| YP | Nathan |
| Mother of YP | Sharon |
| Girlfriend of YP | Chelsea |
| Step-Grandfather of YP | Don |
| Arresting officer | Jim, Constable Kennedy |
| YP's niece | Valerie |
| Other characters not given a turn in the conference | Martin, Barry, Tony, Dan, Barbara, Angela |
| **Locations** | Davidton, Weathersbury, Hardacre, Doonbeg Hospital, Morwood |

## Shopping Trolley YJC

| Role | Name |
|---|---|
| YP | Toby |
| Convenor | |
| Victim's representative | Michael |
| Youth Liaison Officer | |
| Mother | |
| Arresting officer | Bob |
| **Location** | Manduka Police Station |

## Mobile Phone YJC

| Role | Name |
|---|---|
| Convenor | |
| YP | Brody |
| Mum | Valerie |
| YLO | Stephanie |
| | Jane |
| Researcher? | Michele |
| Researcher? | Paul |
| | Niece |
| Extra characters | Tuvale (victim not present) |

## Batteries YJC

| Role | Name |
|---|---|
| Convenor | |
| YP's Stepfather | |

## Affray YJC

| Role | Name |
|---|---|
| ECLO | Amir |
| YP | Aatif |
| Convenor | |
| Arresting officer | |

| | |
|---|---|
| YLO | |
| Other characters | Misbah, Tahseen |
| **Locations** | Falconswood Park, Paulberg |

## Running Shoes YJC

| Role | Name |
|---|---|
| Convenor | |
| YLO | |
| YP | |
| Other characters | Brendan |
| **Locations** | Bunderna, Smallton |

## School Library YJC

| Role | Name |
|---|---|
| Convenor | |
| YP1 | |
| YP2 | |
| **Locations** | Bridgeton |

## Train Tracks YJC

| Role | Name |
|---|---|
| Convenor | |
| Young Person | Amy |
| Young Person's Support Person | Kate |
| Mother | |
| Victim | Michael |
| Other characters | Mr Glenn Matthews (person who the final letter of apology is directed to) |
| | Murray Hartfield (monitor of the Young Person's outcome plan) |
| | Sharp's (corporate victim) |
| **Locations** | Marie PCYC |

# Appendix B: Conventions Used in This Book

## Transcription Conventions

The transcription conventions used in this book are adapted from those of Eggins and Slade (1997/2006: 2–5).

(a) (…)
   An ellipsis surrounded by parentheses indicates inaudible or non-transcribable talk.
(b) (word)
   A word surrounded by parentheses indicates an uncertain transcription and the transcriber's best guess of what was said.
(c) [laughs]
   Square brackets indicate paralinguistic and non-verbal phenomena. Such information is only included where it is judged important in making sense of the interaction.
(d) -
   Hyphens indicate a false start where a speaker rethinks or rephrases what they were saying out loud. For example:
   **ECLO:**     Yeah. OK. What a- where is she now?

(e) ...

    Ellipses indicate hesitation or intervals within turns.

(f) ==

Double equals signs indicate an overlap of speech. There are four kinds:

  (i) Simultaneous or concurrent turns. When two entire turns occur simultaneously, == is placed before each turn. For example:

    **Convenor:**    Is that OK?
    **Victim:**    == That's fine
    **Convenor:**    == That's fine?

  Here, this indicates that both the Victim and the second turn of the Convenor occur simultaneously.

  (ii) Overlapping utterances. == is used to show the point at which the second speaker begins talking during the first speaker's turn. For example:

    **Convenor:**    He's you daughter's == boyfriend?
    **Mother of YP's girlfriend:**    == Daughter's boyfriend.

  Here, this indicates that the second turn begins during the first turn, after the Convenor says *daughter's*.

  (iii) Contiguous turns. When there is no interval between two turns produced by different speakers, the run-on is indicated by == at the end of the first speaker's turn and the beginning of the second speaker's turn. For example:

    **Convenor:**    So you met your mates. ==
    **YP:**    == Yeah, met my mates there.

  Here the == indicates that the second turn occurs straightaway without any gap between the first and second turns.

Backchanneling indicated by utterances such as *ah*, *mmm* and *hmm* are only transcribed when occurring between turns, unless it is judged important for understanding the interaction. These phenomena do not relate to the analysis used throughout the book and so for ease of readability they have not been tracked.

(g) <<...>> indicates elided material.

## Genre Structure Notation

The notation used to indicate the structure of genres is as follow:

(a) Official Welcome
   Initial upper case indicates a genre stage (also known as a function).
(b) socio-legal framing
   Lower case indicates a genre (also known as a class).
(c) ^
   A caret indicates a sequence. For example, Official Welcome ^ Legal Invocation indicates that the Legal Invocation comes directly after the Official Welcome.
(d) •
   A bullet indicates that there is a freedom of sequence. For example: Consent Check • Confidentiality Reminder indicates that Consent Check and Confidentiality Reminder can occur in any sequence in relation to each other.
(e) Goal Affirmation$^n$
   A superscript $^n$ indicates that there may be any number of this stage.
(f) [Consent Check • Confidentiality Reminder]
   Square brackets indicate that the stages within the square brackets are grouped together in relation to those outside the brackets. For example:

Goal Affirmation$^n$ ^ [Consent Check • Confidentiality Reminder • Conference Protocol$^n$]

(g) This example indicates that each of Consent Check, Confidentiality Reminder and Conference Protocol occurs after the Affirmation (due to the ^), but due to the bullet • they may occur in any order.

An example of an expanded genre structure is:

Official Welcome ^ Legal Invocation ^ Role Declaration ^ Goal Affirmation$^n$ ^ [Consent Check • Confidentiality Reminder • Conference Protocol$^n$]

This example indicates that first there is a sequence of Official Welcome followed by a Legal Invocation followed by a Role Declaration followed by any number of Goal Affirmations. Following this, there is any sequence of a Consent Check, Confidentiality Reminder and any number of Conference Protocols.

**Exchange structure notation**
**(See Chap. 2 for a more detailed overview of exchange structure)**

Exchange structures are divided into two broad types, depending on what is being exchanged. These are knowledge exchanges and action exchanges. As the names suggest, knowledge exchanges are those which negotiate knowledge or information, while action exchanges negotiate actions. The following is an example of a knowledge exchange:

**Convenor:** So did you commit the offences you are charged with?
**YP:** Yes.

In this exchange, a proposition is being negotiated during a knowledge exchange. This can be contrasted to an action exchange:

**Convenor:** I need you to speak a bit louder.
**YP:** OK.

In this exchange, the negotiation is not about information as in the first example, but about an action; in this case, the action of speaking louder. The conventions for knowledge and action exchanges are as follows:

(a) knowledge exchanges

Each move type is listed in the sequence in which they can occur. All moves except K1 are optional.

(i) Dk1

Delayed primary knower. This move is given by the person who has control over the knowledge being exchanged (known as the primary knower). Delayed primary knowers are optional, but if they occur, they come first in a knowledge exchange and work to preempt or prompt that the primary knower has information they wish to negotiate.

(ii) K2

Secondary knower. The secondary knower is the person with whom the primary knower is exchanging information. Often, though not in all cases, the secondary knower is the one who asks a question.

(iii) K1

Primary knower. The primary knower is the nucleus of the exchange that gives or affirms the information negotiated in the exchange. This element is obligatory in a fully formed exchanged.

(iv) K2f

Secondary knower follow-up. This is a move by the secondary knower that follows the primary knower (K1) and is often used to confirm the knowledge given in the K1 move.

(v) K1f

Primary knower follow-up. This is the final move in an exchange and is often used to answer the question posed by the K2f.

The following is an example of a full knowledge exchange involving all the move types described:

| ECLO | Dk1 | Mate, what's your mum got on her head? |
|---|---|---|
| YP | K2 | Scarf |
| ECLO | K1 | Yeah |
| YP | K2f | It is, isn't it? |
| ECLO | K1f | Yep |

(b) Action exchanges

Each move type is in the sequence in which they can occur. All moves except A1 are optional.

(i) Da1

Delayed primary actor. This move is made by the person who may eventually perform the action (the primary actor). It works to prompt or ask the secondary actor (A2) if they would like the action to be performed.

(ii) A2

Secondary actor. This is the person who will receive the goods or for whom the action is performed. This move typically works to ask for or indicate an agreement for the action to occur.

(iii) A1

Primary actor. This move is the nucleus of the exchange and is the one in which the action is performed (or promised to be performed). This move is obligatory in a fully formed action exchange.

(iv) A2f

Secondary actor follow-up. This is a move by the secondary actor that follows the action. It often involves thanking the primary actor.

(v) A1f

Primary actor follow-up. This is a move that completes the exchange and often functions to welcome or reassure the thanks given in the A2f.

The following is an example of a full action exchange involving all the move types described:

| Convenor | Da1 | Would you like some water? |
|---|---|---|
| YP | A2 | Yes please |
| Convenor | A1 | Here you go |
| YP | A2f | Thanks |
| Convenor | A1f | No worries |

(c) Other moves

Each move can be inserted at any point within either action or knowledge exchanges. In general, these moves work to interrupt or block the culmination of the exchange and each may be chosen any number of times.

(i) tr, rtr

Tracking (tr) and response to tracking (rtr). These moves clarify the meanings being negotiated. For example:

| ECLO | K2  | Any of your friends go?  |
|------|-----|--------------------------|
| YP   | tr  | At the police station?   |
| ECLO | rtr | Yeah                     |
| YP   | K1  | No                       |

(ii) ch, rch

Challenge and response to challenge. These moves function as a resistance to the exchange, frustrating and at times completely derailing the exchange. For example:

| Convenor | K2 | And what were they doing? |
|----------|----|---------------------------|
| YP       | ch | I don't know              |

(iii) bch

Backchanneling. These moves work to signal to the speaker that the listener is attending to what they are saying. Unlike tracking and challenging moves, they do not predict a response. Backchanneling moves will only be transcribed when they occur between moves, unless they are deemed important for understanding the exchange. For example:

| YP       | K1  | And I was heading down the road |
|----------|-----|----------------------------------|
| Convenor | bch | Mmhmm                            |

(iv) check, rcheck

Check and response to check. Checks are used by speakers to make sure the listeners are following what they are saying. Response to check moves involves verbal or non-verbal reassurance. For example:

| YP | K1 | I was going to a mate's house, |
|---|---|---|
|  | check | right? |
| **Convenor** | rcheck | [nods] |

(v) invite

Invite. Invite moves are used in action exchanges to check that the listener is both following and willing to undertake the action. For example:

| Convenor | A2 | So I need you to go and talk with |
|---|---|---|
|  |  | your mum over there |
|  | invite | Ok? |
| YP | A1 | [nods] |

(d) Retrospective and prospective moves: ↓ and ↑

Retrospective and prospective moves are those moves which explicitly mark the role of the move as functioning to organize the following moves prospectively (↓) or the preceding moves retrospectively (↑). Prospective and retrospective arrows always modify other types of move detailed earlier and occur in exchanges associated with regulative discourse (see Chap. 3).

(i) ↓

Prospective move. These moves indicate an explicit marker that prospectively organizes the following moves in relation to the unfolding genre.

(ii) ↑

Retrospective move. These moves indicate an explicit marker that retrospectively organizes the preceding moves in relation to the unfolding genre.

An example of both a retrospective and prospective move in an exchange associated with regulative discourse is given as follows:

| Convener | ↓ A2 | So what I need you to do is |
|---|---|---|
|  | A1 | you've already admitted your guilt to this offence and you're here of your own free will? |
| YP |  | Yep. [nods] |
| Convener |  | Yep |
|  | ↑ A2f | OK |

## Intonation Conventions

The intonation conventions used in this book are adapted from those of Halliday and Greaves (2008: 211).

(a) //
   Double forward slash indicates a tone unit boundary (which is also always a foot and syllable boundary).
(b) /
   Single forward slash indicates a foot boundary (which is also always a syllable boundary).
(c) */**bold**
   Asterisk and bolding indicates the tonic syllable. (*//**bold** if initial in tone unit)
(d) ^
   Caret indicates a silent Ictus.
(e) ..
   Double period indicates a pause.
(f) << >>
A tone unit within double angled brackets indicates an enclosed tone unit.

Elements of structure of a tone unit include an optional Pretonic followed by a Tonic: (Pretonic)^Tonic. Elements of structure of a foot include an Ictus followed by an optional Remiss: Ictus^(Remiss).

# References

Aertsen, I., & Willemsens, J. (2001). The European forum for victim–offender mediation and restorative justice. *European Journal on Criminal Policy and Research, 9,* 291–300.

Ahmed, E., Harris, N., Braithwaite, J., et al. (2001). *Shame management through reintegration.* Cambridge/Oakleigh: Cambridge University Press.

Antaki, C., & Widdicombe, S. (1998). Identity as an achievement and as a tool. In C. Antaki & S. Widdicombe (Eds.), *Identities in talk* (pp. 1–14). London: Sage.

Austin, J. L. (1962). In J. O. Urmson (Ed.), *How to do things with words. The William James lectures delivered at Harvard University in 1955.* Oxford: Clarendon Press.

Baldry, A., & Thibault, P. J. (2006). *Multimodal transcription and text analysis: A multimedia toolkit and coursebook.* Oakville: Equinox.

Bateman, J. (2008). *Multimodality and genre: A foundation for the systematic analysis of multimodal documents.* Basingstoke/New York: Palgrave Macmillan.

Bateman, J., & Schmidt, K.-H. (2013). *Multimodal film analysis: How films mean.* London: Routledge.

Bauman, R. (1977). Verbal art as performance. *American Anthropologist, 77,* 290–311.

Bauman, Z. (2004). *Identity: Conversations with Benedetto Vecchi.* Cambridge: Polity Press.

Bednarek, M., & Martin, J. R. (2010). *New discourse on language: Functional perspectives on multimodality, identity, and affiliation*. London: Continuum.

Bell, C. (1992). *Ritual theory, ritual practice*. New York/Oxford: Oxford University Press.

Bell, C. (1997). *Ritual: Perspectives and dimensions*. New york/London: Oxford University Press.

Benwell, B., & Stokoe, E. (2007). *Discourse and identity*. Edinburgh: Edinburgh University Press.

Berger, P. L., & Luckmann, T. (1966). *The social construction of reality: A treatise in the sociology of knowledge*. Garden City/New York: Anchor Books.

Bernstein, B. (1975a). Class and pedagogies: Visible and invisible. *Educational Studies, 1*, 23–41.

Bernstein, B. (1975b). *Class, codes and control, volume 3: Towards a theory of educational transmissions*. London: Routledge & Kegan Paul.

Bernstein, B. (1990). *Class, codes and control 4: The structuring of pedagogic discourse*. London: Routledge.

Bernstein, B. (1996/2000). *Pedagogy, symbolic control and identity: Theory, research, critique*. London: Taylor and Francis.

Bernstein, B. (2000). *Pedagogy, symbolic control and identity: Theory, research, critique*. London: Taylor & Francis. [Revised Edition].

Berry, M. (1981). Systemic linguistics and discourse analysis: A multi- layered approach to exchange structure. In M. Coulthard & M. Montgomery (Eds.), *Studies in discourse analysis* (pp. 120–145). London: Routledge.

Blagg, H. (1997). A just measure of shame? Aboriginal youth and conferencing in Australia. *British Journal of Criminology, 37*, 481–501.

Blagg, H. (2008). *Crime, aboriginality and the decolonisation of justice*. Sydney: Hawkins Press.

Bourdieu, P. (1991). *Language and symbolic power*. Cambridge, UK: Polity Press.

Bourdieu, P. (1998). *Acts of resistance: Against the tyranny of the market*. New York: New Press.

Bourdieu, P., & Thompson, J. B. (1991). *Language and symbolic power*. Cambridge, MA: Harvard University Press.

Bradt, V., Roose, L., & Nicole, R. (2007). Relevant others in restorative practices for minors: For what purposes? *Australian & New Zealand Journal of Criminology, 40*, 291–312.

Braithwaite, J. (1989a). *Crime, shame and reintegration*. Cambridge/Sydney: Cambridge University Press.

Braithwaite, J. (1989b). *Crime, shame, and reintegration*. Cambridge [Cambridgeshire]/New York: Cambridge University Press.

Braithwaite, J. (2002). *Restorative justice & responsive regulation*. Oxford/New York: Oxford University Press.

Braithwaite, J. (2003). The fundamentals of restorative justice. In S. Dinnen, A. Jowitt, & T. N. Cain (Eds.), *A kind of mending: Restorative justice in the Pacific Islands* (p. xi, 308 p). Canberra: Pandanus Books.

Braithwaite, J., & Daly, K. (1998a). Masculinities, violence and communitarian control. In D. Chappell & S. Egger (Eds.), *Australian violence: Contemporary perspective II* (pp. 221–252). Canberra: Australian Institute of Criminology.

Braithwaite, J., & Daly, K. (1998b). Masculinities, violence and communitarian control. In S. L. Miller (Ed.), *Crime control and women: Feminist implications of criminal justice policy* (pp. 151–180). Thousand Oaks: Sage.

Braithwaite, J., & Strang, H. (2001). *Restorative justice and civil society*. Cambridge/Melbourne: Cambridge University Press.

Brown, P., & Levinson, S. (1978). Universals in language usage: Politeness phenomena. In E. Goody (Ed.), *Questions and politeness* (pp. 56–289). Cambridge: Cambridge University Press.

Butler, J. (1988). Performative acts and gender constitution: An essay in phenomenology and feminist theory. *Theatre Journal, 40*, 519–531.

Butler, J. (1990). *Gender trouble and the subversion of identity*. London: Routledge.

Campbell, C., Devlin, R., & O'Mahony, D., et al. (2005). *Evaluation of the Northern Ireland youth conference service*. NIO research and statistical series: Report 12. Belfast: NIO.

Caple, H. (2008). Intermodal relations in image nuclear news stories. In L. Unsworth (Ed.), *Multimodal semiotics: Functional analysis in contexts of education* (pp. 123–138). London: Continuum.

Caple, H. (2013). *Photojournalism: A social semiotic approach*. London: Palgrave Macmillan.

Chan, J. (2013). Ethnography as practice: Is validity an issue. *Current Issues in Criminal Justice, 25*, 503–516.

Christie, N. (1977). Conflicts as property. *British Journal of Criminology, 17*, 1–15.

Christie, F. (1997). Curriculum macrogenres as forms of initiation into a culture. In F. Christie & J. R. Martin (Eds.), *Genre and institutions: Social processes in the workplace and school* (pp. 134–160). London: Continuum.

Christie, F. (2002). *Classroom discourse analysis*. London: Continuum.

Clancey, G., Doran, S., & Maloney, E. (2005). The operation of warnings, cautions and youth justice conferences. In J. B. L. Chan (Ed.), *Reshaping juvenile justice: The NSW young offenders act 1997* (pp. 47–72). Sydney: Sydney Institute of Criminology.

Cléirigh, C. (2011). *Gestural and postural semiosis a systemic-functional linguistic approach to 'body language'*. Unpublished manuscript.

Collins, R. (2014). *Interaction ritual chains*. Princeton: Princeton university press.

Conley, J. M., & O'Barr, W. M. (2005). *Just words: Law, language, and power*. Chicago: University of Chicago Press.

Consedine, J. (1999). Restorative justice: Could Ireland lead the way? *Studies: An Irish Quarterly Review, 88,* 132–137.

Coupland, N. (2007). *Style: Language variation and identity*. London: Cambridge University Press.

Cuneen, C. (2002). Restorative justice and the politics of decolonization. In E. Weitekamp & H. J. Kerner (Eds.), *Restorative justice: Theoretical foundations* (pp. 32–49). Cullompton: Willan Publishing.

Cuneen, C., & White, R. (2007). *Juvenile justice: Youth and crime in Australia*. Oxford: Oxford University Press.

Daly, K. (2001a). Conferencing in Australia and New Zealand: Variations, research findings, and prospects. In A. Morris & G. Maxwell (Eds.), *Restorative justice for juveniles: Conferencing, mediation and circles* (pp. 59–84). London: Bloomsbury Publishing.

Daly, K. (2001b). Conferencing in Australia and New Zealand: Variations, research findings, and prospects. In A. Morris & G. Maxwell (Eds.), *Restorative justice for juveniles: Conferencing, mediation and circles* (pp. 59–83). Oxford/Portland: Hart Publishing.

Daly, K. (2003). Mind the gap: Restorative justice in theory and practice. In A. von Hirsch, J. V. Roberts, A. E. Bottoms, et al. (Eds.), *Restorative justice and criminal justice: Competing or reconcilable paradigms* (pp. 219–236). London: Bloomsbury.

Daly, K., & Stubbs, J. (2007). Feminist theory, feminist and anti-racist politics, and restorative justice. In G. Johnstone & D. W. Van Ness (Eds.), *Handbook of restorative justice* (pp. 149–170). Cullompton, Devon: Willan Publishing.

Davies, B., & Harré, R. (1990). Positioning: The discursive production of selves. *Journal for the Theory of Social Behaviour, 20,* 43–63.

Davis, S. (2002). *"Offending behaviour": Episode four of "crime and punishment"*. Documentary broadcast on the program Radio Eye, Australian Broadcasting Commission.

Dickson-Gilmore, E. J., & La Prairie, C. (2005). *Will the circle be unbroken?: Aboriginal communities, restorative justice, and the challenges of conflict and change*. Toronto: University of Toronto Press.

Douglas, M. (1973). *Natural symbols*. New York: Random House.

Dreyfus, S. (2011). Grappling with a non-speech language: Describing and theorising the nonverbal multimodal communication of a child with an intellectual disability. In S. Dreyfus, S. Hood, & M. Stenglin (Eds.), *Semiotic margins: Meaning in multimodalities* (pp. 53–72). London: Continuum.

Eades, D. (2008). *Courtroom talk and neocolonial control*. Berlin: Mouton de Gruyter.

Eades, D. (2010). *Sociolinguistics and the legal process*. Bristol: Multilingual Matters.

Efron, D. (1941). *Gesture and environment: A tentative study of some of the spatio-temporal and "linguistic" aspects of the gestural behavior of eastern Jews and southern Italians in New York city, living under similar as well as different environmental conditions*. New York: King's crown Press.

Eggins, S. (1994). *An introduction to systemic functional grammar*. London: Pinter.

Eggins, S., & Slade, D. (1997). *Analysing casual conversation*. London/New York: Cassell.

Etzioni, A. (1998). *The essential communitarian reader*. Lanham: Rowman & Littlefield.

Firth, J. R. (1957). *Papers in linguistics, 1934–1951*. London: Oxford University Press.

Fitzpatrick, T. (1995). *The relationship of oral and literate performance processes in the commedia Dell'arte: Beyond the improvisation-memorisation divide*. Lewiston/Lampeter: Edwin Mellen Press.

Formentelli, M. (2007). The vocative mate in contemporary English: A corpus based study. In A. Sansò (Ed.), *Language resources and linguistic theory* (pp. 180–199). Milano: Franco Angeli.

Foucault, M. (1977). *Discipline and punish: The birth of the prison*. New York: Vintage.

Geertz, C. (1973). Thick description. In C. Geertz (Ed.), *The interpretation of cultures: Selected essays*. New York: Basic Books. <<need pages>>.

Geertz, C. (1983). *Local knowledge: Further essays in interpretive anthropology*. New York: Basic books.

Gibbons, J. (2003). *Forensic linguistics: An introduction to language in the justice system*. Oxford/Malden: Blackwell Publishing.

Gilbert, L. (1983). *Educating Rita*. Burbank, California: Columbia Pictures.

Goldin-Meadow, S., & Singer, M. A. (2003). From children's hands to adults' ears: Gesture's role in the learning process. *Developmental Psychology, 39*, 509–520.

Hadley, M. L. (2001). *The spiritual roots of restorative justice*. New York: State University of New York Press.
Hage, G. (2006). Against paranoid nationalism: Searching for hope in a shrinking society. Melbourne: Pluto Press.
Halliday, M. A. K. (1967). *Intonation and grammar in British English*. The Hague/Paris: Mouton.
Halliday, M. A. K. (1970). Language structure and language function. In J. Lyons (Ed.), *New horizons in linguistics* (pp. 140–165). Harmondsworth: Penguin.
Halliday, M. A. K. (1975). *Learning how to mean – Explorations in the development of language*. London: Arnold.
Halliday, M. A. K. (1977). *Learning how to mean: Explorations in the development of language*. New York: Elsevier.
Halliday, M. A. K. (1985). *Spoken and written language*. Geelong: Deakin University Press. [Republished Oxford University Press 1989].
Halliday, M. A. K. (2008). *Complementarities in language*. Beijing: The Commercial Press.
Halliday, M. A. K., & Greaves, W. S. (2008). *Intonation in the grammar of English*. London/Oakville: Equinox Pub.
Halliday, M. A. K., & Matthiessen, C. M. I. M. (1999). *Construing experience through meaning: A language-based approach to cognition*. London: Cassell.
Halliday, M. A. K., & Matthiessen, C. M. I. M. (2004). *An introduction to functional grammar*. London: Arnold.
Halliday, M. A. K., & Matthiessen, C. M. (2013). *Halliday's introduction to functional grammar*. London: Routledge.
Halliday, M., & Matthiessen, C. M. (2014). *An introduction to functional grammar*. London: Routledge.
Harris, N., & Burton, J. (1997). The reliability of observed reintegrative shaming, shame, defiance and other key concepts in diversionary conferences. *RISE Working Papers, Research School of Social Sciences, ANU, 5*, 1–50.
Harris, N., Walgrave, L., & Braithwaite, J. (2004). Emotional dynamics in restorative conferences. *Theoretical Criminology an International Journal, 8*, 191–210.
Hasan, R. (1985). *Linguistics, language and verbal art*. Geelong: Deakin University Press. [Republished by Oxford University Press 1989].
Hasan, R. (2005). *Language, society and consciousness*. London: Equinox. (The collected works of Ruqaiya Hasan, edited by J. Webster, Vol. 1).
Hasan, R. (2009). *Semantic variation: Meaning in society and sociolinguistics*. London: Equinox. (The collected works of Ruqaiya Hasan, edited by J. Webster, Vol. 2).

Hayes, H. (2006). Apologies & accounts in youth justice conferencing. *Contemporary Justice Review, 9*, 369–385.

Hayes, H., & Daly, K. (2003). Youth justice conferencing and re-offending. *Justice Quarterly, 20*, 725–763.

Hinckfuss, J. (2012). *Rethinking English for academic purposes: Towards a performance-centred pedagogy*. Thesis, Department of performance studies, University of Sydney.

Hood, S. (2011). Body language in face-to-face teaching: A focus on textual and interpersonal meaning. In S. Dreyfus, S. Hood, & M. Stenglin (Eds.), *Semiotic margins: Meaning in multimodalities* (pp. 31–52). London: Continuum.

Hoyle, C., & Noguera, S. (2008). Supporting young offenders through restorative justice: Parents as (in)appropriate adults. *British Journal of Community Justice, 6*, 67–85.

Hoyle, C., Young, R., & Hill, R. (2002). *Proceed with caution: An evaluation of the Thames Valley police initiative in restorative cautioning*. York: York Publishing Services.

Hudson, J., Morris, A., Maxwell, G. M., et al. (1996). *Family group conferences: Perspectives on policy & practice*. Annandale: Federation Press.

Hymes, D. (1962). The ethnography of speaking. *Anthropology and Human Behavior, 13*, 11–74.

Jackson, M. (1996). *Things as they are: New directions in phenomenological anthropology*. Bloomington: Indiana University Press.

Jayyursi, L. (1984). *Categorization and the moral order*. Boston/London: Routledge and Kegan Paul.

Johnson, D. (2002). *Lighting the way: Reconciliation stories*. Sydney: The Federation Press.

Johnstone, G. (2011). *Restorative justice: Ideas, values and debates*. London and New York: Routledge.

Jordens, C. F. (2003). *Reading spoken stories for values: A discursive study of cancer survivors and their professional carers*. Doctoral dissertation. Sydney: School of Public Health, Faculty of Medicine, University of Sydney.

Jordens, C. F., & Little, M. (2004). 'In this scenario, I do this, for these reasons': Narrative, genre and ethical reasoning in the clinic. *Social Science & Medicine, 58*, 1635–1645.

Kendon, A. (2004). *Gesture: Visible action as utterance*. Cambridge: Cambridge University Press.

Knight, N. K. (2008). Still cool… and American too!': An SFL analysis of deferred bonds in internet messaging humour. Systemic Functional

Linguistics in Use, Odense Working Papers in Language and Communication 29: 481–502.

Knight, N. K. (2010). Wrinkling complexity: Concepts of identity and affiliation in humour. In M. Bednarek & J. R. Martin (Eds.), *New discourse on language: Functional perspectives on multimodality, identity, and affiliation*. London: Continuum.

Knight, N. K. (2013). Evaluating experience in funny ways: How friends bond through conversational hum. *Text & Talk, 33*, 553–574.

Kress, G., & Van Leeuwen, T. (2006). *Reading images: The grammar of visual images*. Oxon: Routledge.

Labov, W. (1972). *Language in the inner city: Studies in the Black English vernacular*. Philadelphia: University of Pennsylvania Press.

Labov, W. (1982). Speech actions and reactions in personal narrative. In *Analyzing discourse: Text and talk* (pp. 219–247). Washington, DC: Georgetown University Press.

Labov, W. (1984). Intensity. In D. Schiffrin (Ed.), *Meaning, form, and use in context: Linguistic applications* (pp. 43–70). Washington, DC: Georgetown University Press.

Labov, W. (2006). *The social stratification of English in New York City* (2nd ed.). Cambridge: Cambridge University Press.

Labov, W., & Waletzky, J. (1967). Narrative analysis: Oral sessions of personal experience. In J. Helm (Ed.), *Essays on the verbal and visual arts* (pp. 12–44). Seattle: University of Washington Press.

Lambert, C., Johnstone, G., Green, S., et al. (2011). *Building restorative relationships for the workplace: Goodwin Development Trust's journey with restorative approaches*. London: Goodwin Development Trust and University of Hull.

Lewis, J. L. (2008). Toward a unified theory of cultural performance: A reconstructive introduction to victor turner. In G. St John (Ed.), *Victor turner and contemporary cultural performance* (pp. 41–58). New York: Berghahn.

Lewis, J. L. (2013). *The anthropology of cultural performance*. New York: Palgrave Macmillan.

Martin, J. R. (1984). Language, register and genre. In: F. Christie (Ed.), *Children writing: Reader* (pp. 21–30). Geelong: Deakin University Press. (ECT Language Studies: children writing), [revised for Burns, A., & Coffin, C. (Eds.). (2001). *Analysing English in a global context: A reader* (pp. 2149–2166). Clevedon: Routledge (Teaching English Language Worldwide)] [Japanese translation by Hiro Tsukada published in Shidonii Gakuha no SFL: Haridei Gengo Riron no Tenkai. Tokyo: Liber Press. 2005.] [further revised for Coffin, C., Lillis, T., & O'Halloran, K. (Eds.). (2010). *Applied linguistics methods: A reader* (pp. 2012–2032). London: Routledge.] [reprinted in J R Martin 2012 Register Studies [Volume 2004 in the Collected Works of J R Martin edited by Wang Zhenhua. Shanghai: Shanghai Jiao Tong University Press. 2047–2068].

Martin, J. R. (1992). *English text: System and structure*. Philadelphia: John Benjamins Pub..

Martin, J. R. (1996). Evaluating disruption: Symbolising theme in junior secondary narrative. In *Literacy in society* (pp. 124–171). London: Longman. [Reprinted in Text Analysis 2012. 213-248].

Martin, J. R. (2008a). Innocence: Realisation, instantiation and individuation in a Botswanan town. In K. Knight & A. Mahboob (Eds.), *Questioning linguistics* (pp. 27–54). Cambridge: Cambridge Scholars Publishing.

Martin, J. R. (2008b). Intermodal reconciliation: Mates in arms. In *New literacies and the English curriculum: Multimodal perspectives* (pp. 112–148). London: Continuum.

Martin, J. R. (2016). Meaning matters: A short history of systemic functional linguistics. *Word, 61*, 1–23.

Martin, J. R., & Doran, Y. J. (2015a). Around grammar: Phonology, discourse semantics and multimodality. In *Critical concepts in linguistics: Systemic functional linguistics* (Vol. 3). London: Routledge.

Martin, J. R., & Doran, Y. J. (2015b). Context: Register and genre. In *Critical concepts in linguistics: Systemic functional linguistics* (Vol. 4). London: Routledge.

Martin, J. R., & Doran, Y. J. (2015c). Grammatical descriptions. In *Critical concepts in linguistics: Systemic functional linguistics* (Vol. 2). London: Routledge.

Martin, J. R., & Doran, Y. J. (2015d). Grammatics. In *Critical concepts in linguistics: Systemic functional linguistics* (Vol. 1). London: Routledge.

Martin, J. R., & Doran, Y. J. (2015e). Language in education. In *Critical concepts in linguistics: Systemic functional linguistics* (Vol. 5). London: Routledge.

Martin, J. R., & Plum, G. A. (1997). Construing experience: Some story genres. *Journal of Narrative and Life History, 7*, 299–308.

Martin, J. R., & Rose, D. (2003/2007). *Working with discourse: Meaning beyond the clause*. London/New York: Continuum.

Martin, J. R., & Rose, D. (2008). *Genre relations: Mapping culture*. London: Equinox.

Martin, J. R., & Stenglin, M. (2007). New directions in the analysis of multimodal discourse. In T. Royce & W. Bowcher (Eds.), *Materialising reconciliation: Negotiating difference in a post-colonial exhibition* (pp. 215–238). Mahwah: Lawrence Erlbaum Associates.

Martin, J. R., & White, P. R. R. (2005). *The language of evaluation: Appraisal in English*. New York: Palgrave Macmillan.

Martinec, R. (2000). Types of process in action. *Semiotica, 130*, 243–268.

Martinec, R. (2001). Interpersonal resources in action. *Semiotica, 135*, 117–145.

Maruna, S., Wright, S., Brown, J., et al. (2007). *Youth conferencing as shame management: Results of a long-term follow-up study*. Cambridge: ARCS.

Maton, K. (2007). Knowledge-knower structures in intellectual and educational fields. In F. Christie & J. R. Martin (Eds.), *Language, knowledge and pedagogy* (pp. 87–108). London: Continuum.

Maton, K. (2009). Progress and canons in the arts and humanities: Knowers and gazes. In K. Maton & R. Moore (Eds.), *Social realism, knowledge and the sociology of education: Coalitions of the mind* (pp. 154–178). London: Continuum.

Maton, K. (2013). *Knowledge and knowers: Towards a realist sociology of education*. London: Routledge.

Maton, K., & Chen, R. T. (2016). LCT in qualitative research: Creating a translation device for studying constructivist pedagogy. In K. Maton, S. Hood, & S. Shay (Eds.), *Knowledge building: Educational studies in legitimation code theory* (pp. 27–48). London: Routledge.

Maton, K., & Doran, Y. J. (in press). Semantic density: A translation device for revealing complexity of knowledge practices in discourse, part 1 – Wording. *Onomázein: Journal of Linguistics, Philology and Translation, 35*, 46–76.

Max Planck Institute for Psycholinguistics. (2008). *ELAN*. Nijmegen: The Language Archive.

Maxwell, G., & Morris, A. (2001). Family group conferences and reoffending. In A. Morris & G. Maxwell (Eds.), *Restorative justice for juveniles: Conferencing, mediation and circles* (pp. 243–266). Oxford: Hart.

Maxwell, G., & Morris, A. (2002). The role of shame, guilt, and remorse in restorative justice processes for young people. In E. Weitekamp & H. J. Kerner (Eds.), *Restorative justice: Theoretical foundations* (pp. 267–284). Cullompton: Willan Publishing.

McAuley, G. (2008). Not magic but work: Rehearsal and the production of meaning. *Theatre Research International, 33*, 276–288.

McCold, P., & Wachtel, B. (1998). *Restorative policing experiment*. Pipersville: Community Service Foundation.

McDonald, J., & Moore, D. (2001). Community conferencing as a special case of conflict transformation. In H. Strang & J. Braithwaite (Eds.), *Restorative justice and civil society* (pp. 130–148). Cambridge: Cambridge University Press.

McGarrell, E. F. (2000). *Returning justice to the community: The Indianapolis juvenile restorative justice experiment*. Indianapolis: Hudson Institute.

McGrath, A., & Weatherburn, D. (2012). The effect of custodial penalties on juvenile reoffending. *Australian & New Zealand Journal of Criminology, 45*, 26–44.

McLaughlin, E. (2003). Introduction: Justice in the round: contextualising restorative justice. In E. McLaughlin, R. Fergusson, G. Hughes, et al. (Eds.), *Restorative justice: Critical issues* (pp. 1–19). London: SAGE.

McNeill, D. (1992). *Hand and mind: What gestures reveal about thought*. Chicago: University of Chicago press.

Miller, D. R., & Bayley, P. (2016). *Hybridity in systemic functional linguistics: Grammar, text and discursive context*. London: Equinox.

Moore, D. B., & McDonald, J. M. (2000). *Transforming conflict in workplaces and other communities*. Bondi: Transformative Justice Australia.

Moore, D., & McDonald, J. (2001). Community conferencing as a special case of conflict transformation. In J. Braithwaite & H. Strang (Eds.), *Restorative justice and civil society* (pp. 130–148). Cambridge/Melbourne: Cambridge University Press.

Moore, D., Forsythe, L., & O'Connell, T. (1995). *A new approach to juvenile justice: An evaluation of family conferencing in Wagga Wagga*. Criminology Research Council grant. http://www.criminologyresearchcouncil.gov.au/reports/moore/

Moore, D. B., McDonald, J. M., & Transformative Justice Australia. (2000). *Transforming conflict in workplaces and other communities*. Bondi: Transformative Justice Australia.

Morgan, S. (1987). *My place*. Fremantle: Fremantle Arts Centre Press.

Morris, D. (1979). *Gestures, their origins and distribution*. New York: Stein & Day Pub.

Muntigl, P. (2004). *Narrative counselling: Social and linguistic processes of change*. Amsterdam/Philadelphia: John Benjamins Pub.

Nathanson, D. L. (1997). From empathy to community. *The Annual of Psychoanalysis, 25*, 125–143.

Norris, S. (2012). *Multimodality in practice: Investigating theory-in-practice-through-methodology*. London: Routledge.

NSW Department of Juvenile Justice. (1999). In Justice NDoJ (Ed.), *A guide to youth justice conferencing*. Sydney: NSW Department of Juvenile Justice.

NSW Department of Juvenile Justice. (2000). In Justice NDoJ (Ed.), *Youth justice conferencing policy and procedures manual*. Sydney: NSW Department of Juvenile Justice.

O'Halloran, K. L. (2004). *Multimodal discourse analysis: Systemic-functional perspectives*. London: Continuum.

O'Toole, M. (2011). *The language of displayed art*. London: Routledge.

Painter, C. (1998). *Learning through language in early childhood*. London: Cassell.

Painter, C., Martin, J. R., & Unsworth, L. (2013). *Reading visual narratives: Image analysis of children's picture books*. London: Equinox Publishing.

Palk, G., Hayes, H., & Prenzler, T. (1998a). Restorative justice and community conferencing: Summary of findings from a pilot study. *Current Issues in Criminal Justice, 10*, 125–137.

Palk, G., Hayes, H., & Prenzler, T. (1998b). Restorative justice and community conferencing: Summary of findings from a pilot study. *Current Issues in Criminal Justice, 10*, 138.

Pavlich, G. C. (2005). *Governing paradoxes of restorative justice*. London: Psychology Press.

Plum, G. A. (1988). *Text and contextual conditioning in spoken English: A genre approach*. Linguistics, University of Sydney.

Poynton, C. (1990a). *Address and the semiotics of social relations: A systemic-functional account of address forms and practices in Australian English*. University of Sydney, 1991, xii, 277 leaves.

Poynton, C. (1990b). *Address and the semiotics of social relations: A systemic-functional account of address forms and practices in Australian English*. Department of Linguistics, Faculty of Arts, University of Sydney, Sydney, 284.

Prichard, J. (2002). Parent-child dynamics in community conferences, Äî some questions for reintegrative shaming, practice and restorative justice. *Australian & New Zealand Journal of Criminology, 35*, 330–346.

Rappaport, R. (1999). *Ritual and religion in the making of humanity*. Cambridge, UK: Cambridge University Press.

Retzinger, S., & Scheff, T. (1996). Strategy for community conferences: Emotions and social bonds. In B. Galaway & J. Hudson (Eds.), *Restorative justice: International perspectives* (pp. 315–336). Monsey: Criminal Justice Press.

Rose, D., & Martin, J. R. (2012). *Learning to write, reading to learn: Genre, knowledge and pedagogy in the Sydney school*. London: Equinox.

Rossner, M. (2011). Emotions and interaction ritual: A micro analysis of restorative justice. *British Journal of Criminology, 51*, 95–119.

Rothery, J. (1994). *Exploring literacy in school English (write it right resources for literacy and learning)*. Sydney: Metropolitan East Disadvantaged Schools Program.

Rothery, J., & Stenglin, M. (1997). Entertaining and instructing: Exploring experience through story. In F. Christie & J. R. Martin (Eds.), *Genre and institutions: Social processes in the workplace and school, Open linguistics series* (pp. 231–263). London: Pinter.

Rothery, J., & Stenglin, M. (2000). Interpreting literature: The role of appraisal. In L. Unsworth (Ed.), *Researching language in schools and communities* (pp. 222–244). London: Cassell.

Russell, E. (2004). *The shack that dad built*. Surry Hills: Little Hare Books.

Sacks, H. (1992). In G. Jefferson (Ed.), *Lectures on conversation. Volumes I and II*. Oxford: Blackwell.

Sacks, H. (1995). *Lectures on conversation*. Oxford: Blackwell Publishing.

Schechner, R. (2004). *Performance theory*. London: Routledge.

Scheff, T., & Retzinger, S. (1991). *Violence and emotions*. Lexington: Lexington Books.

Schegloff, E. A. (2006). Interaction: The infrastructure for social institutions, the natural ecological niche for language, and the arena in which culture is enacted. In N. J. Enfield & S. C. Levinson (Eds.), *Roots of human sociality: Culture, cognition and interaction* (pp. 70–96). Oxford: Berg.

Schegloff, E. A. (2007). A tutorial on membership categorization. *Journal of Pragmatics, 39*, 462–482.

Sherman, L. W., Strang, H., & Woods, D. J. (2000). *Recidivism patterns in the Canberra reintegrative shaming experiments (RISE)*. Centre for Restorative Justice, Research School of Social Sciences, Australian National University, Canberra.

Silverman, D. (2006). *Interpreting qualitative data: Methods for analyzing talk, text and interaction*. London: Sage.

Smith, N., & Weatherburn, D. (2012). Youth justice conferences versus children's court: A comparison of re-offending. *Crime and Justice Bulletin. Contemporary issues in crime and justice, 160*, 1030–1046.

Snow, P., & Powell, M. (2008). Oral language competence, social skills and high-risk boys: What are juvenile offenders trying to tell us? *Children and Society, 22*, 16–28.

Stenglin, M. (2004). *Packaging curiosities: Towards a grammar of three-dimensional space*. Department of Linguistics, University of Sydney, Sydney.

Stenglin, M. (2008a). Binding: A resource for exploring interpersonal meaning in three-dimensional space. *Social Semiotics, 18*, 425–447.

Stenglin, M. (2008b). Interpersonal meaning in 3D space: How a bonding icon gets its 'charge'. In L. Unsworth (Ed.), *Multimodal semiotics: Functional analysis in contexts of education* (pp. 50–66). London: Continuum.

Stenglin, M. (2009). Space odyssey: Towards a social semiotic model of three-dimensional space. *Visual Communication, 8*, 35–64.

Stenglin, M. (2012). *Transformation and transcendence: Bonding through ritual.* Paper presented at the International Systemic Functional Congress, University of Technology, Sydney, 16–20 July 2012.

Stenglin, M., & Djonov, E. (2010). Unpacking narrative in a hypermedia 'art-edventure' for children. In C. R. Hoffman (Ed.), *Narrative revisited: Telling a story in the age of new media.* Amsterdam: John Benjamins.

Strang, H., & Braithwaite, J. (2001). *Restorative justice and civil society.* Cambridge: Cambridge University Press.

Strang, H., Barnes, G., Braithwaite, J., et al. (1999). *Experiments in restorative policing: A progress report on the Canberra reintegrative shaming experiments (RISE).* Canberra: Research School of Social Sciences, Australian National University.

Tangney, J. P. (1991). Moral affect: The good, the bad, and the ugly. *Journal of Personality and Social Psychology, 61*, 598.

Tann, K. (2010a). Imagining communities: A multifunctional approach to identity management in texts. In M. Bednarek & J. R. Martin (Eds.), *New discourse on language: Functional perspectives on multimodality, identity, and affiliation* (pp. 163–194). London: Continuum.

Tann, K. (2010b). *Semogenesis of a nation: An iconography of Japanese identity.* Sydney: Department of Linguistics, University of Sydney.

Tann, K. (2013). The language of identity discourse: Introducing a systemic functional framework for iconography. *Linguistics & The Human Sciences, 8*, 361–391.

Taussig, I. (2012). Youth justice conferences: Participant profile and conference characteristics. *Crime and Justice Bulletin.* http://www.ntyan.com.au/images/uploads/news_docs/BB75.pdf

Tillich, P. (1963). *Christianity and the encounter of the world religions.* New York: Colombia University Press.

Tomkins, S. S. (2009). Affect theory. In K. R. Scherer & P. Ekman (Eds.), *Approaches to emotion* (pp. 163–195). New York/London: Psychology Press.

Tönnies, F. (1887a/1974). *Community and association* (translation of Gemeinschaft und Geseellschaft). London: Routledge & Kegan Paul.

Tönnies, F. (1887b/2001). *Tönnies: Community and civil society.* Cambridge: Cambridge University Press.

Trimboli, L. (2000). *An evaluation of the NSW youth justice conferencing scheme.* Sydney: NSW Bureau of Crime Statistics and Research.

Trimboli, L., & New South Wales. (2000). *An evaluation of the NSW youth justice conferencing scheme*. Sydney: NSW Bureau of Crime Statistics and Research.

Trudgill, P. (1974). *The social differentiation of English in Norwich*. Cambridge: Cambridge University Press.

Turner, V. W. (1974). *Dramas, fields, and metaphors: Symbolic action in human society*. Ithaca: Cornell University Press.

Turner, V. W. (1979). *Process, performance, and pilgrimage: A study in comparative symbology*. New Delhi: Concept Publishing Company.

Turner, V. W. (1982). *From ritual to theatre: The human seriousness of play*. New York: Performing Arts Journal Publications.

Van Gennep, A. (1960). *The rites of passage*. Chicago: University of Chicago Press.

Van Ness, D., Morris, A., & Maxwell, G. (2001). Introducing restorative justice. In A. Morris & G. Maxwell (Eds.), *Restorative justice for juveniles: Conferencing, mediation and circles* (pp. 3–16). Oxford: Hart.

Van Stokkom, B. (2002). Moral emotions in restorative justice conferences: Managing shame, designing empathy. *Theoretical Criminology, 6*, 339–360.

Ventola, E. (1987). *The structure of social interaction: A systemic approach to the semiotics of service encounters*. London: Pinter (Open Linguistics Series).

Wagland, P., Blanch, B., & Moore, E. (2013). Participant satisfaction with youth justice conferencing. In *Crime and justice bulletin: Contemporary issues in crime and justice*. Sydney: NSW Bureau of Crime Statistics and Research.

Weatherburn, D., Vignaendra, S., & McGrath, A. (2009). *The specific deterrent effect of custodial penalties on juvenile re-offending*. Report to the Criminology Research Council.

Webber, A. (2012). Youth justice conferences versus children's court: A comparison of cost-effectiveness. *Crime and Justice Bulletin, 164*, 1030–1046.

Weitekamp, E. (1999). He history of restorative justice. In G. Bazemore & L. Walgrave (Eds.), *Restorative juvenile justice: Repairing the harm of youth crime*. Monsey: Criminal Justice Press.

Wilkie, M. (1997). *Bringing them home: Report of the national inquiry into the separation of aboriginal and Torres Strait islander children from their families*. Sydney: Human Rights and Equal Opportunity Commission.

Young, R. (2001). Just cops doing "shameful" business? In A. Morris & G. Maxwell (Eds.), *Restorative justice for juveniles: Conferencing, mediation and circles* (pp. 195–226). Oxford: Hart.

Zappavigna, M., Dwyer, P., & Martin, J. R. (2007). "Just like sort of guilty kind of": The rhetoric of tempered admission in Youth Justice conferencing. In

M. Zappavigna & C. Cloran (Eds.), *Proceedings of Australian systemic functional linguistics Congress*. Woollongong. http://www.asfla.org.au/category/asfla2007/

Zappavigna, M., Dwyer, P., & Martin, J. R. (2008). Syndromes of meaning: Exploring patterned coupling in a NSW youth justice conference. In A. Mahboob & K. Knight (Eds.), *Questioning linguistics* (pp. 03–117). Newcastle upon Tyne: Cambridge Scholars Publishing.

Zappavigna, M., Cléirigh, C., Dwyer, P., et al. (2009). The coupling of gesture and phonology. In M. Bednarek & J. R. Martin (Eds.), *New discourse on language: Functional perspectives on multimodality, identity, and affiliation* (pp. 237–266). London: Continuum.

Zehr, H. (1990). *Changing lenses: A new focus for crime and justice*. Scottdale: Herald Press.

Ziegler, A. (1999). Facing the demons.

Ziegler, A., Kramer, K., O'Connell, T., Marslew, K., & Marslew, L. (1999). *Facing the demons*. [audiovisual recording]. Sydney: Dee Cameron productions.

Zimmerman, D., & Weider, L. (1970). Ethnomethodology and the problem of order. In J. Douglas (Ed.), *Understanding everyday life* (pp. 285–295). Chicago: Aldine.

# Index[1]

**A**

admonition genre, 104–17, 124, 152, 257–62, 265
affect theory, 17
affiliation, 120, 123, 151, 200–2, 227, 235, 238, 262, 272, 279, 287
  bond, 7, 15, 92, 195n12, 199, 215, 216, 227, 240, 246
apology, 9, 33, 34, 38, 52, 54, 100–4, 118, 119, 200, 247, 269, 277, 291
appliable linguistics, 297
attitude, 67, 70, 71, 109, 158, 160–2, 167, 168, 194n1, 201, 202, 215, 217–19, 221, 223–5, 227, 240, 241n1, 241n2, 255, 273
Austin, J., 36

Australian Capital Territory, 6
axiology, 201

**B**

Bauman, R., 37, 40n13
Bayley, P., 61
Bednarek, M., 287
Bell, C., 291
Benwell, B., 245
Berger, P.L., 245
Bernstein, B., 140–2, 187, 192, 273
Blagg, H., 10, 39n8
bondicon, 275, 276, 279, 281–3, 285
bonding icon. *See* bondicon
Bourdieu, P., 2, 193, 194, 270
Bradt, V., 95

---

[1] Note: Page numbers followed by "n" refer to notes.

Braithwaite, J., 7–9, 11, 13–17, 50, 98, 166, 278, 291–4
Brown, P., 235
Butler, J., 36, 246

**C**

Campbell, C., 12
Caple, H., 274
Chan, J., 40n11
Children's Court, 13, 287
children's magistrate, 8, 31, 52
Christie, F., 73, 74, 141, 142
Christie, N., 7
Circle Sentencing, 5
Cléirigh, C., 203, 205, 208, 211, 212
Collins, R., 37
commissioned recount, 73–85, 91, 92, 96, 101, 102, 125n10, 125n11, 130, 145–54, 161–87, 212–15, 237, 238, 247, 248, 250, 254–7, 260–2, 277, 296
Communitas, 271, 278, 279, 281–3, 285, 286, 294, 295
community, 2, 4–9, 15, 22, 39n3, 54, 55, 63, 87, 93, 105, 118, 119, 122, 123, 134, 139, 142, 143, 151–3, 169, 171–4, 190, 193, 227–40, 260, 271, 275, 276, 278, 281–3, 285, 286, 288, 291–4, 297
Consedine, J., 7
Coupland, N., 245
coupling, 188, 195n12, 200–2, 215–27, 232, 237, 240, 241n2
Cuneen, C., 10, 11, 39n8, 142, 193, 298n4

**D**

Daly, K., 6, 9–11, 98, 130, 193, 200, 269, 296, 298n4
Davies, B., 246
Davis, S., 27, 161, 191
Dickson-Gilmore, E.J., 10, 193
Djonov, E., 274
Douglas, M., 290
Doxa, 270, 279, 281–3, 286, 295
Dreyfus, S., 203
Dwyer, P., 1, 20, 25, 35, 57

**E**

Eades, D., 4
Eggins, S., 26, 31, 40n12, 71, 131, 181
empathy, 15, 16, 33, 96, 180, 283, 284
Ethnic Community Liaison Officer, 2, 133, 144, 151, 153, 205, 263
Etzioni, A., 7
exchange structure
    action exchange, 131–3, 135, 136, 139, 145
    integrative move, 143, 144, 148
    knowledge exchange, 131–3, 135, 150, 153, 154
    primary knower, 132–4, 152, 153
    secondary knower, 132–4, 150, 151

**F**

Family Group Conferencing, 6, 39n5
Firth, J.R., 32, 246
Fitzpatrick, T., 41n13

forensic linguistics, 3, 4, 295, 297
forgiveness, 3, 7, 15, 16, 18, 33, 38, 247, 277, 298
Formentelli, M., 238
Foucault, M., 18, 262

G

Geertz, C., 24, 25
Gemeinschaft, 227, 228, 270, 271, 278, 279
generic structure, 125n8
gesture, 3, 33, 35, 36, 38, 57, 65, 203, 205, 206, 208, 209, 217, 219, 222
Gilbert, L., 101
Goffman, E., 37

H

Halliday, M.A.K., 26, 28, 32, 91, 131, 141, 144, 147, 203, 204, 206, 208, 211, 237, 273, 297
Harris, N., 16–18, 247
Hasan, R., 195n10, 246
Hayes, H., 247, 269, 291
Hinckfuss, J., 37
Hood, S., 203, 217, 218
Hoyle, C., 18, 95
Hudson, J., 9, 39n5
Hymes, D., 40n13, 41n13

I

iconisation, 270, 272–7, 281, 283–7, 294–7
iconography, 270–2, 279, 281, 282, 284

identity, 4, 15, 16, 36, 38, 66, 166, 192, 194, 212–16, 227, 232–5, 240, 245–65
impact genre, 92–5, 97
intermodality, 36

J

Jackson, M., 24
Jayyursi, L., 246
Johnson, D., 183
Jordens, C.F., 181

K

Kendon, A., 203, 209
Knight, N.K., 201–3, 240
Kress, G., 35

L

Labov, W., 61, 183, 195n8, 245
Lambert, C., 7
La Prairie, C., 5, 10, 193
Legitimation Code Theory, 251
Levinson, S., 235
Lewis, J.L., 287, 288, 290, 292
lexical metaphor, 273
liminality, 291, 292
   liminoid genres, 292
linguistic service, 130, 138–40, 144–6, 149
Luckmann, T., 245

M

McAuley, G., 22
McCold, P., 12

McDonald, J., 3, 17, 19
McGarrell, E.F., 13
McGrath, A., 38n1, 39n2
McLaughlin, E., 7
McNeill, D., 203
macro-genre, 37, 49–125, 246–8, 255
Martin, J.R., 25, 26, 32, 40n12, 60, 61, 70, 74, 92, 125n5, 131, 136, 138, 147, 157–9, 161, 170, 176, 181, 184–6, 195n10, 195n13, 199, 206, 208, 217, 228, 247, 262, 273, 274, 287, 291
Martinec, R., 35, 203, 208
Maton, K., 251–4, 261, 262, 265
Max Planck Institute for Psycholinguistics, 204
Maxwell, G., 5, 12, 15, 16, 39n5, 298n4
Miller, D.R., 61
Moore, D., 3, 17, 19, 291
Morgan, S., 181, 182
Morris, D., 5, 12, 15, 16, 39n5, 203, 298n4
Muntigl, P., 142, 181

N

Nathanson, D.L., 155
New South Wales (NSW), 2, 5, 6, 8, 12–15, 19, 20, 23, 38n1, 39n2, 51–3, 55, 60, 63, 80, 90, 104, 124n1, 154, 258, 269, 280, 290, 296
New Zealand, 6, 7, 10, 12, 15, 39n5, 258, 290
Norris, S., 35
NSW Department of Juvenile Justice, 59, 60

O

O'Barr, W.M., 4
O'Halloran, K.L., 35
Oracle, 270–2, 280
O'Toole, M., 35
outcome plan, 3, 8, 18, 37, 53–6, 59, 73, 100, 101, 104, 117–19, 121, 130, 184

P

Painter, C., 36, 204
Palk, G., 12, 269
paralinguistic, 18, 36, 63, 203
passion play, 38, 269, 277, 279, 294, 297
Pavlich, G.C., 9
pedagogic discourse, 139, 148, 154, 155, 187
personae, 201, 231, 240, 245, 251, 255–7, 261–4
Plum, G.A., 181
Police Youth Liaison Officer, 2, 52, 147, 175
Powell, M., 124n3
Poynton, C., 233–5, 237, 238
Prichard, J., 95

R

rallying, 285, 291
Rappaport, R., 290
re-affiliation, 130, 235, 260
recidivism, 12–14
redemption, 260
reflective recount, 84–90, 92, 99, 187

regulative discourse, 129, 130, 140, 142, 145, 147–9, 153, 154, 193
reintegration, 4, 15, 38, 50, 98, 117–23, 143, 154, 173, 175, 176, 190, 232, 240, 260, 265, 278, 288, 291, 296
reintegrative shaming, 15–17, 25, 50, 65, 66, 175, 269, 278, 294
rejoinder macro-genre, 83, 91, 92, 95, 97, 100, 101, 103, 104, 125n11, 175, 187–90, 255, 260, 261, 265
remorse, 3, 15, 16, 18, 33, 38, 55, 88, 166, 191, 200, 247, 256, 257, 275, 277
reoffending. *See* recidivism
Retzinger, S., 15, 16, 18, 33, 203, 247
RISE study, 13, 16, 18
ritual, 25, 36, 38, 107, 265, 270, 287–95, 297
Rose, D., 26, 60, 61, 70, 74, 92, 125n5, 131, 176, 181, 184, 185, 208, 228, 262
Rossner, M., 37
Rothery, J., 186

S

Saussure, F., 246
Scheff, T., 15, 16, 18, 33, 203, 247
Schegloff, E.A., 228
scripts, 4, 50
shame, 14–17, 98, 155, 247, 276
Sherman, L.W., 12, 13
Silverman, D., 23, 24
Smith, N., 13, 14

Snow, P., 124n3
socio-legal framing genre, 62–71, 125n8
South African Truth and Reconciliation Commission, 6
Spatialization device, 227, 231, 232, 286
Stenglin, M., 186, 270, 274, 291
stigmatizing, 15, 16
Stokoe, E., 245
Strang, H., 5, 8, 269
system network, 28, 135, 158, 181

T

Tangney, J.P., 15, 16
Tann, K., 227–9, 232, 240, 270–2, 278–80
Taussig, I., 55
Thames Valley, 6
Tillich, P., 288
Tomkins, S.S., 17
Tönnies, F., 227, 270, 271
topology, 254–6, 261, 264
transcription, 22, 56, 125n7
Trimboli, L., 12, 14, 269
Trudgill, P., 245
Turner, V.W., 36, 271, 287, 288, 291, 292, 295

V

Van Gennep, A., 293
Van Leeuwen, T., 35
Van Ness, D., 6
Van Stokkom, B., 49, 50, 247
Ventola, E., 130, 131, 138

Victim-Offender Mediation, 5
vocative, 234, 238

W

Wagland, P., 14
Weatherburn, D., 13, 14, 38n1, 39n2
Webber, A., 40n9
Weider, L., 245
Weitekamp, E., 7, 298n4
White, P.R.R., 10, 39n8, 142, 157–9, 161, 170, 199, 206, 217, 273
Wilkie, M., 195n7

Y

Young Offenders Act, 2, 8, 20, 51, 52, 55, 56, 58, 64, 65, 67, 90, 104, 112, 120, 130
Young, R., 18

Z

Zappavigna, M., 20, 25, 195n13, 203, 250
Zehr, H., 5, 8, 9
Ziegler, A., 40n10
Zimmerman, D., 245